# LITERACY
# IN PROCESS

**The Heinemann Reader**

# LITERACY IN PROCESS

edited by

### Brenda Miller Power
*University of Maine*
*Orono, Maine*

### Ruth Hubbard
*Lewis and Clark College*
*Portland, Oregon*

Heinemann
Portsmouth, NH

**Heinemann Educational Books**

361 Hanover Street   Portsmouth, NH 03801-3959

Offices and agents throughout the world

The following have generously given their permission to reprint borrowed material:

Page 114: Excerpt from "The Unknown Citizen" by W. H. Auden. Copyright 1940 and renewed 1968 by W. H. Auden. Reprinted from *W. H. Auden: Collected Poems* edited by Edward Mendelson, by permission of Random House, Inc.

Page 198: Questions from *The Child as Critic*, 2d edition, by Glenna Davis Sloan, 1984. Reprinted by permission of Teachers College Press.

Pages 198−99: Questions from *Child and Story* by Kay Vandergrift, 1980. Reprinted by permission of Neal-Schumann Publishers, Inc.

Pages 249−50: Excerpt from "The Moustache" by Robert Cormier. From *Eight Plus One* by Robert Cormier. Copyright © 1975 by Robert Cormier. Reprinted by permission of Pantheon Books, a division of Random House, Inc.

Page 247: "The Little Boy and the Old Man" from *A Light in the Attic* by Shel Silverstein. Copyright © 1981 by Evil Eye Music, Inc. Reprinted by permission of HarperCollins, Publisher.

Pages 251−52: Excerpt from "don't send me flowers when I'm dead" by Eva J. Salber, 1983. Reprinted by permission of Duke University Press.

Every effort has been made to contact the copyright holders for permission to reprint borrowed material where necessary. We regret any oversights that may have occurred and would be happy to rectify them in future printings of this work.

**Library of Congress Cataloging-in-Publication Data**

Literacy in process : the Heinemann reader / edited by Brenda Miller
   Power and Ruth Hubbard.
       p.     cm.
   Includes bibliographical references.
   ISBN 0−435−08532−8
   1. Literacy.   2. Reading—Study and teaching.   3. English
language—Composition and exercises—Study and teaching.   I. Power,
Brenda Miller.   II. Hubbard, Ruth, 1950−       .
LC149.L4993   1990
428.4−dc20
                                                   90−37651
                                                       CIP

A portion of the editors' proceeds from the sale of this book go to the Center for Teaching and Learning in Edgecomb, Maine.

Designed by Wladislaw Finne
Printed in the United States of America
92 93 94 95      10 9 8 7 6 5 4 3 2

*to our teacher and friend,*
*Patricia McLure*

*Literacy is something bigger and better than mechanical skill in reading and writing. Literacy is a potent form of consciousness. Once possessed, it makes us productive. It irradiates the universe we have created. It remakes our lives. It gives us power for good and ill—more often for ill in proportion as we misunderstand it. I hope by understanding it better, we may finally have more of it.*
Robert Pattison,
*On Literacy*

# CONTENTS

# INTRODUCTION

*Sacajawea, the Shoshone woman who was the guide and translator for the Lewis and Clark expedition to explore the Oregon territory, has always been a heroic figure for me. Near the end of her life, she was asked how she found her way through thousands of miles of unexplored territory, through many languages and cultures she didn't know. She said simply, "The far vision, the close look." Her words have implications for us in literacy education. The "far vision" is the theory we construct, our philosophy, and our grand aims. And the "close look" is the steps we have to take day by day to get there, the classroom realities. We always have to keep both of these in mind.*

*Tim Gillespie, teacher-researcher*

This book is a collection of writings by theorists and practitioners who explore literacy instruction by emphasizing processes as well as products. By including the writings of both major theorists and current master teachers, we hope readers will be able to bring into clearer focus both the "far vision" and the "close look" of this holistic philosophy. Our aim is to demonstrate practical theory. Throughout the book, you will read about changes in the field of literacy education; hear the voices of teachers, researchers, and teacher educators as they discuss their own reading and writing; and learn what's exciting to them—as well as what they fret about.

The four parts of this book reflect Pattison's dynamic view of what it means to be literate and to work with young readers and writers. We begin with personal literacy in Part I, because this is where understanding how to teach reading and writing begins. Teachers who see themselves as evolving readers and writers are well equipped to understand their students' language processes. They explore with their students what literacy can mean in their own lives and in a society that values reading, writing, and reasoning abilities. In this view of literacy, everyone is in the process of becoming more literate.

Like their students, teachers look back on their history as readers and writers. They also maintain a day-to-day commitment to the same process of reading, writing, and responding to texts that they ask of their students.

Schools are changing because of teachers' changing sense of themselves as learners. Reforms in literacy instruction are theory-driven, and it is teachers who are actively reading and applying new theories and research findings. Researchers and teachers are understanding in new ways the complexity of cultural differences, the uniqueness of individuals, and the different functions and purposes of literacy in students' lives. Part 2 explores some of these changing concepts of what it means to be literate and to help students become literate.

As teachers understand the theory underlying their instructional methods, they can begin to develop their own theories and design research studies to test these theories. Part 3 shows how the curriculum is transformed as teachers apply new principles of literacy instruction to their classrooms. Theories of what occurs in the transactions of reading and writing — the "far vision" — are explored in the classrooms by practitioners who take a "close look" at the day-to-day realities of the sometimes rocky paths they negotiate with their students on the road to literacy.

The final chapters in the book get at fundamental issues of how teachers continue to grow and change personally and professionally as they work with young readers and writers. And even as teachers strive to define and develop the best literacy programs possible, they realize that there is something not quite tangible in trying to define good teaching.

No part of this book is meant to stand alone; rather, it should be viewed as interconnected. After all, personal literacy doesn't end as we delve into classroom practices, but continues to inform and enrich our daily professional lives. The selections in this book are not meant to be read in one fixed order only, but adapted to the needs of each reader.

It's difficult to get the "far vision" and "close look" of literacy instruction in focus through one text. Exciting research studies and practical examples of teachers and theorists refining literacy instruction continue to hit the presses monthly, the result being that the works of many fine teachers and researchers are omitted from our text. But our text may help you begin the journey of exploring your own literacy and developing a coherent and specific theory of how you might form a literate community in your classroom. It is only the beginning of the journey. We hope our further resources section at the end of the book helps you to carve out your own "territory of learning" over the next few months and years.

# PART 1

**personal literacy**

The book begins where you must begin—with your own continuing history as a reader and writer. You know that at different times you have been frustrated, delighted, or challenged as a reader and writer. As authors *Tim Gillespie* and *Paulo Freire* share how they developed as readers and writers, you may see parallels to your own learning experiences.

Becoming literate is a process that never ends. There is always more to learn about reading and writing once you have cracked the code of language. *Donald Murray* shares some tips to help you continue your development as a writer. And all teachers must continue that development according to *Ruth Nathan*, who shares how the experience of writing a text in a workshop changes a teacher's perceptions of her students.

That experience of sharing texts in workshops can be positive or negative, depending upon the atmosphere in the class. *Marge Piercy* lays out some ground rules for helping create a supportive environment for sharing texts. Her own history as a feminist affects her perceptions of how to foster response.

In the final chapter of this section, *Brenda Miller Power* shares the histories of two women who found many challenges in their development as readers, writers, and teachers.

# getting under
# the lightning

DONALD M. MURRAY

1

*Writing is primarily not a matter of talent, of dedication, of vision, of vocabulary, of style, but simply a matter of sitting. The writer is the person who writes. The best writing is self-commanded, and most writers have the problems of life: eating, paying the mortgage, getting the kids off to school, responding to those to whom they have commitments. The world intrudes.*

*Only a handful of writers can attend to their own work full-time. Most writers in the United States hold staff writing jobs, teach, doctor, lawyer, sell, buy, serve society in a way which society will reward with salary—and health benefits.*

*At times I found it hard to accept this double life, getting up early to write or staying up late when my peers in other professions could lawyer or doctor or insure from eight to five. But then I would remind myself that writing isn't a profession, it is a calling—and the only one calling is yourself. I had no choice; I had to write.*

*Recently Annie Dillard put all this talk of discipline and work habits in perspective:*

> *Let me close with a word about process. There's a common notion that self-discipline is a freakish peculiarity of writers—that writers differ from other people by possessing enormous and equal portions of talent and willpower. They grit their powerful teeth and go into their little rooms. I think that's a bad misunderstanding of what impels the writer. What impels the writer is a deep love for and respect for language, for literary forms, for books. It's a privilege to muck about in sentences all morning. It's a challenge to bring off a powerful effect, or to tell the truth about something. You don't do it from willpower; you do it from an abiding passion for the field. I'm sure it's the same in every other field.*
>
> *Writing a book is like rearing children—willpower has very little to do with it. If you have a little baby crying in the middle of the night, and if you depend only on willpower to get you out of*

*bed to feed the baby, that baby will starve. You do it out of love. Willpower is a weak idea; love is strong. You don't have to scourge yourself with a cat-o'-nine-tails to go to the baby. You go to the baby out of love for that particular baby. That's the same way you go to your desk. There's nothing freakish about it. Caring passionately about something isn't against nature, and it isn't against human nature. It's what we're here to do.*

*Whether we are motivated by love, hunger for fame, or just plain hunger, the fact is that most of us find it hard to get our rump in the writer's chair and keep it there. I wish more could. I don't need the competition, but most of my students and the teachers with whom I have worked could be writers. But whether they are writers or not, writing is an act of therapy and an act of power. Armed with the craft of writing, each individual can decide to use that craft or not.*

*Our students have important messages to deliver and their own language in which to deliver them. We need to hear their voices and they need to hear their own voices. I hope the following selections will help make more of those voices heard.*

*And I hope that by taking the teacher into the writer's studio, the teacher will see the possibility of the powerful interaction I have experienced between practicing my craft and sharing that craft with my students. Each activity has stimulated the other.*

---

Writing is easy; it's *not* writing that's hard. The writing comes in a bolt; one moment there is nothing and the next there are a thousand words or more, an always unexpected burst of language that is frightening in the power and complexity of its connections, in the sudden clarity where there was confusion a moment before. It's easy to receive the bolt of lightning when it strikes; what's hard is to create conditions that cause lightning to strike — morning after morning — and then wait for the bolt to hit.

Every six weeks or less I get drawn away from the writing — too many interruptions, too much traveling, too much talking about writing, too many meetings, too much nonwriting writing (letters, memos, handouts) — and I have to reteach myself the conditions that allow me to receive writing. These include:

## SITTING

### Waiting

Lightning hits twice, thrice, a thousand times in the same spot. Flannery O'Connor teaches and comforts me: "Every morning between 9 and 12 I go to my room and sit before a piece of paper. Many times I just sit for three hours with no ideas coming to me. But I know one thing: If an idea does come between 9 and 12, I am there ready for it." She was a magnificent sitter; I wish I could sit as well as Flannery O'Connor.

But sitting has its price. Watch writers waddle across campus and you'll notice they grow broad in the beam, their spines shaped like a question mark, their necks crane forward as they peer at you. Writers are sedentary hunters. They wait for the lightning and keep making New Year's resolutions to sit better a dozen times a year — each resolution is aimed at getting the rump in *the* chair on a regular basis. My present resolutions:

- *Only* write before lunch.
- *Never* write after lunch.

If I write in the afternoon and the evening — when I don't write very well anyway — I put off all those things that interfere with writing but have to be done. Soon they build up and steal my mornings. Then I don't write and become mean.

## Immersion

I am involved with the subjects I write about long before I know I am going to write about them. And I am involved to a degree I cannot demand of my students. I am on duty twenty-four hours a day, reading, observing, absorbing, connecting, thinking, rehearsing. The subjects I write about are never far from me: the death of my daughter, the questions about my family and myself I am still trying to answer, the war in which I learned I could kill, the way I see others and myself behaving toward each other, the process of learning to write.

Of course, I suffer all the guilts that my students admit and my colleagues usually try to hide. I do not read enough; I do not read effectively enough; I do not read what I should read. I'm not up on the latest work — or I do not understand it. And yet I realize that never a day goes by that I am not grabbing hold of new information about the subjects on which I write. I am a continual student, and that is the resource from which all my writing is drawn.

## Need

Writing for me is more than a vocation; it is a need; it is the way in which I make meaning of my world, the way I collect and relate, explore and comprehend, speculate and test in a dialogue with myself that never ends. If you don't have to write, don't.

I don't (and didn't) write to win tenure, to get promoted, to make money (with this energy and commitment I could have made eleven killings in real estate). I don't write for fame, since I had a teaspoon of fame early and found it was both irrelevant — the process of doing the writing was long gone and I was doing new work — and unsatisfying — win one award and you want a dozen more.

I write because I have to write. Meet writers and they look ordinary because they are ordinary. It's important for students to become familiar with that ordinariness. We have many writers in our department and our students learn from their ordinariness. "Gee, I look more like a writer than Murray, perhaps I . . ."

But you'll never know writers as well in person — even lovers, wives, children?—as you'll know them from their writing. And you won't know them from their writing either. The more open and revealing writers are, the more they may be hidden, the more successful at camouflaging their necessary loneliness.

Writers are here and there at the same time, living while observing their living. Talking to you we are also often talking to ourselves in an interior dialogue which discusses—silently, secretly—what is being done while it is being done. Writing, for the writer, is an essential kind of talking to yourself. You may like what you hear, be amused, stirred, stimulated, angered, encouraged, startled, comforted, but what you are hearing is only part of the conversation by which the writer lives. If you don't have to talk to yourself, if you have no need to teach yourself by writing, then writing may not be essential to you. Talk, play the flute, paint, build a bridge, do business, bake, hammer, and do not worry that you're not writing. Society has never said it needed writers. We are all self-appointed and rise to speak without being called upon.

I have no choice. I must write to answer questions I am asking myself, to solve problems that I find interesting, to bring an order into an area where the confusion terrifies me. Donald Barthelme said, "Write about what you're most afraid of," and I nod, smiling. I write to hang on.

### Readers

I also write from an external need, to share what I am thinking with that tiny audience of intimates whose respect I need and with whom I am learning. I need to share my writing with my wife, my daughters, Don Graves, Chip Scanlan, Tom Newkirk, Jane Hansen, Carol Berkenkotter (who makes science of pauses, hesitations, and what is left out), and a changing audience of readers, always small, mostly writers themselves, who may respond or not. If hundreds or thousands of other readers tune in later, that's nice, but I really can't see that vague, distant audience who will not see the work until I am two or three projects down the road anyway. Publication is nice, but it is not significant enough to motivate me to place my rear end in the writing chair each morning. I write mostly for myself—and a handful of patient friends.

### Critics

I must confess those friendly readers on whom I depend are appreciators mostly. I am too immature to enjoy criticism; more sadist than masochist. I hunger for appreciation, and my writing takes its largest steps forward after praise, not criticism, no matter how much the constructive—or even destructive—comments are deserved. As a teacher I try to remember that.

I find little criticism relevant to the work in progress. Critics usually have their own idea of what I should say—based on their own beliefs—and how I should say it—based on their own ideas of good writing. Even the praise of nonwriting critics has little relationship to the writing in progress, and it can even be destructive — if that's what they think I am saying, I'm really in trouble.

### Invitations

When I receive an invitation to write a chapter such as this, to produce a journal article, to give a talk, I try to combine an internal need — how *do* I write — with an external need — maybe students *do* need to know what their teachers practice — and I have a condition for receptivity. The lightning may strike again.

### Innocence

I have the advantage in being undereducated for my trade. I'd like to be well educated but I am surrounded by people who are too well educated, who know too well what has been done and what can't be done. If you have the disadvantage of a fine and complete education, move out from that center of comfort to where you don't know everything, where there are dark forests, looming mountains, shadows that move, strange noises in the night.

I write out of what I don't know, not what I know, and that exploration of my ignorance makes each draft, the failed ones even more than the successful ones, fascinating, a challenge for another morning. Of course I keep discovering what others already know — but I have the challenge and the joy of exploration.

## ACTING

### Fragments

I need something to say — an idea, a subject, a theory, a thesis — but what the lightning bolt leaves is usually just a fragment, a puzzling piece of information, a question without an answer, an answer without a question, a detail, an incomplete observation, a partial pattern, an image, a phrase (a fragment of voice), a problem not yet defined, a feeling of anxiety that may be relived by writing. Writers have learned to pay attention to fragments that others do not even see lying at their feet.

### Concentration

Well, yes. Perhaps stubbornness is what I mean, a dumb determination to finish what is started. But that isn't all of it — a good deal of it — but not all of it. With all the necessary distraction and all the unnecessary interruptions, I need to be able, at the time of prewriting and writing, to concentrate on one task over all the others — at least for an hour, an hour and a half, two hours, half an hour, fifteen minutes, ten, less, but still a moment when I fall out of the world, forgetting time, place, duty, and listen to the writing flowing through me to the page.

### Deadlines

I have to have deadlines that are self-imposed or imposed by others, and I confess that the deadlines of others are more powerful than my own. I have to be patient, to wait, to listen, not to force the writing, but the day-by-day, hour-by-hour, and louder and louder and louder goose-step march of an approaching deadline is one of the most powerful lightning rods on my study roof.

### Planning

I spend most of my time planning what I may write, making lists, making notes, making more lists, talking to myself in my head and in my daybook. I try not to be too formal about how I plan — planning should be, above all, play — and I try not to write too early but wait. I will not force the writing — forced writing sounds like forced writing — but hold back until I have to write. The draft must demand to be written. I want to write when I can*not* not write. When the writing will come easily, without effort.

### Drafting

I write fast. I rush forward, writing so fast my handwriting becomes incomprehensible even to me, typing beyond my ability so that the letters and words pile up on the word processor like a train wreck, or dictating so fast I can produce 500 words or 1,000 in an hour; 1,500, 2,000, 2,500, 3,000 in a morning.

The speed itself is important. The best accidents of phrase or meaning — or meaning illuminated by phrase — occur when I am writing too fast.

### Rewriting

I'm doing it less and less. Rewriting means the creation of a new draft with major changes in subject, focus, order, voice. These days I plan more and rewrite less. But when I rewrite, I start back at the beginning, seeing the subject anew, not through the vision of the past draft. Rewriting is mostly replanning.

### Revising

Of course these first drafts — or third or fourth drafts — will have to be fussed with, cut, added, reordered, shaped, and polished so they appear on the page with the effort hidden, all the spontaneous touches neatly in place. That's fun, once you have a draft in hand.

### Voice

Most important of all, voice. I do not begin to write until I hear the voice of the writing, and when that voice fades during the drafting, rewriting/replanning, or revising, I stop, make myself quiet, and listen until I hear it again. The music of the writing, more than anything else, teaches me what I am learning about the subject, what I am feeling about the subject, how I must write the subject to make those thoughts and feelings clear.

And when the writing doesn't go well, the most effective tactic is to listen, quietly, carefully to the writing. If I listen closely enough the writing will tell me what to say and how to say it. As Jayne Anne Phillips says, "It's like being led by a whisper."

## BELIEVING

### Acceptance

Of what I am, not what I wish I were. Acceptance of the writing I am receiving, remembering that intention is the enemy and surprise the friend. William Stafford reminds me:

*I can imagine a person beginning to feel that he's not able to write up to that standard he imagines the world has set for him. But to me that's surrealistic. The only standard I can rationally have is the standard I'm meeting right now ... you should be more willing to forgive yourself. It really doesn't make any difference if you are good or bad today. The assessment of the product is something that happens after you've done it.*

The way I write today is the way I can write today. I must accept what the lightning delivers and make use of it. I can't imagine another text, written by someone other than myself, into being. I must accept myself to write — and accept the fact that writing reveals, not just what I say but who I am. Of course, I am afraid I will be found out — and I will.

### Self-consciousness

I used to worry that my compulsive study of my craft — "Don't think" we used to tell the goalie, knowing that if he thought, the puck would be in the net before the decision was made — would paralyze my writing or at least cause terminal constipation. Perhaps it hasn't helped, but I had no choice; long before I taught or made a profession of studying the writing process, I was a student of my craft. Aren't most writers?

Writing is luck but writers are repeatedly lucky. They hit the lottery number again and again. To be a writer, you have to be unself-conscious enough to allow the writing to strike, to allow it to surprise you, to accept the gift. But you have to be prepared — calculatingly prepared — to be lucky, and you have to have the cunning to allow what is written to appear spontaneously in the reader's mind. William Shakespeare: "The truest poetry is the most feigning."

### Escaping Craft

Skill is our goal and our prison. We have to learn the tricks of our trade. We apprentice ourselves to our craft to learn to write better — and we do. Our words are surer, stronger; our sentences grow lean; our paragraphs are packed. We learn to turn a phrase, to shape, to polish until our writing becomes professional, polished, slick. Our pieces are so well constructed they say what we have already said — better and better and better until we are hidden within our too well-constructed pages. We are safe. Skilled. Craftpersons. Publishing scholars. Pros.

We have constructed a prison around ourselves with our own carefully crafted words and we can't see out, can't hear out; can't see what needs attending to; can't hear the voice of what we might write on the outside. So we have the obligation to break out, to push beyond our skills, to try and write what we cannot yet write but what needs writing in ways that we have not yet found so that we write with less polish and craft and learn the craft of not finishing the writing too much, to make it rough enough (to leave the roughness in [to remember what Amiri Baraka wrote, "Hunting is not those heads on the wall"]) to let our writing be finished enough so that it helps us do our thinking but not so finished that our readers can only stand and gaze in awe at our clever thinking when we should invite them and allow them to do their own thinking, messing around with our drafts so they will not respect the text too much.

would I stop and mess around with a finished text, unpolish it, unshape it, incomplete it?

you know it

if I can learn how.

know your craft

yeah — that's the complicated thing. Exactly. If I get to know how to do that too well, then I'm crafty again, blinded by my carefully unfinished drafts.

But we *do* want to allow the reader to get into the writing with us, so that the writing doesn't get in the way of the experience of writing/reading reading/writing, so we aren't blinded by the conventions, deafened by the traditions, made dumb by our own hard-earned craft.

unfinishing a text

it is necessary and will be necessary again

as we learn how to get out of the way — how to write rough — when we become crafty enough to allow the writing to appear spontaneous. Even when it is really spontaneous, when we have not got in the way, then what we have done is to learn a new craft, a new skill, a new way of digging in where it is safe and the lightning can never find us. so

## Incompleteness

This is a new draft, but it isn't the last word on how writing is made or even how I make writing. It contradicts some things I've said about how I write, and what I say in the future will produce more contra-dictions. I just wrote a new version of *A Writer Teaches Writing* without opening the previous edition; I am writing a novel without referring to the last draft. I don't want to be imprisoned by my own ideas and my own words. I don't want to be either consistent or proudly inconsistent. I want each morning to find out what I have to say that day. Each publication is nothing more or less than an entry in my daybook where I talk to myself about what I don't know and need to know, imagining answers to questions that really can't be answered: How do people stay with us after they die? Why did my family do what it did to itself? Why are we able to make war — and to be proud of it? Why did I survive? How do people take experience and re-create it in the minds of others through some squiggles on paper?

How do we learn from writing? How can we help others learn to learn from writing? I don't want any questions that have answers — they aren't any fun.

### Faith

Hardest of all for me. Faith that I can write, that I have something to say, that I can find out what it is, that I can make it clear to me, to a reader, that I can write so that the reader is not aware of the writer but the meaning.

Faith enough not to read what is written until the entire draft is done and then not to compare it to what might have been or what others have done, but to listen to the writing, to see in it its own meaning, its own form, to hear its own voice. Faith enough to stand out there all alone and invite the lightning.

# 2

# starting support groups for writers

MARGE PIERCY

Every writer needs support and feedback to go on writing. Established writers can get some of that from their audiences, but until then, we can only get support and feedback from the people around us and from each other. In Chicago many years ago I had a support group, and then again for a while in New York. I still have a number of writers to whom I show manuscripts or my novels in second draft or with whom I exchange poems. This description of how to set up a support group was written initially for the Feminist Writers' Guild of New England, published in our newsletter, and then expanded some for the National Feminist Writers' Guild Handbook, *Words in Our Pockets*.

For publication here I have changed little. I have retained the female pronouns of its original publications; I am always reading "he's" that are presumed to include me, so why not vice versa? If these suggestions are to be applied to mixed groups, I think it even more important to stress the importance of not allowing one, two, or three individuals to dominate a group and especially to dominate reading or criticism. I once taught a workshop composed of eight women and two men. The two men always spoke first to every poem, and set the tone of reaction so that the women who were timid and had different aesthetic criteria tended to keep silent. I finally had to establish a rule that neither of the men could speak until two women had addressed any particular poem. After two weeks I could lift the rule because the women had begun to gain confidence and the men had become conscious of their overmastering behavior. The workshop was more useful to everybody in it once it reflected the opinions of more than two members.

Reprinted by permission of The Wallace Literary Agency, Inc. Copyright © 1981, 1982, 1984 by Marge Piercy and Middlemarsh, Inc.

## GROUND RULES FOR A SUPPORT GROUP

### 1. Respect

Everybody should be able to expect the group to listen to her work and accord it respect. We should try to give another writer criticism for succeeding or failing to do what she is trying to do, not for doing something we wouldn't do. We should not expect that other people want to write the way we do or with the style or content of writers we admire. We should respect women who write directly from their own experiences and women who write from their imagination or their research. A support group is no place to win converts to your ideas.

### 2. Equal Time

This is an ideal but not a rigid one. Everyone in the group should be able to claim equal time for her work. However, if somebody has low or slow output, the group should not put more pressure on her than she wishes. With a poetry group we might go around the room each time and read one poem by each of maybe half the group. In a drama, fiction, or article group, we might do two or three people each meeting until everyone has been heard and then repeat.

### 3. Everyone Participates

No one has the right to ask support, feedback or criticism if she is not willing to listen carefully and/or read carefully the work of others and give her responses freely. When we feel we don't know how to express what we sense about somebody's writing, we have to risk trying to say what we mean. We have to risk sounding silly or clumsy or wrong. Silence is not fair to the others in the group; being shy is a luxury. We must share our reactions to others' work so that we can give help as well as receive it. Learning to express my feelings and reactions, my evaluation of another woman's work is important to me because from that exercise I will learn observations I can bring back to my own work. Having to say what I feel is good discipline, and support groups are an environment, unlike a class or a formal workshop or writer's conference, where it should be easy for us to expose our reactions to each other, where we have a right to expect support and respect.

Not every writer can afford to be taking writing workshops all the time, nor are they necessarily the best source of feedback. Often what you learn when you "study" writing with somebody is their mannerisms and their prejudices. Some writing workshops tend to produce a product; a large number of the students who pass through them emerge with similar notions about poetry or prose revealed in their work. Sometimes you will do better with a group of peers.

Often what you learn in a workshop or in a support group is the questions to ask yourself when your poem or piece of fiction is not coming along right. What variables should you consider changing? That way you learn how to revise.

### 4. We Try to Help

The rule of thumb is always to think what to say to help the other become a better writer. Being witty at the expense of another group member or using their work to put out a pet theory about writing is not being helpful. Each group will set its own emotional tone: how blunt or how gentle people feel comfortable with. But everyone in the group must be able to live with that feeling tone. We should not lie to each other, as that does not help. But we should think how to give feedback that is truly useful.

We must try to be open to each other's criticism too. It's useless to be in a group at all if all we want is adulation. If every criticism is met with "But that's the way it was!," "That's just how I felt!," "That's how it came to me," you can't learn and there's no motivation for others to boil their brains trying to help you.

### 5. Copies

Each person should take the responsibility for making copies of her own work. Xeroxing is so popular, people often forget that carbon paper exists. Any typewriter will make six or seven legible copies if onion skin or carbon copy manifolds are used. If you give copies to your group, you can expect much better feedback. Many people simply can't get more from a poem or story the first time they hear it than a general emotional sense. That's fine for a reading, but defeats the purpose of a support group.

### 6. Who Talks

As said above, everybody should make a strong attempt to communicate about each piece of writing. It's also our duty to keep any one or two writers who are more articulate or experienced from dominating the group so that their taste has too much influence.

### 7. Support in Work Habits

Many of the problems writers face are not in our work, but in our lives. People around us give us little or no support for being writers, for writing. We can give each other that support. We may have trouble sitting down to write. We can encourage each other. We can work in the same building or at certain hours. We can share or circulate child care among our group. We can work out patterns of assistance that help individual women work. Some women want to be nagged. They want a phone call at 10:00 saying, "Have you got to work yet?" Some women need to be praised. They want a phone call at 5:00 saying, "How much did you get done? That's wonderful." Some women want to be let alone while working. They need encouragement in taking the phone off the hook and refusing to answer the door. Some of us need places outside our homes in which to write: we can share office space. Sometimes writers get stuck and need help getting unstuck. Sometimes being listened to about personal problems helps. Praise may be needed. Sometimes a writer needs a sounding board for ideas or needs some help or suggestions for solving a problem that has stymied her.

## MECHANICS OF STARTING

1. Somebody must take early responsibility. We need a leader for the first meeting or two. After that, we should rotate the chair.

2. Limit the size of your group. The group can be bigger for poetry than for prose. You do not want a group so big it takes two months before you get to read your work. People will drop out if that is so.

3. Make a real commitment to coming. Death, serious illness, and having to be out of town are valid excuses. Going to a movie, a party, not feeling like it, let other people down who want to read that night, who need help, who need encouragement.

4. Always inform the group if you won't be there.

5. Don't set a time for a meeting when people in your group usually are writing. If the group cuts into work time, it will be resented.

6. Things to do at the first meeting if you don't start right in with reading: You might want to discuss, going around the room:

*What writing experiences you have had,*
*What you want to write and why,*
*What do you want/need from the group,*
*What obstacles do you experience in writing,*
*What has helped you to define yourself as a writer and*
*What has hurt you,*
*What do you hope and/or fear from the group?*

7. In fiction or nonfiction groups, an agreement should be made about roughly how many pages somebody is going to read. It doesn't work well for somebody to read for two hours or even one hour. No matter how interesting it may be (especially to the author), everybody tunes out eventually and starts thinking about their dental appointment, kids, lovers, and how long it will be till they get to read.

8. Save some time in every other meeting at least to go around and get out anything that's needed. Groups can foul up on little bad interactions if there's no way to work out problems or hurt feelings that arise.

## THINGS A GROUP CAN DO EVENTUALLY

Our support group can also provide the beginnings of a group who gives readings. It's much easier for a group of lesser known writers to get a reading someplace together than for each woman individually to secure such a reading. You can each coerce enough close friends to come out to hear you to put together a decent-sized audience. Your writing often improves when you have to read it aloud. Once you have got over your initial fear and nervousness, you can hear what works and what doesn't in prose as well as in poetry.

Your support group can also put out a magazine, a journal, an anthology, or a chapbook. You can sell it at readings you do together as well as hustling it around in the usual bookstores.

Finally, your support group gives you an audience, something which an apprentice writer needs more than anything else except time and determination.

# effective teacher-child conferences
# the importance of writing yourself

RUTH NATHAN

3

If you are a teacher, holding a conference with a writer is not easy. The problem is twofold. Authors break easily, and teachers tend to criticize. Authors, especially authors who happen to be children, do not want advice right away. Authors want readers to tell them they've done a good job. Recently a fourth grader put it rather simply: "I want people to say, 'Oh, that's *excellent*.'"

Authors understand that advice, while necessary, must be given at the right time and by a trusted individual. Because this is so, it is essential that you write if you are going to be a good writing teacher. It doesn't really matter if you write well; that's almost (but not totally) irrelevant. What does matter is that you *attempt* to write something well, and then that you read your draft to someone else. In other words, practice putting yourself on the line. It is knowing how a writer feels when a piece is shared, the chemical twang, the wildly beating heart, the mental involvement, the "I'm out there and feeling vulnerable" sensations that you *must* comprehend if you want to do a decent teaching job.

Another equally important reason for writing if you are going to teach the subject is that only after you have seriously attempted to get an idea across on paper does the difficulty inherent in the writing process become obvious. For example, ideas, far too many of them, enter your mind all at once; and you (unlike the computer on your desk) must eke them out one at a time—slowly. Furthermore, you don't have gestures to help you get your point across, as you do when you talk. Gestures, and other cues like intonation, help your audience understand you. When you write, all you have is a blank sheet of paper and your ability to handle the English language. If you are a novice writer (or if you are a small talker), you undoubtedly fail in your initial attempts to say what you mean. The point is, the difficulty in producing a memorable and interesting, funny, or informative piece is only apparent if and when you attempt to write yourself.

Reprinted with permission from "The Reading and Writing Process: A New Approach to Literacy" Resource Guide. Developed by Donald Graves and Jane Hansen; produced by James Whitney; written by Ruth Hubbard and Brenda Miller Power. Copyright © 1988 by Heinemann Educational Books, Inc.

As long as you write, you will have absolutely no reason to be afraid of teaching writing. In addition to being a sensitive listener and a person aware of the difficulty inherent in writing well, you can be a good conference partner. This is simply because, whether experienced at writing or not, you are an experienced listener: You know when you are confused, you know when you need more information, you recognize when a story is incomplete. In other words, you have the power to help others develop their writing ability not only because you write, but because you can respond as an interested reader; that is, as a reader who wants to comprehend a message.

# the importance of the act of reading

PAULO FREIRE

4

In attempting to write about the importance of reading, I must say something about my preparation ... something about the process of writing this [text], which involved a critical understanding of the act of reading. Reading does not consist merely of decoding the written word or language; rather, it is preceded by and intertwined with knowledge of the world. Language and reality are dynamically inter-connected. The understanding attained by critical reading of a text implies perceiving the relationship between text and context.

As I began writing about the importance of the act of reading, I felt myself drawn enthusiastically to rereading essential moments in my own practice of reading, the memory of which I retained from the most remote experiences of childhood, from adolescence, from young manhood, when a critical understanding of the act of reading took shape in me. In writing this [chapter], I put objective distance between myself and the different moments at which the act of reading occurred in my experience: first, reading the world, the tiny world in which I moved; afterward, reading the word, not always the word-world in the course of my schooling.

Recapturing distant childhood as far back as I can trust my memory, trying to understand my act of *reading* the particular world in which I moved, was absolutely significant for me. Surrendering myself to this effort, I re-created and relived in the text I was writing the experiences I lived at a time when I did not yet read words.

I see myself then in the average house in Recife, Brazil, where I was born, encircled by trees. Some of the trees were like persons to me, such was the intimacy between us. In their shadow I played, and in those branches low enough for me to reach I experienced the small risks that prepared me for greater risks and adventures. The old house—its bedrooms, hall, attic, terrace (the setting for my mother's ferns), backyard—all this was my first world. In this world I crawled, gurgled, first stood up, took my first steps, said my first words. Truly, that special world presented itself to me as the arena of my perceptual activity and therefore as the world of my first reading. The *texts*, the *words*, the *letters* of that context were incarnated in a series of things, objects, and signs. In perceiving these I experienced myself, and the more I experienced myself, the more my perceptual capacity increased. I learned to understand things, objects, and signs through using them in relationship to my older brothers and sisters and my parents.

The *texts*, *words*, *letters* of that context were incarnated in the song of the birds — tanager, flycatcher, thrush — in the dance of the boughs blown by the strong winds announcing storms; in the thunder and lightning; in the rainwaters playing with geography, creating lakes, islands, rivers, streams. The *texts*, *words*, *letters* of that context were incarnated as well in the whistle of the wind, the clouds in the sky, the sky's color, its movement; in the color of foliage, the shape of leaves, the fragrance of flowers (roses, jasmine); in tree trunks; in fruit rinds (the varying color tones of the same fruit at different times — the green of a mango when the fruit is first forming, the green of a mango fully formed, the greenish-yellow of the same mango ripening, the black spots of an overripe mango — the relationship among these colors, the developing fruit, its resistance to our manipulation, and its taste). It was possibly at this time, by doing it myself and seeing others do it, that I learned the meaning of the verb *to squash*.

Animals were equally part of that context — the same way the family cats rubbed themselves against our legs, their mewing of entreaty or anger; the ill humor of Joli, my father's old black dog, when one of the cats came too near where he was eating what was his. In such instances, Joli's mood was completely different from when he rather playfully chased, caught, and killed one of the many opossums responsible for the disappearance of my grandmother's fat chickens.

Part of the context of my immediate world was also the language universe of my elders, expressing their beliefs, tastes, fears, and values which linked my world to a wider one whose existence I could not even suspect.

In the effort to recapture distant childhood, to understand my act of reading the particular world in which I moved, I re-created, relived the experiences I lived at a time when I did not yet read words. And something emerged that seems relevant to the general context of these reflections: my fear of ghosts. During my childhood, the presence of ghosts was a constant topic of grown-up conversation. Ghosts needed darkness or semidarkness in order to appear in their various forms — wailing the pain of their guilt; laughing in mockery; asking for prayers; indicating where their cask was hidden. Probably I was seven years old, the streets of the neighborhood where I was born were illuminated by gaslight. At nightfall, the elegant lamps gave themselves to the magic wand of the lamplighters. From the door of my house I used to watch the thin figure of my street's lamplighter as he went from lamp to lamp in a rhythmic gait, the lighting taper over his shoulder. It was a fragile light, more fragile even than the light we had inside the house; the shadows overwhelmed the light more than the light dispelled the shadows.

There was no better environment for ghostly pranks than this. I remember the nights in which, enveloped by my own fears, I waited for time to pass, for the night to end, for dawn's demilight to arrive, bringing with it the song of the morning birds. In morning's light my night fears sharpened my perception of numerous noises, which were lost in the brightness and bustle of daytime but mysteriously underscored in the night's deep silence. As I became familiar with my world, however, as I perceived and understood it better by *reading* it, my terrors diminished.

It is important to add that *reading* my world, always basic to me, did not make me grow up prematurely, a rationalist in boy's clothing. Exercising my boy's curiosity did not distort it, nor did understanding my world cause me to scorn the enchanting mystery of that world. In this I was aided rather than discouraged by my parents.

My parents introduced me to reading the word at a certain moment in this rich experience of understanding my immediate world. Deciphering the word flowed naturally from *reading* my particular world; it was not something superimposed on it. I learned to read and write on the ground of the backyard of my house, in the shade of the mango trees, with words from my world rather than from the wider world of my parents. The earth was my blackboard, the sticks my chalk.

When I arrived at Eunice Vascancello's private school, I was already literate. Here I would like to pay heartfelt tribute to Eunice, whose recent passing profoundly grieved me. Eunice continued and deepened my parents' work. With her, reading the word, the phrase, and the sentence never entailed a break with reading the *world*. With her, reading the word meant reading the *word-world*.

Not long ago, with deep emotion, I visited the home where I was born. I stepped on the same ground on which I first stood up, on which I first walked, began to talk, and learned to read. It was that same world that first presented itself to my understanding through my reading it. There I saw again some of the trees of my childhood. I recognized them without difficulty. I almost embraced their thick trunks — young trunks in my childhood. Then, what I like to call a gentle or well-behaved nostalgia, emanating from the earth, the trees, the house, carefully enveloped me. I left the house content, feeling the joy of someone who has reencountered loved ones.

Continuing the effort of rereading fundamental moments of my childhood experience, of adolescence and young manhood — moments in which a critical understanding of the importance of the act of reading took shape in practice — I would like to go back to a time when I was a secondary school student. There I gained experience in the critical interpretation of texts I read in class with the Portuguese teacher's help, which I remember to this day. Those moments did not consist of mere exercises, aimed at our simply becoming aware of the existence of the page in front of us, to be scanned, mechanically and monotonously spelled out, instead of truly read. Those moments were not *reading lessons* in the traditional sense, but rather moments in which texts, including that of the young teacher Jose Pessoa, were offered to us in our restless searching.

Sometime afterward, as a Portuguese teacher in my twenties, I experienced intensely the importance of the act of reading and writing — basically inseparable — with first-year high school students. I never reduced syntactical rules to diagrams for students to swallow, even rules governing prepositions after specific verbs, agreement of gender and number, contractions. On the contrary, all this was proposed to the student's curiosity in a dynamic and living way, as objects to be discovered within the body of texts, whether the student's own or those of established writers, and not as something stagnant whose outline I described. The students did not have to memorize the description mechanically, but rather learn its underlying significance. Only by learning the significance could they know how to memorize it, to fix it. Mechanically memorizing the description of an object does not constitute knowing the object. That is why reading a text as pure description of an object (like a syntactical rule), and undertaken to memorize the description, is neither real reading nor does it result in knowledge of the object to which the text refers.

I believe much of teachers' insistence that students read innumerable books in one semester derives from a misunderstanding we sometimes have about reading. In my wanderings throughout the world there were not a few times when young students spoke to me about their struggles with extensive bibliographies, more to be *devoured* than truly read or studied, "reading lessons" in the old-fashioned sense, submitted to the students in the name of scientific training, and of which they had to give an account by means of reading summaries. In some bibliographies I even read references to specific pages in this or that chapter from such and such a book, which had to be read: "pages 15 – 37."

Insistence on a quantity of reading without internalization of texts proposed for understanding rather than mechanical memorization reveals a magical view of the written word, a view that must be superseded. From another angle, the same view is found in the writer who identifies the potential quality of his work, or lack of it, with the quantity of pages he has written. Yet one of the most important documents we have — Marx's "Theses on Feuerbach" — is only two and a half pages long.

To avoid misinterpretation of what I'm saying, it is important to stress that my criticism of the magical view of the word does not mean that I take an irresponsible position on the obligation we all have — teachers and students — to read the classic literature in a given field seriously in order to make the texts our own and to create the intellectual discipline without which our practice as teachers and students is not viable.

But to return to that very rich moment of my experience as a Portuguese teacher: I remember vividly the times I spent analyzing the work of Gilberto Freyre, Lins do Rego, Graciliano Ramos, Jorge Amado. I used to bring the texts from home to read with students, pointing out syntactical aspects strictly linked to the good taste of their language. To that analysis I added commentaries on the essential differences between the Portuguese of Portugal and the Portuguese of Brazil.

I always saw teaching adults to read and write as a political act, an act of knowledge, and therefore a creative act. I would find it impossible to be engaged in a work of mechanically memorizing vowel sounds, as in the exercise "ba-be-bi-bo-bu, la-le-li-lo-lu." Nor could I reduce learning to read and write merely to learning words, syllables, or letters, a process of teaching in which the teacher *fills* the supposedly *empty* heads of learners with his or her words. On the contrary, the student is the subject of the process of learning to read and write as an act of knowing and of creating. The fact that he or she needs the teacher's help, as in any pedagogical situation, does not mean that the teacher's help nullifies the student's creativity and responsibility for constructing his or her own written language and for reading this language.

When, for instance, a teacher and a learner pick up an object in their hands, as I do now, they both feel the object, perceive the felt object, and are capable of expressing verbally what the felt and perceived object is. Like me, the illiterate person can *feel* the pen, perceive the pen, and say *pen*. I can, however, not only feel the pen, perceive the pen, and say *pen*, but also write *pen* and, consequently, read *pen*. Learning to read and write means creating and assembling a written expression for what can be said orally. The teacher cannot put it together for the student; that is the student's creative task.

I need go no further into what I've developed at different times in the complex process of teaching adults to read and write. I would like to return, however, to one point referred to elsewhere in this book because of its significance for the critical understanding of the act of reading and writing, and consequently for the project I am dedicated to—teaching adults to read and write.

Reading the world always precedes reading the word, and reading the word implies continually reading the world. As I suggested earlier, this movement from the word to the world is always present; even the spoken word flows from our reading of the world. In a way, however, we can go further and say that reading the word is not preceded merely by reading the world, but by a certain form of *writing* it or *rewriting* it, that is, of transforming it by means of conscious, practical work. For me, this dynamic movement is central to the literacy process.

For this reason I have always insisted that words used in organizing a literacy program come from what I call the "word universe" of people who are learning, expressing their actual language, their anxieties, fears, demands, and dreams. Words should be laden with the meaning of the people's existential experience, and not of the teacher's experience. Surveying the word universe thus gives us the people's words, pregnant with the world, words from the people's reading of the world. We then give the words back to the people inserted in what I call "codifications," pictures representing real situations. The word *brick*, for example, might be inserted in a pictorial representation of a group of bricklayers constructing a house.

Before giving a written form to the popular word, however, we customarily challenge the learners with a group of codified situations, so they will apprehend the word rather than mechanically memorize it. Decodifying or *reading* the situations pictured leads them to a critical perception of the meaning of culture by leading them to understand how human practice or work transforms the world. Basically, the pictures of concrete situations enable the people to reflect on their former interpretation of the world before going on to read the word. This more critical reading of the prior, less critical reading of the world enables them to understand their indigence differently from the fatalistic way they sometimes view injustice.

In this way, a critical reading of reality, whether it takes place in the literacy process or not, and associated above all with the clearly political practices of mobilization and organization, constitutes an instrument of what Antonio Gramsci calls "counterhegemony."

To sum up, reading always involves critical perception, interpretation, and *rewriting* of what is read.

# one teacher's learning

TIM GILLESPIE

**5**

*One must always tell what one sees. Above all, which is more difficult, one must always see what one sees.*

*Charles Peguy*

---

I want to try to tell, in this essay, some things I see about teaching writing from points of view outside the classroom, from my perspective as a learner, a parent, and a writer.

Sometimes, however, I get so caught up in my teaching that I don't see what I see from these other vantage points. I'll try to remedy a writing class problem by consulting experts, scanning research, reading books on pedagogy. There's nothing wrong here; my teaching is often enriched. But I think I may be starting in the wrong place. Thus, when, as it sometimes happens, the recommended techniques don't work so well, or the textbook activities fall flat, or the pedagogy apparently fits students other than the ones in *my* classroom, I'm really stuck if I'm ignoring what I have learned as a student or parent or writer.

For example, I'm trying to learn to *wait* in my teaching, to look twice before I jump in with advice or assistance, so my student writers have a chance to see if they can first do it themselves. I learned this lesson again recently on a morning walk—learned it better, perhaps, than if I'd been thinking about teaching.

I came upon a fixture in my neighborhood, an elderly gentleman who often stands on the corner watching traffic or inches along the sidewalk by the nearby market. I don't know him, but I see him there frequently. He walks painfully, a cane in each of his big tanned hands. He's unmistakable for the dented old fedora he always wears and the red-and-black checked shirt he tucks into his blue bib overalls. I've decided he was a farmer once but has somehow ended up in a

Reprinted with permission from *Language Arts* 64: 738−42. Copyright 1987 by the National Council of Teachers of English.

residential care center for seniors in the middle of the city. Out of habit, though, he still gets out in the day's weather early.

I was out early, too, on a walk to the store for some milk. When I came out with my grocery bag, he was standing there, facing the side of the store in a clumsy posture, head down. The ends of both his canes were awkwardly banging together on the sidewalk as if he were trying to grasp something, the rubber tips jerkily scraping the gum-stained cement again and again.

I looked down. A quarter was leaning against the wall, its serrated edge glinting copper in the sunlight. He was trying to pick up the coin with his canes. On one try he seemed to have it, but when he started to lift the quarter between his cane tips it flipped out and rolled away from the wall. He had to drag himself a couple of steps to try again, only now with a greater challenge—the coin lay flat on the sidewalk, clumsy even for those who could bend and use their fingers.

I couldn't walk past. The old guy's dropped his quarter, I thought. He's poor, he needs it. He can't lean over to get it. He's frustrated, humiliated. He needs some help, my help.

I didn't ask, just leaned over to grab the coin for him. "Here, let me get it for you." He touched the back of my outstretched arm with one rubber cane tip. I looked at his face for the first time. "Don't," he said, with a small grin. "I'm just trying to see if I can do it."

So here's a lesson. A student, a writer, sometimes just needs to see if he can do it, needs to scrape at the improbable, needs to feel the inching handicap of words in the face of all the glittery promising stuff he'd like to say and grasp and hold. All before I jump in to help. Learning to wait is part of the art of teaching.

The place I think I learn most about teaching is at home, in the presence of all the miracles of language development I witness in my own children. A couple of years ago, for example, I had this conversation with my youngest son, who was somewhere in that magical span of wordweaving between ages one and two:

"Daddy," he told me, "Wanna moobuh. Up." He was tugging at my pant leg, animated, looking way up into my face. I was impressed; this was one of the longer utterances he'd strung together.

"Joshie, what do you want?"

"A moobuh, Daddy."

"A 'moo-buh'?"

"Yes, Daddy." There was a sweet urgency in his face.

"Hm . . . moo? You mean a moo-cow, Joshie, a cow? You want a cow?"

No, Daddy, a moo-buh, a look."

What's he want, I wondered. Couldn't be an amoeba. A move? A mood? "A *moon*, Joshie?"

"Yes, Daddy!" He danced a little jig of excitement: to be understood!

"You want to see the moon outside, Joshie?"

No, a moon-*buh*, Daddy. Up inna."

A moon *bug*? No. "A moon *ball*?" Maybe, I thought, he means the rubber ball with the stars around it, confusing stars and moon.

"No, Daddy. Up. A moon-buh. A look."

"It's up?" I look up, scan the room, see a washtub of Joshua's books on top of the piano. "Moon *book*, Joshie? You want a moon book?"

"Yes, Daddy. Moon book. Up inna."

"That's right, the books are up there in the tub, up on top of the piano."

"Yes, Daddy. Look."

I go over and scan the books, find our Margaret Wise Brown favorite. "Oh, Joshie, I bet you want me to read you this *Goodnight Moon* book,"

Joshua is gleeful, beaming—as overjoyed, it seems to me, by being understood as by having the power to get me up to grab the book off the piano for a lapside read-aloud.

I'm struck, then, by the comparison to teaching writing. What compels this child's energy, this willingness to try again to be clear, to compose and revise with tireless verve? How can I replicate this willingness in my writing class?

The answer lies, I think, in the interaction. My son and I are involved in a fond conspiracy to make sense, an ongoing interchange to create meaning together, fueled by the good will of our relationship and the belief we can reach understanding, and driven by the desire to get something done. The growth in proficiency of Joshua's language skills and vocabulary are both functions of his urge to make sense, to be understood. We start at this pragmatic level, with the *reasons* Joshua has for making language.

These lessons for my writing classes—to cultivate trust, to provide interaction, to start with writing's purposes rather than its protocols— are reinforced in my home, learned from my sons, with a special lastingness.

I learned another powerful lesson about teaching writing when I began to cross-country ski a decade ago.

An insight about grammar, of all things, struck me as I stood, puffing slightly, poised on the edge of a deep, snow-lined crater on Mt. Hood, held only in the narrow friction between my spindly skis and the sleek snow dropping away, gleaming blue below me in the bowl's shadow. My breath was visible in the air, small ragged periods punctuating my heartbeat. So, I thought, maybe learning to write is like learning to ski.

It was snowing lightly, fat wet flakes, and it was cold. My goggles, I remember, were a bit fogged, and I couldn't see perfectly where I wanted to go. Perched on the lip of that crater, I thought, "This is ridiculous. These skis are for distance, not downhill."

I pictured myself stepping out over the abyss, into the hip-deep powder, angling across the precipitous curve of the bowl. "Just keep your weight on your back leg," Viljo had said earlier that winter.

Viljo, my instructor, a ruddy and vigorous fellow who'd grown up on skis in his Finnish village, was a masterful teacher. In our first session at the Scandia Hall, he had set up displays of various bindings, poles, clothes, and skis. We had learned the names for all the gear. Then he'd demonstrated some basic principles (the arm held straight, the glide, the weight over the skis, a simple step-turn, the snowplow). Flipping off the lights, he'd shown a film. Skiers on majestic slopes demonstrated rudimentary moves. What Viljo had shown on the wood floor we now saw in the snow of the film. The narrator's polished voice reinforced our new knowledge. By the end of our hour-and-a-half orientation, we were ready. We knew the equipment. We could recognize correct technique and could analyze its component parts. We had a skiing vocabulary. In short, we knew a great deal *about* cross-country skiing.

There is a significant point lurking here, I told myself, standing on the edge of the crater. I tried to remember some of the principles I'd learned from the movie and lecture. Poised there, I knew what I was going to try to do and I knew generally where I wanted to end up at the bottom of that monstrous bowl. The *how* of it all was a little hazy.

I stepped off the crater rim with the smallest push of the poles and dropped with a stomach-lurching slam, but I did remember for a moment, I did put my weight way back on those skinny edgeless skis, did keep one ski far forward of the other but parallel as the tightest of paragraphs. I enjoyed the roostertail of snow beside me as I found the balance, caught the rhythm, the glide, the adrenaline-pumping pace of grace and speed — and then some earthly bump, some imperfection in the slope or me, some unanticipated flaw in material or technique broke the smooth surface, ripped into the seamless flight, set me off balance, bounced me around, knocked legs akimbo, pitched me forward to cartwheel, roll, fall, tumble woodenly, ripped the poles out of my hands, the ski off one foot, snowballed me over and over, punched the breath out of me. I landed groaning in a heap below, snow crammed under my goggles and up my back.

Here's what I learned so forcefully: *knowing about* is different than *doing*. Studying the parts of ski equipment and performance is knowing about. Skiing is doing. Studying grammar and technique is knowing about. Writing is doing. The former is not useful without plenty of the latter. I can know the vocabulary, describe the techniques and equipment, label and name the parts with astonishing accuracy, but I still don't know how to ski until I practice on the snow time and time again, and sometimes fall. The same with writing.

One more thing. Viljo, watching with a chuckle from the bottom of the bowl, skied over to me in the groaning heap. He did not say, "You did it wrong." He said, "Wasn't that fun? You got almost halfway down. Your weight was back. You could lean more on your poles maybe. Next time you might get even farther."

I brushed the snow off and headed back up to the edge of the crater.

So, I'm working as a teacher to reclaim the authority of my own experience. My teaching partner, the poet and essayist Kim Stafford, says it this way: "Whenever I can't figure out how to help one of my students solve a writing problem, I think long and hard about my own work first. My writing teaches me what books on teaching writing can't always."

I want to be open to learning as much as I can from any source, but I also don't want to be completely dependent on received knowledge. I don't want to give up the power of my own judgment in the face of expertise, but would rather weigh and assess any new learning in the light of my own perceptions and discoveries. I want to start with an acknowledgement of whatever expertise I have earned myself—from my classroom observations, my teaching history, and my students' claims, to be sure, but also from my reflections on my own experiences as a writer, parent, and learner. I want to make sure to see what I see.

**on paying attention
to the magic
an interview with Tim Gillespie**

RUTH HUBBARD

**Ruth Hubbard**: Let's start with your own literacy history. When did you start writing, Tim?

**Tim Gillespie**: When did I start writing? I don't know ... I've always written, but I don't know where it came from. I remember in fifth grade writing a poem when my youngest brother was born. I wrote it at home. It was self-sponsored, not school-determined. It was a long poem—rhyme and meter, or maybe semi-meter. I brought it to school and my teacher liked it. Somewhere, somehow, I guess I just found that it was something I enjoyed or got reinforcement for. It feels like an illness some days.

I mean, here I am at 10 o'clock, most every night when the impedimenta of daily living has been dispensed with—the dishes are washed and the kids are in bed and the bills are paid—and I'm drawn to the writing task—the writing table. And I ask myself, "Why am I doing this?" I could be reading a good book or watching TV, or doing something more sensible. I never signed a contract to do all this writing. What is this—compulsive?

**RH**: It's kind of addictive.

**TG**: Yeah, it has its addictive qualities. I figure it's my way of learning my way through the world.

**RH**: Who helps you with your writing now?

**TG**: Well, I get a lot of good help. Jan, my wife, is a good reader and I've been in a writing group for six years now. It's a varied group—some writers, some teachers, an architect, an anthropologist. The poet Kim Stafford is in it. Some people publish, some don't. Everyone works on different things.

**RH**: If you know you're going to be meeting with others, it keeps your writing going.

**TG**: It's a great incentive.

**RH**: Can you think of a teacher who has been influential in your life?

**TG**: Well, plenty. I've been lucky, but I think of one in particular: my eighth-grade teacher in a gigantic urban elementary school in Los Angeles County. We had thirty-seven or thirty-eight eighth graders in an all-day self-contained classroom. This guy named

Donald Seif—Mr. Seif—what a teacher he was! In this old dingy beat-up building with floor-to-ceiling windows and bolt-to-the-floor desks with the old open lids and the inkwells. There was no more ink, but there were holes where they used to be. Just wretched conditions. It was a very interesting mixed population. A lot of Hispanic kids, Asian kids. The middle-class kids on one side of the freeway and some real economically disadvantaged kids on the other. This guy was a miracle worker! He taught us algebra; he had us reading books we wanted to read; he had us putting on plays in class. We wanted to start a mathematics club and he said, "Great," and gave class time for it. He was very much into transferring responsibility to his students. I remember this being a year where lots was accepted—and lots was *expected*

**RH**: A combination of high expectations from you but a lot of choice and responsibility on your part?

**TG**: I think that's a good way to characterize it. And fun. This guy loved to laugh. He was a member of the community. He'd take a part in the plays, he'd read the books.

**RH**: That joy in literacy is so important and it often seems to get left out.

**TG**: I agree. But Mr Seif loved to read. He knew books. He was sharing his enthusiasm rather than jumping us through the hoops of mandated requirements. It makes it easier to go into work each day when you feel you're sharing what you love, rather than just keeping a lid on things. I heard Don Graves say this year, "Why should kids have all the fun?" I think that's a very wise question.

**RH**: You mention Don Graves. Who else would you include as a theorist who has had an influence on you?

**TG**: I think my first educational hero was James Moffett ... *Teaching the Universe of Discourse* was way ahead of its time. I read it early in my career as an English teacher and was really fascinated by this way of thinking about the teaching of writing. Moffett honored the students' words and worlds. My current heroes are Nancie Atwell, Jane Hansen, Don Murray, James Herndon for his classroom testimony. And I think more and more now I'm influenced by eloquent teachers who tell good stories about their classrooms, teachers who respect and who are articulate about our practitioners' lore. Nancie Atwell, for example, and folk like Carol Avery, that wonderful first-grade teacher in Pennsylvania—people who respect the narrative wisdom of teachers. Those are the educators whose work I like to read most now.

**RH**: Their voices are so strong in the stories they tell about classrooms—and literacy too. Talking of stories, you tell some wonderful ones in your article. I think of Josh asking to be read the "moon" book, and other examples of literacy in the home. Your kids are older now; is parenting still affecting your literacy instruction?

**TG**: I think I learn more about literacy as a parent than in any other role. At least, the teaching ratio is pretty good. Somehow, it's easier to pay attention at home to the magic we find in our own children's words. I mean, we collect malaprops from our kids and post them on the refrigerator! When Joshie points to a whirlybird in the sky and says, 'Look, Daddy, an ecilopter,' we're so delighted by that. I've always felt that, yes, this is the way it works, with this kind of mutually delighted collaboration toward making sense. I learned at home with my own children that language starts in joy and moves toward precision. So why can't those sparks also fly in a classroom? Sure, there are more kids in a classroom, but I find being a parent a pretty good metaphor for teaching. And now that my kids are a bit older, they're facing different things.

**RH**: Can you share an example?

**TG**: We were just throwing a story around about Joshua last week. It's fun for me to see Joshua, who's five, make a creative effort to figure out the world. These are the concepts that he's messing with all the time:

*"Daddy, we live in Portland, right?"*
*"Yup."*
*"So we don't live in Oregon?"*
*"Portland's inside of Oregon."*
*"Well . . . how does that work?"*

He wants to *know*. "Wait a minute. Oregon's bigger than Portland? How do you be inside of it? How does it all fit together?"

There's something in good chat—and *fond chat*—that is the key to much learning. It's engaged talk, but it's not always exactly directed at some specified end. So I'm continually reminded that I'd like to bring good conversation to the kids that are in my own classroom.

**RH**: How about your reading? What are some books that have had a real influence on you?

**TG**: I mostly read fiction, and most everything influences me. Oh, let's see. All I can talk about is what I've been reading the last few months. There's Louise Erdrich's *Love Medicine, The Beet Queen*, and I've been reading lots of books by Bobbie Ann Mason. In the most recent past, Toni Morrison's *Beloved* had a huge impact. I think books have always been a major influence on me. Reading Mark Twain's *The Mysterious Stranger* when I was in eighth grade changed my life. It was so expansive and I had that eighth-grade teacher—Mr. Sief—who supported me in reading these things and I guess it was one of those times when I left the last page of the book thinking, "The world is different than the world I have received as a given. I mean, there are more possibilities here." It was like someone shook me up and said, "Here's a new way of seeing things." Literature for me has always been a way of traveling and my way of learning and finding empathy. To go back to Toni Morrison, for example, her manner of engagement with the dilemmas of slavery in *Beloved* are so moving.

**RH**: It was a difficult—and wrenching—book for me to read. At one point I had to put it down, it was just so disturbing.

**TG**: Well, it *is* disturbing. I read that Toni Morrison said that she felt her goal was to conclude the slave narratives that were never completed. None of them told it all—they shied away from telling the final truths that were too hard to tell. But she did.

And, I have to admit, I've got my own personal vices for some of the literature I read. A couple of really trashy detective fiction writers. So I figure the kids need to read some schlock, too—it's part of being literate. And I've read an awful lot of children's literature and now adolescent literature through my children. I get all my good young adult fiction recommendations from my older son. When my eleven-year-old, Nathan, introduces me to Lloyd Alexander, I'm so grateful. That literature is so wonderful. Nancie Atwell's metaphor for the dining room table as a way of talking and about encouraging literature is one that I really buy. That's what I want my dining room table to be like, as well as my classroom.

**RH**: What are you working on now?

**TG**: Well, for one thing, I'm working on my own fiction. I've been fortunate to have a year sabbatical to work on a piece of fiction. I'm still trying to decide what I have learned about writing fiction that will help me with kids in a classroom. I'm not sure what conclusions I've made. It really strikes me in writing my own fiction that I have to rub against the rules—or any preconceived sense of what fiction must be like. I agree with Henry James's contention that a novelist's first responsibility is to exercise the freedom inherent in the form. That is, to be willing to break the rules. So in the classroom, I want to make sure my students understand that writing fiction is not a matter of following rules, even some that I think we've begun to enshrine in process-oriented approaches like "show don't tell." I don't think that advice is always appropriate for a fiction writer's goal. Sometimes it is, but sometimes it isn't. As a fiction writer, I have a particular story I'm struggling to tell. And the story itself is helping me to invent the best way of telling it. My characters, for them to live for me, and I assume, then, for them to live for the reader, I have to follow them. I'm just trying to catch up with them. They're following a path through this story that I've dreamed up. So, I don't know what kind of discovery that is and how that's going to help me in the classroom, other than to say "Beware of excessively imposing rules on young fiction writers."

But then, it's not always comfortable from a teaching standpoint to walk in and say, "We're writing fiction, kids, break the rules." How do I pass that advice on to other teachers or share [it] with my colleagues?

**RH**: I guess you encourage them to experiment with you—and keep track of what happens so you can share the wide range with other teachers.

**TG**: I think so. And I need to provide the context where kids have the time and have the choice if they want to explore some fiction writing and have lots of models and rich literature in the classroom so they see how many possible directions there are to go and get a sense of freedom of the form. And then provide them with response. I think those are things I have learned from writing fiction of my own.

**RH**: What's going on in the field of literacy that's really exciting to you?

**TG**: I'm really excited about the democratization in the field of literacy research, particularly. Or a diffusion of authority, at least. I can see it first in the honoring of classroom teachers, in the fact that we have greater access to eloquent teacher voices, those storytellers I talked about earlier. The whole teacher-as-researcher movement and the notion of collaborative research again honors the experiences of teaching, which I think is really terrific. Ethnographic or descriptive research itself honors the classroom environment and it basically looks at that environment as the seedbed of whatever theory or research we will end up living by.

I like honesty about life in school. Teachers are victims of so many theories or strategies or activities or programs or reading series that are abstractions of the messy realities of the classroom. I think we've all had the experience of setting up the perfect curriculum in the summer, designing the perfect environment, and then somehow the wrong kids walk in the door in September! "Wait a minute! This must be for other kinds of kids." James Herndon has a funny line: "Well, my ideas were correct—they just didn't work."

But, I think the greater availability of these ethnographic or descriptive or anthropological-type research descriptions of the classroom—they democratize our thinking about teaching. Knowledge is not just received from experts, it is earned by researchers watching real teachers, watching us. And I like that a lot.

**RH**: It's an exciting trend to give more validity to what teachers construct out of the experiences in their classroom—that kind of grounded theory. Now, on the other hand, is there anything you find disturbing?

**TG**: What do I fret about in literacy instruction? It seems to me we use ideas up at such a prodigious rate in our culture and things pass through so fast that I worry that something is being missed. I'm always seeking those "eternal verities," to use Faulkner's term. So much happens in educational thinking and scholarship and research; so many ideas keep coming and they just wash over us. I mean, from a classroom teacher's perspective, it feels like you're standing in the ocean and a wave comes and then another wave comes and another wave comes—the latest pedagogical trend or movement—many are refreshing, most powerful. The wave may have been the minimum competency movement one year, may have been behavioral objectives, may have been ITIP. One year it was assertive discipline, then one year it's writing process, then the next year it's discipline-based art education, then the next year it's whole language. A reasonable response to this continual washing and rewashing is to plant your feet and to say, "If I just stand here and hang in, this latest wave will pass. It'll kind of knock me a little bit, and I won't have to pay much attention 'cause the next one's gonna come and this one will be gone." Good ideas have the same dimension as faddish ideas. I want to learn from every new thing that comes by, but I also don't want to lose essential principles. I wonder, for example, what writing as a process means to people? What's the core truth that needs to be retained? A couple of years back, for instance, I went to talk to a principal who said, "I'm so excited after our workshop. I've been so excited about the writing-process approach and finally, after all this time, I've got my whole building into writing process! So now I know that every kid in every classroom in my building is prewriting Monday, drafting on Tuesday, revising Wednesday, editing Thursday, and sharing Friday."

So, I think, "Well, that's not exactly my sense of what writing-process theorists were trying to say." Then, two days later I visited a friend who's a middle-school teacher who said, in almost exactly the same language, "I'm so excited about this writing process. It's really changed my life. Now I just have my kids write for half an hour every day in their journals. They just write and choose all their own topics and they're creating all this stuff and they're excited about writing. I've never seen so many words generated and I never have to read anything; they just write in their journals all the time."

So within about three days, I had heard the term "writing process" used to justify instructional techniques in a range from very teacher-centered and lockstep to very unstructured and chaotic with no teacher involvement whatsoever. So I fret because I think we do use up ideas at this ferocious rate. And these ideas that I really love and care about are going to get used up, spit out, misunderstood and left behind in the rush for the new, the fashionable, the current.

RH: What are those core ideas, then, that you believe in for your teaching?

TG: Well, this is something I learned from a student I had a few years ago. Brian was one of these kids that really touches your heart because he was so bright and so alienated simultaneously. He hated school, you know, and rebelled against school and was started on a cycle of drugs and crime. He had all this wonderful potential so he made me angry and he made me want to save him and all those things we feel as teachers. But he had a habit of every day asking, "What's this for?", "Why am I doin' this?", "What's the purpose of this?", "What's the point?", "How'm I gonna use this?" You know, those very inconvenient questions.

But, it was also a very good discipline for me as a teacher to think what *is* this for? What is my final goal for him? What do I want him to have? How do I justify whatever it is we're doing? What does he need? What does *he* think he needs? And because of his daily obnoxious questioning, I became convinced that the lion's share of time in school needs to be spent practicing literacy skills in pretty close to the form in which they'll be encountered in the real world. In other words, why *were* we doing all these little worksheets on inferences and comprehension? Why wasn't he reading something about motorcycles? Because that's what he needed to know about, and maybe some good fiction and some current events so he'd be up on the world. Why wasn't he reading real things? And instead of doing exercises in writing, why wasn't he *writing*? Because that would be something that would give him more tools to bring with him out into the world.

So, Brian taught me that school can consist of the practice of things as they are encountered in the real world. And to me that's the lesson of whole language.

# personal histories and professional literacies

BRENDA MILLER POWER

*Those who forget history are condemned to repeat it.*

George Santayana

Some years ago I was a student in a graduate reading research seminar. One week our assignment was to bring in a favorite book — reading that was special to us at some point in our lives.

There were twenty-five students who were also public school teachers in that class. Of those students, eighteen brought in books they had read as young children. Again and again the teachers lamented the fact that they didn't have time to read. Most students in that class rarely read anything but assignments for class, or perhaps the newspaper.

I am now an instructor of teachers of reading and writing. The pattern I saw in that reading research seminar repeats itself in the classes I teach. Many teachers I work with rarely find time to read and write except when performing professional tasks. And many intensely dislike or fear the task of writing.

Specific experiences propelled these teachers into the teaching profession or away from reading and writing tasks in their lives. They all have histories as readers and writers. These personal histories as readers and writers consciously and unconsciously help shape the way we work with students struggling to read and write.

I want to share the stories of two women teachers, Ellen and Jan, whose histories as readers, writers, and teachers are radically different. Working with women like Ellen and Jan has shown me the importance of emphasizing personal history in the literacy methods courses I teach.

I think for many of us defining literacy in our classrooms and lives begins with these unique human stories. Dr. Oliver Sacks, a neurologist who is famous for his case studies recounted in the collection *The Man Who Mistook His Wife For A Hat* (1985), notes the importance of personal, human tales in our presentation of cases:

*To restore the human subject at the center — the suffering, afflicted, fighting human subject — we must deepen a case history to a narrative or tale: only then do we have a "who" as well as a "what"—a real person.*

Through case studies I do of students like Ellen and Jan, my sense of what it means to be literate is often redefined, and implications for changing my teaching practices have emerged.

## ELLEN AND THE POLITICS OF MOTHERHOOD

Ellen's story begins two years ago when I was rummaging through a trashcan in a first-grade classroom. Patricia McLure was the teacher in this room at Mast Way School in Lee, New Hampshire. I was a researcher in the room. One of the children in the class, Lindsay, had just thrown away a piece of paper. I was learning to save everything, and Lindsay's work was particularly interesting. What Lindsay had discarded is shown in Figure 7–1.

In this picture, Lindsay is holding her beloved dog with one hand, and a book about a dog written by a classmate in the other. Reading about the dog is integrated with her love for the dog and connects her to the classroom community of readers and writers.

I had tried for weeks to define what it means to be literate for a first grader. In Lindsay, I felt I'd found a child who could help me with that definition. She used her reading and writing to integrate her life experiences and make sense of them. She was innovative in the class, experimenting with ghostwriting, science writing, writing auto- biographical material, and even cue cards for a special presentation done for her classmates.

Lindsay was also assertive in class, unafraid to challenge the fairness of others. She knew what she wanted, and reading and writing were

**Figure 7–1**
Lindsay's Drawing

tools for her to have her wants met. She had the components for literacy in first grade that Carol Avery (1987) writes of—she took a major role in forming questions, exploring ideas, and drawing conclusions in order to be responsible for her own learning.

I knew the environment in Pat's class had a lot to do with Lindsay's literacy. Pat allows the children time and choice during reading and writing periods. The children can choose their topics and books, work areas, and different genres to explore. But Lindsay's assertiveness and sense of purpose were marked even in a classroom where these traits were encouraged for all. I knew that Lindsay's home environment might also play an important role in defining her sense of the purpose of literacy (for further research on home-school literacy links, see Heath [1983] and Wells [1986]), and I wanted to find out how.

I interviewed Lindsay's mother, Ellen, about Lindsay. I discovered quite a bit about Lindsay's interests in reading and writing. But more importantly, I learned about Ellen's history as a reader and writer. Ellen's history shaped her decision to become an English teacher, and it also plays a critical role in defining her attitudes toward parenting.

Ellen spoke of her own parents' expectations for her. When she became a parent herself, she was determined that her two daughters would have a different view of the world. When I asked her about her career and background, Ellen spoke of the conflicts she felt as a woman in our culture:

*I went to college to find an educated man to marry. That's what my parents expected. And once you graduated from college, well, hopefully you would have met someone your senior year, not gotten married before your senior year. I graduated in English lit, and was fortunate to find someone at the right time, and then I did get married. But then he was going on for his Ph.D., and didn't want to have kids yet, so I didn't know what to do with myself. I mean, I was a college graduate—I didn't want to be a waitress. So I was left in this quasi-land. "Well," some people said, "go back to school. Maybe you should be a teacher." Okay, fine. I really fell into teaching in a backhanded way. And like I said, I felt so frustrated all of my life with that attitude. I'm not the type of person to say, "Oh well, whatever moves me, I guess I'll do that." There are those people who enjoy living like that, moving from one thing to the next. But I'm not that type of person. I've always been goal-oriented. It was frustrating to me as a young adult not to have those goals, not to have been educated by my parents to think in terms of life goals ... When I was growing up, the only thing that was expected of me was to be taken care of through college and then someone would marry me and take care of me for the rest of my life. I mean, what a nowhere type of world that is. That's very Victorian. Very, very Victorian.*

Many of the teachers I work with fell into teaching in a similar way; teaching was viewed as an acceptable profession for women in our society for many generations. It was viewed as an adjunct to raising children. Ellen's memories of what she was told it meant to be a woman in her society, and the expectations of that culture, made her determined that things would be different for her daughters:

*I'm very interested in [my children] being able to perceive themselves as strong people, as people being able to make their way in the world, and being comfortable with that. I refuse to allow [what happened to me] to happen to them. I really want them educated about the world that they're growing up in as females, and that they have to be strong.*

Even when Lindsay and her sister were toddlers, Ellen and her husband encouraged them to be independent in many different ways. It surprised Ellen to remember how aggressively she promoted their independence:

*This is awful—when they were little and we'd be out, well, they'd have to go to the bathroom. This is [when they were] very little, just out of diapers, two-and-a-half or three years old. They'd say, "I have to go to the bathroom." And I'd say, "I'm shopping here. I'm going to have to drop everything in order to trot over to a sales clerk and see if they have a bathroom. I'm not going to do that. You go ask. You're the one who has to go to the bathroom—you go ask. You find out where it is, then I'll take you . . . I always encouraged them. "You have a question, you ask. You don't have to hold my hand to go up there." They learned if they really had a question to ask it. If they didn't ask, they didn't want it answered.*

Ellen recognizes issues of power and control even in the practical matter of asking to use a restroom. Her beliefs about questioning and assertiveness at these basic levels were extended into literacy as her children were introduced to reading and writing. Lindsay proved to be unenthusiastic about learning to read in kindergarten. Ellen's hard work in encouraging Lindsay to be independent almost backfired on her at this point:

*[Lindsay] liked memorizing books, but as far as the challenge of reading the book herself went, she'd want me to read it to her first, and then she'd memorize it. So then I'd say, "Okay, Lindsay, I will buy two books. One I'll read to you, one you'll read to me." She fought it tooth and nail. She said, "Well then, don't buy me any books," even though she wanted one.*

It was at this point that Lindsay entered first grade. In Pat McLure's class, Lindsay had the opportunity to read books to the whole class. Ellen sensed Lindsay's whole attitude toward reading, particularly reading aloud, changed because of this:

*The sharing in front of the class [became important to Lindsay]. It was the normal thing to do to read a book to the class. You were on the spot, center, and you had everyone's attention.*

Reading became a way for Lindsay to have the attention of the entire class, to share favorite stories and connect with classmates in different ways. Writing soon began to fulfill these same purposes, not only through sharing writing in school, but through writing done at home. At one point in the year, Lindsay watched a televised version of the radio program "Prairie Home Companion." She so enjoyed it that she decided to write a letter to Garrison Keillor, the host of the show. She wrote that she thought it was funny to see him wearing glasses on television and that she liked one of the funny things he had said. Ellen noted that Lindsay enjoys writing letters, which she often sees her mother doing:

*I write letters to companies. Once Lindsay had a good coat for over a year, and the zipper broke. I got in touch with the manufacturer ... sent in the coat, and in five days, a brand new coat arrived. Lindsay was thrilled. A brand new coat! And she knew I didn't have to spend any money for it at all, except to send the coat back. And another time I had a broken fryer, after owning it four years. There was a problem with the plug. And there's no one who can fix those things, but I've learned to write to the company and ask what they can do for me. I sent the fryer back and they sent me a new one. Not only am I delighted, but my children say, "This is wonderful" ... So much of the world today says, "Oh well, I have to buy a new one," or, "This is totally disposable." The kids realize that it isn't disposable, that you can do something about it. You can write or call the company and find out what they will do. And I'm usually pretty insistent. I say, "You've got to help me. I'm a consumer!"*

In talking to Ellen, I realized many of the goals she has for her children fit into the process curriculum I have seen in some elementary classrooms. Ellen expects her children to be responsible — as much as they are able at their age — for getting their questions answered. She expects them to determine what questions are important to them and to believe they have the power to have those questions answered. She challenges them to stretch beyond the limits they set for themselves, and applauds their attempts to communicate with others through their reading and writing. She wants her children not necessarily to accept things as they are, but to believe they have the power to change the status quo.

What Ellen showed me in discussing how she raises her children is the power of her own experience in affecting how she deals with them. She demonstrates the importance of our decisions as educators in the day-to-day challenges we face in our classrooms. All the small details of classroom and home life — decisions about how much responsibility we will give our students in determining the curriculum; our reactions when a fryer, desk, or zipper breaks; the cultural assumptions behind the questions we ask male and female students — shape our students' notions of who they are and what power they might have in the world. Ellen encourages her children to question even as she continues to question:

*I was never asked what I wanted to be when I grew up, and I feel very badly about that, because I grew up in a society where you were just kind of a female. Other than getting married and having children, I don't think that you were expected to do any more . . . I expect my girls to be more than that, and so I'm constantly asking them . . . trying to get them thinking, to challenge themselves, "Well, is that what I'm interested in?" Not that they have to, at the early age of seven, decide what they're going to do for the rest of their lives, but they're questioning themselves, "What is it like to do this? How am I different from that person? What does this person do?" They can start to think what their interests are, and be a responsible person. They can internalize that.*

## FAILING MR. VINCENT: JAN'S STORY

Questions about literacy and personal history start from a different source for Jan Nelson, a junior high school English teacher. I met Jan in a graduate writing instruction course I taught with my colleague, Meg Peterson. Jan wrote often about her experiences as a reader and writer in high school. Much of her current beliefs about teaching stem from those experiences. The name Eric Vincent came up often in our classroom discussion and in Jan's writing. Mr. Vincent was Jan's high school English teacher for three years, and for three years, the class followed a set format. In Jan's words:

*We wrote essays based on books, genre, and topics of Mr. Vincent's choice. After handing us the prerequisites for the next writing project, Mr. Vincent would read us his college notes on the book he had assigned. We would spend the remaining class time working on grammar and mechanics exercises from* Warriners. *From this amalgamation of information we were expected to crank out a three-page paper each week.*

  *Mr. Vincent's authority came from his lecture notes. His influence came from the [college] degree he had to dazzle us and our parents. His power came from the grades he assigned us. His control stemmed from his written or oral comments. These comments were often demeaning and sarcastic, and seemed designed more for his private amusement than to [help us.]*

Eventually, Jan failed a year of Mr. Vincent's English course and had to go to summer school. She realized during her time in his classes that she was not a writer:

*I felt I had to compromise my views in order to graduate and not surprisingly, the years of 65s on my papers privately convinced me that I could not write. I was, in fact, silenced as a writer . . . When I think back on my initial decision to become an English teacher, I am still surprised by both the decision itself and the strength of the force which drove me to that decision. Unlike some of my friends who teach because they were inspired by a superior teacher, I chose teaching because I knew I could do a better job than Mr. Vincent and others like him. I wanted to make a difference. I was not sure how; I just knew that I would try.*

Jan's words may reveal an important reason why change in classrooms over generations is rare. Most of us who work as teachers come to the educational system because we are comfortable in it. Many of us were inspired by favorite teachers. We adapted to our "Mr. Vincents." We accepted such treatment from certain teachers. Like many others in our culture, we may have identified such wielding of authority as the heart of what it means to teach. Jan wanted to be a different kind of teacher. But her early years of teaching still left her uncomfortable with her role in the classroom:

*Teachers . . . who wished to have some sort of meaningful interaction with students would make themselves available between classes or in an adviser's or coach's capacity. The teacher as a professor and the teacher as a person were personalities divorced, undermining the credibility of education in the eyes of a student. It seemed clear that the place in school for the energy-filled adolescent to make sense of and mesh with the adult world had to take place outside of the classroom, outside of the curriculum . . . [In my first three years of high school teaching] I was a great field hockey coach, and put in long hours on lesson plans, ditto masters, and correcting mounds of papers. My classroom methods still reflected those of my models. I did little more than maintain the status quo and at times felt lucky to be able to accomplish even that.*

During the next seven years of teaching, Jan did develop a systematic writing program for her students. But she was not happy with it, and she began to seriously question her career choice:

*I worked out as painless a writing program as I could devise. I would discuss (lecture!) and demonstrate thesis statements and then have students write one "perfect" thesis statement. I would then discuss and demonstrate supporting statements, concluding "clincher" sentences, have students write the same . . . mostly what I got back from my students was stiff, forced dreck. Humor was almost nonexistent. I could see evidence of counted words, even though I gave no word number requirements . . . Writing had been the modern interpretation of flogging in my own school career, and I'd be darned if I would further equate the pencil to the hickory stick. [I knew things would have to change in my class] if I were to remain a teacher.*

It was at this point that Jan began the writing course with Meg Peterson and me. As her writing program changed, she began to see herself and her students differently. The balance of power began to change in the class in ways she had always wanted:

*[At the start], I began each class with the proposal that we would write for ten minutes on a topic of our choice and then stop. Ten minutes seemed reasonable. I figured anyone could do something mildly distasteful for ten minutes. The results were astounding. In each class, students asked if they could have more writing time. Voices cropped up from nearly everyone within the next two weeks.*

*Humor and questioning began to have a place in their writing ...
Students with the slimmest backgrounds in writing took greater risks
as their efforts and progress received peer acknowledgment.
My role in this community of writers became far different from that of
Mr. Vincent. My authority seems to flow from my writing along with
my students. I am a beginning writer, so I model and share the same
writing experiences as my students. They see me write topic lists,
map, freewrite, and experiment with leads. They show great interest
in the many pieces I have started and then put aside in my writing
folder, some to develop at a later time, and some to be left
unfinished. They are encouraged to know that experimentation is not
synonymous with failure ... Together we learn that writing is a craft
before it becomes an art. The fact that I write along with my students
works as an impetus, encouraging them to stretch their wings and
take part in a community of writers.*

There are many paradoxes in Jan's words. She views herself as "a
beginning writer," even though she can write accomplished prose. I
think in some ways she is trying to rewrite her history as a teacher
and writer. But the desire to rewrite it comes from a keen sense of
that history Jan possesses as a teacher and writer.

## IMPLICATIONS FOR WORKING WITH TEACHERS

The acknowledgment that teachers gain insight into how to teach
reading and writing through their own reading and writing certainly
doesn't break any new ground. Numerous researchers have documented the importance of teachers writing to understand how to
teach (see Hansen 1987; Graves 1983; Calkins 1986). From the Bay
Area Writing Project's inception decades ago to current summer
writing institutes across the country, the basic principle of English
teachers learning by doing is entrenched in learning theory.

But I think there are also deeper issues of personal reading, writing,
and teaching history that can be dealt with through methods courses.
I currently teach two sections of a writing methods course for prospective elementary school teachers. In the course, the first half of every
meeting is devoted to a writing workshop. Students write, share
writing in small groups, and then later they may share their writing
with the whole class.

What comes out of these small groups is the history of a piece of
writing—how the idea for the piece came about, the stumbling
blocks and breakthroughs encountered during its creation, the differences in processes of writers in the group. From the history of a piece
of writing, we build to the histories of the writers. Histories as writers
lead to histories as teachers.

The first assignment for the class is a short personal narrative.
Students also write and photocopy copies of a weekly letter to the
class, in which they also may share their writing and teaching processes. These weekly letters serve to help the class form a community
around a common text we are creating together. Students also keep a

journal that I respond to, forming a dialogue between me and each student.

After the narrative assignment, students write a short case study of a writer they observe in a public school. This writing often leads to reflections about differences between the observed writer's process and their own. For the final assignment in the course, students write a history of themselves as readers and writers, tracing back to the breakthroughs and stumbling blocks in their literacy experiences.

What both Jan and Ellen want for the children they work with and for themselves is to integrate experiences with actions they take in their lives. I want the same thing for my students. It is important that the writing of papers isn't disconnected from the experiences of the class. I know most of the students' experiences in courses involve a final major paper, project, or test worth almost half of their grade. They are accustomed to scurrying off alone to write after the semester reaches the midway point. In the course I teach, writing is a continuous process — there is always a draft of a letter, the close of a paper, or the germ of an idea in a journal in progress. If we want teachers we work with to value the learning around texts in a classroom community, we have to enable them to experience that themselves. Jan wanted a different model of learning in her own classroom, but she was never exposed to that.

By working with teachers like Ellen and Jan, I've learned the importance of history in teaching, and for this reason we have to help teachers acknowledge their histories. At times this is painful, especially for teachers like Ellen who may have fallen into teaching because there were few alternatives for women. At times this is exhilarating — for example, when a teacher brings in Robert Louis Stevenson's *A Child's Garden of Verses* and remembers for the first time in years what a delight reading once was. For teachers who have trouble finding time for personal reading and writing, rediscovering the value of written words may begin with these recollections.

## REFERENCES

Avery, Carol. 1987. First grade thinkers becoming literate. *Language Arts* 64: 611−618.

Calkins, Lucy. 1986. *The art of teaching writing*. Portsmouth, NH: Heinemann.

Graves, Donald. 1983. *Writing: Teachers and children at work*. Portsmouth, NH: Heinemann.

Hansen, Jane. 1987. *When writers read*. Portsmouth, NH: Heinemann.

Heath, Shirley Brice. 1983. *Ways with words*. Cambridge, MA: Harvard University Press.

Hubbard, Ruth. ed. 1983. *Children who write when they read: A collection of narratives from the first year of the Mast Way reading and writing research project*. Durham, NH: Writing Process Laboratory, University of New Hampshire.

Sacks, Oliver. 1985. *The man who mistook his wife for a hat*. New
    York: Summit Books.
Wells, Gordon. 1986. *The meaning makers: Children learning
    language and using language to learn*. Portsmouth, NH: Heinemann.

# PART 2

## changing concepts of literacy

As you think about your development as a reader and writer, your attitudes about learning to read and write may change. These changes are accelerated when you begin to look closely at young readers and writers. *Harste*, *Woodward*, and *Burke* share a careful glimpse of one young girl trying to adjust to the demands of school reading and writing tasks. Viewing school through the child's eyes makes it clear that traditional methods of teaching reading and writing must change.

*Donald Graves* also looks at a young child, Billy, as he struggles to learn to read and write. Billy's teacher has made changes in her classroom to help Billy grow, and Graves writes about the principles this teacher follows. Many of these principles are supported by the work of *Kenneth Goodman*, who defines whole language—that term you will read over and over again in this book. A holistic literacy program considers how children read, write, listen, and speak as they try to make sense of language. *Ruth Hubbard* shows how different children tackle the complex task of translating thoughts to words and images.

As teachers and researchers work to change concepts of what it means to be literate, they are looking at how readers and writers approach different texts. *Louise Rosenblatt* writes about how different texts and needs affect the way you read and write. For instance, you probably read this text differently than you might approach a Danielle Steele novel.

In order for children to see the importance of literacy, they need to have some real power and responsibility in the classroom. *Patrick Shannon* outlines the history of literacy instruction, a history that needs to change if children and teachers are to take control of the literacy curriculum. Once the balance of power changes in classrooms, literacy is redefined.

# examining
# instructional assumptions

JEROME HARSTE, VIRGINIA WOODWARD,
AND CAROLYN BURKE

**8**

*Both teachers and learners operate on the basis of language assumptions. Teachers are asked, before seeing the sty in their students' eyes, to first know themselves.*

Alison, age 6, could hardly wait for first grade to start. Her mother explained her anxious anticipation tongue-in-cheek, saying, "She's caught it from me! She's no more enthusiastic than *I* am that school is going to start!"

A letter from her new teacher welcoming her to her new classroom made her impatience even more obvious.

Finally the day came when Alison and her mother could privately go to find her room, meet the teacher, and explore the school. Alison was in ecstasy! She got to register her name and birthdate on the class birthday cake, explore the reading center, tell about her summer, find out what supplies to buy, and clarify both for herself and her teacher what bus she would be riding. Alison was now more than ready.

So was her mother. This teacher was a marvel! She obviously loved children and was ensuring that they would have a good year. Alison had already made her mark on "her new classroom."

That was some time ago. School is now in full swing. Alison is still enthusiastic. She loves school—the books, the teacher—and willingly shares her observations and experiences:

"Recess is *'the pits'!*"

"The boys chased me today and I fell. Do you know my friend was being so *'unconcentrative'* that she didn't even come to help?"

She also brings home her reading and writing worksheets, her art work, and other items produced or completed each day in school.

We would like to share these with you as we think that they are typical of many of the language activities found in first grades. They

Reprinted with permission from *Language Stories & Literacy Lessons* by Jerome Harste, Virginia Woodward, and Carolyn Burke. Copyright © 1984 by the authors; published by Heinemann Educational Books, Inc.

may even be better activities than those found in many classrooms, though we wish to argue that they are not good enough; that they reflect unfounded assumptions about written language growth and development, and that they debilitate rather than facilitate the process of language literacy.

## IDENTIFYING THE TEACHER'S ASSUMPTIONS

One of the first activities which Alison completed is that shown in Figure 8—1.

When questioned at home about why she had elected to draw the bottom half of her body, Alison responded, "It's okay, teacher said so. Someone asked and teacher said we didn't have to draw our 'whole self' if we didn't want to."

The teacher, in all likelihood, responded in this manner assuming some children wanted to draw their heads rather than their complete figure. It is interesting to note that Alison, given the option, elected to draw her bottom half and leave her top half unrepresented, extending, as it were, off the page.

At first, we might think, "A creative response to a good instructional activity." But is it? After all, this was an activity designed to help children learn to control the reading/writing process. Did it do for language what it did for art? In order to answer this question it becomes necessary to examine the activity more closely. We need to identify what teacher-held assumptions underlay the creation and selection of this activity.

This is readily done by identifying the set of written language principles related to learning which undergird this activity as opposed to other activities which might have been selected. We can easily think of both more open and more closed activities which were

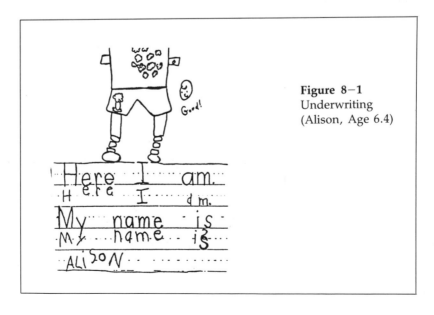

**Figure 8—1**
Underwriting
(Alison, Age 6.4)

available options to the teacher. For example, the teacher did not elect to give the children a sheet of paper, ask them to draw a picture of themselves and then write or pretend to write an autobiographical story to share (a more open activity), nor did the teacher focus the children's attention upon an isolated letter or letter-sound correspondence pattern (a more closed activity). An analysis, then, of this activity and of the teacher's responses to it, suggests the following assumptions about written language learning:

*Assumption 1: One of the first tasks in learning to read and write is to be able to discriminate visually between the letters of the alphabet.*

*This is best taught by activities such as underwriting which force the child to attend to the distinctive features of each letter.*

*Assumption 2: Language activities designed for children should be manageable to insure completion and hence success.*

*One way to accomplish this is to use simple whole texts which contain a limited number of basic vocabulary items (Here I am. My name is . . .).*

*Assumption 3: Errors should be marked to give corrective feedback and to stop bad habits from forming (see the teacher's correction of s in Figure 8−1).*

*Assumption 4: Initial language activities should be personally meaningful to the child.*

*This is best done by focusing on topics of interest to the child (in this activity, the topic self).*

*Assumption 5: Children do not need as much support in art as they do in writing.*

*The incorporation of art allows for self-expression and creativity.*

The question now becomes, "In order to make these assumptions, what does one have to believe?"

The more obvious belief underlying Assumption 1 is that children need to be able to note differences between the various letters of the alphabet in order to read and write. Less obvious perhaps is the implicit belief that first graders do not already possess this ability to discriminate between the letters of the alphabet, i.e., that visual discrimination of letters must be formally taught.

Each of these beliefs merits investigation. They may be as much folklore as developmental givens. The rampant popularity of a belief is never a criterion for acceptability, but rather for testing.

A rather extensive listing of further beliefs which we have identified as inherent in this single instructional activity is the following:

*Access to the reading/writing process hinges on mastery of the distinctive features of print (see Assumption 1). The word is the key unit in language (see Assumption 2).*

*Words selected for initial instruction must be chosen on the basis of frequency of usage (see Assumption 2).*

*Errors must be pointed out by a guiding adult since children do not have information which they can use for self-correction (see Assumption 3).*

*The goal of early language learning is an error-free performance on basics since without this children will never be able to access the process (see Assumption 3).*

*Activities which make personal sense support the child's access to basic literacy processes (see Assumption 4). This means, insofar as language learning is concerned, that topics should be chosen carefully so that children find them personally meaningful but that the actual language introduced must be carefully selected and controlled by the teacher (see Assumptions 2 and 4). Art is an easy activity for the child (natural); reading and writing are hard activities (unnatural) (see Assumption 5).*

*Art is learned; reading and writing must be taught (see Assumption 5). Creativity must wait upon control. Because children have already learned the basic forms of art, i.e., they have control of the basic conventions, creativity can be expected. Once children control the conventions of written language, they can and will become creative written language users as well (see Assumption 5).*

Some may argue that this kind of analysis is highly speculative, and infers much from a single instructional activity. With this we would have to agree. These same persons would feel more comfortable, as indeed we would, if the identified language learning principles re-occurred in subsequent activities. To show that this is indeed the case, three additional activities completed during the first week of school are illustrated.

The activity illustrated in Figure 8−2 is closely tied to that already discussed in Figure 8−1. In this instance, children were given ditto master copies of story parts, of which the page shown is one. The children were asked to arrange the pages in order, paste them to the blank pages of a stapled book, draw a picture to fit the text, and overwrite the script on each page. Though this assignment involves more procedures, what has been said about the beliefs inherent in the first activity holds for this activity too. The significant creative decisions about the written language—the writing of the story—have been made by the teacher. The student is left simply to recreate the decreed text order and to copy the print. Only the art is left open to the creative efforts of the student.

The activity which generated the product illustrated in Figure 8−3 initially appears somewhat different, but closer examination indicates that it too shares the beliefs reflected in the first two assignments. This assignment is a Parent-Teacher Notice which the children were asked to copy off the blackboard and take home as a reminder of an upcoming meeting. In this instance, the teacher gave the children a sheet of lined paper with their name on it. She asked the children to

**Figure 8—2**
Overwriting
(Alison, Age 6.4)

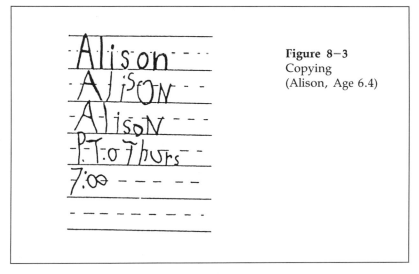

**Figure 8—3**
Copying
(Alison, Age 6.4)

underwrite their name twice, and then to copy the message written on the blackboard.

An analysis of the beliefs which guided this activity suggests that all of the original beliefs still hold, and that a further clarification has been achieved. Presumably the teacher is concerned with how Alison spatially controls the writing of her name and feels that she needs to practice it. Often this concern for the child's inability to stay within the lines is predicated on the belief that handwriting signals muscle and eye coordination and that such coordination is prerequisite to learning to read and write.

Figure 8—4 illustrates this teacher's application of the language experience approach to teaching reading. Rather than transcribe what the children have actually said, Alison's teacher has transformed

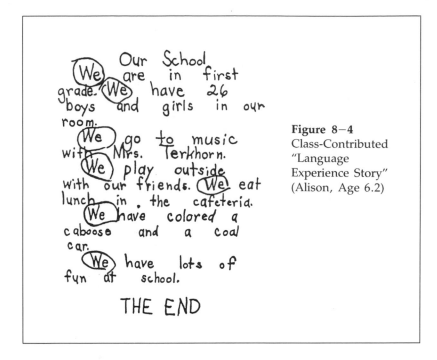

Our School
(We) are in first
grade. (We) have 26
boys and girls in our
room.
(We) go to music
with Mrs. Terkhorn.
(We) play outside
with our friends. (We) eat
lunch in . the cafeteria.
(We) have colored a
caboose and a coal
car.
(We) have lots of
fun at school.

THE END

**Figure 8−4**
Class-Contributed
"Language
Experience Story"
(Alison, Age 6.2)

each new suggestion into a common pattern for the purpose of teaching the word *we* and controlling the complexity of the syntactic patterns used. After the teacher composed this text, she gave each child a ditto copy of the class-contributed "language experience story" and asked the class to circle the word *we* each time it appeared. Although the instructional activity has changed, the underlying assumptions governing the activity remain intact from the first three lessons.

An analysis such as we have been doing here is intended to indicate that what Alison's teacher believes about the reading and writing process strongly affects both her choice of instructional activities and her handling of such activities. Her behavior is orderly, consistent, and predictable. This is so in spite of the fact that she maintains that she is eclectic and applies "a variety of approaches to the teaching of reading." Despite the supposed surface structure variety in activities, her invariant assumptions continue to show.

From data such as these, we have come to believe that looking at teacher behavior in terms of beliefs held and assumptions made is more cogent and powerful than looking at behavior in terms of the supposed approach being used (Harste and Burke, 1977). This teacher presumably changes her approaches, but because she does not change her beliefs, her classroom practice is unaffected (as is, in all likelihood, the outcome of her instruction, but that's another equally important and complex issue which we will not develop here).

These data support the position that the teaching of reading and writing is theoretically based, that all of us as teachers have a theory of how to teach reading and writing in our heads which strongly affects our perception and behavior. We define theory simply as a set of interrelated beliefs and assumptions through which perception and behavior are organized. What this means practically is that in order to change behavior we must change beliefs. To that end we will now turn to an examination of the language encounters which Alison had prior to and outside of her school-related experiences.

## IDENTIFYING THE LANGUAGE LEARNER'S ASSUMPTIONS

### Reading

Alison, we wish to argue, has been a user of written language for a long time. One of the earliest instances of Alison's use of written language occurred when she was 3 years old. At the time, Alison and her family were on the way to the zoo. As they approached the beltway which would take them to the zoo, Alison's father, pointing to an overhead sign signaling "West 465," asked, "Alison, what do you think that says?"

Alison responded, "It says . . . uh . . . 'Daddy, turn right here to go to the zoo.'"

While some might argue that this isn't reading, we wish to disagree. Alison has made a decision which puts her in the semantic ball park. She assumes that the print *out there* relates to the activity in which she and her family are engaged. And she's right in all but the pickiest sense. Alison's response demonstrates her expectation that written language is meaningful. We do not know how or when children come to this important conclusion. All we know is that children as young as 3 have already made it, and that somehow readers who end up in remedial classes have lost it or lost faith in it.

We believe it is through the expectation that written language makes sense that control is gained. Once the sense-making intent of written language has been perceived, ideation and hypothecation become the process forces of control. To illustrate this point further, we can share another one of Alison's early encounters with print. This encounter occurred on a "dessert trip" to Baskin-Robbin's. She was 4 years old at the time.

After eating her ice cream cone, Alison looked around the room attempting to find a trash can where she could deposit her soiled napkin. After exploring logical locations, she found it, studied the wooden flap engraved with the word *PUSH*, performed the required action, and deposited her napkin.

Alison's mother, who had been observing her problem-solving behaviors now asked, "Alison, what does that say on the trash can?"

"Push," came the response.

"How do you know?" came her mother's next question.

To which Alison responded by taking her index finger and running it over the *P*, the *U*, the *S*, and the *H* in turn, and saying, "Because it's got all the right letters!"

It was from knowing what written language does that Alison had grown in her control of the form. From earlier cognitive decisions, such as that illustrated in the trip to the zoo which put her in the semantic ball park, she could and did test language hypotheses which put her—to carry the metaphor another step—not only on base, but gave her the metalinguistic control to speak about the game itself.

The importance of this process of ongoing hypothesis-testing is best illustrated by yet another language story. Alison was 4 years, 1 month at the time. In this instance she was shown a Wendy's cup, like the one illustrated in Figure 8—5, and asked, "What do you think this says?"

Alison ran her finger under the word *Wendy's*, and responded, "Wendy's," and under the word *Hamburgers*, and said, "Cup." Alison then paused a moment as if in reflection, and added, "That's a long word with a short sound!"

In this instance, the hypothesis which Alison has formulated about graphic-sound correspondence is an incorrect one. Yet her very mention of it signals us that she has also formulated the correct alternative and is attempting to orchestrate this decision with the sense-making intent she knows exists.

Need we help her? Not in a traditional corrective sense. All we need to ensure is that she has continuing encounters with the process, for each encounter will allow her to test out the validity of her current hypotheses and to reconstruct a new set at a level far above our assumptive imaginations.

Alison was reading before she went to first grade. Her first-grade teacher, through the use of standardized tests, has placed her at the preprimer level. At home she reads such texts as *It's the Easter*

Figure 8—5
Wendy's Cup
(Alison, Age 4.1)

*Alison's Response*

"*Wendy's*"

"*Cup*"

*Beagle, Charlie Brown* (Schulz, 1976) — she's not likely to encounter equivalent print settings in school until fourth grade.

Why the discrepancy? It's those assumptions again. The tests Alison has taken in school strip language of its context, forcing her to deal with letters and words not only outside of a supportive linguistic environment, but also outside of a supportive context of situation. Without the latter, Alison has neither a point of anticipation, nor a point of contextualization.

Written language learning is a social event of some complexity, and written language use reflects the orchestration of this complex social event. Both the complexity and the orchestration support the development of user control. Knowing that Alison is the reader she is would leave us puzzled at her production of backward *s*'s in writing (as illustrated in Figure 8—1) unless we give up the assumption that control of form is prerequisite to the language process. It is because Alison is, and has been, a reader and a writer that she has a growing control of its form, and not vice versa.

## Writing

Alison is, and has been, as impressive a writer as she is a reader. Her explorations of written language began long before what she produced became representational in any adult sense. What Alison reaffirmed in her movement into writing is that children must encounter the language process in its complexity in order to learn control. As with reading, it was Alison's early access to what written language does which allowed her that control.

One evening, at 4 years, 3 months, Alison encountered a wordless book and made up an appropriate story. The next evening, wanting to reread the book, she asked her mother, "What was that story I read last night?"

"Well, I'm sure I don't know. If you want to remember your stories, you need to write them down. Then you can reread them whenever you want to."

Alison's story about Daddy coming home and taking the family to McDonald's (in Figure 8—6) was placeheld by using the letters of the name simply reshuffled in order. For months, whenever she encountered this book, she would get her paper out and faithfully read this text, with minor variations:

*One day Daddy came home and*
*he said, "Hi Family, I'm home,"*
*and he's gonna take us to*
*McDonald's. I'm gonna have a*
*Fun Meal.*

This sample illustrates Alison's public announcement of her discovery of the finite symbol system in written language; namely, that one continuously reorchestrates the same set of letters to produce an infinite set of words. Alison, as was always the case, demonstrated this growth using print of high personal worth — her name.

**Figure 8–6**
Story to Wordless Book
(Alison, Age 4.3)

As with reading, adult recognition of the writing process often seems to hinge on how representational or conventional the product is. This is clearly unfortunate, for it leads to the dismissal of early writing efforts as unworthy of attention.

Alison is clearly a writer, orchestrating aspects of this particular social event much as any writer would. She has already grasped a lot: the meaning relationship between picture, text and her world; directionality (both top-down and left-to-right), the function of print in this setting; the organizational scaffolding of a story; the use of structure components to placehold meaning. Each of these insights is a signal of her developing written language literacy. The fact that her writing is not yet representational (the symbols she uses to placehold *McDonald's* or *Daddy* do not look identifiable as such to our literate eyes) is not nearly as significant as are these other factors.

Alison's orchestration of these multiple insights is clear evidence of her sophistication. In light of all that she has managed to do, why should the questions most frequently generated about her accomplishments be, "Did she spell correctly?" and "Did she make her letters right?"

At 4 years, 8 months, Alison placeheld all written messages using a cursive script such as that illustrated in Figure 8–7. While a first look at Alison's product might indicate that she knew little about writing, such a conclusion would turn out to be assumptive and false. What this product represents is simply Alison's testing of alternative available hypotheses. Although we cannot know specifically what she is testing, we can feel fairly comfortable in light of her earlier behavior in

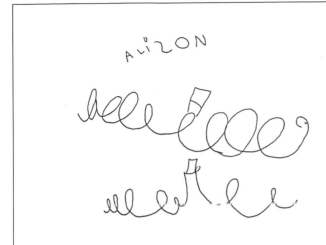

**Figure 8–7**
Cursive Story
Script
(Alison, Age 4.8)

saying that she has tentatively set aside some of what she already knows (her knowledge of letterness and the finite symbol system of English) to test other aspects of the process. Alison has not had a setback. Current models would suggest that she evidences linear growth and is bringing more and more aspects under control in an incremental fashion. Data such as these clearly challenge extant notions of development.

If one views each instance of written language use as the orchestration of a complex social event, then what the initiate written language user is faced with is a problem of some magnitude. As the language user perceives various elements in this event, new hypotheses are generated and tested. These hypotheses are concerned with pragmatics (what the rules of language use are relative to a particular situational context), semantics (how I can say what I mean), syntax (how I get the flow of my message captured on paper), graphics (how I represent what I wish to say), and the orchestration of these systems (how I draw on all these systems simultaneously). Within each of these areas there is, of course, a range of hypotheses which need formulation and fit. Additional hypotheses arise as the user orchestrates more and more elements. What looks like regression, given the assumptions underlying one theory, signals growth from another theoretical perspective.

Growth, while constant—and we believe this to be the mode for *all* of us as written language users—looks sporadic because of the postulates which undergird our assumptive yardsticks. Current yardsticks divert attention away from growth and toward "developmental stages," which attempt to calculate growth by marking surface level features of conventional form. Such a focus draws our attention away from the universals of written language literacy, which operate across language users at all ages and simply express themselves in a variety of alternative forms. It limits our thinking about literacy. Literacy

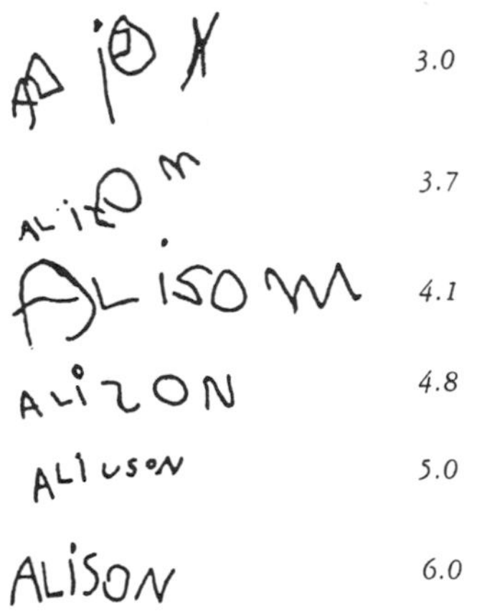

**Figure 8–8**
Signatures
(Alison)

becomes a step-by-step progression of control, not a vehicle for exploring and expanding our world.

As an example, let's take spelling, often measured as a simple yes-no decision. Alison has used the conventional spelling of her name since she was 3 years old, as is illustrated in Figure 8–8. Yet her most interesting signature is not her first or last, but the one she experimented with during a two-week period shortly after she turned 5. At this point, when Alison wrote her name, she added a *u* in the middle. When asked why she added the *u*, she replied, "Because I wanted to." After several weeks of experimenting with this signature, she abandoned it in favor of the spelling her parents had elected at her birth.

Isn't it fascinating? Everything Alison had discovered about print compelled her to say that there ought to be a *u* in her name. And there well could be. It was of the options her parents could have taken when they selected the original spelling of her name.

Alison feels very comfortable with what she's discovered about how print operates. Like all of us, she's most satisfied and most interested in her latest discovery and tries it on for fit. Similar trends will be seen in the writing of all of us—a favorite word, a favorite syntactic pattern, a favorite organizational style. The issue is not so much what is being tested or how much conventional congruency is achieved, but that the universality of growth, and fit, and continued growth is expressed.

At 5 years, 6 months, Alison was asked to make a finger puppet out of paper, to add a smiling face, and to write about something that made her happy. She produced the product illustrated in Figure 8–9. Without apparent warning, Alison moved so naturally from the writing illustrated in Figure 8–7 to that represented in Figure 8–9 that her

**Figure 8–9**
Finger Puppet
(Alison, Age 5.6)

behavior quite surprised us. She has continued to write in this latter fashion ever since.

Alison's "What Makes Me Happy" (MN I C FLOMRS — When I see flowers) is an impressive display of rule-governed, orchestrated behavior. The message is the product of her integrated processing of pragmatics (she used language appropriate to this setting), semantics (she said something which made personal sense), syntax (she managed to capture the flow of her thought on paper using the standard conventional form of wordness), and graphics (she abstracted out the salient letter-sound relationships which undergird written language and placeheld these relationships with letter forms). Given such a magnificent breakthrough, we find it quite frustrating that the only comment made by one professional, with whom we shared this piece, was that her "W's were upside down."

On her sixth birthday, Alison wrote her grandmother a letter thanking her for the present which she had sent (see Figure 8–10). Once again Alison's knowledge of written language proves to be extensive, showing a complex mapping of letter-sound relationships, syntax, and meaning. When her writing here is compared to that done on the finger puppet, it becomes clear that Alison also has some awareness of the function of written language in alternative settings. That is, her letter sounds like a letter, while the message on her puppet was a response to the implied lead, "What makes me happy . . ." We might also note Alison's conventional spellings of *loved* and *your*, indicating that she is using not only a phonetic mapping in her spelling, but also a visual memory of what these words look like. Alison orchestrates these elements so smoothly that they go easily undetected as the magnificent achievements which they are. The fact that such phenomena are sorted out so readily by children at such an early age leads us and others to conclude that, "Writing is Natural" (K. Goodman and Y. Goodman, 1979).

Alison's behavior here is a vivid display of the interrelatedness of

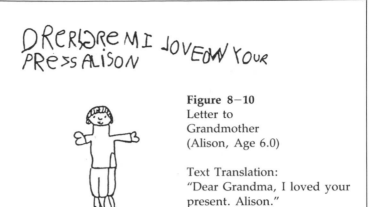

**Figure 8–10**
Letter to
Grandmother
(Alison, Age 6.0)

Text Translation:
"Dear Grandma, I loved your
present. Alison."

reading and writing. It is through having encountered the words *loved* and *your* in reading that Alison fine-tunes her writing strategies. Alison simultaneously orchestrated spelling by the way it sounds, by the way it looks, and by the way it means. All of the growth illustrated in the examples above occurred prior to Alison's entrance into first grade—growth which went untapped in the instructional activities which Alison's teacher provided for her.

When Alison returned home from school with the written product shown in Figure 8–11 her father gave her a piece of paper and asked her to write, "Here is my house and family," the very script which she had underwritten on the school worksheet.

**Figure 8–11**
Underwriting
(Alison, Age 6.4)

HoRoˢ Mi HoˢADNO foMLE

**Figure 8–12**
Uninterrupted
Writing
(Alison, Age 6.4)

Alison, we lamentingly report, burst into tears and said, "I can't write."

After being comforted, she was told, "Sure you can, you've been writing a long time now."

"But I don't know how to spell and write good," came the still tearful reply.

"Oh, yes you do. You're only in first grade. If your writing looked like ours, there would be no reason for you to be there. You know we can read anything you write."

With this Alison produced the text illustrated in Figure 8–12.

We say, "How sad that Alison had to have this moment of doubt." Her assumptions did not match the instructional assumptions being addressed and hence she decided she was wrong. In this instance instruction was a debilitating rather than a facilitating experience.

**CONCLUSION**

Data collected from Alison and some sixty-seven other 3-, 4-, 5-, and 6-year-olds (Harste, Burke, Woodward, 1981, 1983) leads us to conclude that many of the instructional assumptions currently made by teachers are faulty at best and debilitating at worst. In no instance — and our data have been collected from boys and girls in high, middle, and low SES, black and white, small town and urban inner-city families — would the assumptions underlying Alison's instruction have been appropriate ones from which to operate instructionally.

The error in the instruction provided by Alison's teacher was that her instructional assumptions were never tested through the provision of open-entry student activities which could have provided alternative data and led her to challenge her own beliefs. All of the activities given to Alison by her teacher effectively forced Alison to operate within the teacher's assumptive bounds, never providing her the opportunity to demonstrate what decisions she, as a language user, was interested in and capable of making.

What we recommend instructionally for both teacher and pupil is such open-entry language activities in which constraints are allowed to evolve in a risk-free language environment, where each in a sense (both teacher and pupil) can become an assumption taller than themselves. In many ways, the real issue which we've addressed is:

Whose written language assumptions should be tested — the teacher's or the language user's?

## REFERENCES

Goodman, K. S. & Y. M. Goodman. 1979. Learning to read is natural. In L. B. Resnick & P. A. Weaver, eds. *Theory and practice of early reading*. Vol. 2. Hillsdale, NJ: Erlbaum.

Harste, J. C. & C. L. Burke. 1977. A new hypothesis for reading teacher education research: Both the teaching and learning of reading are theoretically based. In P. D. Pearson, ed. *Reading: Research, theory and practice* (Twenty-sixth Yearbook of the National Reading Conference). Minneapolis, MN: Mason Publishing Co.

Harste, J. C., C. L. Burke & V. A. Woodward. 1981. Children's language and world: Initial encounters with print. In J. Langer & M. Smith-Burke, eds. *Bridging the Gap: Reader meets author*. Newark, DE: International Reading Association.

———. 1983. The young child as writer-reader and informant. Final Report #NIE-G-80-0121. Bloomington, IN: Language Education Departments.

# all children can write

DONALD H. GRAVES

9

I stood at the side of Ms. Richards' third grade classroom watching the children write. We were at the beginning of our 2-year National Institute of Education study of children's composing processes. The school had diagnosed two of the children in Ms. Richards' room as having severe visual-motor problems. They were not hard to find.

Both leaned over their papers, their elbows crooked at right angles to their bodies to protect the appearance of their papers. I walked over to take a closer look at one of the two children's papers. Billy's paper was smudged, wrinkled, letters blackened; in several instances, his paper was thinned and blackened still more where he had gone through several spelling trials on the same word. The more serious aspect of Billy's writing profile was not his visual-motor difficulty, the appearance of his paper, or his numerous misspellings. Billy was a self-diagnosed poor writer. He connected his writing problems with a lack of worthwhile ideas and experiences. In addition, he was well-versed in what he couldn't do.

Billy had been in a separate program emphasizing visual-motor skills, letter formation, and various fine-motor tasks. No question, using a pencil was painful and arduous for him. Teachers complained that Billy rarely completed his work and was constantly behind the others, though he seemed to be articulate. Billy's program was skill-based, disconnected from meaning, and filled with positive reinforcement about his ability to form letters on good days. There was no attempt to connect his writing with the communication of ideas.

Children with learning disabilities often work on skills in isolation, disconnected from learning itself, and therefore disconnected from themselves as persons. Therefore, like Billy, though their skills may improve slightly in isolation, the children do not perceive the function of the skill. Worse, they do not see the skill as a means to show what they know. Skills work merely supplies additional evidence for the misconception that they are less intelligent than other children.

Billy was in a classroom that stressed writing as a process. This meant the children received help from the time they chose a topic to the time they completed their final work. Ms. Richards played the believing game, starting with what Billy knew, particularly his experiences. In fact, Billy's breakthrough as a writer came when his teacher discovered his interest in and knowledge of gardening. As Ms. Richards helped him to teach her about this subject, she learned how to plant, cultivate, water, fertilize, and provide special care for certain varieties of tomatoes. Although Billy wrote more slowly than the other children, he became lost in his subject, forgot about his poor spelling and handwriting, ceased to cover his paper, and wrote a piece filled with solid information about gardening. Once Billy connected writing with knowing—his knowing—it was then possible to work with his visual-motor and spelling problems, but as incidental to communicating information.

Ms. Richards is now one of the thousands of teachers who teach writing as a process in the United States and the English-speaking world. New research and publications, university courses, and numerous summer institutes, are now helping teachers and administrators to find out for themselves what students can do when they focus on the meaning of their writing. Much of the focus of these institutes and courses is on the teachers' own writings: most of us had to rediscover the power of writing for ourselves before we could learn to hear what these young writers had to teach us.

Although writing-process work helps all writers, it seems to be particularly successful with people who see themselves as disenfranchised from literacy. I place in this group learners like Billy who have diagnosed learning disabilities and the accompanying "I-don't-know-anything" syndrome.

The writing-process approach to teaching focuses on children's ideas and helps children teach the teacher or other children in the class what they know, with emphasis first given to ideas and clarifying. This is the first experience many children have with other humans who work hard to point to what they know, instead of what is lacking in the message. Small wonder then that the writing process works best with the disenfranchised, who become a bit giddy at the prospect of seeing their words on paper affecting the thinking of others.

Understanding writing as communication is the heart of teaching the writing process. This article will first focus on the nature of writing, look in greater detail at research on the writing process itself, examine two principles in teaching writing, and then describe four basics in establishing a writing program. It also has a brief section on further reading and recommendations for summer programs for people interested in continuing their study of the writing process.

## WHAT IS WRITING?

Writing is a medium with which people communicate with themselves and with others at other places and times. When I write, I write to learn what I know because I don't know fully what I mean until I order the words on paper. Then I see and know. Writers' first attempts to make sense are crude, rough approximations of what they mean. Writing make sense of things for oneself, then for others.

Children can share their writing with others by reading aloud, by chatting with friends while writing, and (in more permanent form) by publishing. Billy found that writing carried a different authority from spoken words. When he took the gardening piece out in December, he found that words written in September could be savored 3 months later. Furthermore, when he read the published books of other children in his room, he began to realize that this book on gardening was read by others when he wasn't present.

Written language is different from oral language. When Billy speaks, he reinforces his meaning by repeating words and phrases. Unlike when he writes, an audience is present; when the audience wanders or indicates disagreement, he changes his message with words, hand signals, facial expressions, and body posture. This is the luxury of oral discourse. "Error," adjustment, and experimentation are an expected part of oral discourse.

There is a different tradition surrounding most teaching of writing. Only one attempt, one draft is allowed to communicate full meaning (without an audience response). Red-lined first drafts are the norm; we blanche at any misspellings or crudely formed letters.

Still worse, writing has been used as a form of punishment: "Write your misspelled word 25 times." (This is called reinforcement of visual-memory systems.) "Write one hundred times, 'I will not chew gum in school'"; "Write a 300-word composition on how you will improve your attitude toward school." Most teachers teaching in 1985 were bathed in the punishment syndrome when they were learning to write. Small wonder that most of us subtly communicate writing as a form of punishment. We have known no other model of teaching.

## THE WRITING PROCESS

When children use a meaning-centered approach to writing, they compose in idiosyncratic ways. Each child's approach to composing is different from the next. Some draw first, write two words, and in 10 minutes or less announce, "I'm done." Others draw after writing or do not write at all; instead, they speak with a neighbor about what they will write. Some stare out the window or at the blank page and write slowly after 20 minutes of reflection. At some point in their development, writers believe one picture and two words beneath the drawing contain an entire story. In the writer's mind, the story is complete; members of the audience shake their heads and try to work from drawing to text and back to understand the author's intent.

Such idiosyncratic approaches by children seem capricious to outsiders, confusing to children, and bewildering to us as teachers. We intervene with story starters to "get them going," produce pictures as stimuli for writing, and consult language arts texts for language activities. The texts provide "systematic" approaches, often through the teaching of the sentence, advance to two sentences, and finally development of the paragraph. Our detailed observation of young children writing shows they simply don't learn that way. Rather, they write three sentences in one in their first year, not understanding where one sentence ends and the other begins. Studies of children's understanding and use of sentences show they don't acquire full sentence sense until much later (about fifth grade).

The most pernicious aspect of teacher interventions is that children begin to learn early on that others need to supply topics because they come to the page with nothing in their heads. A focus on skills and form to the exclusion of child-initiated meaning further confirms their lack of fit with the writing process.

Prepared materials seek to reduce the stress and the uncertainty that writers face when they encounter the blank page. But the attempt to produce certainty through standardization bypasses the opportunity for child growth. There is good reason to expect tension when a child first writes.

When writers write, they face themselves on the blank page. That clean white piece of paper is like a mirror. When I put words on the page, I construct an image of myself on that whiteness. I may not like my spelling, handwriting, choice of words, aesthetics, or general cleanliness of the page. Until I can begin to capture what I want to say, I have to be willing to accept imperfection and ambiguity. If I arrive at the blank page with a writing history filled with problems, I am already predisposed to run from what I see. I try to hide my paper, throw it away, or mumble to myself, "This is stupid." But with every dangerous, demanding situation, there is an opportunity to learn. Teachers who follow and accompany children as they compose help them to deal with what they see on the page. The reason writing helps children with learning disabilities is that they do far more than learn to write: They learn to come to terms with a new image of themselves as thinkers—thinkers with a message to convey to the world.

## TEACHING WRITING—TWO BASIC PRINCIPLES

After 12 years of working with writing research and the teaching of writing, I have found two principles essential for effective teaching of writing: (1) The teacher teaches most by showing how he/she learns, and (2) the teacher provides a highly structured classroom.

The best demonstration of how teachers learn is through their gathering of information from the children. They place the children in the position of teaching them what they know, usually through conferences. "Now you say that you have to be careful how deep you plant lettuce, Billy. Can you tell me more about that? And do you think the precise depth should be in your piece for the other children? Will they want to know that?" Billy's teacher has shown him how she learns and how he should learn to listen to questions he soon will be able to ask himself.

Ms. Richards, Billy's teacher, has a basic lifestyle of learning from everyone. Whether seated next to someone on a plane, in the teachers' room, or talking informally with children, she wants to be taught; in a lifetime she has learned how important it is to help others to teach her. People leave Ms. Richards' presence surprised they knew so much about their subjects.

Ms. Richards' classroom is a highly structured, predictable classroom. Children who learn to exercise choice and responsibility can function only in a structured room. Furthermore, the up-and-down nature of the writing process itself demands a carefully defined room. Predictability means that writing occurs daily, at set times, with the teacher moving in the midst of the children, listening to their intentions, worries, and concerns. They know she will be nearby attending to their work. She rarely addresses the entire class during writing time. She works hard to establish a studio atmosphere. Predictability also means she won't solve problems for them. Rather, she asks how they might approach the problem. She listens, clarifies their intentions and their problems, and moves on.

Children learn to take responsibility not only for their topics, content of their drafts, and final copy, but also for carrying out classroom decisions. A structured classroom requires an organized teacher who has set the room up to run itself. The teacher has already made a list of the things to be done to help the room function. From September through June, he/she gradually passes on those duties to the children. Attendance, caring for room plants and animals, room cleanliness, lunch lines, desk supervision, and cleaning are but a few examples of these delegations. When room structure and routine do not function well, the teacher and students plan together for the best way to make it function more smoothly. Ms. Richards' room is based on extensive preparation in room design and knowledge of materials, the children, and the process by which they learn to take responsibility.

Teachers who function well in teaching the writing process are interested in what children have to teach them. Writing-process teaching is responsive, demanding teaching that helps children solve problems in the writing process and in the classroom.

## CARRYING OUT A WRITING-PROCESS PROGRAM

I am often asked, "What are the essentials to strong writing programs?" Although the list could be extensive, I think that if teachers understand the following four components, their writing programs will serve the children well. These components are adequate provision of time, child choice of topic, responsive teaching, and the establishment of a classroom community, a community that has learned to help itself.

### Time

Our data show that children need to write a minimum of 4 days a week to see any appreciable change in the quality of their writing. It takes that amount of writing to contribute to their personal development as learners. Unless children write at least 4 days a week, they won't like it. Once-a-week writing (the national average is about 1 day in 8) merely reminds them they can't write; they never write often enough to listen to their writing. Worse, the teacher simply has no access to the children. He/she has to scurry madly around the room trying to reach each child. With little access to the children, the teacher can't help them take responsibility, solve problems for them, or listen to their responses and questions. The very important connection between speaking and writing is lost.

Although teaching writing 4 to 5 times a week helps the teacher, it helps the children even more. When children write on a daily basis, we find they write when they aren't writing. Children get into their subjects, thinking about their texts and topics when they are riding on buses, lying in bed, watching television, reading books, or taking trips. When they write regularly, papers accumulate. There is visible evidence they know and are growing. They gain experience in choosing topics and very soon have more topics to write about than class time can accommodate. Children with learning problems need even more time. They need to learn to listen to themselves with help from the teacher. In summary, regular writing helps:

1. Children choose topics.
2. Children listen to their pieces and revise.
3. Teachers help each other.
4. Teachers listen to child texts.
5. Skills develop in the context of child pieces.
6. Teachers to have greater access to children.

**Topic Choice**

The most important thing children can learn is what they know and how they know it. Topic choice, a subject the child is aware that he knows something about, is at the heart of success in writing. Billy struggled with handwriting and spelling and equated those problems with not knowing topics to write about. When his teacher helped him to discover his knowledge and interest in gardening, he began to write, first haltingly, then with greater flow. He was open to help with spelling and handwriting when he knew he had something to say. Skills are important; learning disabilities cannot be ignored, but neither can teachers or researchers forget that writing exists to communicate with self and others.

"How can I get the child to write? Do you have any good motivators?" are frequent questions asked of me in workshops. The world *get* embraces the problem. There are thousands of "motivators" on the market in the form of story starters, paragraph starters, computer software, animated figures, picture starters, and exciting "sure-fire" interest getters. We forget that children are very sophisticated consumers of motivators from Saturday morning television alone. Worse, motivators teach the child that the best stimulus comes from the outside. Writing actually demands dozens of motivators during the course of composing, but they are motivators that can only be supplied by the writer himself. All children have important experiences and interests they can learn to tap through writing. If children are to become independent learners, we have to help them know what they know; this process begins with helping children to choose their own topics.

Very young children, ages 5 through 7, have very little difficulty choosing topics, especially if they write every day. As children grow older and experience the early effects of audience, even under favorable learning conditions, they begin to doubt what they know. From that point on, all writers go through a kind of doubting game about the texts they produce. They learn to read better and are more aware of the discrepancy between their texts and their actual intentions. If, however, overly severe, doubting teachers are added to the internal doubts of the child, writing becomes still more difficult.

If children write every day and share their writing, we find they use each other as the chief stimulus for topic selection. If teachers write with their children, demonstrating the origin of their topics, and surround the children with literature, topic selection is even easier.

Topic selection is helped through daily journal writing where children take 10 minutes to record their thoughts. Teachers may also give 5- to 10-minute writing assignments, such as: "Write about how you think our room could be improved" (just following a discussion about how the room could be improved with the entire class) or "That upsets you? Well, blast away on paper with the first thoughts that come to mind. But write it for you: If you feel like showing it to me, okay." The teacher finds many occasions where it is useful to record thoughts and opinions on paper. Each of these approaches demonstrates what writing is for, as well as helping the children to have access to what they know and think.

### Response

People write to share, whether with themselves or others. Writers need audiences to respond to their messages. The response confirms for the writer that the text fits his/her intentions. First, the teacher provides an active audience for the writer by confirming what he/she understands in the text and then by asking a few clarifying questions. Second, the teacher helps the entire class to learn the same procedure during group share time. Each writing period ends with two or three children sharing their pieces with the group while the group follows the discipline of first pointing to what is in the text, then asking questions to learn more about the author's subject. All of these responses, whether by the teacher or the other children, are geared to help writers learn to listen to their own texts.

While the children are writing, Billy's teacher moves around the room, responding to their work in progress. Here is an interchange Ms. Richards had with Billy about his piece "My Garden." (The child's text is presented, followed by the conference with the teacher.)

### MY GRDAN

*I help my Dad with the grdan ferstyou have to dig it up an than you rake an get the racks out of it. Than you make ros an you haveto be cerfull to make it deep enuff so the letis will come up.*

Ms. Richards first receives the piece by saying what she understands about what Billy has written. She may also have him read the writing aloud to her:

**Ms. Richards**: You've been working hard, Billy. I see that you work with your dad on your garden. You know just what you do: you dig it up, rake it to get the rocks out, and then you have to be careful how deep you plant things. Did I get that right?

**Billy**: Yup.

**Ms. Richards**: Well, I was wondering, Billy. You say that the lettuce has to be planted deep enough so the lettuce will come up. Could you tell me more about that? I haven't planted a garden for a long time.

**Billy**: Well, if you plant it too deep, it won't come up. Lettuce is just near the top.

**Ms. Richards**: Oh, I see, and did you plant some other things in your garden?

**Billy**: Yup, carrots, beans, turnips (I hate 'em), spinach (that, too) beets, and tomatoes: I like tomatoes.

**Ms. Richards**: That's quite a garden, Billy. And what will you be writing here next?

**Billy**: You have to water it once you plant it.

**Ms. Richards**: Then you already know what you'll be doing, don't you.

There are many problems with Billy's text: misspelled words, run-on sentences, missing capitalizations, and incomplete information. But Billy has just started writing his piece. Therefore, Ms. Richards works on word flow, helping Billy to know that he knows something about his subject and that he has a clear understanding of what he will do next. Later, when his piece is finished, she will choose one skill to teach within the context of his topic. Above all, she works hard to help Billy teach her about his subject, to keep control of the topic in his hands, no matter how uncertain Billy might feel about his subject.

Notice that Ms. Richards has spent no more than a minute and a half in response. She then moves to other children while responding in the same manner, receiving a text and asking questions. As she moves to different children in other parts of the room (she does not move in rotation or down rows; the movement appears to be random), the other children can hear that the teacher expects them to help her with what they know. Lengthy responses tend to take the writing away from the child. For example, if Ms. Richards were to say, "I had a garden once, Billy. I planted all kinds of things too: I planted cabbages, those same turnips, yellow beans, pole beans, and corn.

Yes, it's hard work," she'd be identifying with Billy's garden and the hard work that goes into it, but *she* is now the informant. Such sharing should come only when his piece is completed and his authorship of this piece established.

Ms. Richards' statement is specific. When she receives Billy's text, she uses the actual words he has composed on the page. All writers need to know their words (the actual words on the page) affect other people. Notice that very little praise is given to Billy in this type of response. Instead, the listener, Ms. Richards, points with interest to the words; they are strong enough for her to understand and to remember them. The use of specifics, rather than the exclusive use of praise, is a fundamental issue in helping Billy to maintain control of his piece, as well as to take more responsibility for his text.

### Establish a Community of Learners

Writing is a social act. If social actions are to work, then the establishment of a community is essential. A highly predictable classroom is required if children are to learn to take responsibility and become a community of learners who help each other. Writing is an unpredictable act requiring predictable classrooms both in structure and response.

Children with learning disabilities often have histories of emotional problems. Many have become isolated and feel very little sense of community. They themselves may produce unpredictable classrooms. Their histories in taking responsibility are equally strewn with failure. Notions of choice and responsibility are threatening and require careful work on a broad front. The following ingredients help to build a structured, predictable community of more independent writers.

1. Write daily at the same time if possible, for a minimum of 30 minutes.
2. Work to establish each child's topical turf, an area of expertise for each writer.
3. Collect writing in folders so that writers can see the accumulation of what they know. Papers do not go home; rather, the collected work is present in class for student, teacher, parent, and administrator to examine. Some writing is published in hardcover or some more durable form.
4. Provide a predictable pattern of teacher participation by sharing your own writing, moving in the midst of students during writing time, and responding in predictable structure to your students' writing.
5. End each writing time with children responding to each other's writing in a predictable format: receiving, questioning.
6. Set up classroom routines in which you examine the entire day to see which responsibilities can be delegated to the children. Solve room problems in discussion. The group learns to negotiate, whether in working with a draft or solving a classroom problem.
7. Continually point to the responsibilities assumed by the group, as well as the specifics of what they know.

The writing classroom is a structured, predictable room in which children learn to make decisions. The external structure is geared to produce a confident, internal thinking framework within which children learn what they know and develop their own initiative.

## CONTINUING EDUCATION OF PROFESSIONALS

Most teachers have been drawn into process work because they have seen significant personal growth by their students with learning problems. Students who lacked confidence and initiative and were disenfranchised from literacy learn to write, share their writing with others, and take charge of their own learning. Although some teachers may wish to start work on the writing process based on this article, I suggest additional reading and work with their own writing.

The single most important help to teachers who work with young writers is work with the teacher's own writing. Both the National Writing Project and our work here at the University of New Hampshire stress work with the teacher's own writing. Thus teachers become acquainted with writing from the inside by actually doing it themselves. It would be unheard of for a piano teacher, a ceramicist, or an artist working with water colors to teach someone their craft without practicing it themselves. Most of us have had little instruction in learning the craft of writing. We've written term papers, letters, and proposals, but we haven't worked with someone who has helped us to know what we know, then showed us how that knowledge is increased through the writing process.

I strongly encourage teachers to become involved in summer programs or consult their own universities to see if writing-process programs or courses are available. The following intensive summer programs concentrate on the teacher's own writing and the teaching of writing:

- Dean Timothy Perkins, Northeastern University, 360 Huntington Avenue, Boston, MA 02115
- Prof. Thomas Newkirk, English Department, Hamilton Smith Hall, University of New Hampshire, Durham, NH 03824
- Prof. Lucy Calkins, Teacher's College, Columbia University, New York, NY 10027

The National Writing Project has programs in almost all of the 50 states offering 3- to 4-week summer programs. Information about the National Writing Project is available from Dr. James Gray, National Writing Project, University of California at Berkeley, Berkeley, CA 94720.

### For Further Reading

The following books will be helpful in acquiring more detail on teaching writing and organizing classrooms, as well as general background on learning and language theory.

Calkins, L. M. (1983). *Lessons from a child*. Portsmouth, NH: Heinemann.

Graves, D. (1983). *Writing: Teachers and children at work*. Portsmouth, NH: Heinemann.

Hansen, J., T. Newkirk & D. Graves. (eds.) (1985). *Breaking ground: Teachers relate reading and writing in the elementary classroom*. Portsmouth, NH: Heinemann.

Harste, J., C. Burke & V. Woodward. (1984). *Language stories and literacy lessons*. Portsmouth, NH: Heinemann.

Newkirk, T., & N. Atwell. (eds.). (1982). *Understanding Writing*. Chelmsford, MA: The Northeast Regional Exchange.

For teachers who wish to work with their own writing, I suggest the following:

Murray, D. M. (1983). *Write to learn*. New York: Holt, Rinehart, Winston.

Zinsser, W. (1980). *On writing well*. New York: Harper and Row.

## FINAL REFLECTION

Before children go to school, their urge to express is relentless. They learn to speak and to carry messages from one person to another. They burst into their homes to tell what just happened outside. They compose in blocks, play games, mark on sidewalks, and play with pencils or crayons. For most children, early audiences are receptive: adults struggle to make sense of the child's early attempts to communicate.

When children enter school, their urge to express is still present. A few enter already scarred from attempts to communicate with others. But the urge to be, to make a mark on the universe, has not left them. As children grow older and spend more time in school, many become still more disenchanted with writing. They can't keep up with the rest of the class and equate their struggles with handwriting, spelling, and early conventions as evidence that their ideas are unacceptable and that they are less intelligent than others. Even for these children, the urge to express, to make worthwhile contributions, to express a meaning that affects others, does not go away.

The most critical factor for children with learning disabilities is the meaning-making question. Teachers need to first believe they know important information, then work overtime to confirm for the child the importance of that information. The children see their teachers write: they see and hear them struggle for meaning on an easel or overhead projector as they compose before them. The children become apprentices to the use of words.

When children write, they make mistakes on the road to communicating their messages. The teacher's first response is to the meaning. Before a piece is completed, the teacher chooses one skill that will enhance the meaning of the piece still further. From the beginning, the teacher works to build a strong history for writers through collections of all their work, some publishing, and the writers' effective sharing with other members of the class.

Most teaching of writing is pointed toward the eradication of error, the mastery of minute, meaningless components that make little sense to the child. Small wonder. Most language arts texts, workbooks, computer software, and reams of behavioral objectives are directed toward the "easy" control of components that will show more specific growth. Although some growth may be evident on components, rarely does it result in the child's use of writing as a tool for learning and enjoyment. Make no mistake, component skills are important; if children do not learn to spell or use a pencil to get words on paper, they won't use writing for learning any more than the other children drilled on component skills. The writing-process approach simply stresses meaning first, and then skills in the context of meaning. Learning how to respond to meaning and to understand what teachers need to see in texts takes much preparation.

The writing process places high demands on the teacher. The room is carefully designed for developing student independence: Decisions are discussed, responsibilities assigned and assumed. Routines are carefully established with writing becoming a very important part of the room's predictability. Initially, response to the child's writing is predictable with receiving of the child's text, followed by questions of clarification, and the child's next step in the writing process.

Teachers who use the writing process to greatest advantage spend time working with their own writing. They read and become involved in many of the National Institutes that are helping teachers use writing as a tool for their own learning. Soon they find their students' learning careers change as well.

# a lot of talk about nothing

SHIRLEY BRICE HEATH

# 10

Inside a third-grade classroom described by the principal as a class of "low achievers," several pairs of children are working over tape recorders in dialogues with each other. One small group of children is dressed in costumes performing "Curious George" scenes for a few kindergarteners who are visiting. Yet another group is preparing illustrations for a story told by one of their classmates and now being heard on tape as they talk about why their drawings illustrate the words they hear. A lot of talk about nothing? Why are these children who presumably lack basic skills in language arts not spending their time with obvious instruction from the teacher in reading, writing and listening?

These are students in the classroom of a teacher-researcher who has adapted information about the oral and written language experiences of these children at home into a new language arts curriculum for school. She has developed for her children a program in which they spend as much of the day as possible talking—to each other and the teacher, and to fifth- and sixth-graders who come into the class one-half hour each day to read to small groups. This teacher has 30 children and no aides; she enlisted the help of fifth- and sixth-grade teachers who were willing to have some of their students write stories for the younger children and read to them several days of each week. The kindergarten teacher helps out by sending a few of her children for the third-graders to read to each week.

Talk in the classroom in about personal experiences, stories, expository textbook materials and, perhaps most important, about their own and others' talk. Their teacher gives no reading or writing task which is not surrounded by talk about the content knowledge behind the task and the kinds of language skills—oral and written—needed to tackle the task.

Since the beginning of the year, the teacher has asked visitors from the community into her class to talk about their ways of talking and to explain what they read and write at home and at work. The children have come to think of themselves as language "detectives," listening and learning to describe the talk of others. Grocery clerks have to use many politeness terms, and the questions they ask most often of customers require only a yes or no answer. On the other hand, guides at the local nature museum talk in "long paragraphs," describing what is around them and usually asking questions only at the end of one of their descriptions. The children have also learned to analyze their talk at home, beginning early in the year with a simple record of the types of questions they hear asked at home, and moving later in the year to interviews with their parents about the kinds of talking, reading and writing they do at their jobs.

The teacher in this classroom comments on her own talk and the language of textbooks, of older students, and of the third-graders themselves during each day. "Show and tell" time, usually reserved for only first-graders, occurs each day in this class, under the supervision of a committee of students who decide each week whether those who participate in this special time of the day will: (1) narrate about an experience they or someone else has had, (2) describe an event or object without including themselves or another animate being, or (3) read from their diary or journal for a particular day. The children use terms such as *narrative, exposition,* and *diary* or *journal* with ease by the end of the year. Increasingly during the year, the children use "show and tell" time to talk, not about their own direct experiences, but about content areas of their classroom. Also by the end of the year, the children are using this special time of the day for presenting skits about a social studies or science unit. They have found that the fifth- and sixth-graders can offer assistance on these topics, and planning such a presentation guarantees the attention of the upper classmen. By the end of the year, most of these children score above grade level on reading tests, and they are able to write stories, as well as paragraphs of exposition on content areas with which they feel comfortable in their knowledge. This is clearly no longer a class of "low achievers."

## TEACHERS AS RESEARCHERS

All of these ideas sound like pedagogical practices that many good teachers bring intuitively to their instruction. What was different about the motivations of this third-grade teacher for approaching language arts in these ways? The teacher described here was one of a group of teacher-researchers who cooperated with me for several years during the 1970s. I worked as an ethnographer, a daily participant and observer in homes and communities similar to those of the children in their classrooms, studying the ways in which the children learned to use oral and written language. As I studied the children at home, the teachers focused on their own language uses at home and in the classroom. We brought our knowledge together for comparison and as the baseline data from which to consider new methods and approaches in language arts.

We do not need educational research to tell us that different types of attention spans, parental support systems, and peer pressures can create vast differences among children in the same classroom, school, or community. But what of more subtle features of background differences, such as the amount and kind of talk addressed by adults to children and solicited from children? How can teachers and researchers work together to learn more about children's language experiences at home? And what can this knowledge mean for classroom practice?

For nearly a decade, living and working in three communities located within a few miles of each other in the southeastern part of the United States, I collected information on ways in which the children of these communities learned to use language: (1) Roadville is a white working-class community, (2) Trackton is a black working-class community in which many of the older members have only recently left work as sharecroppers on nearby farms, (3) the townspeople, black and white residents of a cluster of mainstream, school-oriented neighborhoods, are school teachers, local business owners, and executives of the textile mills.

Children from the three groups respond differently to school experiences. Roadville children are successful in the first years of the primary grades. Most Trackton children are not successful during this period, and only a few begin in the higher primary grades to move with adequate success through their classes. Most of the mainstream children of the townspeople, black and white, are successful in school and obtain a high school diploma with plans to go on to higher education. Children from backgrounds similar to those of these three groups make up the majority of the students in many regions of the southeastern United States. They bring to their classrooms different patterns of learning and using oral and written language, and their patterns of academic achievement vary greatly.

Intuitively, most teachers are aware of the different language background experiences children bring to school, but few means exist for providing teachers with information about these differences and their implications for classroom practice. Recent development of the notion of "teacher-as-researcher" has begun to help bridge the long-standing gap between researcher and teacher. This approach pairs the roles of teacher and researcher in a cooperative search for answers to questions raised by the teacher about what is happening in the classroom and why. Answering *why* questions more often than not calls for knowledge about the background experiences of both children and teachers. Thus, researcher working with teacher can help bridge yet another gap — that between the classroom and the homes of students.

Throughout most of the decade of the 1970s, I worked in the Piedmont Carolinas with teachers in several districts as research partners. Together, we addressed the questions teachers raised during the sometimes tumultuous early years of desegregation and ensuing shifts of curricular and testing policies. These teachers accepted the fact that language was fundamental to academic achievement, and their primary concerns related to how they could help children learn to use oral and written language in ways that would bring successful classroom experiences. They asked hard questions of language research. Why were some children seemingly unable to answer straightforward questions? Why were some students able to give elaborate directions and tell fantastic stories on the playground, but unable to respond to assignments calling for similar responses about lesson materials? Why did some children who had achieved adequate success in their first two or three years of school begin to fail in the upper primary grades?

In the 1960s, social scientists had described the language habits of groups of youngsters who were consistently failing to achieve academic excellence. The teachers with whom I worked were familiar with these studies, which had been carried out primarily in black urban areas. Most accepted the fact that children who spoke a nonstandard variety of English had learned a rule-governed language system and, moreover, that these students reflected learned patterns of "logic," considerable facility in handling complicated forms of oral discourse, and adeptness in shifting styles. But knowing this information about language learned at home did not answer the kinds of questions noted above about classroom performance. Neither did it provide for development of improved classroom materials and practices.

## ETHNOGRAPHY OF COMMUNICATION

Late in the 1970s, as some language researchers tried to describe the contexts in which children of different cultures learned to use language, they turned to ethnographic methods. Participating and observing over many months and even years in the daily lives of the group being studied, these researchers, who were often anthropologists, focused on oral and written language uses. My work in Roadville, Trackton, and among the townspeople centered on the children of these groups as they learned the ways of acting, believing and valuing around them in their homes and communities. Following the suggestions of anthropologist Dell Hymes, who first proposed in 1964 that ethnographers focus on communication, I lived and worked within these three groups to describe where, when, to whom, how, and with what results children were socialized as talkers, readers and writers. The three communities — located only a few miles apart — had radically different ways of using language and of seeing themselves in communication with their children.

Roadville parents believe they have to teach their children to talk, and they begin their task by talking with infants, responding to their initial sounds as words. They respond with full sentences, varying their tone of voice and emphasis, and affectionately urging infants to turn their heads in the direction of the speaker. As they talk to their infants and young children, they label items in the environment, and as children begin to talk, adults ask many teaching questions: "Where's your nose?" "Can you find Daddy's shoes?" Adults fictionalize their youngsters in talk about them: "He's a little cowboy; see those boots? See that cowboy strut?" Parents read to their children and ask them to name items in books, answer questions about the book's contents and, as they get older, to sit quietly listening to stories read to them. Parents buy coloring and follow-the-number books for their children and tutor them in staying within the lines and coloring items appropriately. All of these habits relate to school practices, and they are transferred to the early years of reading and writing in school. Yet, by the fourth grade many of these children seem to find the talking, reading and writing tasks in school foreign, and their academic achievement begins to decline.

In nearby Trackton, adults immerse their children in an ongoing stream of talk from extended family members and a wide circle of friends and neighbors. Children become the responsibility of all members of the community, and from birth they are kept in the center of most adult activities, including eating, sleeping, or playing. Adults talk about infants and young children, and as they do so, they fictionalize them and often exaggerate their behaviors and physical features. They nickname children and play teasing games with them. They ask young children for specific information which is not known to adults: "Where'd that come from?" "You want what?" By the time they are toddlers, these children begin to tell stories, recounting events or describing objects they have seen. Adults stop and listen to their stories occasionally, but such stories are most often addressed to other children who challenge, extend, tease, or build from the youngster's tales. By about 2, children begin to enter ongoing conversations by actively attracting adults' attention with some physical gesture and then making a request, registering a complaint, or reporting an event. Very quickly, these children are accepted as communicating members of the group, and adults respond directly to them as conversational partners.

Most of these children first go to school with enthusiasm, but by the end of the first half of the first grade, many are coming home with reports that their teacher scolds them for talking too much and working too little. By the third grade, many Trackton children have established a record of failures which often they do not break in the rest of their school careers.

After hearing from me how children of these comminities learned to use language, some of their teachers agreed to work with me to study either their own uses of language with their preschoolers at home or those of their mainstream friends. They found that when talking to very young infants, they asked questions, simplified their sentences, used special words and changed their tone of voice. Moreover, since most of these mainstream mothers did not work outside the home while their children were very young, they spent long hours each day alone with their pre-schoolers as their primary conversational partners. They arranged many outings, usually with other mothers through voluntary associations, such as their church groups or local social memberships.

These teachers' findings about mainstreamers' uses of language with their pre-schoolers indicated that they and the Roadville parents had many language socialization habits in common. Parents in both communities talked to their children and focused their youngsters' attention at an early age on labels, pictures in books, and educational toys. Both groups played with their children and participated in planned outings and family recreation with them. Yet mainstream children and Roadville children fared very differently in their progress through the middle primary grades.

A close look at the home habits of these two groups indicated that a major difference lay in the amount of running narrative or ongoing commentary in which mainstream parents immersed their young children. As these youngsters pass their first birthday, mothers and other adults who are part of their daily network begin to provide a running commentary on events and items surrounding the child. In these commentaries, adults tell the child what is happening: "Mummy's going to get her purse, and then we're going to take a ride. Mummy's got to go to the post office." As soon as the child begins to talk, adults solicit these kinds of running commentaries: they ask children what they are doing with their toys, what they did when they were at someone else's house, and what they had to eat on a trip to the grocery store. These requests for running descriptions and cumulative accounts of past actions provide children in these families with end-less hours of practice of all the sentence-level features necessary to produce successful narratives or recounts of experiences.

In using their own experiences as data, children begin their devel-opmental progression of story conventions and narrative structures which they will be asked to replay in school from the first day of school through their college courses. They learn either to use an existing animate being or to create a fantastic one as the central actor in their stories; they take these actors through events in which they may meet obstacles on their way to a goal. The scripts of the stories that the children have heard read to them and the narratives that have surrounded them and storied their own and others' experiences are replayed with different actors and slightly different settings. Gradually, children learn to open and close stories, to give them a setting and movement of time, and occasionally, even to sum up the meaning of the story in a moralistic pronouncement ("He shouldn't have gone without his mother"). Some children move from linking a collection of events related to one another only by their immediacy of experience for the child to tying a story together by incorporating a central point, a constant goal or direction, and a point of view which may not be that of the child as experiencer and narrator.

When children are very young toddlers, parents talk of and ask children about events of the here-and-now: the immediate tasks of eating, getting dressed, and playing with a particular toy or person. Of older toddlers, adults increasingly ask questions about events that occurred in the past—tasks, settings, and events that the child is expected to recount from memory. These recountings are, however, then interpreted by adults or older siblings in a future frame: "Do you want to go again?" "Do you think Billy's mother will be able to fix the broken car?" Questioners ask children to express their views about future events and to link past occurrences with what will come in the future.

In many ways, all of this is "talk about nothing," and adults and older siblings in these mainstream households model and elicit these kinds of narratives without being highly conscious of their having a didactic purpose or a heavily positive transfer value to school activities. Yet when teacher-researchers examined closely the instructional situations of the classrooms into which these children usually go, they found that, from first-grade reading circles to upper-primary social studies group work, the major activity is producing some sort of commentary on events or objects. In the early primary years, teachers usually request commentary in the form of labels or names of attributes of items or events ("What did the boy in our story find on his walk?"). Later, the requests are for descriptive commentary ("Who are some community helpers? What kinds of jobs do they do for us?"). Gradually the requests are mixed and students have to learn when it is appropriate to respond with labels or features (brief names or attributes of events or objects), fantastic stories, straightforward descriptions, or interpretations in which they comment on the outcome of events, the relative merits of objects, or the internal states of characters.

## A CLOSER LOOK

On the surface, these summaries of the early language socialization of the children from these three communities support a commonly held idea about links between language at home and at school: the more parents talk to their children, the more likely children are to succeed in school. Yet the details of the differences and similarities across these three communities suggest that this correlation is too simple. Trackton children hear and take part in far more talk around them than the children of either Roadville or the townspeople. Yet, for them, more talk does not have a positive transfer value to the current, primary-level practices of the school. Roadville children have less talk addressed to them than the townspeople's children. Yet, from an early age, they are helped to focus on labels and features of items and events. They are given books and they are read to by parents who buy educational toys for their children and spend many hours playing with their toddlers. As the children grow older, these parents involve their children in handicrafts, home building projects, and family recreational activities such as camping and fishing. Both Trackton and Roadville parents have strong faith in schooling as a positive value for their children, and they believe success in school will help their children get jobs better than those they have held as adults. Yet, neither Roadville nor Trackton children manage to achieve the same patterns of sustained academic success children of townspeople achieve with relatively little apparent effort. Why?

A primary difference seems to be the amount of "talk about nothing" with which the townspeople surround their children and into which they socialize their young. Through their running narratives, which begin almost at the birth of the child, they seemingly focus the attention of their young on objects and events while they point out verbally the labels and features of those that the child should perceive and later talk about. It is as though, in the drama of life, these parents freeze scenes and parts of scenes repeatedly throughout each day. Within the frame of a single scene, they focus the child's attention, sort out labels to name, and give the child ordered turns for sharing talk about these labels and the properties of the objects or events to which they refer; adult and child thus jointly narrate descriptions of scenes. Through this consistent focus, adults pull out some of the stimuli in the array surrounding the child and make these stand still for cooperative examination and narration between parent and child. Later occurrences of the same event or object are identified by adults who call the child's attention to similarities and differences. Thus, townspeople's children are not left on their own to see these relations between two events or to explore ways of integrating something in a new context to its old context. These children learn to attend to items both in real life and in books, both in and out of their usual locations, as they practice throughout their pre-school years running narratives with adults

In much of their talk, mainstream adults ask: "What do you call that?" "Do you remember how to say the name of that?" Thus, children are alerted to attend to the particulars to talk about talk: names, ways of retelling information, and ways of linking what one has told with something that has gone before. Thus, mainstreamers' children hear a lot of talk about talk and are forced to focus on not only the features and names of the world around them, but also on their ways of communicating about that world. From the earliest days of their infancy, these habits are modeled repeatedly for them, and as soon as they learn to talk, they are called upon to practice similar verbal habits. Day in and day out during their pre-school years, they hear and practice the kinds of talk in which they will display successful learning in school.

The teacher in the third-grade classroom described at the beginning of this essay recognized that her students needed intense and frequent occasions to learn and practice those language uses they had not acquired at home. She, therefore, created a classroom that focused on talk—all kinds of talk. The children labeled, learned to name the features of everyday items and events, told stories, described their own and others' experiences, and narrated skits, puppet shows, and slide exhibits.

Many classrooms include such activities for portions of the day or week; others provide some of these activities for some children. A critical difference in the case given here, however, and one driven by a perspective gained from being part of a research team, was the amount of talk about talk in this classroom. School-age children are capable of—and can be quite proficient at—stepping back from and commenting upon their own and others' activities, *if* the necessary skills are modeled and explicated. In this classroom, and in others which drew from ethnographic data on the home life of their students, teachers and visitors to the classroom called attention to the ways they used language: how they asked questions, showed politeness, got what they wanted, settled arguments, and told funny stories. With early and intensive classroom opportunities to surround learning with many different kinds of talk and much talk about talk, children from homes and communities whose uses of language do not match those of the school *can* achieve academic success. A frequently heard comment, "Talk is cheap," is, in these days of bankrupt school districts and economic cutbacks, perhaps worth a closer examination — for more reasons than one.

# 11

## whole language:
## what makes it whole?

KENNETH GOODMAN

Before we get to specifics, let's consider what distinguishes whole language approaches from other reading-writing methods. Most of the discussion will center on reading, simply because there has been so little teaching of writing, particularly in elementary schools. Perhaps no one could figure out how to make a basal writing series! So we have limited ourselves to isolated spelling and handwriting instruction. It should be said, however, that considerable writing in a holistic way is beginning to be done in elementary schools, mainly because of Donald Graves and his colleagues.

## WHAT IS NOT WHOLE LANGUAGE?

Teaching practices, reading programs, and curricula in schools vary widely at the moment, and many of them are simply incompatible with whole language instruction. Whole language firmly rejects such things as these:

- Isolating skill sequences.
- Slicing up reading and writing into grade slices, each slice neatly following and dependent on prior ones.
- Simplifying texts by controlling their sentence structures and vocabulary, or organizing them around phonic patterns.
- Equating reading and writing with scores on tests of "sub-skills."
- Isolating reading and writing instruction from its use in learning, or in actual reading and writing.
- Believing there are substantial numbers of learners who have difficulty learning to read or write for any physical or intellectual reason.

### Skills-Technology Views

Contemporary reading instruction has been dominated by several key factors:

THE DEVELOPMENT OF A TECHNOLOGY OF READING INSTRUCTION

This technology grew between 1920 and 1960. Linguists, psycho-linguists, and sociolinguists were busy elsewhere, and North American educators and researchers put great faith in technology. Behavioral psychology strongly dominated. The technology incorporated narrow views of language and language learning.

TESTS: THE FOCUS OF THE TECHNOLOGY

Standardized reading tests assume that reading can be subdivided neatly into sub-skills that can easily be sequenced and measured. Learning to read means scoring better on tests of these sequenced bits and pieces: letter-sound relationships, isolated words, abstract definitions, fractured sentences, and paragraphs pulled out of the middle of longer coherent texts. With faith in technology, teachers, school boards, and legislators came to rely more and more on tests. At their worst, tests decide promotion or failure, admission to special programs and ability tracks, and the effectiveness of teachers. In extreme cases, they have even become the curriculum. This very abusive use of tests has driven teachers to seek alternatives that are more positive, more humane and fairer to learners, more soundly based on modern research and theory, and more effective in producing learning. Teachers know they know more about their pupils than the tests can show them.

BASAL READERS IN EVERY CLASSROOM UP TO GRADE 8

Basals, basals, everywhere! Basals vary somewhat in the criteria used to organize and sequence them, but essentially they are organized around controlled vocabulary. So, learning to read becomes learning to recognize words: the most common words appear in primers and early books, while less common words are introduced gradually over the years; behavioral psychology is used to develop rules for how often a word must be repeated in a text once it is introduced, and how many words should be introduced per page; separate basals are created for each grade.

A VIEW OF WORDS AS THE KEY UNITS IN LEARNING
TO READ AND WRITE

There have been noisy public battles between those advocating explicit phonics approaches and those advocating teaching words as whole. The latter use a range of ways to "attack" words in order to learn them, including phonics. The former argue that once kids know "the sounds of the letters" they can read and don't need anything else. But both agree that learning to read is a matter of learning words. In fairness, it should be said that whole-word advocates tend to be more concerned with giving kids good stories. There are even some who have tried to combine a strong explicit phonics program with having the pupils read real stories.

DIRECT INSTRUCTION FOR READING

The technology has produced workbooks, ditto masters, extra practice for learners who get low test scores, and supplementary "enrichment" materials for the high scorers. Strangely, the huge allocation of time for reading instruction does not mean that a lot of time is spent on actual reading. Little time is left after skills drill exercises, phonics drills, and workbook exercises with nothing longer than a line or two. Writing gets even less time, as does oral language, science, social studies, humanities, arts, or thinking about real problems.

SEVERELY LABELED CHILDREN

Readers are labeled remedial, disabled, or dyslexic if they don't do well in tests and technologized reading programs. They then get more isolated drills on phonics and word attacks, and even less time for learning language while using language to learn. What they suffer from most is the fact of being labeled.

DISLIKE OF READING

Large numbers have managed to survive the technology and learn to read and write with at least moderate effectiveness, but in the process have learned to think of reading and writing as unpleasant activities to be done only when absolutely necessary. They can read and write, but they usually choose not to do so if the choice is their own to make.

## Breaking Some Icons

There are some aspects of the reading technology that have become so firmly entrenched in conventional reading instruction that they need special attention to indicate why they have no place in whole language programs:

READINESS

Some good reasons lay behind special readiness programs. Children need time to mature; rushing them is counter-productive. So when Washburne said that a mental age of 6 was necessary for success in learning to read, many people eagerly accepted that, though even at the time questions were raised about the validity of the research. Similarly, people could see that when children start school they haven't yet developed fine muscle control, so they should perhaps not be expected to write with adult pencils and pens. Unfortunately, bad reasoning combined these facts with a lack of understanding of human language development and use. What resulted were non-language activities and abstractions that had nothing to do with children's readiness for written language development.

Real readiness is intrinsic when language is real. Good kid-watchers know when children see a need for reading and writing, have confidence in themselves, and want to join "the literacy club." Whole language teachers don't rush children, but neither do they distract them from natural functional language use and development. They simply support them as they build on what they already know.

PHONICS

Phonics is the set of relationships between the sound system of oral language and the letter system of written language. Phonics methods of teaching reading and writing reduce both to matching letters with sounds. It is a flat-earth view of the world, since it rejects modern science about reading and writing and how they develop. Phonics programs tend to be unscientific even in their presentation of phonic relationships. It simply isn't true that "when two vowels go walking, the first does the talking" except in a limited number of cases, which must be already known to the reader in order for the rule to be sensible.

Besides, English vowels don't just come in long and short varieties. The difference in the vowels in the following list of words will vary from dialect to dialect: *frog, fog, bog, dog, smog, cog, hog, jog.* But not one of the sounds is a "long o." Phonics programs can't deal with dialect differences unless they acknowledge that each dialect has a different set of phonics rules. Moreover, phonics methods ignore normal shifts in pronunciation that happen as words add affixes. Notice the letter "t" in *site, situate, situation.* The "t" stays in each word even though the sound shifts as the affixes are added. That's good, because it preserves the meaning relationship between these related words.

But even a more scientific phonics approach would be insufficient as a method for teaching reading and writing. The logic of phonics instruction is that letters can be coded as sounds, or sounds as letters. Then these can be blended to produce reading or writing. But that doesn't produce meaningful language—it only produces strings of sounds or letters.

Instead, children discover the alphabetic principle when they learn to write. There are relationships between letter patterns and sound patterns. They do what they do in all language learning: they search for rules. That leads to invented spelling. But spelling is standardized in English (and most other languages), so the rules produce only a possible spelling, not necessarily the standard one. Thus children learn to keep their eyes open for standard spellings as they read, and to suspend the rules when they don't work. Gradually they move toward conventional spelling in their writing.

Readers are seeking meaning, not sounds or words. They may use their developing phonics generalizations to help when the going gets tough. If they are lucky enough not to have been taught phonics in isolation, with each letter equally important, then they will not be diverted from developing the strategies necessary to select just enough graphic information to get to the sense they are seeking.

In a whole language program readers and writers develop control over the phonic generalizations in the context of using written language sensibly. These self-developed rules are not overlearned and artificial as they would be if they were imposed by a structured reading and spelling program. Whole language programs and whole language teachers do not ignore phonics. Rather they keep it in the perspective of real reading and real writing.

## WHAT ARE THE PRINCIPLES OF WHOLE LANGUAGE?

Whole language is an attempt to get back to basics in the real sense of that word—to set aside basals, workbooks, and tests, and to return to inviting kids to learn to read and write by reading and writing real stuff.

### Principles for Reading and Writing

- Readers construct meaning during reading. They use their prior learning and experience to make sense of the texts.
- Readers predict, select, confirm, and self-correct as they seek to make sense of print. In other words, they guess or make hypotheses about what will occur in the text. Then they monitor their own reading to see whether they guessed right or need to correct themselves to keep making sense. Effective reading makes sense. Efficient reading does it with the least amount of effort and input. Rapid readers tend to have high comprehension because they are both effective and efficient.
- Writers include enough information and detail so what they write will be comprehensible to their readers. Effective writing makes sense for the intended audience. Efficient writing includes only enough for it to be comprehensible.
- Three language systems interact in written language: the graphophonic (sound and letter patterns), the syntactic (sentence patterns), and the semantic (meanings). We can study how each one works in reading and writing, but they can't be isolated for instruction without creating non-language abstractions. All three systems operate in a pragmatic context, the practical situation in which the reading and writing is taking place. That context also contributes to the success or failure of the reading or writing.
- Comprehension of meaning is always the goal of readers.
- Expression of meaning is always what writers are trying to achieve.
- Writers and readers are strongly limited by what they already know, writers in composing, readers in comprehending.

### Principles for Teaching and Learning

- School literacy programs must build on existing learning and utilize intrinsic motivations. Literacy is an extension of natural whole language learning: it is functional, real, and relevant.
- Literacy develops from whole to part, from vague to precise, from gross to fine, from highly concrete and contextualized to more abstract, from familiar contexts to unfamiliiar.
- Expression (writing) and comprehension (reading) strategies are built during functional, meaningful, relevant language use.
- Development of the ability to control the form of reading and writing follows, and is motivated by, the development of the functions for reading and writing.
- There is no hierarchy of sub-skills, and no necessary universal sequence.
- Literacy develops in response to personal/social needs. Children

growing up in literate environments become literate before they come to school.

- There is no one-to-one correspondence between teaching and learning. The teacher motivates, arranges the environment, monitors development, provides relevant and appropriate materials, and invites learners to participate in and plan literacy events and learning opportunities. Ultimately, it is the learner who builds knowledge, knowledge structures, and strategies from the enriched environment the teacher helps to create.
- As teachers monitor and support the development of reading and writing strategies, learners focus on the communication of meaning. So there is a double agenda in literacy instruction. The kids focus on what they are using reading and writing for. The teachers focus on development and use.
- Risk-taking is essential. Developing readers must be encouraged to predict and guess as they try to make sense of print. Developing writers must be encouraged to think about what they want to say, to explore genre, to invent spellings, and to experiment with punctuation. Learners need to appreciate that miscues, spelling inventions, and other imperfections are part of learning.
- Motivation is always intrinsic. Kids learn to read and write because they need and want to communicate. Extrinsic rewards have no place in a whole language program. Punishment for not learning is even more inappropriate.
- The most important question a teacher can ask a reader or writer is, "Does that make sense?" Learners need to be encouraged to ask the same question of themselves as they read and write.
- Materials for instruction must be whole texts that are meaningful and relevant. From the first school experiences, they must have all the characteristics of real functional language. There is no need for special texts to teach reading or writing.
- Away with exercises that chop language into bits and pieces to be practiced in isolation from a whole text!
- Predictability is the real measure of how hard a text is for a particular reader. The more predictable, the easier.
- No materials are acceptable if they divert the attention of writers from expression and readers from comprehension.

## WHAT'S WHOLE ABOUT WHOLE LANGUAGE?

We can summarize what's whole in language in the following points:

- Whole language learning builds around whole learners learning whole language in whole situations.
- Whole language learning assumes respect for language, for the learner, and for the teacher.
- The focus is on meaning and not on language itself, in authentic speech and literacy events.
- Learners are encouraged to take risks and invited to use language, in all its varieties, for their own purposes.

- In a whole language classroom, all the varied functions of oral and written language are appropriate and encouraged.

## Evaluation

In all that, whole language teachers are concerned with helping learners build underlying competence. They have no interest in getting them to behave in predetermined ways in class and on tests. For example, spelling competence is not a matter of memorizing words for the Friday spelling test, but a matter of first trying out words as they are needed in writing, and then learning the limits of invented spelling against social convention. The basic competence of children who can comprehend when they read English is not reflected in tests of word recognition or phonics "skills." Moreover, pupils can give right answers on tests for wrong reasons, and wrong answers for right reasons. Whole language teachers know that the language miscues pupils make often show their underlying competence, the strengths they are developing and testing the limits of.

KID-WATCHING

Before the testing movement became the multi-million dollar activity it has become, there was a developing child-study movement among researchers and educators. It's simply true that one can learn much more about pupils by carefully watching than by formal testing. Whole language teachers are constant kid-watchers. Informally, in the course of watching a child write, listening to a group of children discuss or plan together, or having a casual conversation, teachers evaluate. It even happens while children are playing. It happens more formally in one-to-one conferences with pupils about their reading or writing, as teachers make anecdotal records of what they observe: It may involve instruments like the Reading Miscue Inventory or a writing observation form. The key is that it happens in the course of ongoing classroom activities.

Whole language teachers evaluate and revise their plans on the basis of the kid-watching they do. But the most useful form of evaluation is self-evaluation. Teachers continuously evaluate themselves and their teaching. They also help pupils develop ways of evaluating their own development, of knowing when they are and when they are not successful in using language and learning through it.

Evaluation has certain general purposes in any program. It is useful in planning and modifying instruction so it will be more effective. It is also useful in getting a sense of the progress pupils have made in their growth, and some sense of the needs they have. Most of these purposes can be accomplished through ongoing kid-watching.

At times it may be useful to use more formal devices to get indications of the strengths and weaknesses of the learners. Unfortunately, most standardized tests of reading and writing focus strongly on isolated skills and words. If they use connected texts, these are often short, disjointed, and deliberately obscure to make them harder, so that the scores are stretched out and produce a bell-shaped performance curve. To the extent that standardized tests test things other than effective use of language, they are inappropriate for judging whole language programs and useless in serving the legitimate aims of evaluation.

Instead, most whole language teachers have pupils fill portfolios with their own writing, records of their reading experiences, and examples of other learning activities.

# 12

## inner designs
RUTH HUBBARD

Six-year-old David gripped his pencil tightly as he leaned over his writing booklet. Carefully, almost painfully, he wrote 'C-A-T.' Then, looking around the room, he tapped his pencil on the desk and slid his chair back and forth across the floor. In a few seconds, he straightened up, then again wrote, 'C-A-T.'

As an avid writing process enthusiast, I was disappointed ... and worried about him. Instead of drawing, or taking risks with invented spelling, I was afraid David was returning to the safety of a known word, written over and over again, meaninglessly.

As I looked at David again, he was writing 'C-A-T' for the fifth time. I was about to turn away when I noticed a smile on David's face as he moved his lips and wrote. I wondered what was going on in that little boy's mind. So I decided to ask him.

I pulled up a chair next to him and asked, "Can you tell me about what you're writing?"

His smile widened. "I'm writing and thinking about all the different cats I know."

"Wow! You know a lot of cats!"

He grinned and nodded. "There's Joey, another Joey, Kitka, and Minudo. Oh, my other friend has one." He picked up his pencil and wrote again. 'C-A-T.' Ignoring my presence, he was again immersed in his writing.

Finally, he pushed back his chair and reread his page to me. "1-2-3-4-5-6-7-8 cats!"

As David read each page to me, he pointed to a written 'C-A-T' — indistinguishable to me, but to David, each was a distinct, individual cat.

"Joey was one," David reminisced. "He's dead now. Buried with a rock at his head in our backyard. Kitka and Joey used to fight 'till they got used to each other."

Pointing his finger to each CAT, he counted again, and said in summary, "That's eight cats I've remembered today."

Reprinted with permission from *Language Arts* 66 (2):119−36. Copyright © 1989 by the National Council of Teachers of English.

What I would have missed if I had focused only on David's product! He had recreated in his mind images and memories of a young lifetime of cats. I was intrigued. After opening up that window to what was going on in his mind, I've continued to ask children, to learn the thinking strategies they employ as they write and as they read, and to begin to get past my egocentric—or perhaps adult-centric—view of their processes.

## TOO MUCH "SPINNING WORDS ABOUT WORDS"

*Thinking—How shall I define it? It is a soundless dialogue, it is a weaving of patterns, it is a search for meaning. (Vera John-Steiner 1985)*

As each of us attempts that search for meaning, we need a medium in which our ideas can take shape. But there is not just one medium; productive thought does not follow a uniform pattern. Instead, our ideas may take form in images, movement, or inner speech. And the search begins young; crucial foundations for thinking begin in childhood.

In her pioneer work on creative thinking, Vera John-Steiner discusses the "inner languages" that adults employ as they think, but little investigation has been done of the diverse thinking strategies that young children use, and these strategies have enormous influence on emerging literacy skills.

The writing, reading, and drawing of children have been sources to analyze their thinking to some degree. Teachers of young children often look at their children's progress from draft to draft in writing, as well as their children's comprehension of more difficult texts as their reading improves. Children's thought has also been studied in terms of reading and writing by investigating their "metalinguistic aware-ness,"—the ability to use language to discuss and analyze language. Yet these studies do not get at the root of children's *thinking* as they read and write. As writer/artist Leo Lionni complains, "The study of literacy is all too often spinning words about words without looking back to the images that precede words and to the feelings that precede both" (Lionni 1984, p. 732).

In investigating the reading-writing-thinking triangle, I decided to explore these "inner languages" as they evolve in children. How is what they are actually *doing* in the process of reading, writing, and planning revealing their thinking strategies? And, if we begin to ask children about their thinking processes, what can they tell us? My research focused around the broad question: What is the nature of children's thinking in relation to the reading/writing process?

## CONTEXT OF THE STUDY

I gathered data in Leslie Funkhouser's second/third-grade classroom at Mast Way School in Lee, New Hampshire. The students work on their reading and writing every morning in a workshop community. The philosophy and teaching style of Ms. Funkhouser made this classroom of seven- to nine-year-old children ideal for investigating thinking strategies. Her class is definitely learner-centered: the students are expected to make choices both in their reading material and in the topics about which they write. They are also encouraged to solve problems using the strategies that work best for them. Although I gathered data on the entire class of twenty-six students, I focused on four children who were chosen on the basis of the differences in their observed strategies and their willingness to interact with me, and explain or demonstrate their thinking. I have organized the findings of this exploratory study into two sections. In the first section, I discuss the three major categories that I found classwide in my observations: the reach for metaphor, the prevalence of planning strategies, and the recognition of literary space. Then I focus on the four case-study children and their "inner languages."

## CLASSWIDE FINDINGS
### The Reach for Metaphors

*I just feel it like it's something sort of magic in my brain. Like I fall in a hole and an adventure happens there while I'm writing. (Christy)*

When adults talk about their thinking processes, they often find it difficult to explain those inner workings without resorting to metaphors (Paivio 1983; John-Steiner 1985). Basil Bernstein uses the image of the springs of a trap to explain how his thoughts forcefully propel him: "My basic metaphor is that of being caught in the jaws of a trap; but, the springs of the trap can drive one's thoughts going, in flight. So you can feel briefly, the sense of your own trajectory" (John-Steiner, p. 18). And Allan Paivio uses the metaphor of the well to explain memory, with words the hooks to pull up the desired image (1983).

Children, too, are often blocked in their attempts to explain what's going on in their minds, and reach for metaphors to explain their processes. In some children, like Ilana, this isn't surprising; her writing is rich with metaphorical comparisons, such as "The porcupine fish looks like a prickly balloon." And when she talked to me about thinking processes as she wrote, she told me, "It's hard to explain what's going on up there. It's like taking a little piece of your mind and putting it down and making it into a piece of paper."

But other children who don't typically write in this manner also found in metaphor the right vehicle for expression. David, for example, explained his writing process in terms of a tape recorder. "When you write about this book, what's going on in your head?" I asked him as he prepared to write in his reading journal.

"It's like I rewinded the book and press play when I write about it. I go "whoop" to the front of the book, press play, then you see it again. I press stop once in a while so I can write a little bit."

Tracy found she can't always hold an image in her mind well

enough to write about it. She explained it this way: "Sometimes I try to make up a story in my head. I sometimes have trouble making the picture stay, like the picture sort of falls off the table."

Pieces of paper, tape recorders, falling into holes or off of tables — this preliminary evidence suggests that children as well as adults turn to symbolic images to make abstract ideas more concrete and manageable. And this carries over into the next category I found classwide.

### The Prevalence and Variety of Planning Strategies

*When I make plans, I hold it in my head. I have a lot on my mind and it slips sometimes. (Jillana)*

Many children recognize the need to plan and plot their work; different children rely on various planning strategies as they read and write.

Planning is essential to Jillana's writing and doesn't always come easily. "The hardest part is how you have to think ahead of time," she told me one morning, then to prove her point, she picked up a book she had recently read to show me that other writers also plan their plots. She explained to me that in *Junk Day on Juniper Street*, the author must have thought ahead of time about what was going to happen. She pointed out that early in the story, a junky old chair is mentioned.

"See?" She stressed to me. "Now, what good is that chair? The author thought ahead of time what he wanted to do with that chair, 'cause ..." — she flipped through the pages to the end of the story, then triumphantly showed me the final page where a man contentedly rocks in the chair — "at the end of the book, it's important."

I questioned her about how *she* thinks ahead of time when she writes. Using her book *The Lost Bunny Rabbit* as an example, she explained her process to me.

"I thought, 'They'll look for [the lost bunny] in the forest.' I thought to have it be a meeting. Then I thought, 'You're in court.' I like to put in some different things that nobody ever wrote about. My Dad's on the jury now, so I thought about court so I just added it."

Chapter titles serve as important preplanners for her. "I like to have chapters," she told me. "I make up the chapters as I go along." Jillana doesn't create a list of chapter headings to map out the whole story, but she does plan by the individual chapter headings. One chapter, for example, is called, "The Search Party." There is no previous mention of one, and it takes her two pages of writing to introduce the search party, yet the title was written first.

Jillana is not the only child who finds chapter titles helpful to preplan writing. One day, Rachel was writing in her book called *My Family*, and shared what she had written so far. I began with a list of three chapters she planned to write about, then proceeded through the first two chapters — the third was not yet written. When I asked her how writing the chapter headings first helped her, she explained, "It just helped me to decide. And the people will know what will be in the book. This is the first time I did it."

"Would you do it again?" I asked.

She nodded. "Yes, 'cause it helped me."

Other children, like Nadine, use drawings to help them organize their thoughts for writing. She explained to me, "The pictures help me think of what I'm doing." I found almost daily examples of this kind of preplanning. For some children, however, the drawings themselves are an important part of their writing and require preplanning, too. Ilana explained to me one morning how she had mapped out her drawing on one page of her book. (See Figure 12−1.) Because she knew she wanted the dog in the middle of the page, she didn't draw the whole deer, which she wanted to be secondary in importance on the page. She also thought of the illustration in terms of an actual photograph.

"You know, if there was a camera here," she told me, "soon the camera wouldn't see the things. It's only for that minute. It only saw part of the deer."

For some children, the piece of writing determines the planning strategy. Rachel and Christine were writing an elaborate fairy tale together and decided to map out the entire plot. "Sometimes we think the same," Christine explained. "but we need to draw the picture and see if it comes out the way we imagined it." Their story, *The Magic Princesses*, contained several twists and turns of fate and exciting adventures, which were carefully orchestrated in advance in the form of a sort of writing map (see Figure 12−2).

"We're planning this now," Rachel told me. "We'll have to get through it. There are people at each of the places, and that bird could eat you! We didn't write this yet. We're going to describe it, so we drew it out first."

Examples of the children planning their writing were abundant, and the importance of planning strategies was reflected in the writing

**Figure 12−1**

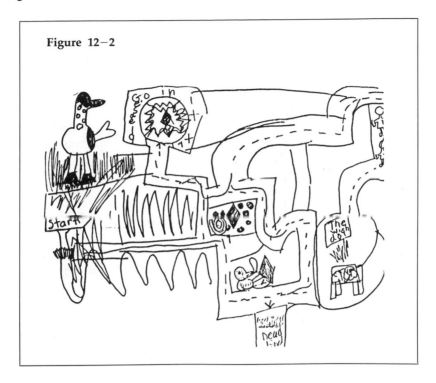

**Figure 12—2**

inventory I administered to the children. When I asked them, "What does someone have to do in order to be a good writer?" their replies often focused on thinking ahead:

**Tracy**: They have to plan what they're going to write . . . think hard.
**Dwayne**: They have to think a lot before they start. They have to make it fit so it sounds good. Good start and ending.

Another question I asked them — "How do you decide what to write about?" — also brought out their need for thinking ahead, as these examples show:

**Angela**: I think for a minute or two . . . You get the thought of what you're going to write after you think for a while.
**Kristy**: I think of it in my mind. I picture it in my mind, then write.
**Rachel**: I think about it. Last time, it took me the whole writing period to decide.

Some planning strategies for reading appeared in these inventories as well, such as looking through a book to gauge its length so there would be enough time to read it, thinking about a friend who would want to share the book, or planning to read another book by the same author. Strategies for planning in reading, however, were slight compared to the range and diversity of planning strategies in writing.

### The Recognition of Literary Space

*When I'm reading, I think ahead. I dream I'm actually the main character doing that in real life. Like* The Secret of the Old Barn. *I feel like I was Angie. There's this old house with these old people in it. Angie was telling Mark about it, and taming the animals. I felt like I was doing that. The pictures when I read—they're exactly like my dreams—in color. (Christy)*

Literary space refers to a psychological "place"—a state of mind in which a reader blurs the distinction between reality and art (Jacobsen 1982). I found that the children I worked with often inhabit and describe this "literary space" which represents a deep involvement with literature.

I first noticed this recognition of literary space when I talked with Adrienne one day and asked her, "When you read this book, what was going on in your head?"

Adrienne struggled to explain the mental space she occupied. "I knew I was reading the book," she told me, "but I sort of felt like I was the girl with the dog. It was a choose-your-own adventure, and if I picked page nine, then that's what I would do if I was her."

Her description struck me as just the kind of experience with literature that Norman Holland (1975) describes in adult readers. "People get involved . . . in three closely related ways: they cease to pay attention to what is outside the work of art; they concentrate their attention wholly on it; then—and this is the special and important thing—they begin to lose track of the boundaries between themselves and the work of art . . . What is 'out there' in the literary work feels as though it is 'in here' in your head" (pp. 66–67).

Jillana, too, began to lose track of those boundaries as she read a book about Georgie the ghost. "I felt like I was the ghost helping people," she told me. "I felt like I came out of a bottle and began serving food. I've served people before and I've cooked a lot, so I could remember that, but I felt like I *was* the ghost, doing that." This is an experience that happens often to Jillana, and she wrote about it one day in her reading journal. "When you read you kind of picksher the sory in your mind as if you were the carikder and you kind of get a tast to the story." (February 12, 1986)

When Stacy reads, she often pictures the scene in her mind. "When I read," she told me, "I get the idea of like the picture moving in my mind. When I read this," she pointed to her *Curious George* book, "I can see the man walking in with the yellow hat. I think I sorta read it inside—what I imagine the voice to be."

When I asked Ilana to tell me about what was going on in her mind as she read *Best Friends for Frances*, she decided to draw a picture. "This is me frances," she wrote next to the drawing of Frances the badger. "I feel like Frances going to Thelma's house."

Drawing this picture of her experience while reading caused Ilana to reflect on "where she is" when she writes. She was in the midst of writing an adventure story about a fictional character named Samoida, and drew a picture of the literary space she inhabits in the act of composing (see Figure 12–3).

Some children seem to be in a very similar "psychological space"

Figure 12–3

when they write, then, as well as when they read. Stacy inhabited a colorful summer world with her grandmother as she wrote about it. "When I wrote about my grandmother," she told me, "it was summer when we go shopping for my school things, and when I close my eyes, I see that. Everything in my mind is so colorful."

And Jillana told me about the image she conjures up as she writes about turtles. ". . . [T]his turtle . . . I remember. My Dad held him and it peed on him. Things like that get stuck in my head and I can never take them out. He had an orange face, and squares with green and orange in them. He was wicked queer. So, if I write about a turtle, that's the turtle I see."

This points out an important difference between the memory images that the children use as they write and the images that are created by reading. The memory images, like Jillana's turtle, present themselves whole simultaneously. The literary images, on the other hand, seem to build up and grow — constantly modified and amended by new statements in the text. And these reading images that they create are different for each child, even within the same text.

I encountered a striking example of these differences during a discussion one day after I had finished reading a chapter from *Little House in the Big Woods* by Laura Ingalls Wilder. Turning my own question back on me, Jon asked, "What was going on in *your* head just now while you read this?" I replied that I pictured the dance floor and saw Grandma and she jigged to the music.

"Well, how did the Grandma look to you?" he pursued.

I started to describe her as a plump woman with rosy cheeks, when

Shonna interrupted to protest, "But the Grandma I saw was thin." After a few moments' discussion of the various mental images we all held of Grandma, Jamie asked me if I felt like I was the Grandma.

"No," I told him. "I think I felt more like Ma."

Heather and Stacy immediately chimed in, "Oh, I felt like I was Laura!"

This type of conversation shows the kind of reading "identity theme" that Norman Holland (1973) talks about in adult response to literature. "Each of us reads in his characteristic way—that is, as an expression of his particular identity theme, just as each of us has his own way of walking, speaking, joking ... looking at a landscape. This reading style is deeply ingrained, more deeply even, than a professional's training as a reader."

Children, too, I found, express those different styles, and *do* recognize the existence of a special "literary space" in their reading and writing.

## INDIVIDUAL CHILDREN AND THEIR MODES OF THINKING

### Verbal Thought: The Voice Within

*There has never been a line read that I didn't hear. As my eyes followed the sentence, a voice was saying it silently to me. (Eudora Welty)*

Children internalize their social dialogue—this inner speech becomes the basis of their verbal thinking (Vyotsky 1962). And for some children, this is the primary way of representing the world to themselves. Jason is one such child. His reading world is filled with sound: rarely do mental images appear.

One morning, Jason told me about the book he was reading—an exciting fantasy about a boy who turned into a television set. When I asked him how he pictured the boy in the story, he looked puzzled. He shrugged, "I guess he must look like me."

I asked him to close his eyes, then continued. "What do you see when you think of this book?"

Jason waited a few seconds, then with his eyes closed, he shrugged again. "Black." He continued apologetically, "Sometimes I see pictures, but mostly, I like hear it. I read like, 'da-da-da,' but in my mind I hear it. I hear their words with the right tone of voice—not my voice—their voices."

Jason's inner voice is important in his writing, too. He told me he needs to put word bubbles in his illustrations to show what the characters are saying. In one "true story" that he wrote about a skiing trip, he explained that "as I went over a jump, I was going, 'Hey, Ma, look!' so I put that in a word bubble." And in one fictional piece called *Mr. Frog*, he felt his final published book was lifeless until he added the sound to the illustrations. As he expressed it, "If you don't have the sound of what the snake and frog were saying or 'sss-

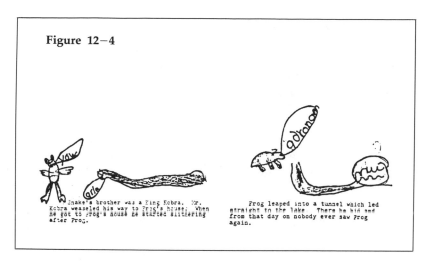

Figure 12–4

ing' or *whatever*, it's boring. It's just not like I imagined it" (see Figure 12–4).

But Jason doesn't rely only on the convention of word bubbles to supply the sound he wants to his pieces of writing: his inner speech is often reported in the form of a monologue. In one such piece, the main character is "Detektiv Jason." And he tells the story like this:

*I Lookt all ofer town. I sad to myself now If I wer a dog were wold I hiyd Iv got It. Iv seyn lots of dogs in the aley downtown maybey that's war she is lyl go look. I dont belev it ther are over 1000 dogs her and not one is christey.*

Even in pieces where he is not one of the characters, Jason finds ways to make the sound heard. He relies heavily on conversations, and in one book, the entire story is told through the dialogue among three characters, as this excerpt illustrates:

*Hey garfeld! What doo you want otey! sumem to eat. go ask Jon. whot can he doo! don't ask me! ask him! o,k, how do I get in. the back dor is opin. not tonit he closd it it was 30 digres last nit try the back wirdo ok all riyt!*

Other children in the class could identify with Jason when one day he talked about the "voices." Ilana told us her Care Bears talk to her as she writes about them, and "they have nice friendly voices." Kristy is even aware of her inner voice as she writes: "I think, 'Well, maybe I should write this,' like I'm talking to myself." And when I read Jason a quote from novelist Margaret Drabble, who reported, "I can hear all my sentences being said. I can hear them in my head to a marked extent," he knew just what she meant.

He smiled, "You took the words right outa my mouth!"

### Movement and Gesture

*. . . [E]ven when I am preoccupied by a philosophical problem, I*

*imagine myself working with a structure which is real, physical.
(Richard Gregory)*

Piaget has written extensively on the ways in which children's knowledge is tied to action; he describes how children use their bodies to search for information and knowledge (Evans 1973). Some children, like Jamie, do rely more heavily on their arms and legs—on movement—as they continue to solve problems in their reading and writing.

When Jamie writes and talks about writing (and to an extent, reading), he relies on gesture. When he wrote his story about karate, he didn't picture the moves, he acted them out, looked at his body position, then drew the pictures. His procedure was interesting to watch. That morning, he sat at his desk thinking for several moments, and although he was lost in thought, he seemed to jerk his head as he pondered. Finally, he took his writing folder and retreated to a table in the back of the room. After setting everything on the table, he gave a powerful kick to the side, then froze. He looked down at his extended leg and the angle of his foot, reflected for a moment, then drew a picture. Under the picture, he wrote, "This is a side blade kick." He continued that morning and several other mornings to execute, then draw and label, several kicks and blocks, among them: the front kick, the side kick, the flying side kick, the high block, and the low block (see Figure 12−5).

When Jamie tells his stories, he tends to act them out, using his hands to stir the air, for example, when he tells about cooking. Rudolf Arnheim contends that people can sharpen mental images and focus thinking by simplifying them into an expressive gesture or posture. "Thoughts need shape, and shape must be derived from

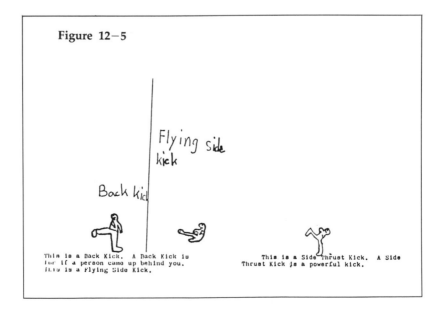

**Figure 12−5**

some medium," he writes (1967, p. 116). For some children, like Jamie, that medium is gesture.

### Dream States Reveries and Dreams as Thought Processes

*What psychoanalysts stress, the relations between dreams and our conscious acts, is what poets already know. (Anais Nin)*

One child in the class, Christy, helped to focus my attention on the importance of the dream state in relation to reading and writing processes. She shared a piece with me one morning called *My Imagination*:

*I've been dreaming about going up into outer space but my big brother always inturuptes me when I'am dreaming about going into outer space. My big brother dreams about being a famous soccer player. I was building a space ship when my brother came out . . .*

When we talked about the piece, she told me that she often writes about her dreams. "I always wrote about what happens in my dreams in my October folder," she explained. "It's like when I write poems."

Because Christy is one of the few children in the class who writes poetry, I followed up by asking her how she writes poems. Dreaming, sleeping, writing, and images all flow together when Christy ponders her poetry writing process: "I like writing poems," she began. "I just started to dream it up and make it rhyme. After a while, I read it to my mother. I think about it, then after school, I always fall asleep. Sometimes, I dream about what I wrote in writing time. I felt like I was in another world when I wrote about the teddy bear. The whole place in my mind was covered with teddy bears."

"Tell me about your thinking as you were writing it," I prompted her.

She thought a minute. "I see it in my brain and I sort of hear voices. I just feel it like it's something like sort of magic in my brain. Like I fall in a hole and an adventure happens there while I'm writing. It's real fun—sometimes poems, sometimes a story."

On another day, Christy hit on the elusive qualities of our dream images when we write. She explained to me, "In my head, it's like feelings. Like I'm dreaming. It's quiet. It's like a picture of somebody moving their mouth even, but no sound. It's tiny little pictures—kind of blurry like I'm not really seeing them clearer. They just stay blurry, but bright."

This perception is strikingly similar to one of the major findings in Calvin Hall's study, *What People Dream About* (1951). He found that most dream images were quite indistinct—"generic" he called them, for so many subjects described them as unclear or indistinct. (Examples would include coins of no particular denomination, or figures which might be either male or female.)

But the color remains clear and bright, Christy insists. "That's why I have fluorescent crayons—to color the pictures in writing, fluorescent like my dreams."

Stacy was writing near us and our conversation struck a familiar chord in her. "When I dream, too," she told us, "everything in my mind is so colorful. When I dreamed about mice trying to eat me, they were like brown and white and they had this yellow on them. They were colorful. They scared me and I woke up."

But for some children, the colors don't stay clear and bright in their minds. Dwayne told me that when he was writing about fish, he could see them in his mind, swimming around in the tank, but the images were blurry. "The colors aren't quite the same," he told me. "They're different, sort of, in my head."

As some children write, they turn to daydreaming. "I wrote about the tree and it was like I was pretending to be the tree myself," Jillana explained one day. "Sometimes I hear my brain saying things. I imaginate things. I dream about what I'm going to do when I grow up."

References to this dream state are not restricted to writing: several of my examples under "literary space" come under this category. And Tracy even made it part of her reading definition: "Reading is when you pick up a book, look at the words, and start feeling like your a character in the book," she wrote. "It's sort of like a dream."

## Visual Thought: The Design Within

*Sitting at a writing table writing words on paper, what is it that forms these words? What is going on in my mind as I write them? I have no doubt that in my case it is a matter of a series of visualizations. Not two-dimensional, as if looking at a television screen; three-dimensional, perhaps, as if I were a thin, thin, invisible ghost walking about on a stage while a play is in actual performance. (C. S. Forester)*

C. S. Forester made conscious use of images in his writing, Coleridge reported that he filled his memory with images before writing, while Blake "copied" his mental images. For these writers, observational learning was very important. And for eight-year-old Chris, too, the visual aspects of learning are paramount. For him, the verbal components of the learning process are slighter, and his inner representation is more likely to deal with images.

During reading time one day, Chris told me about the book he had just finished reading—*The Snow Lion*. He began to explain to me how the pictures in the book helped the story.

**Chris**: Well, you need this picture 'cause he's sweating and that shows he's hot. And here, it shows he's playing, shows the mice pulling on his whiskers.

**Ruth**: What does the snow lion look like to you when you imagine him?

**Chris**: The snow lion I can imagine looks a lot different from the pictures. My snow lion looks a lot more like a lion at the zoo.

**Ruth**: Have you been to the zoo?

**Chris**: No, I've never been to the zoo, but I've seen lions on TV.

**Ruth:** Are the pictures in your mind more real, more like real animals and real nature?

**Chris:** The lion is, but not the jungle. I think the jungle looks like cartoon jungles. That's the picture in my head. I've never been to a jungle.

In this interchange, Chris quickly moves into the differences between the pictures in the book and his own mental images. Much of Chris' visual memory is based on television imagery: he pictures the lion to look like "lions on TV," and because he has "never been to a jungle," he again relies on the television version of a jungle—a cartoon rendering. The pictures in the book don't interfere with his reading— in fact, he comments on how they help make the story clearer. On the other hand, the illustrations never take precedence over how he pictures the story in his mind.

Chris also relies heavily on pictures to help his writing. The stories in Chris' mind are filled with movement and he uses his drawings to make them come alive when words can't express it for him. *When I Learned How to Ski*, for example, is sparse on text and heavy on pictures. Chris uses four separate pictures of himself to tell the story, "I wiped out." And they show the progression well: we see Chris going over a mogul, flying into the air, heading toward the ground, and then landing—one ski over his head, the other flying off, with his poles and glasses swirling around him (see Figure 12—6).

Just as some children, like Jason, are sensitive to the way others use sound to communicate information, Chris notices how people use images to tell stories. He is particularly interested in cartoons and their conventions. Garfield cartoons are immensely popular with the seven- to nine-year-old set. Jason loves the stories for the richness of the dialogue; Chris, on the other hand, focuses on the pictures. He composed a miniature Garfield cartoon book, which helped establish his popularity in the class.

**Figure 12—6**

In Chris' book, it is the pictures that tell the story with the words there to elaborate on the context, with the knocks at the door, or slamming, gulping, and burping. Words are secondary in the books Chris writes; his pictures tell the story.

## DISCUSSION

### Patterns of Thought

Through a closer look at some of the modes of creative thought in one classroom, I have tried to point out some of the different strategies that children use. But there is an inherent danger: to label a child according to one modality or another and attempt to teach to that alone, or to revert to the old "learning style" battles, attempting different kinds of "remediation." Although I have stressed the strong preferences in the children I have discussed, what I found in most children was a merging of different patterns of thought, which varied with the task at hand. Ilana is one child who uses whatever will help her to communicate her thoughts. In order to express what reading is, for example, she used everything she had at her disposal: the written word, a detailed drawing, and an oral explanation.

First, she wrote the following text in her reading journal:

*Ilana*
*2/11/86*
*WHAT READING IS*

*Reading is when you pick up a book and you read the words intell you come to the end of the sentence. Then you read the next sentence intell the next sentence is done. Then you keep on doing that.*

Ilana wasn't sure that that carried the meaning she intended, so she carefully set to work on a detailed drawing of "what reading is" (see Figure 12−7).

When she finished, she brought the piece to me, and explained, "Now this girl, she picked up the book and she's already read this page and she's sounding out these words." Ilana pointed to the words on the right-hand page of the book.

"This teacher is teaching how to spel 'you' — 'y-o-u,'" she continued, then pointed to one girl she had drawn on the page. "This girl is leaning on her hands, looking up at the teacher."

Then she described the context of the classroom. "These are different books by different authors, and they have the stickers, just like ours. That girl is another one sitting at her desk reading. That girl in the middle is sounding out words, 'cause she's new."

She concluded by explaining why she decided to set up her drawing that way. "I thought of a school building and I thought if someone new was reading a book, how it would be. So she's right smack in the middle of reading a tough book for her."

Ilana, and other children whom I investigated, use their different

Figure 12–7

coding systems in cooperation. Other investigators, such as Paivio (1983), have reported similar findings in adults. Walter Grey (quoted in G.R. Taylor 1979) reported from his study that "15% of the population thinks exclusively in the visual modes, another 15% thinks only in verbal terms, and the remaining 70% uses a mixture of approaches" (p. 82).

### The Inner Design

One of the difficulties in any of these studies of the mind, however, is tapping the actual "inner design." There is a difference between the covert forms of thought involved in the process of composing and the results that are displayed in the final product. I take the term "inner design" from the Italian painter Frederico Zuccari, who referred to our inner model as the "disigno interno" to distinguish it from the "disigno esterno" on the canvas (see Arnheim 1969). These final products—on the canvas or on the printed page—are only a representation, or perhaps interpretation, of what goes on in our minds.

Children try to give shape to what they see and imagine. There is a need, then, for researchers to begin to study the inner symbol systems that children create to store and organize their thoughts. I think of these in terms of a thought image, for it shifts the bias from verbal to visual. Rather than discussing different "language of thought," I prefer to use the term "inner designs," for just as images are designs, a verbal language is also a pattern and a design—a set of signs and shapes.

This preliminary study has yielded the following four conclusions:

1. There is a great diversity in children's thinking strategies within the same classroom.
2. Children *can* express verbally the mental processes that they employ when reading and writing.
3. The inner languages — or inner designs — that a child uses are similar for both his or her reading and writing processes.
4. Words and images work together for children, but with varying degrees of emphasis for the different children.

But this is not the notion of thought in our educational system. The whole physical organization of our classrooms is based on the assumption that children need to rely mostly on language — directive language in the voice of the teacher. And as Vera John-Steiner points out, a steady diet of this instruction shapes the children's representations of thought. "One of the important bases for the development of a preferred mode of thought," she declares, "is to be found in the prevalence of certain activities in childhood" (1985; p. 35). So for many children, their unique strategies and modes of thinking are channeled narrowly into one direction. Because other modalities are not encouraged to grow, the children's rich ways of planning, solving problems, and storing memories are stunted in most cases. They are there for the children in the early years, then fade through disuse and lack of encouragement.

I would propose instead that classrooms begin to structure their time and space according to the varied needs of the children. If the children are able to engage in more independent projects — alone, as well as in collaboration with each other — they will be better able to focus on the structure of that particular problem and use their own strengths and individual strategies in order to really learn.

And sharing their strategies is also important. The children I observed benefited from the discussions of thought processes we engaged in. They often tried others' strategies — modifying them, adopting them, or perhaps discarding them if they were not helpful. This caused them to consciously reflect on the choices in meaning making that they rely on as they read and write. The types of questions that I asked as a researcher were incorporated into the classroom structure. Leslie Funkhouser reported later in the year — in a jokingly complaining tone — "Those guys, they're really something else. Ever since the research project, they drive me crazy, always asking, 'What was going on in your head while you were writing that?,' reading the quotes on the bulletin board [about how people think and solve problems], and Ilana's even out there interviewing her parents about how they think!"

These children are hard at work — selecting, condensing, and interpreting their impressions. They have varied inner processes which they use to try to give shape to what they see, hear, and imagine. It is our responsibility to set up our classrooms to aid them in their pursuit of knowledge by helping them to make the most of their own unique "inner designs."

## REFERENCES

Arnheim, R. *Visual Thinking*. Berkeley, California: University of California Press, 1969.

Evans, R. *Jean Piaget: The Man and His Ideas*. New York: Dutton, 1973.

Forester, C. S. *The Hornblower Companion*. Toronto: Little Brown and Company, 1964.

Gregory, R. *The Intelligent Eye*. New York: McGraw-Hill, 1970.

Hall, C. "What People Dream About." *Scientific American*, 184 (1951): 60−63.

Holland, N. *Dynamics of Literary Response*. New York: W. W. Norton and Company, 1975.

Holland, N. *Poems in Persons*. New York: W. W. Norton and Company, 1973.

Jacobsen, M. "Looking for Literary Space: The Willing Suspension of Disbelief Re-visited." *Research in the Teaching of English, 16*, (1982): 21−38.

John-Steiner, V. *Notebooks of the Mind*. Albuquerque, New Mexico: University of New Mexico Press, 1985.

Lionni, L. "Before Images." *The Horn Book*. (1984): 726−734.

Nin, A. *Anais Nin, Diary, vol. IV*. New York: Harcourt Brace Jovanovich, 1967.

Paivio, A. "The Mind's Eye in Arts and Science." *Poetics, 12*, (1983): 1−18.

Taylor, G. R. *The Natural Gift of the Mind*. New York: Dutton, 1979.

Vygotsky, L. *Thought and Language*. E. Hanfman and G. Vakar (Trans.). Cambridge: M.I.T. Press, 1962.

Welty, E. *One Writer's Beginnings*. New York: Warner Books, 1985.

Yaden, D., and Templeton, S. (Eds). *Metalinguistic Awareness and Beginning Literacy: Conceptualizing What It Means to Read and Write*. Portsmouth, NH: Heinemann, 1986.

# 13

# the reading transaction: what for?

LOUISE M. ROSENBLATT

To be asked the question, "Reading, what for?" in the context of a conference on young children's use of language is a reminder of the importance of theory underlying practice. In a developmental frame-work, it is customary to describe the adult stage toward which children are presumably progressing. The picture of the adult or skilled reader is invoked, not in order to impose the adult pattern on children's early reading but, rather, in order to derive developmental, or directional, criteria. Unfortunately, it is all too possible to have short term successes in the teaching of reading, while using methods and materials that turn the youngsters away from growth toward our long-term goals. Hence, I understand the need for the question "Reading, what for?" to be answered in terms of the adult reader.

Reading is a relationship between a human being and a text, and the purpose of that activity involves the whole person. To ask what kinds of readers we hope our young people will become is to ask what kinds of human beings we hope they will become. It is easy to suggest negative answers to such questions. For example, Auden's "The Unknown Citizen" (1945) begins

*He was found by the bureau of statistics to be*
*One against whom there was no official complaint,*

and lists among his virtues

*He was fully sensible to the advantages of the installment plan*
*And had everything necessary to the modern man,*
*A phonograph, a radio, a car and a frigidaire.*
*The researchers of public opinion are content*
*That he held the proper opinions for the time of year. . . .*

and ends

*And our teachers report that he never interfered with their education.*
*Was he free? Was he happy? The question is absurd:*
*Had anything been wrong, we should certainly have heard.*

Reprinted with permission from *Developing Literacy: Young Children's Use of Language*, edited by R. Parker and F. Davis. With permission of Louise M. Rosenblatt and the International Reading Association.

For the development of that kind of reader in that kind of society, a minimum concept of literacy, a listing of skills, might possibly suffice. If we envision the ideal of a humane, democratic society composed of mature people, we cannot simply list advanced high-level skills. We must draw upon abstractions such as to be "free," to be "happy." We must speak of our hope for people with a sense of personal identity, who reject a life of dehumanized uniformity, who seek an expansion of knowledge and awareness, and who possess the imagination to feel themselves part of the human community. In more usual terms, they are capable of fulfilling their responsibilities as members of families and as citizens, capable of participating in the intellectual and artistic life of our society. This also assumes the ability to reflect critically on their own values, their own world.

Reading can in many ways serve the needs and foster the development of such people. Reading is "for" the knowledge, the experience, and the wisdom that the printed word makes possible for us, giving us communication with other minds across time and space, enabling us to share in their thoughts and their worlds. Our libraries are overflowing with the great heritage of works of the past; the avalanche of new publications justifies talk of a "knowledge explosion"; rising levels of education and leisure arouse hopes of increasing recourse to the arts, especially literature. But in this troubled century, we cannot point complacently to our great wealth encased in books. Their potentialities for good or evil remain moot, until we see in what kinds of relationships with readers these texts are brought to a "life beyond life."

The question "What for?" is asked, consciously or unconsciously, by every reader encountering a text. Ultimately, there are as many answers as there are individual personalities, stages of development, and changing needs and interests. Yet this matter of purpose seems most often neglected in the theory and teaching of reading. Models of the reading process typically focus on cognition (Williams, 1971, pp. 7–142, 145). They rarely include motivation, and even then in a very generalized sense. The reader's attitude toward reading in general is very important. I am concerned, however, with the way in which purpose affects the actual process: the actions, procedures, or strategies of the reader during the reading event. I shall deal here only with the evocation of meaning; matters such as validity of interpretation and evaluation have been treated elsewhere (Rosenblatt, 1969, 1978, 1983).

## READING AS TRANSACTION

"Transaction" underlines my rejection of the epistemological dualism that would place the human being against nature as two separate or autonomous entities. Current ecological views of the human being in a two-way relationship with nature (Bateson, 1979; Toulmin, 1972), and current philosophy of science (Weizsäcker, 1980), with its recognition of the observer as an explicit factor in any observation or proposition, illustrate the transactional concept. Dewey (1896) reacted early against the stimulus-response view of the organism passively receiving the stimulus, and showed that, in a sense, the organism seeks out the stimuli to which it responds. As "interaction" suggested the dualism which he had long opposed, Dewey, in *Knowing and the Known* (1949), chose "transaction" to indicate a two-way, reciprocal relationship; thus "knowing" assumes a transaction between a knower and a known.

"Transaction" especially seems to be needed for a description of the act of reading. Reading is always a particular event, involving a particular reader, a particular item of the environment—a text—at a particular time, under particular circumstances. A person becomes a reader by virtue of a relationship with a text. A text is merely ink on paper, until some reader (if only the author)[1] evokes meaning from it. The transactional theory resists the formalist tendency to concentrate on the text as all-important and the reader as passive, and also avoids the alternative extremism of some recent "subjective" literary theorists who see the reader as all-important and the text as passive or secondary. Reader and text are mutually essential to the transaction; meaning happens during the transaction between the reader and the text.

## DYNAMICS OF LANGUAGE

The reader's give-and-take with the text reflects the transactional nature of all language. It cannot be conceived simply as a code, a *langue* existing apart from *parole*, the linguistic acts of individual human beings (Saussure, 1916, 1966). Language is socially-generated and socially-acquired, a public system of communication. As Bruner (1977) phrases it, "In contemporary jargon, language is never to be understood as context independent." But it is easily forgotten that language is always individually internalized. One can understand why psychologists, despite their theoretical break with behaviorism, tend to persist in old experimental methods that deal mainly with public utterances. Equally essential is a conceptualization of the processes by which the individual participates in the public system. The view of language that stems mainly from William James (1890) provides such a matrix for thinking about the process of reading.

James's brilliant metaphor of the stream of thought or consciousness (which now typically serves as a point of departure for cognitive psychologists emerging from the behaviorist interlude) encompasses not only ideas but "every form of consciousness indiscriminately" — sensations, images, precepts and concepts, states or qualities of states, feelings of relations, feelings of tendency. We sense our bodily

---

[1] The author's text also emerges from a personal and social transaction, but as the reader encounters only the text, we can deal simply with the reading act, through which communication takes place. Also, the interrelationship between writing and reading in the child's development cannot be treated here, but is dealt with in Rosenblatt, "Writing and Reading" (1989).

selves as the seat of our thinking: for example, James (1890, pp. 245–246) suggests that we compare our internal states when we look at a tree stump and think of it as a chair, and when we think of it as a table. Such inner dynamics are present, he asserts, whether we think of the objects our words point to, or of the relationships among them:

*There is not a conjunction or a preposition, and hardly an adverbial phrase, syntactic form, or inflection of voice, in human speech, that does not express some shading or other of relation which we at some moment actually feel to exist between the larger objects of our thought. If we speak objectively, it is the real relations that appear revealed; if we speak subjectively, it is the stream of consciousness that matches each of them by an inward coloring of its own. . . . We ought to say a feeling of* and, *a feeling of* if, *a feeling of* but, *and a feeling of* by, *quite as readily as we say a feeling of* blue *or a feeling of* cold.

Vygotsky (1962) also postulates the existence of a "dynamic system of meaning, in which the affective and the intellectual unite." He contrasts referential meaning and "sense":

*The sense of a word . . . is the sum of all the psychological events aroused in our consciousness by the word. It is a dynamic, fluid, complex whole, which has several zones of unequal stability. Meaning is only one of the zones of sense, the most stable and precise zone. A word acquires its sense from the context in which it appears; in different context, it changes its sense. The dictionary meaning of a word is no more than a stone in the edifice of sense, no more than a potentiality that finds diversified realization in speech. (p. 146).*

This view of language is carried further by Werner and Kaplan (1963) in their study of the development of language and the expression of thought. We see the infant engaged in active sensory-motor exploration or transaction with the environment, internalizing "a primordial matrix composed of affective, interoceptive, postural, imaginal elements" (p. 18). From this, an innerdynamic or form-building or schematizing activity carries on the twin process both of shaping a sense of an external object or referent and a symbolic or linguistic vehicle and of establishing a semantic correspondence between them. A word and its referent acquire meaning when they are linked to the same internal organismic state.

Thus the child's early vocables are shown as referring to a complex inner state corresponding to a total situation. "Early vocables are evoked by total happenings and are expressive not only of references to an event external to the child, but also reflect the child's attitudes, states, reactions" (p. 141). Development into two-vocable utterances and beyond depends on differentiation of reference, a process of delimitation and specification. The child must learn to sort out the various elements of the organismic state associated with a situation and must learn to distinguish between the referential, the external object or situation designated by the word, and the inner state, the attitudes and associations, linked with it. "With the progression toward the use of conventional [linguistic] forms, the inner form of the symbol (the connotational dynamics) becomes more and more *covert* in character—carried by 'inner gestures,' 'imagery,' 'postural-affective sets,' 'feelings,' etc." (p. 238). Increasing distance between these two aspects of meaning—the word and the inner state—does not imply a rupture between them, since this would deprive the word of its meaning and it would degenerate into a mere noise or mark. Even the referential aspect remains anchored to its organismic matrix; i.e., cognition is always accompanied by a qualitative or affective element, no matter how much, in some circumstances, this element is ignored (Dewey, 1963).

Halliday (1975, 1978) has helped us to see the child's earliest vocalizations as a process of "learning to mean"; the child develops a sense of the different functions of language through a set of personal utterances, before assimilating the linguistic system of the environment. Yet Halliday's list of functions does not fully take care of the aspect we have been stressing—the attitudes and qualitative states bonded to verbal symbols. The two approaches seem needed, to account for both the public and personal functions of language.

## SELECTIVE ATTENTION IN READING

Given the view of language sketched thus far, it becomes possible to look more closely at the reading process. The assertion that the reading transaction involves the whole person takes on fuller import. The reader brings to the text the internalized sum, the accumulation or memory of all such psychological events, such past organismic encounters with language and the world. In the reading transaction, the words of the text may be said to activate elements of memory, to stir up the organismic state linked to the words and their referents. We must keep in mind that potentially this includes not only those aspects that circumscribe the public referents or objects to which the verbal symbols point but also the personal referents—sensuous, affective, imaginal, and associative. Thus, the evocation of meaning from the text requires a selecting-out from the reservoir of thought and feeling, the acceptance of some elements into the center of attention, and the relegation of others to the periphery of awareness.

"Selective attention" is James's term (1890) for such sorting-out activity, an often-neglected concept basic to his idea of the stream of consciousness. "Consciousness," he tells us, "is always more interested in one part of its object than another, and welcomes or rejects or chooses, all the while." This results in the "selection of some [elements of the inner stream] and the suppression of the rest, by the reinforcing and inhibiting agency of attention." This "choosing activity" is central to thinking, and hence central to reading, which is a form of thinking in transaction with a text.

Reading consists of a continuing stream of choices on the reader's part. As the reader approaches the text, there is the need to develop guides for the selective process, guides that set up expectations and narrow the range of options from which to choose. Just as in the sequence of verbal symbols the article *a* suggests the syntactic category from which to choose the meaning of the next word, so the reader seeks cues to the formation of a guiding semantic principle — tentative, open to constant revision — that will guide the process of selective attention. As the verbal symbols activate areas of consciousness, the reader selects out and focuses attention on those elements that suggest a tentative framework that narrows the range of further choices, which again set up certain expectations, as a structure or meaning is developed. If expectations are inappropriate to subsequent verbal symbols in the text, revision of the guiding principle of selection, or perhaps a complete rereading, occurs. Selective attention thus serves the choosing, structuring, synthesizing activity which produces meaning.

## THE EFFERENT AND THE AESTHETIC

The most decisive act of selective attention still remains to be defined. The general intention to make meaning out of the verbal symbols, though necessary, is not sufficient for a fully successful reading. The *kind* of meaning must be delimited. Either before the encounter with the text, or early in the reading event, the reader must select a general stance, a mental set, toward the internal states that will be activated by the pattern of words.

Every linguistic act we have seen encompasses both public and private elements — the general terms I have used to include aspects variously referred to as cognitive and affective, referential and emotive, denotative and connotative. The reader must choose the purpose, the mental set, that will determine the relative degrees of attention to be bestowed on the public and private aspects of the field of consciousness activated by the words. I term this the reader's choice of a predominant "stance" appropriate to his purpose. This will direct the whole selective process.

One part of the continuum of potential stances covers the mental set I term the "efferent" stance, from the Latin *efferre*, "to carry away." In such reading, attention is focused mainly on building the public meaning that is to be carried away from the reading: actions to be performed, information to be retained, conclusions to be drawn, solutions to be arrived at, analytic concepts to be applied, propositions to be tested. Such a stance usually dominates the reading of a textbook, a cooking recipe, a scientific report. The personal, sensuous, associative elements of consciousness are subordinated or ignored.

In contrast to the efferent focus of attention on what is to be retained *after* the reading, in the predominantly aesthetic stance, the reader focuses attention primarily on what is being lived through *during* the reading. The span of attention opens to attend not only to the public referents for the verbal symbols, but also to the sound and rhythm of the words in the inner ear and the sensations, images, associations, overtones, and memories that make up the qualitative state produced in consciousness by those words in that particular order. ("Aesthetic" is used to refer to attention to feeling, the qualitative, the experiential; whether a work of art emerges is a different, evaluative question.) When we read aesthetically, our attention is concentrated on what we are evoking from the page, on what we are seeing and feeling and thinking, on what is aroused within us by the very sound of the words, and of what they point to in the world of humankind and nature. The new experience we shape out of these elements, through a process of selection and synthesis, is for us the poem or story or play. Moreover, we respond to the very literary work that we are creating under guidance of the text (Rosenblatt, 1978).

Every reading act falls somewhere on the continuum between the efferent and the aesthetic poles. Most readings probably fall somewhere near the middle of the continuum; i.e., attention encompasses both public and private areas of consciousness that are resonating to the words, but in different proportions, according to the reader's purpose.

In predominantly efferent reading (for example, the reading of a book about ecology), the cumulation of information would be the predominant interest, but some associative, affective elements might be appropriately admitted into the range of attention. Similarly, in aesthetic reading, there is always an efferent, referential component, but attention centers mainly on the spectrum of feelings, sensations, associations, and ideas, in which the referential meanings are embedded.

Note that "efferent" and "aesthetic" refer to the reader's stance and not to the text. No matter what the intentions of the author or the linguistic potentialities of the text, any text can be read either efferently or aesthetically. A reader's purpose toward the same text may vary. The text of a poem, therefore, can be read efferently, if only its "literal" meaning is desired, or a novel can be analyzed efferently as a social document. And it is a cliché to speak of mathematicians who look at their solutions aesthetically and admire their "elegance." Unfortunately, there has been a failure to do justice to this aspect of the reading process.

The reader may clearly adopt one or the other, either the aesthetic or efferent, as the predominant stance. Much reading seems muddled or counterproductive at present because of the reader's confusion about stance. Thus, a political statement may be read with too much dominance given to the affective, associative elements, when the reader's purpose presumably is to discover verifiable reasons for, say, what taxation policies should be adopted. Much reading of advertisements fits that pattern. Even more pervasive is the efferent reading of stories, poems, and plays, with the consequent loss of their essential experiential qualities and values as works of art.

The fact that the text of a poem or a story may be read efferently—

producing what often is referred to as its literal meaning—should not be interpreted as confirmation of the popular notion that the literary or aesthetic character of a work is a kind of ornamentation superimposed on the literal meaning—a view that I have termed the "jam on bread" theory of poetry. Aesthetic reading requires an integrated apprehension of the referential impregnated with all the qualitative, experiential constituents of the "sense" of words. Instead of thinking of the aesthetic as the literal plus the poetic, it might be more accurate to think of the referential as the aesthetic minus the personal, private aspects of meaning. However, both of these formulations fail to do justice to the reading act. We are not dealing with literal or affective, efferent or aesthetic, entities but with complex states of mind. Out of these, by a process of selection and under the guidance of the text, the reader carves structures of thought and feeling. Efferent reading involves objective referents plus attitudes and feelings; aesthetic reading involves emotion and thoughts about the world impregnated with affect. The difference lies in the proportions; the emphasis, dependent on the purpose of the reader.

Mature readers are able to adopt the stance that will enable them to carry out the selective and synthesizing process appropriate to their purposes. In most instances, the aim is to adopt the stance most appropriate to the text—to discover what the author may have intended. Often, this reflects the purpose which led the reader to that text—such as the search for information, the need for clarification of an issue, with the attendant adoption of the efferent stance. The desire for the pleasure, the experiences, the relaxation, and the insight, offered by novels, poems, or plays may lead to such a text, with the consequent adoption of the predominantly aesthetic stance. Sometimes an external cue, such as the description on a dustjacket, triggers the stance.

When the text is encountered without such prior selection of stance, the reader seeks cues within the text itself that signal which stance to adopt. Obvious cues of this sort are the wide margins and uneven lines that alert us to the possibility of evoking a poem. We may be invited to conjure up the characters and situations of a novel through such cues as the diction, the dialogue, the situations described, the narrative tense. Conventions such as the "once upon a time" opening, highly metaphoric expressions, verse forms, rhyme, or content such as fantasy may announce the need for the adoption of the stance.

In another context, it would be possible to translate the usual descriptions of critical reading into terms of the predominant stance. All reading transactions require careful elimination of irrelevant, projective, elements that are not supported by the text. The danger of excessive selectivity, of ignoring parts of the text, must be equally avoided. Efferent reading requires a stringent selectivity, an abstracting of the public meaning from its personal resonances, a testing of whether any attitudes or qualitative states aroused during the transaction are consonant with the efferent purpose.

The aesthetic stance requires keen attention to the inner reverberations of sound and sense, a readiness to hold in the memory the states of mind and the images evoked, and to build out of them an emergent structure that becomes the lived-through story or poem. Critical reading is a matter of critical attitudes toward the reader's personal contribution, as well as toward the structure of ideas or experience that is being created out of the transaction with the text.

The mature, skilled reader usually selects the appropriate stance automatically, as with other reading skills. But this act of selective attention must be learned by the child. Adults may give explicit indications as to stance or indirect suggestions, through the atmosphere surrounding the reading, through the reactions of adults to texts, through the kinds of expectations of performance implied in the questions habitually raised before and after readings. The false assumption that the text dictates the reader's stance has unfortunately resulted in concern with the question of what texts to present to students, with little or no help in differentiating the appropriate stance.

## THE EFFERENT BIAS

An inordinate overemphasis on the efferent has been the consequence. Our technologically-oriented society, our mainly extrovert culture, has favored language in its public, impersonal, instrumental, scientific manifestations. This imbalance prevailed long before the current swing toward the narrowly practical and the scientific in our schools and universities and the decline in support of the arts. During the past half-century, the post-Sputnik pressure for scientific and technological advance has reinforced this aspect of our national ethos. Perhaps this partially explains why the teaching of reading in the schools has been based on models of the reading process that have not taken into account aesthetic reading. At best, the aesthetic (or literary) has been considered a variation on the efferent process requiring only the addition to it of new skills or strategies, not a different stance.

Preoccupation with different methods of inculcating the skills, essential though that is, has centered almost entirely on the cognitive, informative aspects of reading. Tests of reading comprehension reflect this bias toward the efferent. Basal reading texts and their teacher manuals manifest the same partiality. Stories and poems, introduced because of the young child's obvious interest, are nevertheless surrounded by the same kinds of questions as would apply to a purely informative text. The implication is clearly that stories and poems should be approached in the same way as such texts. I cannot resist citing again the poem in a third-grade workbook headed with the question, "What facts does this poem teach you?" This question, in its call for an efferent stance even in the reading of a poem, epitomizes the general cumulative effective of most reading instruction, even when poems and stories are included. (Of course, once the aesthetic reading of that text had been honored, it might be entirely appropriate to discuss the new information received through the experience. But that is not why or how the poem should have been read in the first place.)

Even when, in later school years, the curriculum includes the "study of literature," the approach is often primarily efferent, with the accent on students' reporting their memory of details, and recounting the sequence of ideas or events. A similar approach prevails as students move into high school and college. Even when they achieve an aesthetic experience, they are often hurried away from it to efferent concerns, paraphrases, analyses, proofs that they have read the text and have understood it (efferently). Students are seldom encouraged to savor the experience, to linger on, recall or reenact the nuances, tones, and states of consciousness produced by the lived-through images, ideas, and events. Criticism should have such experience as its object.

Recent studies explicitly centered on children's entrance into the realm of literary or linguistic art are hampered by dependence on the (until recently) dominant formalistic literary theory, which identified literary art with product rather than process, and by traditional psychological methodology. Experimental designs purporting to deal with some element of art (e.g., metaphor) often seem rather to test the children's efferent, metalinguistic capacities, their ability to abstract or to categorize (Verbrugge, 1979). Since the literary and philosophical experts have shared the general preoccupation with efferent analysis, one cannot be astonished that psychological studies of art reveal the same bias.

The neglect of the aesthetic admittedly reflects unfortunate trends in our culture, and applies to all uses of language, spoken and written. The situation raises questions relating to mental health (Jones, 1968), and to fostering involvement of both hemispheres of the brain (Sagan, 1977). The importance of the affective and the imaginative in furthering cognitive growth is evidently only starting to be investigated (Ives & Pond, 1980; E. Saltz et al., 1977).

As late as 1968, Rommetveit, one of the few psychologists interested in "the capacity of words to encode and evoke affective states" (p. 141), pointed out that research in this area was fairly recent. The preoccupation with children's efferent use of language may have been reinforced by Piaget's studies of cognitive development. Bruner (1977) chose 1975 as the date to mark the beginning of "a new and interesting period . . . in which experience and function had emerged afresh as central to our understanding of what makes it possible for the child to pass so quickly, and so seemingly effortlessly, into the initial use of language." It is encouraging to note psychologists' increasing interest in the development of affect or emotion (Emde et al., 1976; Lewis & Rosenblum, 1978; Pliner et al., 1973). The problem of the development of awareness and expression of affect remains to be explored.

## THE AESTHETIC AS BASIC

It does not seem too bold to hypothesize that in the earliest years, the capacity for the aesthetic mode of approaching experience may be

primary. Children's prelinguistic and early language processes re-
semble or parallel the aesthetic stance. The following suggests the
purposiveness of these processes, and reaffirms the importance of the
inner organismic matrix in the early years.

*Beginning about the last quarter of the first year and continuing
through the second, increased differentiations of self and other, the
sharpening of self-awareness and the self-concept, and the ability
to form and store memories enable the infant to begin the
development of affective-cognitive structures, the linking or
bonding of particular affects or patterns of affects with images and
symbols, including words and ideas. . . .*

*Since there is essentially an infinite variety of emotion-symbol
interactions, affective-cognitive structures are far and away the
predominant motivational features in consciousness soon after the
acquisition of language. (Izard, 1978, p. 404)*

Poet Dylan Thomas told a friend, "When I experience anything, I
experience it as a thing and as a word at the same time, both
amazing" (Tedlock, 1963, p. 54.). Doesn't this suggest a parallelism
with the child's early "cognitive-affective structures," the child's seeing
the word "cow" as an attribute along with its color, shape, or
threatening bigness? (Bates, 1979, p. 60). Another trait related to the
aesthetic stance is children's attention to and delight in the sound of
words and recurrent rhymes and rhythms. Accounts of children's
earliest responses to stories and poems read to them support this view
of the interplay of experience and language, the "backward and
forward flow between books and life" (White, 1954, p. 13).

Children's early receptivity to the aesthetic has been noted by
parents and teachers, and is reflected in the constantly increasing
publication of children's books and writings about them. Traditionally,
children are offered verses, poems, and stories, and their playacting
is encouraged. However, children's tastes for these are usually phrased
as delight in the imaginative or fantasy. This is surely a powerful
interest, and I should be the last to minimize its importance. Yet
imagination is required for the real as well as the fictive, and my
concern is with stance, which transcends or cuts across the distinction
between the real and the make-believe. Emphasis on the text rather
than stance has undoubtedly contributed to the tendency to equate
the imaginative with the aesthetic. Not enough attention has been
paid to the fact that stories about both the real and the make-believe
are apprehended by the child with the same immediacy, the same
linkage of word, object, and inner feeling that can be termed aesthetic.

The confusion of the aesthetic with the fictive, make-believe, may
also underlie the belief that the child's early aesthetic predisposition
is a passing phase. "With the start of school," we are told, "there is a
subtle yet decisive shift in the child's explorations. An interest in
stories and games continues. . . . But at the same time the child with-
draws from the worlds of the imaginative and the fantastic, electing
to remain securely surrounded by events and objects of the real

world . . ." (Winner & Gardner, 1979; Chukovsky, 1963). One can understand that the child's problem of delimiting the objects and nature of the real world may at a certain stage foster a preoccupation with clarifying the boundary between reality and fantasy. Yet, if literary art is equated with such elements as fictive content or metaphor, the reported distrust of fantasy may be confused with a rejection of aesthetic experience. The possibility of the aesthetic approach to texts presenting the real or the historic is overlooked.

This leads one to question to what extent rejection of fantasy is the product of the eagerness of home and school to precipitate efferent delimitations and to reward success in the efferent approach. How much of this loss of interest is due to education (Jones, 1968, p. 65)? The anthropologists remind us how alert young humans are to the subtlest signals that enable them to become assimilated to their cultural environment (Bateson & Mead, 1942; Benedict, 1934; Geertz, 1973). Surely, children are not insensitive to the fact that the greatest rewards come from demonstrating efferent understanding, that a poem or story is often to be read as a means of proving skills of efferent comprehension.

Of course, children need to conceptualize the real world; as adults they will need to handle abstractions. How can the referential, logical thinking of children be fostered without sacrifice of the rich organismic, personal, experiential basis of both efferent and aesthetic thinking? Isn't it our task to keep alive children's explorations of the world through seeing, hearing, touching, manipulating, and awareness of corresponding inner states? These are the roots of thought and language, both realistic and fantastic, aesthetic and efferent. Instead of accepting the notion of a remission of aesthetic sensibilities, we should make sure that our early reading programs do not permit them to wither away.

We are told that in adolescence children again become receptive to fantasy and the metaphorical (Winner & Gardner, 1979). Children's personal and interpersonal concerns at that stage provide a potential bridge into literary works. Some children, through fortunate home, school, and community influences, have retained their early capacity to respond aesthically. But for most children, there has been an erosion of the habit of attention to inner states associated with the printed word. High school and college teachers sometimes resort to desperate strategies to interest students in literature, and especially to induce them to read poetry. An important impediment is the instructor's own persistence in promoting and rewarding formalistic efferent ap- proaches. Aesthetic transactions with texts lead to personal involve- ment in the lived-through situations, characters, experiences. This is propitious to critical reflection both on the author's art that made them possible and on their significance for the reader's own lives (Rosenblatt, 1983).

Reading becomes no more than an empty skill, a rote exercise, if it does not relate to the needs, interests, and aspirations of the reader. Just as children develop language through their earliest efforts to understand and control the world and the self, so as readers (from the very beginning) they should be helped to feel that the transaction with the text has a meaningful personal purpose. The selection of a stance becomes a particular reflection or dimension of their broader life purposes. Such readers will acquire the capacity to appropriately handle personal responses to the printed word, and to manage critically the whole gamut, from the impersonal public knowledge of the scientist's text to the lyricism of the poet's.

## REFERENCES

Auden, W. H. *Collected poetry*. New York: Random House, 1945.

Bates, E. *The emergence of symbols*. New York: Academic Press, 1979.

Bateson, G. *Mind and nature*. New York: E. P. Dutton, 1979.

Bateson, G., & M. Mead. *Balinese character*. New York: New York Academy of Sciences, 1942.

Benedict, R. *Patterns of culture*. Boston: Houghton Mifflin, 1934.

Bruner, J., E. Caudill & A. Ninio. Language and experience. In R. S. Peters (Ed.), *John Dewey reconsidered*. London: Routledge & Kegan Paul, 1977.

Chukovsky, K. *From two to five*. M. Morton (Trans.). Berkeley, California: University of California Press, 1963.

Deese, J. Cognitive structure and affect in language. In P. Pliner et al. (Eds.), *Communication and affect*. New York: Academic Press, 1973.

Dewey, J. Qualitative thought. *Philosophy and civilization*. New York: Capricorn, 1963.

Dewey, J. The reflex arc concept in psychology. *Psychological Review*, 1896, *3*, 357−370. (Reprinted as "The unit of behavior" in *Philosophy and civilization*.)

Dewey, J., & A. F. Bentley. *Knowing and the known*. Boston: Beacon Press, 1949.

Drucker, J. The affective context and psychodynamics of first symbolization. In N. R. Smith and M. B. Franklin (Eds.), *Symbolic functioning in childhood*. New York: Halstead, 1979.

Emde, R. R., T. J. Gaensbauer & R. J. Harmon. *Emotional expression in infancy*. New York: International Universities Press, 1976.

Gardner, H., & D. Wolf. (Eds.). *Early symbolization*. San Francisco: Jossey-Bass, 1979.

Geertz, C. *The interpretation of cultures*. New York: Basic Books, 1973.

Halliday, M. A. K. *Learning how to mean*. New York: Elsevier, 1975.

Halliday, M. A. K. *Language as social semiotic*. London: Edward Arnold, 1978.

Ives, W., & J. Pond. The arts and cognitive development. *High School Journal*, 1980, *63*, 335−340.

Izard, C. E. *Human emotions*. New York: Plenum Press, 1977.

Izard, C. E. On the ontogenesis of emotions and emotion cognition relationships in infancy. In M. Lewis and L. A. Rosenblum, *The development of affect*. New York: Plenum Press, 1978.

James, W. *The principles of psychology*. New York: Henry Holt, 1890.

Jones, R. M. *Fantasy and feeling in education*. New York: New York University Press, 1968.

Lewis, M., & L. Rosenblum. *The development of affect*. New York: Plenum Press, 1978.

Ornstein, R. E. *The nature of human consciousness*. San Francisco: W. H. Freeman, 1973.

Pliner, P., L. Krames, & T. Alloway. *Communications and affect*. New York: Academic Press, 1973.

Rommetveit, R. *Words, meanings, and messages*. New York: Academic Press, 1968.

Rosenblatt, L. M. Toward a transactional theory of reading. *Journal of Reading Behavior*, 1969, *1*, 31–47.

Rosenblatt, L. M. *The reader, the text, the poem*. Carbondale, Illinois: Southern Illinois University Press, 1978.

Rosenblatt, L. M. *Literature as exploration*, 4th ed. New York: Modern Language Association, 1983.

Rosenblatt, L. M. Writing and reading. In J. M. Mason (Ed.), *Reading and writing connections*. Boston: Allyn & Bacon, 1989.

Sagan, C. *The dragons of eden*. New York: Random House, 1977.

Saltz, E., D. Dixon, & J. Johnson. Training disadvantaged preschoolers in various fantasy activities: Effects on cognitive functioning and impulse control. *Child Development*, 1977, *48*, 367–380.

Saussure, F. de. *Cours de linguistique générale*. Paris: Payot, 1916. Course in general linguistics. Wade Baskin (Trans.). New York: McGraw Hill, 1966.

Tedlock, E. (Ed.). *Dylan Thomas*. New York: Mercury, 1963.

Toulmin, S. E. *Human understanding*. Princeton: Princeton University Press, 1972.

Verbrugge, R. R. The primacy of metaphor in development. In E. Winner and H. Gardner, *Fact, fiction, and fantasy in childhood*. San Francisco: Jossey-Bass, 1979.

Vygotsky, L. S. *Thought and language*. Cambridge, Massachusetts: MIT Press, 1962.

Weizsäcker, C. F. *The unity of nature*, F. J. Zucker (Trans.). New York: Farrar, Straus & Giroux, 1980.

Werner, H., & B. Kaplan. *Symbol formation*. New York: Wiley, 1963.

White, D. *Books before five*. New York: Oxford University Press, 1954.

William, J. P. Learning to read: A review of theories and models. In F. B. Davis (Ed.), *The literature of research in reading*. New Brunswick, New Jersey: Rutgers Graduate School of Education, 1971.

Winner, E., & H. Gardner. *Fact, fiction, and fantasy in childhood*. San Francisco: Jossey-Bass, 1979.

# 14

## transactions in literacy
## an interview with
## louise rosenblatt

BRENDA MILLER POWER

**Brenda Miller Power**: Can you tell me a little bit about your personal history of learning to read and write?

**Louise Rosenblatt**: Well, I suppose the fact that I didn't go to school until I was seven is an important part of my history. My parents didn't believe I should be subjected to that sort of thing too early. We lived near the seashore and as a psychologist friend has said, I spent my time collecting experiences. Sometimes when I think of entering school at age seven I believe that I must have been stupid not to have taught myself to read and write by then. But I came back after a week in school and I was reading. I was in a school system that recognized that I was older than my classmates and [it] adjusted to my abilities. It was a school system that did many things that are now being urged by reformers.

**BP**: Can you remember any specific reading or writing experiences?

**LR**: I remember enjoying fairy stories *and* realistic stories. My parents felt I should have both. I can remember reading conventional stories about boys and girls. I read a wide range of things. I remember in an early grade writing some kind of a drama. It was an allegory. It had something to do with grammar and English, and I remember writing this little story about it. I can still see some of my fellow pupils dressed up. One of them had on a cap and gown and another was dressed as a doctor.

**BP**: Can you remember teachers who influenced you?

**LR**: I had very warm relationships with my teachers. I remember my first-grade teacher, but I didn't stay there long. I think I was moved into third grade after a few weeks. I can remember teachers vividly, but I can't recall their influence. My home influence was strong. My father was a self-educated person. He didn't go to school long, but he read quite a bit. He was very interested in the problems of society. I heard about all sorts of theories; conflicting theories, like Darwin's theory of natural selection and Peter Kropotkin's theory of mutual aid. In a way those home experiences are what I recall more than experience with teachers.

In high school, I remember my French teacher, Ruth Buvington, and my English teacher, Mrs. Bilden. Mrs. Bilden was a recent

Barnard gradùate. I remember acting in a play that she directed, and it was she who urged me to go to Barnard College. Mrs. Bilden became a personal friend as well as a teacher. We would take walks and chat. I first heard about Greenwich Village and contemporary poets from her.

**BP**: What about in college?

**LR**: In college the thing I recall that was important in influencing my theories was the fact that I studied anthropology with Franz Boas and Ruth Benedict. When Margaret Mead was a senior, I was her sophomore roommate. I had a rich intellectual life at college. I became an honors student in English. What followed was unusual: for the final two years, I was freed from course requirements and could read what I wanted to and visit courses I chose. I wrote papers and took a final examination.

**BP**: It sounds like the English system.

**LR**: Yes, I believe that was what it was modeled after. When I graduated, my great problem was to decide between anthropology and literature. I was offered the opportunity to go to France or England. I went to France and eventually took my doctorate in comparative literature at the University of Paris.

**BP**: It's hard to imagine studying with Boas and Benedict, living with Margaret Mead, and then choosing literature over anthropology.

**LR**: It was never a clear choice. When I finished my doctorate and went back to teach English at Barnard, I studied two more years with Boas and Benedict. Sapir came down from Yale and spoke to my classes. I was studying primitive linguistic with Boas. All those experiences in anthropology influenced my theories.

**BP**: One of the places those theories were presented was in your book *Literature As Exploration*. I'd have to say that was the single most influential book I read during my master's program. Ruth Hubbard used the book with her graduate students last term, and they also commented that it was the most compelling text in the course. Why do you think the book endures?

**LR**: Perhaps I should turn around and ask you that question. All I can say is that the book came very much from my own experience. There are all sorts of reasons why I was ready to write it in 1938. I had ten years of experience in literature and anthropology. Dewey's ideas were in the air at that time. I had had a traditional training as a literary scholar, and I wrote a traditional dissertation that happened to be on a relevant subject; the relationship of the artist to society. I think I've always been concerned with human beings in society, and what they do with their lives. When I was teaching, I felt that in my classroom people were struggling with problems of personal relations when they read and talked about works like *Romeo and Juliet*.

*Literature As Exploration* was published in 1938 when democracy was being threatened throughout the world. I believe very strongly in democracy, and I think it's easy now for many people to take it for granted. All of those things went into the book. I recently wrote a retrospective essay about how I came to write *Literature As Exploration* for a book, *Responding to Literature*, which was published by the National Council of Teachers of English.

**BP**: It's interesting that you see the book as rooted in your life experience of a particular place and time. What sets the book apart [from others] for me is its timeless quality — the ideas don't seem to date at all, and it lacks the jargon of many educational texts.

**LR**: That's kind of you to say. I think my basic point of view hasn't changed greatly from when I wrote that work, and it's been explicated further in the many writings which haved followed it, especially *The Reader, the Text, the Poem*.

The important idea behind my theory is that of transaction. John Dewey made the distinction between the Newtonian emphasis on the *interaction* between man and nature as separate and distinct entities, and *transaction*, which stresses a situation in which the influence is reciprocal or circular. When we say, "He's a different person with John than he is with George," we are assuming the fact that personalities are flexible, and that in a particular situation, the interplay can be seen as mutual or reciprocal. The ecologists are showing us that we transact with the environment. In reading, meaning is neither in the reader nor in the text, but emerges in the transaction between reader and text.

I find it difficult to talk about reading without talking about speech and writing. For some reason or other, I've always been asked to write about my theories of reading. But I've always seen it as part of the total activities of the human being. We are constantly in relationship with the environment. I like the fact that you described literacy instruction as holistic, rather than using the term *whole language*.

**BP**: Why don't you like the term *whole language?*

**LR**: That term emphasizes language rather than the whole person using language in a total situation. What the transactional theory leads you to recognize is that you always need to think of the context, but in a very rich way. The term *whole language* might lead to a focus on language rather than experience, the experience of which language is a part. I don't support anything that separates language from context. Most whole language proponents would agree with me, but I think that the implications of terminology are important.

**BP**: Are there any trends now in literacy research that you find interesting?

**LR**: If you have a theory, then you tend to look at work being done to see the extent that it takes care of what you care about. The great danger in much of the work being done now in reading and literature is that it will all fall back into preoccupation with the text. A lot of literary people are concerned with analyzing conventions and codes and are forgetting the reader. In research, one thing that pleases me is when there are references that show that the researcher is recognizing two ways of reading, efferent and aesthetic. Also, I like the ethnographic approach. It provides something extremely important, a rich context for studying transactions. There are some controlled experiments in some areas, like in medicine, that are important. But even then, to apply the experiment, you have to work in terms of the individual patient. The application varies. It isn't that you should never use the experimental approach in education, but researchers need to realize that they shouldn't extrapolate too simply from the controlled conditions of the experiment to the classroom.

Literacy is not a problem just for the schools, although their role is central. The literacy crisis has its roots in economic, social, and cultural concerns that must be changed. Teachers as professionals as well as parents and all who are concerned about the coming generation must not permit a fixation on the role of the schools to obscure the necessity for facing these broader issues. Meanwhile, the schools must take into account the particular kinds of difficulties individual students bring [to the classroom] because of these problems.

**BP**: How did you teach?

**LR**: I guess it was what they now call the collaborative method. My teaching was always in college. But when I was in the Commission on Human Relations I went around to schools, seeing experimental schools and regular classrooms. I thought about what I liked, and what was missing. It made me think about what you do after you create the personal environment and personal reading in your classroom. After you have that personal basis for exchanges, you can help students develop the ability to handle the problems of reading and writing and speaking in society more effectively. One of the things I think I should say is that I was also teaching writing, and I was also concerned with the way people read nonfiction. I'm not just concerned with literature. When I came to try to develop an explanation of how we make a poem out of a text, it had to be a whole theory for literary and nonliterary texts.

What is most lacking today among reading specialists is recognition that there are two ways of reading a text. Students have been taught to read everything in the same way, and not to be aware of their purpose in reading. They need to learn that you don't read an advertisement aesthetically when what you need is the facts about the product. And if you want to read a poem aesthetically, you shouldn't be worrying about remembering the color of the horse in the poem for the so-called comprehension test. And so they are misled when they respond aesthetically or efferently to a work at the wrong time. For example, I was recently in an automobile accident. I wrote my report for the police describing the accident efferently. But when I wrote to a friend about it, I wrote aesthetically, describing the look and feel of the experience. Students need to be able to understand both kinds of tasks, not just in reading, but in listening, speaking, and writing.

# 15

# the struggle for control of literacy lessons

PATRICK SHANNON

Much of the recent debate concerning how best to improve student literacy through schooling focuses on the definition and optimal conditions for learning (e.g., Anderson, Hiebert, Scott, & Wilkerson 1985; Smith 1986; Stanovich 1986). Advocates of various positions in this debate are often labeled skills-based, interactionist, and whole language (process approach). Rhetorically and sometimes in practice, these positions seem quite distinct concerning whether learners receive, construct, or transact new knowledge from text, whether skills, strategies, or purpose is the foundation of literacy use, or whether teachers should be stimuli, conductors, or enablers for student learning. The positions seem rarely to touch and never to overlap. Yet when basals are in use, the positions in this debate are virtually indistinguishable in terms of who controls the lessons.

Just who should be in control during literacy lessons? The answer in theory depends on how one thinks literacy is learned; that is, which position one accepts in the debate. With their reliance on direct instruction, the skills-based (e.g., Cohen 1981) and interactionist (e.g., Pearson 1985) positions begin from a common set of instructional assumptions. To illustrate, I begin with reference to a statement by Andrew Carnegie (1900) in order to capture the spirit of the good intentions of direct instruction's advocates.

*This, then is held to be the duty of the man of wealth.... To consider all surplus revenues which come to him as trust funds ... for his poorer brethren, bring to their service his superior wisdom, experience, and ability to administer. Doing for them better than they would or could do for themselves.*

Carnegie's statement provides a clear picture of the instructional philanthropy that direct instruction advocates would provide for students during reading lessons. First, the advocates decide which knowledge is worth knowing ("trust funds"), which just so happens to be what the advocates know ("men [and women] of wealth"). Second, they see direct instruction as their obligation ("the duty") as

Reprinted with permission from *Language Arts* 66 (6): 625–34. Copyright 1989 by the National Council of Teachers of English.

participants in reading lessons because of their previous success in school literacy matters ("superior wisdom, experience, and ability to administer"). Finally, the advocates believe that, were it not for direct instruction, students would not learn to use literacy wisely ("doing for them better than they would or could do for themselves"). Explicit in Carnegie's remarks—and implicit in those of direct instruction advocates—is the assumption that the poor, however defined, do not have the wherewithal to make sense of their lives or texts without direct aid from their betters.

Of course, the form that this aid takes varies according to the specific type of direct instruction a teacher employs. Here the skills-based and interactionist positions begin to diverge, although not as much as advocates of the two positions claim (Shannon 1984). Both keep control of literacy lessons apparently, but not really, in the hands of teachers.

## THE SKILLS-BASED POSITION

Perhaps skills-based advocates are the most straightforward about where control of literacy lessons should lie (e.g., Becker 1977; Bloome 1976). Because they believe that the tight sequencing of standardized skills is of primary importance in student learning to be literate, skills-based advocates make no apologies for requiring teachers to follow a set plan developed by curricular developers outside of a classroom and school context. The University of Oregon's direct instruction model (Becker & Carnine 1980) may be the classic example of this position with its scripted lessons and hand signals for response. The scripters (reading experts from the University of Oregon and Scientific Research Associates) are in complete control of these lessons. True to their beliefs, these advocates of skills-based lessons offer clear-cut unambiguous directives to teachers in order to ensure that all children will learn to read and write.

Less explicit, but not less controlling are traditional American basals such as Houghton Mifflin (1983). In the introductory information at the beginning of each teacher's manual, the publishers, editors, and authors announce that "when it comes to offering teachers guidance, Houghton Mifflin proves that giving you more can help you work less!" Note the switch in rationale for reading directives coming from outside the classroom from learning being too important to leave in teacher's hands (as with the University of Oregon model) to the attraction of leisure time. In this way the basal takes on the guise of modern "labor-saving" technology. With the allure of saving teachers' time from planning in order to give them more time for teaching, Houghton Mifflin seems to be putting teachers in control of lessons.

But here's an indication of just how much "help" the publishers, editors, and authors are willing to provide. This information appears in each teacher's manual in order to direct teachers' attention to how to use the Houghton Mifflin program. They are discussing the typeset of the manuals.

*Regular type is used for statements and questions that you direct to students. Ellipses ( . . .) following questions and directive statements indicate that you should give students time to think and time to follow your directions before you continue. Boldface type indicates material addressed solely to you. Boldface italic type within parentheses indicates expected student responses.*

Clearly, Houghton Mifflin is just as directive as the University of Oregon model. Within the skills-based position, publishers attempt to make all the important decisions concerning goals, content, sequence, and even the language of literacy lessons, leaving teachers with control over only the pace with which they follow directions as they lead their students through the basal materials.

## THE INTERACTIONIST POSITION

There is little difference between the skills-based and the interactionist basals (Durkin 1987). First, most leading interactionist literacy scholars work for basal publishing companies. Richard Allington, Donna Alverman, Richard Anderson, David Pearson, Robert Tierney, Peter Winograd, and Karen Wixson revolve their new direct instruction activities around basal series. Take one of the most appealing interactionist strategies, reciprocal teaching (Palincsar & Brown 1984). One student is expected to imitate the teacher's questioning behaviors with a small group of peers in order to develop greater student understanding of a text. (See Weber 1986 for further discussion of this point.) But who wrote the questions? Who thought that interrogating readers after reading was an appropriate activity? Whose answers will be honored as "correct" responses? Because the teacher behavior being imitated is driven by basal materials, even when the teacher's manual is not used by the student the basal publishers direct the activity (Harste, in press).

I do not dispute that students can learn to imitate their teachers and that they may understand the text better after the exercise, but I do dispute the interactionist claim that students are in control of their learning when they engage in reciprocal teaching or any other basal reader lesson. Regardless of the content put into American basals in their traditional or modern form, basals keep control at the publishing house.

Perhaps the logic of control in the new McGraw-Hill series (1989), with interactionist coauthors Elizabeth Sulzby, William Teale, and Timothy Shanahan, will make my point clearer. McGraw-Hill's components are virtually indistinguishable from Houghton Mifflin's. Each has an anthology of stories, workbooks, teacher's manuals for coordination of components and lessons, computer disks, tests in many forms, kits, and many types of worksheets. Moreover, both have the same "let us do the work for you" philosophy.

*Whether you are a new teacher or an experienced teacher, you can become overwhelmed when you open any basal reading teacher's edition. A typical lesson plan runs for at least 20 pages. You are faced with the tedious and time-consuming problem of breaking the plan into manageable segments for your students. McGraw-Hill reading has solved this problem for you. Most lessons are one or two pages long. Each lesson has a distinct beginning and end. Planning is made easy because the pattern of lessons for each unit is the same. The focus is simply stated, and your choices are clear.*

Two points are important to notice in this passage. First, note the not-so-subtle message that teachers making their own decisions concerning what should be included in literacy lessons is an arduous task, one to be avoided at all costs because it is "tedious and time-consuming." Second, McGraw-Hill has really only solved a problem that other basals have created for teachers in the first place. The control over literacy lessons remains with the publishers, editors, and authors; it is just that the directives come in shorter, simpler, and clearer forms.

Most often educators discuss control during literacy lessons in terms of whether to implement teacher-directed, children-centered, or some type of blended curricula (e.g. Rowe, in press). However, as I have tried to demonstrate above, this is a false issue in most American classrooms because neither teachers nor students are making decisions of any consequence beyond the pace of working through basal materials. When direct instruction basals are in use — be they skills-based or interactionist — publishing companies set the goals, methods, criteria of evaluation, and materials for learning to become literate at school. And this is particularly true in states and districts where basal use is mandatory (Apple, 1982; Farr, Tulley & Powell 1987).

## A WHOLE LANGUAGE POSITION

Whole language philosophy offers teachers and students more control over their lessons (e.g., Goodman 1986; Goswami & Stillman 1987). Advocates start from the premise that literacy lessons are to be negotiations between and among students and teachers. They reject skills-based notions that the content taught and the content learned should (or even can) be isomorphic, as well as the interactionists' contention that instruction should move students methodically toward an already-known goal. The assumptions which underlie these rejections have strong implications for a profoundly different social organization of classrooms in which control is shared more democratically. That is, whole language advocates invite students to use and develop their literate voice as they work on purposeful projects in order to better understand themselves (e.g., Hansen 1986; Harste, Short & Burke 1988). This invitation requires teachers to listen and to foster students' independence through self-selection of reading materials, analyses of authors' tone and intent, writing civic and poetic texts, and large- and small-group discussions based on the students' response to stories read and written.

Teachers do not lose control during whole language lessons. They share it. In a real sense, they become more powerful forces in children's lives because they are willing to share authority and responsibility as both teachers and students become actively engaged in making decisions based on their theoretical frameworks about literacy. Sometimes these decisions are thoughtful and productive; sometimes they are not. But they are intended to be authentic and based on the concrete experience shared in whole language classrooms.

For most whole language advocates, this interest in democratic social arrangement in their classrooms is based on psychological rather than political beliefs (Goodman 1986; Graves 1983; Smith 1986). They recognize that the two parts of the knowing cycle form a dialectic wherein the production of knowledge and the act of coming to know that knowledge must happen simultaneously. To separate the parts of the cycle by deciding what knowledge is essential for students to know prior to a lesson is to ensure that such knowledge will probably not become part of the learners' knowledge structure. The separation of knowledge from knowing defeats the purpose of planning content curricula in the first place.

Who is in control during whole language literacy lessons? It is supposed to be teachers and students together. But if Canadian basals, touted as whole language basals and corrections to the problems of traditional and modern American basals (Goodman, Shannon, Freeman & Murphy 1988), are widely involved in whole language lessons, then it seems unlikely that the potential of whole language theory can be realized. Granted the content of Canadian basals is quite different than that of skills-based or interactionist basals, but in terms of components, directives, and control, Canadian basals are quite the same.

For example, McGraw-Hill Ryerson's Unicorn series (1985) offers teachers all the traditional basal components except for the tests. The rhetoric in the teacher's manual makes Unicorn materials sound reminiscent of their American counterparts.

*The readers offer selections of high interest and literary quality to stimulate children's personal response to literature and language.*

*The Unicorn program develops in all learners language facility in reading, writing, listening, viewing, representing, and thinking.*

*Before presenting the reading selections on pages 8 to 17, provide suitable learning opportunities that extend each child's experience and oral language, introduce some of the new words ...*

At first, I found myself nodding in agreement as I read through the Unicorn teacher's manual because I appreciated its assumptions concerning language learning, but I stopped nodding when I considered who picked the selections that were of high interest, who set the sequence of reading skills that students are asked to consider and reconsider, and who is making the traditional basals' promise that all students will learn to read through the suggested exercises. Only then did I begin to realize the wide gap between the whole language rhetoric and the controlled reality in the Unicorn series. I do not question that the suggested activities are within the content parameters which qualify them as whole language lessons, but I am questioning who is in control when Unicorn is in use? Who is making the decisions? Whose voice is being developed most fully? It doesn't seem to be the students' or the teacher's.

My concern is not just with Unicorn as it was not simply limited to the American series by Houghton Mifflin or McGraw-Hill. Each is a representative example of a different (at least on the surface) type of basal reading series. In Canada, Nelson (1985) and Holt Impressions (1987) basals have all the traditional basal components (including evaluation booklets). They have skills charts (less elaborate than American basals but skills charts nonetheless). Although they offer whole language types of activities, both separate the knowing cycle by stating what the students should learn, and they subvert the democratic relations whole language literacy lessons are supposed to engender. Even the nonbasal publishers such as Canadian Scholastic-TAB, are now producing teacher's manuals for whole language lessons and book sets. Regardless of the type of basal (and perhaps regardless of any commercially prepared materials designed to teach reading) being used, publishers, editors, and authors are in control of school literacy lessons.

Although the control of literacy lessons is more subtle in Canadian classrooms than it is in the United States, it is there all the same when basals are used. Certainly, it's not like the simple control which teachers and students experience when district administrators and principals dictate which basal pages teachers and students are to cover by certain points in the year. Nor is it like the bureaucratic control under which teachers feel compelled by state law to use basals (Shannon 1988). Although there may be some of these rather direct types of control in Canadian schools where whole language lessons are offered, when basals are in use, there is certainly a third type of control, technical control. Because it is embedded within the context of the whole language suggestions in the teacher's manual, it appears to be benign and part of the realities of literacy education in elementary schools.

Just like the industrial and consumer technology that seems to have brought prosperity and efficiency to our daily lives, both American and Canadian basals promise teachers, administrators, and state officials success in making every student literate with the ease of fingertip planning. Because teachers appear to be pushing the buttons of basals, they feel as if they are in control of their lessons, when in fact they are following someone else's directions (Shannon 1987). Because there is the illusion of control and the promise that all participants in basal lessons will become literate, few teachers protest the technical control of literacy lessons through basals. But as McGraw-Hill tells teachers "your choices are clear," to which I would add, "and they are not your own."

## WHY IS CONTROL NECESSARY?

First, skill-based and interactionist advocates believe that the lesson sequence and patterns are too important to leave to chance (See Kameenui's part in Kameenui & Shannon 1988) and, as I implied through the metaphor of instructional philanthropy and which Kameenui states explicitly, advocates of these-positions do not believe most teachers are able to deliver scientifically appropriate lessons to ensure that students will become literate. Perhaps this is why some advocates of these positions become basal authors and why others promote basal use through methods textbooks and classes (Pearson 1987; Winograd, in press).

Second, control of literacy develops a certain dependence among teachers and administrators that results in a reasonable and steady market for publishers (Shannon 1988). Since 1980, corporate mergers and buyouts have concentrated 80 percent of the yearly $400,000,000 American basal market in the hands of five publishing companies (Goodman, in press). Basals are big business and publishers are in the business of selling books. Anything that will diminish teachers' use of basals—such as classroom level control over lessons—is unlikely to find too much support among publishers and editors (Follett 1985).

Third, basals perform a socializing function as well as an academic one. In the United States basals' separation of literacy learning from real literacy use marginalizes students who do not have enough cultural capital to compensate for the abstraction (Bloome & Nieto, in press). In this way, American basals contribute to a hierarchical, class-based distribution of literacy among the student population (Shannon 1985). The illusion of scientific validity of basals maintains the myths among poor and minority students that they are solely responsible for their difficulty in learning to be literate and among middle and upper class students that they are literate simply because they can pass basal tests and other standardized tests.

Canadian basals seem to have evolved beyond this sorting function, although some charge that whole language approaches neglect real cultural, racial, and class differences, and therefore, cannot serve the disenfranchised well (e.g., Delpit 1988). Although Canadian basals may not sort, they do perform a socializing function. I believe they attempt to tame what might be called the "critical" potential of whole language teaching and learning. The control in Canadian basals, I think, is used to give teachers the illusion that they are fulfilling the language and social assumptions of whole language, while preventing any such thing from happening.

What would happen if students in all literacy programs began to take the rhetoric of whole language seriously? If they insisted that they be treated as active learners by everyone: teachers, administrators, parents, or employers? What if they demanded that all their learning environments be coherent, authentic, sensible, and purposeful? What if they expected that their language, experience, history, and culture be validated at school, at home, and at work? What if they believed and wrote and talked and read and acted as if we have free open language, free speech, free thought, and freedom to control our lives? What would it mean for our current social arrangement, if middle-class, poor, and minority students understood the empowerment of literacy by using it critically and independently, as John Hardcastle's (McLeod 1986) students did in inner-city London, to come to grips with imperialism, injustice, and oppression in their lives?

With the control removed from students' and teachers' hands and placed in basal publishers', editors', and authors' hands, there is little chance that the democratic potential of whole language can be realized. Canadian whole language basals, then, provide a kind of repressive tolerance (Marcuse 1961) of whole language wherein the danger, risk, and hope is negated. Whole language lessons from basals promise teachers and students a voice, but it ensures that they have nothing of social or political consequence to talk about. Basals assure that all the risks will be academic and that nothing will change outside the classroom.

To recognize, understand, and perhaps resist the repressive tolerance of basals (and any other attempts to control literacy lessons from without), teachers and others interested in literacy education must broaden their psychological attraction to the democratic relationship among students' and teachers' voices during whole language lessons to include political and sociological analyses. Certainly, the gnosio-logical cycle of knowledge and knowing cannot be separated if students and teachers are to learn to use literacy critically and to control that use themselves. But in order to see possible threats to that cycle and real opportunities for change, we must examine the historical, political, and social roots of our present practices. In this way we will be able to expose the mentality of basal publishers, editors, and authors on the one hand and the state's interest in our using basals on the other when they say, in effect, "it doesn't matter what you want, we can give it to you better than you would or could do for yourselves."

By adding a political and sociological dimension to our psycho-logical attraction to whole language approaches, we can confront the reality of literacy lessons to show both what is offered and what is denied by our present practices and what literacy lessons might become for all participants. Political and sociological imagination can help us recognize the complex contexts in which we work, the present and potential meanings of that work, and some methods through which we might realize these potentials. Only after we open our classroom doors in order to look beyond the student/teacher dyad to examine the social and political relations of our work and literacy will we really be prepared to engage in the struggle for control of literacy lessons.

## REFERENCES

Anderson, R., E. Hiebert, J. Scott, & I. Wilkerson. *Becoming a Nation of Readers*. Washington, DC: National Institute of Education, 1985.

Apple, M. *Education and Power*. Boston: Routledge & Kegan Paul, 1982.

Becker, W. "Teaching Reading and Language to the Disadvantaged: What We Learned from Field Research." *Harvard Educational Review*, 47 (1977) 518–543.

Becker, W. & D. Carnine. "Direct Instruction." In B. Lahey and A. Kazden (Eds). *Advances in Clinical Child Psychology*, vol. 3. New York: Plenum, 1980.

Bloome, B. *Human Characteristics and School Learning*. New York: McGraw-Hill, 1976.

Bloome, D., & S. Nieto. "Basal Readers and Children." *Theory Into Practice*, in press.

Carnegie, A. Speech at the dedication of the Cooper Union, New York City, 1900.

Cohen, S. A. "in Defense of Mastery Learning." *Principal*, 60 (1981): 35–57.

Delpit, L. "The Silenced Dialogue: Power and Pedagogy in Educating Other People's Children." *Harvard Educational Review, 58* (1988): 280–298.

Durkin, D. "Influences on Basal Reader Programs." *Elementary School Journal*, 87 (1987): 331–341.

Farr, R., M. Tulley, & D. Powell. "The Evaluation and Selection of Basal Readers." *Elementary School Journal*, 87 (1987): 267–281.

Follett, R. "The School Textbook Adoption Process." *Book Research Quarterly*, I (1985): 19–23.

Goodman, K. *What's Whole in Whole Language*. Portsmouth, NH: Heinemann, 1986.

Goodman, K. "Access to Literacy: Basals and Other Barriers." *Theory Into Practice*, in press.

Goodman, K., P. Shannon, Y. Freeman, & S. Murphy. *Report Card on Basal Readers*. New York: Richard C. Owen, 1988.

Goswami, D., & P. Stillman. *Reclaiming the Classroom: Teacher Research as an Agency for Change*. Portsmouth, NH: Boynton/Cook, 1987.

Graves, D. *Writing: Teachers and Children at Work*. Portsmouth, NH: Heinemann, 1983.

Hansen, J. *When Writers Read*. Portsmouth, NH: Heinemann, 1986.

Harste, J. "The Basalization of American Reading Instruction." *Theory Into Practice*, in press.

Harste, J., K. Short & C. Burke. *Creating Classrooms for Authors*. Portsmouth, NH: Heinemann, 1988.

*Holt Impressions Language Arts Series*. Toronto: Holt, 1987.

*Houghton Mifflin Reading Series*, Boston, MA: Houghton Mifflin, 1983.

Kameenui, E. & P. Shannon. "Point/Counterpoint: Direct Instruction Revisited." In J. Readence & S. Baldwin (Eds). *Dialogues in Literacy Research*. Chicago: National Reading Conference, 1988.

Marcuse, H. *One Dimensional Man*. Boston, MA: Beacon, 1961.

McLeod, A. "Critical Literacy: Taking Control of Our Own Lives." *Language Arts*, 62 (1986): 31−50.

*McGraw-Hill Reading*. New York: McGraw-Hill, 1989.

*McGraw-Hill Ryerson Unicorn Language Arts Series*. Toronto: McGraw-Hill, 1985.

*Nelson Networks Language Arts Series*. Toronto, Ont.: Nelson, 1985.

Palincsar, A. & A. Brown. "Reciprocal Teaching of Comprehension Fostering and Comprehension Monitoring Activities." *Cognition and Instruction*, I (1984): 117−125.

Pearson, P. D. "Changing the Face of Reading Comprehension Instruction." *Reading Teacher*, 38 (1985): 724−738.

Pearson, P. D. "The Role of Basals in American Reading Instruction." A paper presented at the National Council of Teachers of English Convention, Los Angeles, CA, 1987.

Rowe, D. "Creating Social Environments That Support Critical Thinking." In J. Harste & D. Stephens (Eds). *Teaching Reading Comprehension as Inquiry*. Portsmouth, NH: Heinemann, in press.

Shannon, P. "A Dialectical Look at Direct Instruction." A paper presented at the National Reading Conference, St. Petersburg, FL. 1984.

Shannon, P. "Reading Instruction and Social Class." *Language Arts*, 62 (1985): 604−613.

Shannon, P. "Commercial Reading Materials, a Technological Ideology, and the Deskilling of Teachers." *Elementary School Journal*, 87 (1987): 307−329.

Shannon, P. *Broken Promises: Reading Instruction in 20th Century America*. Granby, MA: Bergin & Garvey, 1988.

Smith, F. *Insult to Intelligence*. New York: Arbor, 1986.

Stanovich, K. "Matthew Effects in Reading: Some Consequences of Individual Differences in the Acquisition of Literacy." *Reading Research Quarterly*, 1986.

Weber, R. "The Constraints of the Questioning Routine in Reading Instruction." A paper presented at the American Educational Research Association Convention, San Francisco, CA, 1986.

Winograd, P. "Improving Basal Reading Instruction: Beyond the Carrot and the Stick." *Theory Into Practice*, in press.

# 16

## "caring where the rockets come down"
## an interview with
## patrick shannon

BRENDA MILLER POWER

**Brenda Miller Power**: Tell me how you came to be an educator.

**Patrick Shannon**: I came to this field strangely, because I had no teacher training when I started to teach. My undergraduate degree is in history and economic theory. After graduating, I started to teach in an experimental program. When that ended, I wrote a letter to David Pearson [of the University of Minnesota and Center For the Study of Reading] and he suggested some schools I might find interesting. My brother Tim is also a teacher, and I had spent time in his classroom when he taught in New York

**BP**: What about your history as a reader and writer?

**PS**: Actually, I'm seriously learning to read and write now. My wife is teaching me to write. She reads what I've written, we talk, and through talking about it I learn. She asks good questions. Now she's becoming dangerous because she is taking classes and reading about writing instruction. I'm afraid it will ruin her.

**BP**: What about reading?

**PS**: I didn't begin to learn to read till quite late either. My undergraduate advisor in college taught me to read when I was a sophomore. He'd give me two or three books on the same subject—different interpretations of the same events. We'd sit down together and try to tie the books to modern political movements. Through that kind of reading I became a reader, though I'm not terribly accurate with the words. My wife still won't let me read to the kids if the kids can see the book. But this same professor gave up on my writing. He even burned one of my papers.

**BP**: You mean burned as in "up in flames"?

**PS**: I remember coming into his office one day and seeing something smoldering in the wastepaper basket. I said, "What's that?" and he said, "Your paper. I burned it for atrocities against the English language." So he gave up on my writing, even if he did teach me to read.

Before I started to really learn to read and write, I only had two serious career goals. I wanted to be centerfielder for the Yankees or a member of The Byrds [rock singing group].

**BP**: And here you are instead. What are you reading now?

**PS**: I'm doing a couple of kinds of reading. The book I'm writing now is tracing roots of whole language and process teaching through the progressive movement. I spent the morning reading a fascinating account of William Kilpatrick's project method from 1917. I probably won't use any of it in the book, but I take off on a tangent and I'll go with it, like I did this morning.

I also read books with my children. My wife and I are reading *The Ordinary Princess* with our daughter Laura, who is four years old. She really believes she is a princess—she always wants to wear pink clothes and all that crap. So we're trying to read her books to show her that ordinary people can be happy, too. We're reading books like *Sheep In a Jeep* and *One Two Three To the Zoo*—those kinds of books—with Tim-Pat, our eighteen-month-old son.

I've also been reading *Billy Bathgate* by Doctorow. It uses gangsterism as a metaphor for political commentary about the individual vs. corporate capitalism. And someone said something about Nixon recently that infuriated me, so I'm back to rereading Vonnegut's *Jailbird*.

**BP**: So even the fun reading comes back to politics?

**PS**: I'm a one trick pony in that respect. I see almost any event as having political implications. Sometimes it drives my wife crazy. She'll point to a tree and say, "Isn't that a lovely tree?" And I respond, "Yes, but *who* do you think planted that tree? And why do you think they picked *that spot*?"

**BP**: What about writing?

**PS**: I've completed the first six chapters of my new book.

**BP**: Does it have a working title?

**PS**: The title is *The Struggle To Continue: Progressive Reading Instruction In America*[1]: The last book, *Broken Promises*, was a statement about the dominant movement in reading instruction. The new book is about the two other movements, whole language-process instruction and critical literacy, which are subdominant, but active. I came up with the title after responding to people shouting back at me after talks. There was criticism that *Broken Promises* presented only a negative picture of reading instruction.

**BP**: Don't you think the people shouting back at talks are often cynical about the prospects for change in the field? I'm not so sure about the usefulness of responding to them.

**PS**: No, I disagree. I think many of the people shouting back are terribly frustrated. They don't like what they're doing, but

---

[1] Since this interview, Patrick Shannon's book *The Struggle to Continue: Progressive Reading Instruction in the United States* has been published by Heinemann.

they don't see any alternatives. They lack a sense of history. They need to see how they are connected to other people from other times and places. I'm telling them that they're not just being strange if they want to teach in a different way, that others have come before them.

I want also to show that there is this dialectic within the literacy reform movements in this century. Critical literacy and whole language-process people really are part of a dialect that has been going on for a long time (scientific management vs. child-centered and social reconstructionists). In the twenties, it was expressed in debates between the radicals and bohemians. There can be a reluctance now for kindred reform groups to criticize each other. And there are good reasons for that — you don't want the subdominate movements to fractionalize so much that they turn on themselves.

**BP**: How do you think your work is perceived by other researchers?

**PS**: I don't have a good sense of how my work is perceived, quite honestly. I think it is largely ignored. I know there is some criticism of *Report Card On Basal Readers* because it comes across as a polemic rather than a research report. Perhaps critics have the right to protest that it is a polemic, because it was written for teachers who are upset with what's going on in their classrooms. We wanted them to know that the [basal reading] method they are using is not the only way to teach reading, and it has a short history. There are other ways to teach.

I would argue that the rest of my work isn't polemical. It is grounded in historical or philosophical contexts. I may have a narrow perspective, but I'm not alone. The power structure within reading education is stacked toward the scientific management point of view. I'd like to think my work is thorough, logical, and tight, and that it asks people to look beyond the immediate particulars of classroom instruction to questions of how we want to live together. I believe you can trace people's actions back to philosophical views, and as researchers we need to keep that in mind, so that we know how our research will be applied. People do this unconsciously, but if this was conscious, we'd be more honest.

**BP**: Can you give me an example of that?

**PS:** A couple of reviews of *Broken Promises* criticize my discussion of whole language as a method rather than a philosophy. But if I discussed whole language at a philosophical level only, I'd have to do the same for basals and the philosophy on which they're based. One of the biggest arguments by basal publishers and authors about why basal instruction isn't more effective is that teachers aren't using the basals properly — that is, according to the philosophy summarized up front. It seems to me like that old Tom Lehrer song about the fellow who invented the rocket for the Nazis — "Once the rockets go up who cares where they come down? That's not my department says Werner Von Braun." If philosophy is made up of action and emotion, if it is real, then you can't separate philosophy from its application.

**BP**: What about your teaching? How do you apply your theory of learning and literacy to your own classroom?

**PS**: I'm hesitant to respond, because I still carry this ideal picture of a teacher in my head from when I started teaching. I came up with that picture when I read in one month *36 Children* by Herb Kohl, *How Children Fail*, by John Holt, and *Understanding Reading* by Frank Smith. I'm still trying to reach that ideal.

I try to get across the points we've just been talking about. I want my students to understand that their practice, the actions they take, have philosophical underpinnings. When you make an act, you make a statement about human beings and life. They need to understand that. I also want them to see that school and life outside of school are not really separate. Teachers aren't terribly different than other people that work—it's just that the context of their work is different.

I used to think I had to tell everyone that. I get closer to getting the students to confront it themselves in each class, every time in some way. Students need to think about how their work is connected to what they did before, and what they will do now.

**BP**: You're asking them to think about political implications of literacy and teaching.

**PS**: I think I'd even take exception, friendly exception, to that phrase "political implications of literacy." Literacy is political. You can't talk about literacy without talking about politics. Earlier when I said I wasn't quite sure how my work is perceived by others, I didn't mention that I don't believe I did a good job of laying the groundwork for considering my work. Much of my work has been an analysis of the dominant tradition in reading. I didn't respond well to criticisms that it was too negative. Now I'm trying to explain that the statements aren't really negative at all. When you're censoring something, or criticizing something, you're also making an affirmative statement about what's important to you. Every criticism is also an affirmation of what you believe should happen instead.

**BP**: Is there anything, any work in reading research, that you find disturbing?

**PS**: I don't see anyone as dangerous now that William Bennett [former Secretary of Education] is out of education. I saw him as a politician in the job. He knew how to use that job to get what he wanted, and he wasn't afraid to step on people's faces. And I mean faces, not toes.

The thing I fear is that people switch research topics in order to get grant money. What that means is that reading education does not direct itself, although we consider ourselves professional. I would argue that we are led by the nose. People are so interested in funding themselves. Look at federal grant proposals and the switching of research that's done. Look at the research published in reading research journals. There ought to be fair fights within our journals.

**BP**: What do you mean by "fair fights"?

**PS**: If you're not working in the empirical/analytic scientific mode, you almost have to publish your work in a book or anthology. Almost anything qualitative is going to come back with "Maybe you should send this to *Language Arts*" scrawled across the bottom by reviewers, as if this is the great dumping ground for qualitative work. But when you think about it, *Language Arts* has a circulation of over 30,000, and *The Reading Teacher* has a circulation of 55,000. These are great publications for reaching a wide audience of the people we want to talk with. But I still think there should be more room for subdominant views in the reading research journals.

**BP**: What stops that?

**PS**: There is the pretense that the work we do is objective. In this respect, I think we're all bad guys. Everyone has an agenda — we're all trying to get a point across by the work we do. If we would admit that, there would be fair fights, more debate, and we'd all be better off.

# PART 3
## literacy in classrooms

As teachers and students come to understand that literacy is indeed, as Robert Pattison reminds us, "a potent form of consciousness, bigger and better than mechanical skill in reading and writing," they are exploring ways to *reinvent the curriculum*. The articles in the first section, chapters 17–22, show how differently we can plan instruction by following the lead of the students we teach. You'll read about ways that teachers can build on what the students *do* know and nudge them further through the use of mini-lessons, invented spelling, reading discussion groups, and student journals. In her interview with Ruth Hubbard, *Yetta Goodman* closes this section, stressing the important contributions the teachers themselves make to the profession as they are more involved in writing and in doing classroom research.

Goodman claims that "teachers can't wait for researchers to give them answers, because they're working in the whole context of the classroom." The articles in the second section, chapters 23–30, show what this kind of teacher-research looks like *in the midst* of teaching and learning in the classroom. The authors in this section share the problems they solve and the discoveries they make as they create reading and writing communities in their classrooms. Their students from first through eighth grade engage in genuine communication about the books they are reading and the stories they are writing. In these classrooms, the students are learning that they don't need to check their culture—or their special ways of knowing—at the door. What they know is clearly a key ingredient in the recipe for process learning.

# mini-lessons: an overview, and tools to help teachers create their own mini-lessons

LUCY CALKINS

**17**

### MINI-LESSONS: AN OVERVIEW

My belief in mini-lessons comes from my own background. My parents were "project people." They believed the nine of us should each have our own projects — and so Joan entered her dog in obedience trials, Ben raised a flock of sheep, Steve played in jazz bands, and I explored the swamp on a homemade raft, or later, wrote and directed plays for the neighborhood children. My parents balanced their interest in projects with an interest in achievement. In whatever our area of interest, they provided us with the best available instruction. I have come to believe in this balance. I learn best when I am deeply absorbed by a topic and when this involvement is guided by well-timed tips from experts.

I learned to write through a balance of high teacher and high student input. I was working in England at the time, teaching in the British Primary Schools and living in the basement of a Cotswold manor house. I had never written for publication, but what I was seeing in the schools seemed so important that I fancied myself writing a book about it. Every day I spent hours poring over my manuscript, investing every ounce of heart and soul into it. Then, in the late evenings, I read great literature, and finally, for a snippet of time before going to bed, I read about the qualities of good writing. It took me three weeks to read Zinsser's *On Writing Well*; I could only digest a few bits of advice at a time or my mind would begin to swirl with too many pointers to remember as I worked on my writing. I read slowly, and took the time to integrate each new bit of information. If I read about leads while I was in the midst of writing a chapter, I'd tuck what I learned into the back of my mind and draw on it, either deliberately or unconsciously, when I began a new chapter.

I want students to experience the balance that was so valuable to me. This is one reason for my belief in mini-lessons. Then too, just as I have come to believe that there is something powerful about the

Reprinted with permission from *The Art of Teaching Writing* by Lucy McCormick Calkins. Copyright © 1986 by Lucy McCormick Calkins; published by Heinemann Educational Books, Inc.

ritual of beginning every football game with a huddle, or opening every program of "Hill Street Blues" with a meeting in the police station, I find that the ritual of beginning every writing workshop with a whole-group gathering brings form and unity to the workshop. In theory, mini-lessons are wonderful.

In practice, they often represent the worst part of a writing workshop. When I bring visitors to see the writing-process classrooms throughout New York City, I sometimes deliberately time our visits so we avoid the mini-lesson. A colleague recently suggested that it might help to change the title, "mini-lessons," to something with less traditional overtones. She explained, "As soon as teachers hear mini-*lessons*, we think of aims and motivations, and of discussions to elicit information from children. What title would be more accurate? Nutshell meetings? Writing huddles? I would want the new title to convey the simplicity and brevity of a good mini-lesson.

About a year ago, I observed Shelley Harwayne teaching a writing workshop. Afterward, I told Shelley that her mini-lesson was fabulous. Apparently this comment perplexed her because as far as she knew, she hadn't given a mini-lesson that day. At the time, Shelley said nothing to me about her confusion. At home that night she reread her notes. "What could Lucy have meant?" Then she realized that instead of what she perceived as a mini-lesson, she had begun the workshop with a quick tip. She had said to the children, "Can I ask just one thing of you before you begin your writing? When you open your folders today, and every day, would you reread what you have written? Before you add to it, have a little conference with yourself. Ask yourself questions: how you feel about the piece, whether there are ways you could make it better. All right, take out your folders and, first, read them to yourselves." To my way of thinking, this was a perfect mini-lesson. Shelley had given students a strategy they could use often. She had not interrupted their ongoing commitment to writing with an elaborate assignment. Best of all, instead of a long whole-class discussion on rereading, she simply told them about this strategy. The mini-lesson had not become a maxi-lesson.

Then too, I would want my revised title for "mini-lessons" to let teachers know that there is nothing wrong with a three-minute lecture. Teaching through recitation is deeply ingrained in most of us. In one study, Hoetker (1982) found that English teachers ask questions at the average rate of one every 11.8 seconds. But mini-lessons become diffuse and clumsy when teachers persist in the question/answer mode that is so pervasive in our schools. To illustrate my point, let me describe a mini-lesson on titles and then show how that lesson might look if taught through recitation. In the first version, the teacher might say something like this:

*Last night I was thinking about the titles you are using for your pieces and it occurred to me that if your piece was about your dog, many of you—without thinking twice—would put the label "My Dog" on the top of the page. You wouldn't stop and think about how to change that label into a* title *which might catch the reader's eye.*

*I mention this because it may help you, as authors, to think about the titles of the books you are* reading. *Jerome is reading a book about two dogs but instead of calling it "Two Dogs," the author, Wilson Rawls, has named it* Where the Red Fern Grows. *It is a curious title, isn't it, but if you read the book you will understand why he selected it. Cynthia's book is about a journey taken by three children but instead of being called "The Trip," it is called,* The Lion, the Witch, and the Wardrobe.

*And so, children, when it comes time for you to work on titles, think hard about a good title. You may want to go to the library and look at the titles there, or you may want to brainstorm a lot of possibilities before selecting one for your piece. Or perhaps it isn't important for you to think about titles now, and that is OK too.*

*If there are any of you who want to work on titles today, why don't you stay after the mini-lesson and we'll form a title-group. The rest of you, off you go. Let's have a good day.*

The same lesson, taught through recitation, might begin like this:

*The teacher has a book with her. She holds the cover up towards the class as she says, "Last night I was thinking about a part of your writing we haven't talked about." Pointing to the title of the book in her hand, she says, "the what, class?"*

*The children respond in chorus, "The name."*

*"Title, we call it," and the teacher writes* title *on the chalkboard. "It occurred to me that instead of giving your pieces catchy titles, you do what?"*

*"Hand it in," Robert guessed.*

*"Yes, you do hand it in and class, I am glad you're now remembering to put your pieces in the box called 'Final Editing,' but before you hand it in, what do you write? (Pause) Not titles, but labels. Your are labeling your stories, telling what they are about. If your piece is about dogs, what would you probably call it, Sarah?"*

*Sarah has evidently not been following the discussion. She fumbles for an answer, and so the teacher calls on two more children. The second one guesses correctly, "Dogs," etc.*

When I listen to recitation mini-lessons, I often find them hard to follow. I often cannot supply the correct answers, and I spend so much time raising and dismissing incorrect answers that I do not follow the teacher's train of thought. Worse still, the mini-lessons drag on and encroach on the time reserved for writing.

Although I find the question/answer format cumbersome, an even more serious problem occurs when people want every student to interrupt whatever he or she is doing to use that day's mini-lesson. For example, in some classes, on the day in which titles are the subject of the mini-lesson, every child is expected to list ten possible titles for his or her piece. Although there are certainly occasions when it makes sense to ask every child to do something — as when Shelley suggested that every child take a moment to reread his or her draft — I think more often, mini-lessons will only be suited to what several children are doing. We need to think of mini-lessons, then, as ways to add information to the class pot. If five children pick up on an idea when it is presented, that idea is in the room. When those five children share their work in peer-conferences and share meetings, the ideas are recirculated. Meanwhile, other children have tucked the ideas into the back of their minds, and they will draw upon them when they are needed.

But all of this avoids the main question: what does one teach in a mini-lesson? People often suggest that I write a book of possible mini-lessons. I will not and cannot do this. I am not in the classroom day by day, and I do not know the rhythms of those classrooms. I cannot know whether children in one room are cranking out purposeless little pieces, or whether the writing folders are sloppy, or whether a child has just turned a personal narrative into a beautiful letter. Only the classroom teacher knows the pulse beat of a class. Mini-lessons are meant as a time for teacher-input, not for my input.

Perhaps, however, I can give teachers the tools and the confidence to invent their own mini-lessons. In the next chapter, I want to suggest categories of mini-lessons and within each category, several possible examples. I will address these categories, although there are many others:

- Early Writing. In this section, I suggest several mini-lessons that are particularly suited to kindergarten and first-grade youngsters. Many of the other mini-lessons are also applicable to this age group.
- The Launch. The hardest days in a writing workshop are the first ones. This section contains transcripts of two "launches" and a list of other ways to begin writing workshops.
- Topic Choice. Although topics are an ongoing concern throughout the year, they are of particular importance at the start of the year. I describe a number of mini-lessons in detail in this section.
- Conferences. I hope this section encourages teachers to develop mini-lessons that help students confer well with each other and with themselves.
- Classroom Procedures. A writing workshop is only as good as the management system that supports it. Mini-lessons can help create and sustain that management system.
- Rehearsal and Revision Strategies. Children often do not know what to do when we ask them to rehearse for writing or to revise their pieces. It is helpful to demonstrate specific strategies such as mapping, listing titles, changing modes, etc.
- Qualities of Good Writing. I think it is extremely helpful for children to think about and learn about the components of good writing. In this section, I try to recommend ways to convey these qualities without turning them into diehard rules, and I suggest some of

those that seem particularly suited to K-8 children and their writing.

- Literature. Talking about good writing is often not as powerful as immersing oneself in it. Some of the most successful mini-lessons center on reading and celebrating good literature.

## TOOLS TO HELP TEACHERS CREATE THEIR OWN MINI-LESSONS

### Early writing

Mini-lessons can help young children understand the functions and power of print. For example, I sometimes gather together a class of kindergarten children and, showing them examples of environmental print, I ask them to read what the print probably says. The letters on the milk carton probably say "milk" and the letters on the can of peas probably say "peas." Usually I end the lesson by switching from reading environmental print to writing it. I ask children what word I should write on a tagboard label hanging on the door, and soon the children and I have labeled the library area, the hamster, the coat hooks, and the math manipulatives. At the end of the mini-lesson I generally ask whether some children want to write more labels during the writing workshop, and the others go off to their drawing and writing.

A natural follow-up for this mini-lesson might be for me to draw a picture and then, sounding out words, to label different parts of the picture. Then I could encourage children to label parts of their own pictures. Alternately, if two or three children had made the breakthrough and were writing words (perhaps with scribble-writing or initial consonants only), I might celebrate and share these in a mini-lesson. Still another mini-lesson might involve the children in brainstorming the sorts of writing they might do in the block area (road signs, maps, titles to the buildings, etc.) or the playhouse area (phone messages, grocery lists, labels for each child's room) and so forth.

Although many young writers will need very little help with spelling, some will need to learn how to listen for sounds. In mini-lessons, I sometimes encourage children to stretch out a word, listening slowly to the component sounds. Recently, after gathering together a group of five-year-olds, Martha Horn, one of the teacher trainers in our project, brought out a miniature chalkboard and told the class they were going to be spellers. "Does anyone have a special word we could spell together?" she asked. The children suggested spaghetti, Tyrannosaurus Rex, and hippopotamus, and then the class worked together to say the words slowly. "Watch my hand, and see if you can say it as slowly as my hand goes," Martha said, stretching out the word with her hand. "Stretch it like a rubber band," she urged, "and listen to the sounds." Then she asked, "What sounds do you hear?" and transcribed the children's guesses on the chalkboard. Her purpose was not to arrive at correct spellings, of course, but to model the process of spelling words. For this reason, if a child called out an incorrect letter, Martha did not correct the youngster.

Soon many children write whole sentences and use those sentences to tell stories, write recipes, compose poetry, and so forth. Mini-lessons can provide a forum for sharing those breakthroughs. Ideally, the mini-lessons should support the less able youngsters while also celebrating and raising the upper level of what children are doing. I particularly liked the way Shelley Harwayne did this on her third day with kindergarteners at P.S. 10. Once the children had quieted down, Shelley said, in her softly energetic voice, "This morning I looked on my bookshelf and saw some books. I thought to myself, 'These authors are doing just the same things as the children at P.S. 10.'" Then, holding up a picturebook she said, "In Tana Hoban's book, she put a picture on each page and one word to tell about the picture." Then Shelley held up a child's writing. "Here is a piece by Sylvia and see, she too has written one word to tell about her picture. She has written 'family'" (spelled FME). In the same way, Shelley showed the class that another young author, Marigold, wrote like Richard Scarey, whose books have lots of labeled pictures on every page. She concluded, "Marigold is doing just what Richard is doing," and then she turned to the final comparison. "I have one more book to show you. This book is called *The Little Bird* and it is written by Dick Bruna. After Dick drew a picture, like many of you are doing, he put some words to tell what is happening in the picture. On this page, he wrote, 'A little yellow bird flies in the air looking for a place to build a nest.'" Then Shelley likened this to Alex's work, showing that he, too, had written a sentence to tell what was happening in his picture. The mini-lesson ended with Shelley congratulating the children on being authors, and sending them on their way.

I have also seen effective mini-lessons in which the teacher begins by telling her children about a visit she took to another writing classroom. By showing samples of what the authors in that room were doing (books with chapters, tiny three-inch square books, poetry, class newspapers, etc.), the teacher encouraged her youngsters to move in new directions.

If many children are uneasy about invented spelling, I sometimes begin a mini-lesson by asking children, "Who is the boss of your book? Who makes the decisions?" Once we establish that each child is the boss of his or her writing, I ask, "Who decides whether you will write with pencil or with marker?"

"We do!"

"Who decides whether you are going to write a big, big book or a very little book?"

"We do!"

After a series of such questions, I come to the crucial question, "Who decides how you will spell a word? If you come to the word 'rattlesnake,' who decides how to spell it?"

"You do!" The children will often answer, which gives me the chance to tell them that no, *they* are the boss of their spelling, and they must not come to me for spelling decisions. "Just do the best you can and don't worry. You are the boss of your writing."

Literature can also be the source of countless other mini-lessons. For example, the teacher might read several pages from a book aloud to show children that writers usually make sure that their words match their pictures. Another day, the teacher might simply read a beautiful passage aloud and in this way, set the stage for the writing workshop. Then too, children can talk about the titles of their reading —and their writing—books, or they can notice page numbers, or think about the ways in which stories end. The teacher might bring in many different kinds of books, ranging from Kunhardt's *Pat the Bunny* to Mayer's wordless books, encouraging young writers to realize that they too, can write different sorts of books. The primary-school teacher will also find that most of the mini-lessons described in the next sections of this chapter can be adapted to the needs of very young children.

## Launching the Writing Workshop

Teachers often ask what I recommend for the first day of writing workshop. In this section, I include a verbatim transcript of the way the teacher trainers in our Writing Project often launch writing when we use demonstration lessons to train teachers in New York City classrooms. I developed this launch six years ago when I first came to New York City, and since then we have been continually refining it. This particular transcript records Shelley Harwayne's work in a sixth-grade classroom. At the beginning of the transcript, Shelley had just come into the room. She glanced around at the children, seated at their desks. "Boys and girls, could I ask you to clear your desks of everything?" When the children had finished this, Shelley said, "In a moment, I am going to ask you to come and sit with me, but when you come, please remember to push your chairs in and to come quietly." Shelley, meanwhile sat on the floor. When the first group of youngsters (row one) came to join her, she motioned for them to pull in close, and to sit on their bottoms, not their knees. When all the children had gathered, she again waited for their total attention before beginning to talk. "We will begin every writing workshop by gathering together like this. There are a couple things I want to ask of you during these meetings. If you whisper to each other or if you all start talking at once, I won't be able to appreciate the things you have to say. So I will ask you not to talk out in the meeting. And second, if you are wearing those sneakers with Velcro straps, could I ask you not to play with the straps during the meeting? In many classes I go into, there are a few children who play with their sneakers and I cannot listen really well when there are those sounds."

From the change in her body posture and in the tone of her voice, it was evident that Shelley was now done with her introductory remarks and ready to begin. "My name is Mrs. Harwayne, and I am a teacher and also an author. All of you will be authors today, so it is important for us to think, 'What does an author do first when he or she is going to write?'"

"Even before that," Shelley responded, and continued, "The author begins by thinking of his or her topic, and all of you will be thinking about that today."

Immediately I saw worry lines on the children's foreheads as they glanced back and forth at each other. It was as if they were thinking, "But I haven't gone on any trips and no one has died." It often seems that our children have watched so much television they are convinced a story will only be interesting if it contains two murders, a suicide, and a trip around the world.

Shelley, wanting to show children that little, everyday topics are worth writing about, continued, "Let me tell you what I was thinking of writing about. The other day my daughter, who is eleven, was in an awful mood. "Come on and play with me, Mom," she kept begging, but I was busy making banana bread so I said no. She kept begging and begging, so finally I scooped up a big handful of walnut shells and tossing them to her, I said, 'Here, play with these.' I never thought she'd buy the idea, but she vanished, and an hour later, she reappeared. She had taken the lid of a shoebox and flipped it over to make a tray, and on the tray was this wonderful collection of walnut-shell animals. With yellow pipe cleaners she had made a giraffe, and with paper ears she had made a bunny. I was so proud of her, and I might write about that."

Then Shelley quickly mentioned other options (one involved a hair cut, another an incident with her cat). She gave several examples in order to demonstrate the brainstorming she does prior to settling on one topic, so that the children would get a sense of the range of options open to them. Then she quickly said, "I am going to ask you to think of things that really happened to you, things you do and things you know about, and to tell them to the person sitting beside you." For a few minutes the room was filled with happy chatter. Quieting the children, Shelley asked, "What did you come up with?" and then called on several children.

Their topics were reasonably focused and so she did not carry the mini-lesson one step further, as we often do, by helping children focus their topics. If children select topics such as summer, my family, and school, I often ask the class to listen well to the question I ask. Then I ask one youngster, "Of all that you have to say about summer, of all the things that happened to you and all that you know and feel, what is the one thing you want to focus on in this piece?"

But Shelley did not do this on this particular day. Instead she simply heard several topics and then reported, "I learn so much about you when I hear your stories. I didn't know Miguel is from Peru, or that Marigold gets bad earaches when she goes on the airplane...." The children interrupted Shelley with giggles. They thought Marigold's earaches were very funny. Shelley responded by becoming serious, almost stern. "Can I stop you?" she said. "When I tell a funny story and you laugh, that is OK. But when I tell a sad story, you should not laugh. Instead, we need to feel with the person. OK, children?"

Then Shelley turned back to the job at hand. "In a bit I am going to get you started, but first, here are some rules, and these will apply to every day in writing workshop. Would you put your name and date on the paper, and please don't erase. Just cross out. This is a rough draft and no one expects it to be perfect. Don't ask for help with spelling! Just take a guess. It is the story that matters for now. Off you go. . . ."

Six or seven teachers observed Shelley on the day she gave this mini-lesson and about a week later, one of them asked if Shelley would do some demonstration teaching in her class. "But don't tell the walnut-figures story," she warned, "I already told that one." It turned out that in trying to model her lesson after Shelley's, the teacher pretended *her* daughter made walnut shell animals. How afraid we are to invest ourselves in something! Now, whenever I tell teachers about a launch, I ask them to brainstorm what stories they might tell the children, and then we consider which of their ideas might be most effective. I encourage teachers sometimes to model functional writing, such as a sympathy letter to a friend, or the notes for a talk, or an article for the local newspaper. We wrestle with the issue of fiction. Although later I stress the importance of fiction, I generally begin the workshop by modeling stories which highlight the day-to-day details of life: how the dog crawls into the bed when it thunders, what it is to watch our forsythia begin to bloom, the day I found a beautiful rock in the water and carried it for nine miles before noticing that when it was dry, the colors grew dull. When modeling, I generally do not share topics that involve big events, or ones that center on retelling a television show or a movie. These topics are not taboo, but children already overuse them.

Recently, my colleagues in the Writing Project have helped me to see that we can launch a writing workshop by demonstrating how writers often use their early bits of writing as a lens for discovering what they really want to say. We can gather students together and say, for example, "I wrote this little piece of writing a while ago and then I fixed it up, copied it over, and put it away. But when I reread it the other day I realized that it doesn't get at the really important thing that I wanted to say. So I put it aside and started brainstorming. . . ."

I hope that it is evident from this example that just as staff members in our Writing Project are continually adapting our ways of launching writing workshops, every teacher too, can invent his or her own ways to bring writing into the room. In our Writing Project, when staff members begin a workshop, we are generally demonstrating how to do this for observing teachers. For this reason, we need to squeeze the introduction to the writing process into a single class. Most of my readers do not have this constraint. You may want to begin the workshop by allowing time, day after day, for children to tell true stories to each other, either as an entire class or in small response groups. At the end of a week, each child could select one story to put into writing. You may want to begin by telling how a well-loved author went about composing his or her book, and suggesting that children could begin writing using a similar rehearsal strategy. Alternately, you could ask youngsters to bring objects in from home and, working in pairs, interview each other to find out the stories behind those objects. Whole-group meetings could be used to demonstrate and teach interviewing skills. After several days, you could encourage children to write these—or other—stories. Or you might begin by telling children that on Wednesday of the following week, a very special thing would begin: the writing workshop. In preparation for the workshop, you might devote twenty minutes a day to readiness activities: discussions of potential topics, introductory remarks about the routines of the writing workshop, opportunities to watch the teacher in the midst of writing.

I hope these suggestions serve as an invitation, encouraging you to invent and adapt your own ideas for launching the writing workshop.

## Topics

When I lead writing workshops for adults, as I often do in conjunction with our summer institute on the teaching of writing, I find that a surprising number of my mini-lessons deal with the issue of topics. I know the reason: I want my students to have successful writing experiences and it seems that when they find the right topic, half the battle is won. The reverse is also true: I have the hardest time helping writers when their drafts are those which Macrorie describes as "all style and no content." For this reason, even after a launch which deals largely with topic choice, I am apt to spend the second day (and perhaps the fourth, and tenth) on topics.

At our Institute last summer, I began the second day's workshop by saying, "At home, I thought a lot about what I could say today that might help you. I tried to put myself in your shoes, to imagine what writing is like for you. I thought about how, for many of you, this kind of writing is very new. You have done a lot of teaching about the characteristics of good writing but less actual writing. This can create an imbalance." I tried to explain. "I worry that rather than approaching your writing by thinking deeply and honestly about your subject, you will approach it by trying to produce a 'good' text. I worry that your focus will be on writing impressive descriptions, a strong lead, a forceful ending and so forth." Then I referred to how Elbow, in his book, reminds us that the way to empower our words is not through "techniques" but through letting words be an extension of ourselves. Elbow likens this to the blind man with his cane. If the blind man focuses on the place where his cane meets the edge of the sidewalk, then the cane becomes an extension of his arm and it is as if his fingertips are feeling the edge of that sidewalk. But if the blind man's focus is on the way he holds the cane, then the cane becomes an awkward piece of equipment (Elbow 1981, 368).

I ended the mini-lesson by saying, "Try to remember that this is also true for your writing. Let the focus of your attention be on your subject rather than on trying to write an impressive piece. This means taking some risks but, as Faulkner says, "If you want to write something really good, you must risk writing a great deal that is really bad."

Another day I began the workshop for adults by reading aloud a passage from Peter Elbow's book, *Writing with Power*. I suspect the passage, one of my favorites, might have meaning for upper-elementary and junior high school children, and so I quote it here:

*New and better ideas ... don't come out of the blue. They come from noticing difficulties with what you believed, small details or particular cases that don't fit what otherwise feels right. The mark of the person who can actually make progress in thinking—who can sit down at 8:30 with one set of ideas and stand up at 11 with better ideas—is a willingness to notice and listen to these inconvenient little details, these annoying loose ends, these embarrassments or puzzles, instead of impatiently sweeping them under the rug. A good new idea looks obvious and inevitable after it is all worked out and the dust has settled, but in the beginning it just feels annoying (Elbow 1981, 131–32).*

I ended the mini-lesson by encouraging teachers to probe their topics, to deal with the contrary feelings, the exceptions, to lift up the rug. "In this way," I said, "you will learn from your writing, and the piece will be more textured and have more insight as a result."

Another year, when working with an advanced group of teachers who were interested in writing articles on teaching composition, I began by giving the teachers an inventory, and I could imagine giving a similar inventory to a class of young writers. When working with the teachers, I simply read through a collection of questions, and after each question, I gave time for them to jot down silently whatever came to mind. These are some of the questions:

- What are some of the discoveries you've made as you've been teaching writing?
- Good writing is based on something we know and care about—list some of the things you have cared very much about in the teaching of writing.
- Trace the journey you have taken in learning to teach writing. What were the turning points? The high moments? The crucial lessons?
- Look back over what you've mentioned thus far. What stands out—from this list, or in your mind's eye—as a possible topic?
- What do you already know about this topic? What don't you know?
- What images, memories, or anecdotes does this topic evoke?
- If you were going to make a movie about this topic, how might you begin it? What would the opening scene show?

Thus far, my illustrations in this section have come from my work with adults. I have done this partly in an effort to elevate mini-lessons, to show readers that mini-lessons are not gimmicks for children. They are as important to my graduate students as they are to children. Also, I want to leave my readers with some work to do, and one challenge will be to find ways these mini-lessons can be adapted so they are appropriate for children.

Finding topics is a multifaceted problem and mini-lessons can be developed to deal with each facet. I can imagine mini-lessons that help children see that the seminal issues in one's life are not "used up" once they have been written about: topics such as a relationship with a sibling, wishing for a pet of your own, or wanting to have an area in which you excel are quarries from which many pieces of writing can be mined. The range of pieces any one child writes will probably be broader if the youngster circles back often to readdress the salient topics of his or her own life.

There will be times during the year when many children feel as Greg did, when he said, "I am broke. I am out of space stories, I am out of war stories . . ." and on these occasions, a mini-lesson might deal with the issue of what to do when you are, in Greg's words, "broke." The class could brainstorm strategies for finding a topic and post this list on the back wall. Included on this list might be: free write, take an interest inventory, confer with a friend, make a list of bad topics and hope a good one pops up on it, reread one's folder to see if previous pieces could be revised, think of an area in which you are an expert, notice what the other kids are writing about, and so forth. Or in a mini-lesson the teacher might encourage everyone to begin keeping a list of potential topics inside their folders. For a few minutes, the children could work in pairs, helping each other come up with the beginning of a list.

Recently I watched a simple lesson in a kindergarten classroom. The teacher, Carol Seltzer, told the class that she was excited by their topics. Then she simply asked youngsters to tell their classmates, in one sentence, what they were writing about. The lesson was particularly effective because each child stood to announce his or her topic. One by one, these youngsters jumped to their feet and, sticking their chests out proudly, said, "This is a make-believe story and I'm writing about how a puppy drowned," "I'm writing about when I had a bad dream and I was all alone on the ocean," "I have a three-months-old cat," or "I went on a house tour." Of course, children who did not have ideas for their writing got ideas from those who did, and the class as a whole enjoyed knowing what others were doing.

Shelley Harwayne recently gave a mini-lesson on topics. She was teaching in a third grade classroom in which the children were in the "when-I" stage: when I went to Great Adventure Amusement Park, when I visited my aunt, when I went to the movie, when I went to Florida. Shelley wanted the children to realize that they could write about the tiny details of life, so she began the mini-lesson by reading aloud a poem called, "Jumping on Mama's Bed." Then she said, "Can you imagine that this writer actually thought of jumping on Mama's bed as a topic?" "It is such a little thing—jumping on

Mama's bed — but you know, sometimes the little things that happen almost every day but are still very important to you, can make wonderful topics."

The class decided to call these "un-topics," and then they shared possible un-topics with each other. "I could tell about my mother's face when she is mad at me," one said. "How my baby brother throws food off his plate onto mine when we are eating," another suggested. "How every time I go to play, I take one thing out and put it on my bed, then another thing out, and soon my whole bed is covered," still another child suggested.

Brian's un-topic was, "I could write about when I shut myself in my closet and play." The children seemed puzzled, so Brian began to explain in more detail. Closing his eyes and feeling the air with his hands, he said, "On this side of the closet is my mother's fan, and there are lots of coats over here." Brian gestured with his hands as he talked, as if reliving the scene in the closet. "Over here, I make a little space between the toy chest and my mother's fan, and that is where I put my teddy bear."

"Isn't there a light in there?" the children asked.

"Oh, no! It is a dark castle. I can't see. I just feel, and I keep my teddy bear close to me. He is my subject and I am king." Brian was ready to write.

## Conferences

I would probably introduce peer-conferences in a classroom by saying, "There are thirty-two writing teachers in this room. Every one of you must be a writing teacher." Then in order to show what this entailed, I might ask the entire class to act as teachers for one child. After the youngster read his or her piece out loud, I would lead the class to respond to the piece, then to ask questions of the writer, and perhaps also to making tentative suggestions. Afterward, by reviewing what the class had done, I would list the steps involved in peer-conferences.

This mini-lesson, like most, could be repeated many times during the year. Each time, I might add a new point of emphasis. For example, children often ask trivial questions. If a writer's piece is about falling down while roller skating, it would not be unusual for a child to respond, "What color were your roller skates?" Mini-lessons can highlight the need to ask important questions. I might suggest that children think of the single most important question they could ask to respond to a particular draft. Then, instead of having the writer answer those questions, we could record them, reflecting on why some are particularly effective. Or I might confer publicly with a child, asking the class to notice especially the questions that I raise. Later I might talk about the differences between my questions and theirs. Another time, I might give each child a slip of paper and ask everyone to imagine that they were sitting in the author's chair and to write down the question they would most want a friend to ask them.

Children not only have a hard time *asking* important questions, they also have difficulty following a line of questioning. It would not be unusual for a discussion to go like this:

**One Child**: Where were you when you caught the fish?
**Writer**: Near a lake.
**Next Child**: What did the bite feel like on your fishing line?
**Writer**: It was a gentle pull. It surprised me because it wasn't a jerk.
**Next Child**: What kind of boat do you have?

In a mini-lesson, I might talk about the importance of pursuing a line of thought. "Keep the idea going," I might say, "Keep it going back and forth between you and the writer, just as if you were keeping a ball going across the net." To illustrate, I could take a segment of the class discussion and role play how it could have been done differently:

**One Child**: Where were you when caught the fish?
**Writer**: Near a lake.
**Second Child**: Can you tell us a little more about where you were, can you set the scene so we can picture it?
**Writer**: Well, it was early morning and the mist was still on this lake near my aunt's house. I had planned to fish in the brook but it was so pretty at the lake, I just put my stuff down and sat on a soggy stump near the edge of the water.
**First Child**: Do you think you should add that because when you told me, I could feel like I was there. I think it would make your story much better.
**Writer**: Tell all of it? My story would get pretty long!
**Class**: So?

One word of caution: we must avoid turning conferences into recitations of preset questions. Too much attention to conferences can make children overly self-conscious. This is probably less apt to happen if we avoid laying down rules and preaching the "right way" to respond, and instead, use mini-lessons to create a *gestalt*, to show our concern about conferences and gently coach children to become more responsive and more helpful listeners.

### Classroom Procedures

When I first began telling teachers about writing-process classrooms, I rarely bothered to address issues of classroom management. My job was to translate research into practice, and I was content to leave the more mundane matters in teachers' hands.

There is nothing worse than a reformed sinner, and perhaps this accounts for why I now spend so much time addressing classroom management. I am finally convinced that the single biggest reason why many writing classrooms flounder is that the workshop context requires new sorts of expectations, rules, and rituals. Writing teachers cannot afford to assume, as I did, that belief in children and knowledge of teaching writing will ensure a productive, smoothly-run workshop. Not only will administrators evaluate writing classrooms according to the level of productivity and the amount of order in the room, but also, children need to know what is expected of them. If we are going to have the luxury of responding well to individuals, the class as a whole needs to carry on without us. For this reason, we need a simple, clear, reasonable management system — and we need to teach it to our children.

The simplest mini-lesson on classroom management is one the teacher trainers in our Writing Project sometimes give after we have worked with children (of any age) for about a week. In the mini-lesson, we simply review the predictable structure of the writing workshop. "Children, you may have noticed that we have been writing from ten o'clock to eleven o'clock every morning. You can count on this time. This will be our special time, set aside for writing. And the writing workshop will always begin with us gathering here on the floor for a mini-lesson, as we are doing right now. During the mini-lesson, I may give you a tip about good writing or I may read some fine literature. Every day it will be a little different but you can count on our meeting together. After the mini-lesson you will have the chance, every day, to work on your pieces and share them with each other and with me. Then, for the last ten minutes of writing time, we will meet again for a share meeting. During this meeting, several children will read their work-in-progress and we will talk about it as we did with Miguel and Marissa yesterday."

This mini-lesson paves the way for others. Another day we may want to focus specifically on the procedures for coming to a mini-lesson. This may entail having the children actually practice pushing in their chairs, leaving pencils and paper behind on the desk, and walking quietly to the meeting area. This may sound very mundane, but an extraordinary amount of classroom time is wasted on transitions. If children know how and when to come to the meeting area, it will save time and spare everyone irritation. The mini-lessons will begin on a better footing.

Children also need to learn that they must return the stapler to the writing area and put caps on marker pens. They need to know that once they complete their final drafts, they must staple all the rough drafts together in order and file them in their cumulative folders. All of these expectations can be subjects for mini-lessons. Once, in an effort to engender respect for rough drafts, I brought in an iron from home. After the children had gathered for the mini-lesson, I used the warm iron to smooth a crumpled page from one child's messy writing folder.

Mini-lessons can also convey procedures for peer conferences. If two children arrive at a peer-conference, each determined to read his or her piece right away, it often leads to trouble. Instead of listening well to the other person, children wait impatiently for their friend to be finished so they can have a turn. In Aida Montero's kindergarten class, children learned in a mini-lesson that they must begin a peer-conference by deciding which youngster will be the writer and which will be the listener. Then the writer sits up on a makeshift author's chair (an overturned plastic milk crate) and the listener sits on the floor below. This outward, physical commitment to a role seems to remind Aida Montero's children of their respective jobs.

Response groups, more common in junior high classrooms, raise a number of procedural issues, and these, too, can be the subject for a mini-lesson. In a mini-lesson the teacher might mention her concern over the fact that one or two students dominate many of the response groups. The class could then brainstorm ways to rectify this situation. There are, of course, hundreds of other possible mini-lessons dealing with classroom management. I hope I have given teachers ideas for inventing mini-lessons suited to their own classroom procedures.

## Rehearsal and Revision Strategies

Several years ago I watched a youngster alternate between writing and crumpling her paper. With tremendous intensity, she would lean low over her paper and carefully write her story. Then, taking the page in both hands, she'd scrunch it this way and that. I was astonished and bewildered by what I saw and so I asked the youngster what she was doing. "Revising," she answered, as she proudly patted the well-worn page. "See, it is all loved up."

We laugh at this story, but I have found that this youngster is not as unusual as we might think. Across the country, many children have sensed that their teachers have new agendas. Nowadays, teachers seem to want (oddly enough) messy drafts, and they seem to want the work to drag on forever. Since children are extraordinarily good at giving us what we want, many youngsters are producing one draft after another. They revise up a storm. A closer look shows that these children often do not know what revision is. Often they write successive drafts, none with any connection to the one before it except that they all address the same general topic. Even more often, the drafts are almost identical, one to the next, save for a few insertions, deletions, or corrections.

We need to demythologize revision and help children see what it entails. The first step may be to take a hard look at the component strategies we use (I recommend Murray's book, *Write to Learn*, and Elbow's *Writing With Power* as reference), which might result in a list such as this one:

- Change the piece from one mode to the next (personal narrative to poem, journal entry to published narrative, etc.).
- Rework a confused section—the ending, the title, the lead, etc.
- Reconsider tone or voice. Try a different sort of voice and see if it is preferable.
- Take a long piece and make it shorter.
- Take a short piece and expand it into a longer one.
- Experiment with different leads.
- Select a functional purpose for the piece of writing and then if necessary, reorient the writing so that it accomplishes the task.
- Predict a reader's questions, then revise in order to be sure they are answered, ideally in the order in which they are asked.

- Reread the draft, evaluating what works and what does not work. After selecting what works, write another draft or portion of a draft, building on that strength. Decide whether to delete, repair, or ignore what does not work.
- Read the draft over, listening to how it sounds.
- Put the draft aside and return to it another day.
- Talk with someone about the topic, then rewrite the draft without looking back at the previous versions.
- Take a jumbled piece and rewrite it in sections or chapters.

Each of these—and other—strategies can be the topic for a mini-lesson. Sometimes during the workshop I deliberately encourage one or two children to try a new strategy. Then, what they do becomes the source for a whole-class lesson. For example, Mrs. Howard sensed that many of her fourth graders were restricted to small scale revisions: they inserted clarifying phrases and omitted needless details, but they rarely approached a second draft with a spirit of openness and adventure. In conference with one child, Susie, Mrs. Howard suggested a larger-scale revision. "Susie," she said, "do you notice that all of your stories seem to be about the same length?" It was a wise observation, for Susie seemed to have developed a scheme for writing two-page stories, and each story was similar to the last. In the discussion that ensued, Mrs. Howard suggested the girl challenge herself by taking the two-page draft of "Seeing My Grandparents," and extending it into a much longer draft.

Susie reread the original draft, circling sections of it with her pencil. "These circled parts are places I can spread out with more detail," she explained as she worked. After circling several sections and rewriting them, she added, "I had no idea there were so many parts I could fix up!" Her voice was high with excitement. "I'm discovering more on this draft than I ever did. I never realized I could change so much!"

The next day she told the class about what she had done and, using the overhead projector, she showed them her first and second drafts. The class noticed the similarities and differences between the circles draft and the final one. Here is a portion of what Susie showed the class that day:

| DRAFT—WITH CIRCLES | FINAL DRAFT |
|---|---|
| *I started walking up to the airport from the plane. We had to go through a tunnel. I squeezed my mother's hand. I couldn't wait to see my grandparents.* | *My mother and I started to get off the plane. My sister, Jill, was right behind us. I looked at Jill. Her face was red from excitement. She smiled at me. I giggled. I could tell she was just as excited as I was.*<br>*By pulling my mother's hand, I hurried her to the entrance of the* |

*airport. As we got nearer, I heard the crowd inside, laughing and talking. I saw a lot of people. They were looking for the person they came to meet. They stretched their necks, searching through the crowd. Everyone was smiling, everyone was happy.*

*We were almost in the end. I saw my grandparents.*

*My grandmother's face was tanned. It made her look so healthy. My grandfather looked pretty much the same except he was tanned too. Somebody steeped in front of me. I lost sight of my grandparents. The crowd was moving very slowly so I wiggled past everybody. I ran straight to my grandparents. First I went to my grandmother. I threw my arms around her.*

The next day Birger reread the draft of his piece, "The Day My Cat Died," and decided he, too, would make the parts longer, as Susie had done. The mini-lesson had worked: a new revision strategy was in the air, and it was spreading like wildfire.

There are other ways to introduce revision strategies. Sometimes it may be more helpful to survey several options rather than discussing one in detail. I could begin a mini-lesson by saying, "I thought it might help you to hear what I saw yesterday as I went from writer to writer. Let me tell you, specifically, about some of the revision strategies which people in this room are using. Several of you, Mohammed, Allison, and perhaps others, are working on different leads. You are listing alternative ways to start your piece, and trying to select the best beginning. This is exactly what some writers do — they call it experimenting with leads — and I think it is a strategy we could add to our chart, 'Revision Strategies.' Marigold has invented her own revision strategy. She read her piece over and decided she could hear a song in it, and so she is making a tune up and changing the words to match the mood and beat of her song. Not everyone will want to write songs, but the idea of changing modes is an important strategy; taking a narrative and turning it into a song, taking a letter and making it into a story, and so forth. So let's add that strategy to our list."

Mini-lessons on revision strategies will not always come from what the children are already doing. I might, for example, encourage children to revise for the sound of their language by reading them Katherine Mansfield's description of how she wrote "Miss Brill." "I chose not only the length of each sentence," she said, "but the sound of every sentence. I chose the rise and fall of every paragraph to fit her, to fit her on that day on that very moment. After I'd written it I read it aloud—numbers of times—just as one would play over a musical composition—trying to get it nearer and nearer to the expression of Miss Brill—until it fitted her."

I also used my own writing as a source for mini-lessons on revision strategies. For example, I sometimes say, "Many of you are starting new pieces today and I thought I'd show you how I often go about beginning a piece." Then, taking a piece of chalk I go to the board as if I was about to write on it. "Let's say I am going to write about my brother's wedding," I say. Then I pick up my chalk, but I do not actually write words on the chalkboard for that is time-consuming and in this instance, unnecessary. Instead, I pretend to write, saying aloud the intended words as I put squiggles on the board.

| ON THE BOARD | ORAL TRANSCRIPT |
|---|---|
| 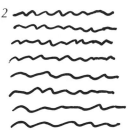 | *"Last weekend I went to Baltimore to attend my brother's wedding. It was great fun. We got there just in time for the service to begin. I was excited."* |

Then I say to the class, "After I start writing, I often force myself to stop and look at what I have said so far." At this point I reread my words to the class. "It's a boring beginning, so I draw a line underneath it and write number two. Then I say to myself, 'How else could I begin my piece?'"

| ON THE BOARD | ORAL TRANSCRIPT |
|---|---|
| 2 | *"As we drove nearer to the stone church, the bells began to ring. It was a glorious day, and everywhere people hurried toward the wedding.*<br>*'Amazing to think my own brother is getting married,' I thought."* |

"Then, after a bit of writing, I stop and see what I've said. I reread it and ask myself, 'Is this a better lead?'" The consensus of the class is yes." I could keep this lead, but I think I'll try a third one first," I say. Then I draw another and line and write number three and begin a third lead.

This mini-lesson might end with my suggesting that those children wanting to experiment with different leads stay in the meeting area to help each other with leads or to begin to study the leads authors use in literature books. I would *not* end by suggesting that every child stop what he or she is doing and try three leads. No one revision strategy is right for every child, and certainly no strategy could be right for every child on any one given day. The purpose of the mini-lesson is to suggest options, to add to the class pot, to give children a repertoire of strategies from which they can draw. Another word of caution. It would be a disaster if teachers of five-, six-, and seven-year-olds expected their children to use revision strategies such as lead-writing. Revision for young children consists mostly of adding on, and mini-lessons might illustrate how one child reread her book, realized she'd forgotten certain information, and added it in the empty spaces on her pages, or how children added pages to a pre-existing book. Kindergarten children are not ready to experiment with different leads!

Although this section is titled "Rehearsal and Revision Strategies," I have ignored rehearsal. This is not accidental. My hunch is that adult writers can do a great many things in their mind's eye through rehearsal. I can jot down a few key phrases, and imagine how the entire draft might go. I can anticipate whether a particular angle or perspective will be effective. But this requires a great deal of abstract thinking. It is something I have learned by taking the longer, harder route of actually writing a draft out, then seeing the problems and revising accordingly. It is probably easier for children to wrestle with their writing problems through concrete revisions rather than doing this mentally, in anticipation, through rehearsal. I do not mean to suggest that children will accomplish *nothing* in rehearsal. Certainly second graders can consider possible topics and select the best. Most third graders can see when a topic needs to be divided into subtopics. Through mapping, they can outline chapter headings or brainstorm a variety of focused topics from which they can choose (See Figure 17−1).

Older children can do much more in rehearsal. My advice for teachers is to think about how they rehearse for writing and then to question whether those strategies seem appropriate for young students. In this way, they can invent mini-lessons on rehearsal that parallel those I have suggested for revision.

## Qualities of Good Writing

"My story is good because it starts exciting, ends exciting, and the excitement keeps on going," eight-year-old Birger told me. Birger often put ten or fifteen exclamation marks on each page of his writing, and he revised even his social studies report on squirrels to add more excitement to it. Birger's understanding of good writing influences everything he does when he writes.

Jen is seven, and she wants very much to be grown-up. She carries a purse now, and envies her friend Melissa for her thin legs. Jen thinks her stories are terrible, "babyish," she calls them. She toils over the shape of each letter and often crumples up her paper in disgust. For Jen as for Birger, a sense of what makes good writing influences everything she does when she writes.

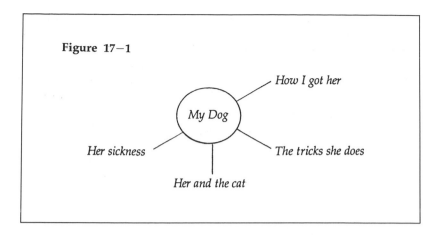

It is only natural, then, that we spend time during mini-lessons helping children deepen their understanding of good writing. During these mini-lessons we will want to tell children about the qualities of good writing that are helpful to us, and we will want to discuss those aspects that seem especially pertinent to the pieces they are writing. But I think that in many of the mini-lessons, we need to give children opportunities to articulate their sense of what good writing is. For example, we might ask each child to think of the *best* book he or she has ever read, and then to tell a friend what made that book so wonderful. If we were to move among the pairs of children, taking note of what they were saying, we could end the meeting with a brief summary of what we heard and the reminder that these same qualities are important in their own writing. Another day, we might ask children to select the best sentence from the book they are reading and read those sentences to each other. These same mini-lessons could be applied to a particular mode of writing. If the class was working on reports, the children could bring examples of good nonfiction writing to class to read and discuss with a partner. If the class was working on poetry, each child could select the best poem he or she had read recently and then in pairs, children could discuss their selections. Similarly, these mini-lessons could use the children's own writing. Which is *their* best sentence? their best piece? their best poem? Why?

These mini-lessons may sound simple, almost mundane, and yet imagine what fun it would be for us to search for our own favorite poem and then to meet with colleagues to share our choices and discuss what drew us to this poem and not to others. Of course, in these mini-lessons there are no right or wrong answers. Their purpose is to think through with the children their beliefs about the components of good writing, and to consider ways to apply those principles to work-in-progress.

The children's values will differ from ours. Many children place high value on good pictures, action, excitement, and funny topics.

We will want to share our criteria for evaluating writing with children, and although each of us will stress the qualities we know and care about, certain characteristics will pertain to most texts. One of these is the inclusion of information. Readers thrive on the concrete and the specific, on the anecdote, statistic, quotation, or example. As Murray points out, "The amateur thinks that the writer has an idea, perhaps a vague thought and a few facts. He doesn't. He has shelves of reports, miles of tape-recorded interviews, notebooks of quotations and facts and ideas and possible constructions. It takes thirty gallons of sap to make a gallon of maple syrup; it takes hundreds of pages of notes to make one *Reader's Digest* article (Murray 1968, 6).

Children may not have miles of tape-recorded interviews, but when they write about topics they know well, they do have a wealth of concrete information. Too often they assume that no one cares about the little details. They are accustomed to adults wanting only cursory answers to their questions. An adult asks, "Did you have a good time at the beach?" and children nod yes. Most children know better than to tell about draping themselves with seaweed and pretending they were brides; they know from past experience that teachers do not want to hear how the sand felt, scratching on their sunburned toes. Yet these are the details that will make their writing powerful, and therefore, as writing teachers, we need to undo the damage and let children know these details are important.

I might show children the importance of detail by telling about one child who rewrote a draft to add detail and improved it significantly. I might read them nine-year-old Susie's two drafts, asking them to notice the wealth of information she added to her second version (Calkins 1983, 2).

DRAFT 1

*I was at a beach in Florida. I pressed my toes into the hot sand. I saw my sister jumping out in the waves with my Aunt. She was jumping around as the waves hit her, she was out deep . . . I wanted to go and play in the big waves but I was nervous to.*

DRAFT 2

*I pressed my toes in the hot sand. I wiggled them around. The gritty sand felt good on my sunburnt toes. I looked out over the ocean. My sister was out deep, jumping over waves with my Aunt. Sometimes the waves got too big and they would knock her over, then my Aunt would pull her up and she'd be dripping wet and they'd start laughing. My shoulders were hot from the burning sun. I would have loved to be out there in the waves but I was too scared.*

Hindly List recently gave a similar mini-lesson. She told a group of fifth graders, "I want to give you a tip about good writing today, so listen closely. I have been going around to classes and often I see pieces like this one:

HAVING FUN AT MY PARTY

*I had so much fun at the party. I got a lot of presents and I ate a lot and the food was delicious.*

You know, I have a hard time picturing exactly what the author meant. I would just love it if the author would use more specifics. I would have liked to hear about the T-shirt with a unicorn on it and the giant Unifix cube she was given. And instead of telling us she ate delicious food, I would have liked to see the seven-layered cake and the four glasses of ice-cold coke. So when you are writing, remember to add details. And if you don't add details *during* writing, you can add them afterward, during revision, when you reread your piece. Let me show you how I do this."

Hindy turned to the draft she had written on the chalkboard. With chalk in hand, she continued, "If I had written this story, I might reread it afterward and think, 'Can I tell more?' 'Can I help the reader see?' When I notice that I haven't told specifically about the presents, I put a little asterisk here (and she inserts a star into the appropriate place in her story) and then, turning the paper over, I put the same code on the back, and beside it, I explain the section more specifically. Whenever I get to spots where I could have been more specific, I insert a secret code, and then in a different place I write what belongs there." Hindly ended the mini-lesson by asking, "Do any of you want to reread your pieces today, searching for places where you could be more specific?" Many childen nodded, and Hindy told them she would be coming around to help and sent them off to work.

Readers may notice several things. Hindy used a hypothetical draft rather than a real one as her negative example. The only time I would use a child's draft as a negative example is when I want to show how the youngster improved his or her own piece, as in Susie's story. Also, Hindy did not label the component of writing she was trying to teach. She did not write "Telling Details" or "Show not Tell" on the chalkboard and ask the children to recite the phrase. Hindy learned not to do this the hard way. Until several years ago, we told children that writers have a saying: "Show not tell." Then we proceeded to illustrate the motto with a mini-lesson such as Hindy's lesson on details. Now I often visit classrooms and hear children parroting "show not tell," and it is clear to me that *labeling* a quality of good writing creates a cliché. Clichés are too easy. They allow people to recite easy dictums rather than responding honestly and freshly to written work.

Readers may also have noticed that Hindy ended the mini-lesson by talking about how the children might go about adding more specific details to their drafts. Had she not ended the mini-lesson this way, few children would have incorporated the lesson on specifics in their work-in-progress. Almost every mini-lesson ought to end with a specific, concrete discussion of what the children can *do* next with their writing.

There are countless other ways to teach children the importance of revealing details, and there are also many other qualities that make writing good. I find it helpful to talk about honesty in writing; it is easy to say "white snow covered the world," but was the snow really white? It is easy to say "I had a terrific time," but weren't there annoying moments, and feelings that shadowed the happiness? Donald Hall emphasizes that honesty is one of the most important qualities of good writing. "Concentration upon honesty is the only way to exclude the sounds of the bad style that assault us all," he writes, and I would tell children this.

Other mini-lessons could center on focus, order, voice, and point of view. I would also suggest that as teachers of writing, we need to read about good writing. I have learned about good writing from people such as Ken Macrorie, Donald Hall, Donald Murray, John Gardner, Robert Graves, Eudora Welty, and William Zinsser, and their books are available in bookstores and libraries. Find them, and use them as resources. Otherwise we will continue to think that the qualities of good writing are those described in language arts text-books. From language arts textbooks, I learned that piling adjectives and adverbs into one's sentences creates "colorful language." It was only when I read Zinsser's book, *On Writing Well*, that I realized writers often delete adjectives and adverbs during editing. Strong, precise nouns and verbs are important to a sentence. Often adjectives and adverbs are only used to prop up a weak noun or verb. In the sentence, "I walked softly into the room," the adverb "softly" supports a weak verb. Why not say, "I crept into the room," or "I tiptoed into the room." In the sentence, "The young dog came to greet me," the adjective "young" supports a weak noun. Why not say, "The puppy came to greet me"?

My point in giving this lesson on strong nouns and verbs is that we need to learn what writers have to say about their craft and to use it as a resource for mini-lessons on the qualities of good writing. But my larger point is that teachers of writing need to be students of writing. We need to read the best literature we can find, we need to study what works in our own texts and in those of others. We also need to invite our students to do the same.

## REFERENCES

Calkins, Lucy McCormick. 1983. *Lessons from a child*. Portsmouth, NH: Heinemann.

Elbow, Peter. 1981. *Writing with power: Techniques for mastering the writing process*. New York: Oxford University Press.

Hoetker, James. 1982. A theory about talking about the theories of reading. *College English* 44, 2 (February): 175−81.

Murray, Donald M. 1968. *A writer teaches writing.* Boston: Houghton Mifflin.

———. *Write to learn.* 1984. New York: Holt, Rinehart & Winston.

Zinsser, William K. 1980. *On writing well.* 2nd edition. New York: Harper & Row.

# 18

SUSAN SOWERS

1. *What is invented spelling?*

Invented spelling is the name for children's misspellings before they know the rules adults use to spell, often before they know how to read. In some respects inventive spellers are learning to write as they learned to talk.

Inventive spellers' errors are systematic. Their judgments result from their tacit knowledge about our system of sounds, but they don't know all our conventions for written language. Like children learning to talk, they construct a series of increasingly elaborate rule systems. We can infer their rules, but children can't formulate the rules they follow. Inventive spellers' errors give us a window on their thinking.

Inventive spellers' errors don't interfere with their learning to spell correctly later. Like early attempts to walk, talk, and draw, initial attempts to spell do not produce habits to be overcome. No one worries when a child's first drawing of a person is a head propped up on two stick legs. As the errors become more sophisticated—two stick arms protruding from the head where the ears should be—no one fears this schema will become a habit, though it may be repeated a hundred times. Although deficient by many measures, the drawings are not interpreted as signs of visual, cognitive, or fine motor problems. They are greeted as a display of intelligence and emerging proficiency.

2. *Why should children be permitted to be inventive spellers?*

Invented spelling is not so much an approach to writing as it is a way of removing obstacles in the path of a young writer. Here are some advantages for learners and teachers:

- *Independence.* An inventive speller doesn't have to ask for the correct spelling of every word he doesn't know.
- *Fluent and powerful writing.* Children can elaborate their stories and play on the paper without interruptions to look up correct

spellings. With invented spelling, writing need not be the shortest distance between the title and "the end."

- *Efficient instruction.* By application of rules about the relationship between sound and symbol, children practice and drill themselves at a pace and a level of difficulty appropriate to their skills. No teacher has the time to motivate, diagnose, and assign the appropriate individualized materials for encoding and decoding that could match the work children do when they write.

  Their greater commitment to their own work also ensures a different quality of attention than they would give to worksheets and workbooks. A beginner may struggle and reread a single sentence thirty or forty times before finishing it. To write "sun," the beginner may say, "Sun. Sssssuuunnn, ssss, ssss," and write S. Then, "Sunnnn, sunnnn, nnnn, nnnn," and he writes N, SN for sun.

- *Early control and responsibility.* Children make the system their own. As they use it for their own objectives, they also extend their knowledge of how the system itself works. Children learn to take risks. The worst outcome of an unsuccessful invention is that communication stops temporarily. But if the invention succeeds, their message will reach its audience. Real rewards await the child who writes fearlessly about a FROSHUS DOBRMN PENSR instead of a BAD DOG.

3. *Other than being "wrong" instead of right, how does invented spelling differ from standard spelling?*
First, children use the names of letters and not just the sounds we say the letters represent. Although we sometimes use this principle—and *I* and *x-ray*, for instance—it is the inventive speller's chief strategy. They may begin "elephant" with L, spell "why" with Y, "bee" with B, and end "thank you" with Q. Children don't know that the relationship between a sound and the letter that represents it is often arbitrary. Y seems a more logical choice to begin the word "went" than W, pronounced "double-u," so many early attempts to spell "went" look like Y, YT or YNT.

Second, the sounds linguists call liquids—spelled with R and L—stand more often as a syllable without a vowel than other consonants. Toni, a first grader, spelled L's and R's without vowels most of the time:

| | |
|---|---|
| ACL | ankle |
| BOTHRING | bothering |
| BUTRFLI | butterfly |
| YACE DODL | Yankee Doodle |
| MAPL | maple |
| OVR | over |
| REVR | river |
| SNRCLS | Santa Claus |

Third, inventive spellers spell long vowels (rain, beet, *b*ike, boat, *c*ube) more accurately than the short vowels (*a*sk, bet, *t*ick, fox, t*u*g).

The long vowels, as many of us were taught and still may teach, "say their names." This fits nicely with the letter-name strategy inventive spellers discover on their own. Inventive spellers determine the spelling of a sound by the position of their lips and tongue when they say the word or sound, that is, the place of articulation in the mouth. We rely, in contrast, on sound, visual memory, or knowledge of word meanings to spell an unfamiliar word. Linguists and six year olds know that the E in "bet" is articulated more like the letter name A than E. Say the sounds together: "-e-" -A and "-e-" -E. Feel and hear the similarity between the short E and long A. As a result, inventive spellers spell "bet" BAT. Similarly, I in "fit" is articulated more like the letter name E than I, so inventive spellers write FET for "fit." Short O and short U are often spelled as O for the same reason. Short A (ask) is also spelled with A. Here are a few examples taken from the writing of Sarah, a first grader:

| SHORT *E* | | SHORT *I* | | SHORT *U* | |
|---|---|---|---|---|---|
| ALVS | elves | HEZ | his | MOD | mud |
| DRRASSIS | dresses | MENIT | minute | ROFE | rough |
| NAKST | next | STEL | still | TROBLE | trouble |

A fourth principle is that M's and N's before most consonants are not spelled because they are not articulated; that is, the tongue does not go to a particular place in the mouth. Instead, the M or N resonates in the nasal passages before the next consonant is articulated. Notice the position of your tongue when you pronounce the N's in "nine" and the position of your tongue when you say the N in "tent." "Nine" will be spelled NIN, but the N in "tent" will not be represented. TAT is a typical spelling for "tent." The N will not be felt. Children typically spell "friend" and "Fred" as FRAD. They do not hear the words as identical, but using their mouths to make judgments, the words feel similar.

The two keys to understanding why inventive spellers spell as they do is that they rely on the place of articulation in the mouth as well as their ears and eyes to spell. More experienced readers rely mainly on their ears, eyes, and knowledge of word meanings, and they make different kinds of spelling errors. Also, inventive spellers rely on matching the name of the alphabet letters to the sound they wish to spell.

4. *Are there stages in invented spelling?*
Two types of development are visible. First, the location of the sound spelled in a word is a clue to the child's maturity. The first step is writing apparently random strings of letters, then beginning sounds, then beginning and ending sounds, then beginning, middle, and ending sounds.

The least mature writers may write a string of apparently random letters. They may attempt to write a story, a sentence, or a phrase and record letters that represent a sound in the stream of language, but those sounds may not occur at the beginning or end of words. Extra letters seem to be mixed in for reasons the child may not remember when he finishes writing. Matching letters with the message may be almost impossible. Sometimes there is no message. The writer intended to write letters and pretend it tells a story. The content must be committed to memory since the clues are not adequate, and often the message is lost. Some teachers believe these children are not yet ready to profit from instruction. Others believe they are. Often with adult amplification of their memories, they can invent reasonable spellings for words.

Next, most first graders can segment a sentence into words and spell the first sound and sometimes the last sound with a letter or two. Although they may not be able to use the terms "word" and "sentence" correctly in talk, their spelling indicates they have an implicit knowledge of word boundaries. Finally, children don't begin to attend to the sounds in the middle of words until they are spelling every sound.

A second pattern of development is the change in the child's locus of control in spelling. First, the mouth dominates, and then the ears and eyes, and finally knowledge of words. When children no longer use the place of articulation in the mouth to determine the spelling, they are no longer inventive spellers. Inventive spellers do, however, use auditory clues and their visual memories as well as their mouths to spell.

5. *Does invented spelling get better on its own?*
Yes, invented spelling improves without special instruction up to a point, and that point differs from child to child. Some children want to spell correctly and observe the spellings in printed books with an eye to their own writing. Some children are happy to use invented spelling as a convenient abbreviation for as long as they are permitted to do so. Children don't automatically and spontaneously arrive at the correct spelling of a word simply because they read.

Some teachers have found that until the end of second grade, their inventive spellers score as well as children who study lists of words for tests. But at about that time, some notice inventive spellers' scores drop in relation to those of the others. This may be because spelling instruction is delayed until a conference about the content and the process of writing has taken place. Certainly, it is wise to confer about content first and mechanics last if we wish to convey to our students the value of content. However, when pressed for time, teachers may overlook spelling and the other mechanics. If we want our children to spell well, we will have to attend to spelling. This does not mean a return to weekly lists of twenty spelling words with a test each Friday. It does mean more systematic attention to spelling and proofreading responsibilities on the child's part.

6. *How do you decide what spelling skills to teach an inventive speller?*
Invented spelling makes diagnosis of the child's rules for spelling possible. Spelling instruction should follow conferring about the content of the writing. Although at times you will want to teach individual

words ("they" instead of THA or "there," "their," and "they're," for instance), usually you will teach principles of spelling. Look for signs that a child has begun to use a rule or principle but does not apply it consistently. Another similar approach is to ask yourself about the spelling on the page, "What does the child now know about spelling?" then, "What does he need to know next?"

A hierarchy of spelling skills is helpful:

1. String of letters.
2. Beginning sounds only.
3. Beginning and ending sounds.
4. Beginning, middle, and ending sounds.

When your assessment of the spelling falls around step 3 or 4, you may begin to be concerned about how many letters of the alphabet the child knows. A typical pattern of learning the letters and using them may look like this:

• Single consonants.
• Long vowels.
• Everything else in no special order: other vowel sounds, digraphs (sh, ch, ck, etc.), consonant blends or clusters (bl, str, sk, etc.).

Try to apply the diagnostic hierarchies to this sample of writing Mike produced in early December of first grade:

*I wt DS A I B the C BC AP.*
*(I went downstairs and I brung the cat back up.)*

This is more than 1, a string of letters. Mike has spelled the beginning and the ends of most words, but A for "and" and C for "cat" are not as complete as the others. DS may be *downstairs* or *downstairs*. Only Mike can tell you. He is the real expert on how he spells, so ask him before assuming anything.

In your diagnosis and in your talk with Mike, focus on what he knows. This is not a matter of kindness or politeness. For years teachers have been urged to look for deficiencies, and we often forget what the children *do* know is also important diagnostic information.

An instructional conversation might consist of these steps:

• *Acknowledge.* You might begin like this: "I see you know how to spell all the beginnings of the words." Perhaps you would read with Mike the sentence emphasizing the beginning sounds. Then, "I see you know 'the' and you heard the 'uh' in 'up', and you spelled it with a vowel, A. And you also heard the endings of most of the words." You might read "went" emphasizing /t/, "back" emphasizing /k/, and "up" with /p/.
• *Ask for information.* Ask Mike about the S in DS, downstairs. Notice you are using the hierarchy, moving from step 2 to 3.
• *Apply.* Now you may ask Mike to apply the knowledge that he already has to a situation he has overlooked. First, he knows how

to represent endings of some words, and he knows the sounds /t/ and /d/. He will probably be able to spell "cat" and "and" with T and D, CT instead of C for "cat" and AD instead of A for "and." Perhaps you think it is important instead to teach "and" as a correct and automatic word like "the." Teaching the ending of B, "brung," is tricky. There is no evidence that Mike knows the NG sounds. You may want to teach him that, too, or teach "brought" with /t/ instead.

- *Practice.* You may ask Mike to think of words that rhyme with "cat" and "and" to spell. This could be a small assignment, but more likely will take place beneath your direct supervision.

Two weeks later Mike brought this to his teacher:

*M i  M m  P t  IP  the  S d c n z  A d  S h n  P t  A P  the c h r s  M s  T n.*
*(My mother put up the stockings and she put up the Christmas tree.)*

Consult the writing and the hierarchy. Now Mike regularly spells the endings of words, step 3. Look at step 4 and ask whether he is regularly spelling the middles of words. If so, does he represent only single consonants? single consonants and long vowels? what else — digraphs, short vowels, consonant clusters? He does represent single consonants and some consonant clusters (ST and CHR) and digraphs (SH) although not all of them. He missed TR in "tree" unless the N is an R that he lost control over. Notice that he ended "she" with N, too. Perhaps he has forgotten E as a letter and as a sound. You must ask Mike.

Begin with the previous pattern. Acknowledge what Mike knows. Often this is helpful to you in focusing on his work. Now you need not mention the beginnings of words or even the ends, but the completeness of the middles of words. Don't fail to congratulate him on "Christmas" — CHRS MS — and the completeness of SDCNZ, "stockings." Ask for information next. Did he remember seeing "Christmas" in print or remember how to spell his friend Chris's name? Ask about N in "she" and "tree." The answers to those questions will determine the content of the rest of the conference, whether you teach E in "she" and "tree" or TR and other consonant clusters or both.

To encourage invented spelling is not to imply that spelling does not matter. The teacher's role is neither passive nor permissive. But rather than demanding perfection of beginning spellers, the teacher can build on their emerging competence. This approach also suggests to students the value of taking risks with writing, and that attitude toward written language may be the real lasting benefit of invented spelling.

# 19

## planning instruction
LYNN K. RHODES AND
CURT DUDLEY-MARLING

Assessing literacy development is a matter of observing children reading and writing in a variety of situations, recording these observations, and making judgments about children's ability to use written language. These observations, however, are useful only if they actually influence instruction on a daily basis. It's possible for teachers to observe children's literacy development regularly and yet fail to use this information effectively when planning instruction, often because they don't see the relevance of the information they've collected.

Making effective use of the information gathered from observational assessment may be difficult for some teachers, especially for those trained and practiced in behavioral approaches to teaching reading and writing. What do you do, for example, about writers whose writing is lifeless or readers who are more concerned with "getting the words right" than with constructing meaning?

In this chapter we'll discuss using assessment information to plan and adapt instruction to the ever-changing needs of developing readers and writers. We'll address the problems in writing goals or objectives that are consistent with the principles of holism.

### WRITTEN GOALS OR OBJECTIVES

Written goals or objectives are a good idea. They help guide instruction and encourage accountability, reassuring parents and administrators that students are receiving instruction tailored to their individual needs. Goals or objectives are also something most good teachers have always included in their teaching, even those not compelled to write them by law. Teachers must have some sense of the reading and writing development of their students if they are to be effective. They should have a good idea of what their students know about reading and writing and what kinds of experiences and feedback they should provide for them to encourage continued literacy development.

Most importantly, however, producing goals and objectives encourages reflection about individual students, a process that facilitates the planning of literacy programs for individual LD and remedial students.

Written goals can provide teachers with a focus for instruction that is responsive to students' ever-changing needs. For example, through observation and record-keeping, a teacher may become aware that a student rarely writes more than a few words at a time. As a result, the teacher establishes a primary goal for this student: to increase writing fluency. Making a written record of this goal will influence the teacher to provide activities that encourage the student to write, and write often. However, if written goals or objectives are going to be useful, they must be referred to often and revised on the basis of ongoing observation. They must not be written and forgotten, something that happens all too often with Individual Education Plans (IEPs) (Dudley-Marling, 1985).

Ongoing evaluation aids teachers in adapting instructional strategies in accordance with changing student needs. If the student who usually writes very little begins to produce a large amount of writing, the teacher may decide, as a result of more recent observations, to have the student focus on writing for different purposes and audiences. At some point the teacher may also identify revising and editing as areas needing attention. The key is that the teacher is always aware of a student's current level of reading and writing development, alert to evidence of continued development, and knowledgeable about the student's course of development in reading and writing. This awareness forms the basis for revising teaching and learning goals.

Setting goals is a good idea, but only if they actually influence instruction. The problem for those whose teaching is based on the philosophy of holism is the behavioral nature of the goals or objectives written for most LD and remedial students.

## BEHAVIORAL OBJECTIVES

Special education and remedial teachers are well acquainted with behavioral objectives. In Canada and the United States, LD and remedial teachers are typically required to develop specific educational plans for each student in the program. Many of these educational plans include specific, measurable, short- and long-term goals or objectives. But writing measurable instructional objectives results in fragmented, behavioral objectives.

"Johnny will pronounce the first one hundred words from the Dolch Word List with 80 percent accuracy by Jan. 1" is a representative short-term, behavioral objective. The expected student performance is stated precisely and is measurable. It's clear what you and Johnny will have to do to show that this objective has been met: you will show Johnny the first one hundred words of the Dolch List and, if he pronounces 80 percent of the words correctly, the goal has been achieved.

Through task analysis teachers identify component parts of the learning process and teach those isolated tasks using appropriate reinforcement (Astman 1984). Mastery of the task is defined in terms of learning those individual subskills thought to make up the task. It follows that writing behavioral objectives for reading and writing is a matter of identifying the component parts of the task of written language. Reading, then, may be defined in terms of sight vocabulary or mastering a finite set of letter-sound correspondences. Once these words or correspondences have been learned to the point of automaticity, it's assumed that students can read.

But, of course, reading is not merely a matter of pronouncing words nor is writing simply a matter of spelling, punctuation, and sentence structure. Reading and writing are systems for constructing meaning and fulfilling intentions. Readers and writers use their world knowledge and their knowledge of language, as well as their knowledge of written language conventions, to make meaning. Reading and writing are different from the sum of their parts and, in any case, the "parts" cannot be removed from the context of the whole without destroying the integrity of written language.

For example, a woman may be able to pronounce the French words on bilingual Canadian Government forms, but if she cannot construct meaning from the French, she is not reading French. She is merely making what for her are meaningless sounds. Of course, an ardent behaviorist might argue that she should now focus on learning the meanings of the French words, and that this process could be task-analyzed and appropriate goals or objectives written, and so on. But again the meaning of a text is not the sum of the meanings of the individual words. Readers construct meaning based on a whole range of cognitive and socio-linguistic factors including, but certainly not restricted to, the meanings of individual words. Readers can only learn how this multitude of cognitive, social, and linguistic factors interact to affect meaning if they encounter words and word meanings within the context of whole texts and within meaningful, communicative contexts. Similar arguments can be made for writing. This still might not deter an especially ardent behaviorist, but we doubt that anything we say could.

Behavioral objectives are well motivated. They presume to ensure maximally efficient instruction by focusing on well-defined, easily achievable "building blocks" of learning. But they depend on a technology that does not exist. Precise descriptions of cognitive, social, and linguistic behavior, including reading and writing, are not possible and probably not desirable. Higher forms of human learning are not reducible to their component parts.

In addition, behavioral objectives trivialize learning, seriously underestimate the potential of learners, including students identified as learning disabled and remedial, and strip away the meaningfulness of what is presented to students. By stripping meaning from reading and writing, behaviorists deprive students of their most powerful vehicle and motivator for learning—making sense of their world. Certainly many students can learn the content of behavioral objectives that have been written for them, but what they learn in this way has little value for them in their lives outside of school. Poplin (1983) captures our feelings about behavioral objectives best when she states, "Anything you can put into a computer or analyze into behavioral objectives is not worth teaching" (10).

The problem for us is to provide alternatives to behavioral goals or objectives for teachers committed to holistic approaches to literacy learning but justifiably concerned with accountability and with fulfilling their legal responsibilities.

## A HOLISTIC APPROACH TO PLANNING INSTRUCTION

As we've said, we do think that developing written goals and objectives and a detailed instructional plan for students, especially students who are struggling to become literate, is a good idea. However, we object to behavioral approaches to describing written language behavior and developing reading and writing objectives. As an alternative, we suggest a four-step approach for planning written language instruction: 1) developing concise summaries of current reading and writing performance, 2) developing learner objectives, 3) developing teaching goals, and 4) providing ongoing evaluation of student learning.

### Developing Summary Statements

For purposes of discussion, we'll talk about planning instruction for students new to your program. The first step in planning instruction tailored to the needs of an individual student is to write concise summaries of the student's current reading and writing development, based on the observations you've made, from which learner objectives can be produced. These summaries are a collection of brief statements that describe what the student does as a reader and writer — statements of effective and ineffective processes and products. Some examples of summary statements are presented in Figure 19–1.

Ideally, these summary statements will be developed only as teachers have the opportunity to work with the student over several weeks, observing the student as s/he reads and writes and as s/he responds to reading and writing instruction. If teachers are compelled to develop an instructional plan after only initial evaluation sessions with a student, they should remember that the behaviors they have observed may not be representative. More reliable information about students' reading and writing performance will come only from daily observation of the student's reading and writing during instructional time.

No doubt some of our readers will be uncomfortable with terms like "usually," "typically," and "seldom," which we used in our examples of summary statements. Those trained to write behavioral objectives have been taught that general terms like "typically" are imprecise and antithetical to good teaching practices. After all, how do you measure "typically"? How will you know if the student has progressed? Many would probably be tempted to translate the kind of general summary statements we're proposing into more precise,

**Figure 19—1** Examples of Summary Statements

John's reading miscues are typically graphophonically similar but do not make sense.

John's reading miscues are seldom corrected.

When John comes to a word he doesn't know, he often asks the teacher or another student to tell him the word.

John's oral retellings consist mostly of the random recall of a few facts.

John's oral retellings do not include any references to his own personal experiences with the topic of the text.

John rarely writes more than one or two sentences at a time.

John does not usually use capital letters or punctuation to mark sentence boundaries in his writing.

John's background knowledge does not include information about "classical" literature, i.e., common fairy tales, folk-tales, and tall tales.

John's spelling depends heavily upon a letter-naming strategy, including those words he frequently sees during reading.

John doesn't initiate the reading or writing of texts outside of school; he does choose to read (but not write) during school "choice time."

When John chooses books to read, he frequently selects those recommended by classmates or previously read by the teacher.

Though John reads and writes far less than his classmates in the same length of time, he concentrates on the reading and writing for the established period of time.

John does not revise or edit as he writes.

behavioral-sounding objectives. What's wrong, for example, with stating that "John's reading miscues do not make sense 76 percent of the time"?

This kind of quasi-behavioral statement would be very misleading. Students' reading and writing performances are variable and context dependent. A student may depend heavily on the sound and appearance of words when she reads her history book at school but focus much more on meaning when she is reading a Nancy Drew story or *Anne of Green Gables*. So statements like "76 percent of her/his miscues do not make sense" imply a false precision. At other times, in other contexts, many more of her miscues may make sense.

As we noted earlier, reading miscue performance (and all other reading and writing performance) will depend on a host of factors, including the text, students' background knowledge, their interest, and so on. The use of general descriptive statements is a recognition of reality, because reading and writing performance, like all higher forms of human learning, are variable and context dependent, and can only be described generally.

### Developing Learner Objectives

Once you've described your individual student's current reading and writing performance, the next step in instructional planning is to think about how you want that reading and writing performance to change. Learner objectives refer to what teachers hope will happen as a result of their teaching interactions with students. They encourage teachers to be aware of learning milestones, which indicate the effectiveness of their teaching efforts. Written learner objectives also facilitate communication with administrators and parents, who may be particularly anxious for evidence of literacy development.

Of course, the overriding objective of written language instruction is that students develop into lifelong readers and writers. This is the ultimate test of a reading and writing program. If students achieve a series of learner objectives but fail to use reading and writing in and out of school for their own purposes, the reading and writing program has not succeeded. Examples of learner objectives, based on the preceding summary statements, are presented in Figure 19−2.

---

**Figure 19−2** Examples of Learner Objectives

John will balance his use of the language systems more consistently while reading.

John will correct oral reading miscues that don't make sense more frequently.

John will rely on independent strategies when he comes to words he doesn't know.

John's oral retellings will include important information from the texts he has read, organized in a logical fashion.

John will make connections between what he reads and his own life, first at the teacher's initiation and then on his own.

John's writing will increase in length and fluency.

John will experience a variety of classical literature.

John will use features of standard English in his spelling; he will begin to use correct spellings of the words he sees most frequently while reading.

John will initiate the reading and writing of texts outside of school; he will occasionally choose to write during school "choice time."

John will add information to his writing drafts when appropriate.

Remember that the learner objectives you establish should be based on the summaries of a student's reading and writing behavior that you have prepared and on what you know about the course of reading and writing development. Your knowledge about development may preclude writing a learner objective for some summary statements. For example, because the teacher knows that fluent writing development precedes the development of the conventional use of capitalization and punctuation, no learner objective was written to correspond with the summary statement on capitalization and punctuation. In other cases, the learner objective should take into account the usual course of development. Developmentally, students learn to add information in revision before they learn to subtract or reorganize information. Thus, the objective written for John regarding revision takes that into account.

The summaries of effective reading and writing (e.g., "he concentrates on the reading and writing . . . ") do not require a corresponding learner objective unless you feel that you need to do something as a teacher to maintain or expand the behavior.

### Developing Teaching Goals

The next step in instructional planning is to develop teaching goals — the general steps a teacher takes to encourage the student's literacy development toward the learner objective. In other words, what will you do to help the student move from the current description of reading and writing performance in the summary statement to the learner objectives you have established?

Teaching goals will include general statements about instructional strategies, suggested materials and resources, and so on. These goals represent an overall plan or a road map for literacy instruction. Some examples of teaching goals are presented in Figure 19–3. Again, they are related to the summary statements and learner objectives presented earlier.

As with learner objectives, it's sufficient to indicate just some of the teaching strategies and resources that will be used with students. It's unreasonable to be expected to indicate all of the instructional strategies that will be used. It's also important to remember that teaching goals will change all the time in response to students' ongoing development. Teaching goals will always include the provision of a literate environment for students, including the establishment of plentiful opportunities for reading and writing.

### Ongoing Evaluation

As we said earlier, developing individual goals or objectives does not make sense unless these goals and objectives are routinely reexamined and revised in light of a student's daily reading and writing instruction. Thus, ongoing evaluation is a necessity in instructional planning if instruction is to meet the needs of students and respond to what they are currently trying to learn and do.

In order to conduct ongoing evaluation, teachers must routinely

---

**Figure 19–3** Examples of Teaching Goals

The teacher will help John discover meaning-based strategies for figuring out words.

The teacher will help John identify miscues that don't make sense and discover strategies for self-correcting those miscues.

When John asks for help with words, the teacher will refer him to the chart of meaning-based strategies for figuring out words that he has generated.

The teacher will encourage John to participate in oral story-telling based on well-structured stories he has read.

The teacher will use prereading strategies with John to encourage him to activate his background knowledge prior to reading.

The teacher will schedule daily writing time in a journal for the entire class.

The teacher will construct a thematic unit featuring classical literature for the entire class.

The teacher will encourage John to think about how words look in print so that he begins to access visual information he has from reading.

The teacher will talk with John's parents about establishing an inviting literacy environment for John at home. The teacher will also establish a literacy environment at school that encourages more person-to-person writing, such as message boards or mailboxes.

The teacher will arrange for others to conference with John about what he has written so that he learns what information can be added to his writing. The teacher will help John learn how to add information to his writing.

---

record their observations of students' reading and writing performance. This needn't take more than a few minutes each day. Teachers can jot a quick note whenever they observe something new about students' reading or writing, and they should be prepared to make a few notes after conferencing with students. Graves (1983) suggests several ways for teachers to make regular notes in students' writing folders. Another possibility for recording observations is to write each student's name on a yellow "Post-it" note before school and then put the Post-it notes on a clipboard. Before the day or the week is through, write something on each student's note. At the end of the day/week, transfer each note to the notebook pages devoted to that particular student and review the note in light of the others already there from past observations. You could use index cards in the same way. It isn't usually necessary to make a detailed record of your observations, but do write enough so that you'll be able to understand the details and significance of your own notes days or weeks later.

As we have said before, assessment and instruction are inseparable. Teachers must also be prepared to spend a routine amount of time reviewing not only observational notes but also learner objectives and teaching goals, and then revising as needed. Evidence that learning is taking place will not be limited to the stated learner objectives. Teachers must be alert to any evidence that learning is taking place, and their alertness improves with consistent and continual review of notes, summaries, and objectives. One way to make certain that you continually review student needs and developmental progress is to schedule a daily review of a certain number of the students you see for instruction.

Careful record-keeping and close monitoring of goals or objectives is the only way teachers can respond flexibly to the needs and development of individual students. It isn't enough for teachers to do all they can and hope for the best; that is a "shotgun" approach to teaching reading and writing. It fails to consider students as people with individual needs and developmental rates and is contrary to the basic principles of special and remedial education. Careful record-keeping is also important for communicating with parents, who deserve a detailed account of their child's literacy development.

## The Individual Education Plan: A Note to Special Educators

As any special educator in the United States is well aware, the main components of the individual education plan (IEP) include statements indicating students' current level of functioning, short- and long-term instructional objectives, and some indication of how short- and long-term objectives will be evaluated. The format we've presented for developing written instructional plans was designed to be as IEP-like as possible. Our format includes statements of current reading and writing performance, and long-term goals or objectives. The evaluation of progress toward objectives is based upon ongoing observation. Our format does not include short-term objectives for learners because we feel that short-term learner objectives are inconsistent with the basic principles of holism.

It's easy enough to state that some isolated skill (e.g., "John will pronounce all of the letters of the alphabet") will be learned by such and such a date, but more meaningful types of learning just don't work this way. It's not possible to predict the rate or precise course of higher forms of learning, including oral and written language, with any certainty.

A teacher we know described the early writing development of one of her students for us. In September she observed that the student's writing was limited to several lines of unintelligible scribbling, which looked like cursive writing, written alternately right to left and then left to right. A few weeks later the teacher observed that the student began to write cursivelike lines only from left to right. After several more weeks, she noticed that letters were beginning to appear in the student's writing and, finally, that the student's name appeared among the letters. Certainly this student's writing showed developmental progress similar to other children's, but the rate of development and precise course could not have been predicted.

Short-term behavioral objectives also imply that teachers are technicians. Presumably, task analysis and appropriate reinforcement techniques allow teachers to influence the rate and course of learning with a high level of success. Anyone who has observed the cognitive development of young students knows that the rate of students' cognitive development is often uneven and unpredictable. It would make no sense to state that we expected a two-year-old to begin using adjectives within a month, and it makes no more sense to us to make similar short-term predictions for students' reading and writing development. We have set aside expectations of a gradual and incremental learning curve; we have observed that many students do not reveal their progress toward literacy in this way.

We have also made some compromises to make our planning format IEP-like. We aren't entirely comfortable with the format we've presented for writing learner objectives. There is a risk that teachers will unduly focus their attention on these objectives and not respond to what students are trying to do or notice other development that may come about as a result of their teaching efforts. For example, Allen and Hansen (1986) talk about a boy who shared a piece of writing about whales that had only three lines of information. A teacher who had written learner objectives like the ones for John about increasing the length of writing and adding information to writing might have responded to the boy's writing by calling attention to these things. In this case, the boy's friends asked him what he wanted to do next and he replied, "Write one on seals. This was the first time I used the card catalogue and I want to use it again tomorrow before I forget" (689). Obviously, the teacher needs to set aside her learner objectives in such a case and respond to the student's initiative even though it may have nothing to do with established learner objectives.

In general, we are confident that the format we have presented for planning instruction satisfies the basic components of the IEP and, more importantly, satisfies the spirit of the IEP, which holds that all students placed in special and remedial education programs should have individualized education plans tailored to their needs as learners. However, in some cases special education teachers (and even remedial teachers) may feel that they are compelled to write short- and long-term behavioral objectives even though they are uncomfortable with behavioral approaches to teaching reading and writing.

In this case, teachers should probably try to shape their goals and objectives into a behavioral format. For example, they might state something like "Johnny will write a story with thirty words by June 1" or "Mary will spontaneously correct 80 percent of any reading miscues that don't make sense by March 1." Given the conditional nature of these goals, they aren't very meaningful, but they will likely satisfy those administrators who insist on behavioral goals and objectives.

## CONCLUSION

In this chapter we've presented a set of procedures for translating the results of assessment into instructional plans. We've recommended that teachers begin by summarizing the results of assessment with brief summary statements and then develop learner objectives. Teachers may then establish goals to help the student develop as a reader and writer in the direction of the learner objectives. Finally, and most importantly, teachers must routinely evaluate student progress, modifying learner objectives and teacher goals as needed.

We've also made every effort to assist special educators by making the format for planning instruction IEP-like, yet faithful to our views on reading and writing development. However, it's worth restating that the key to instructional planning is observation—observing children as they read and write and as they respond to reading and writing instruction. This careful observation of students' reading and writing development will enable teachers to modify and adapt their instructional plans as their students progress. Teachers who do this will provide students with literacy experiences tailored to their dynamic and ever-changing needs.

## REFERENCES

Allen, J., and J. Hansen. 1986. Sarah Joins a Literate Community. *Language Arts* 52: 813–815.

Astman, J. A. 1984. Special Education as a Moral Enterprise. *Learning Disability Quarterly*, 7: 299–308.

Dudley-Marling, C. C. 1985. Perceptions of the Usefulness of the IEP by Teachers of Learning Disabled and Emotionally Disturbed Children. *Psychology in the Schools* 22: 65–67.

Graves, D. H. 1983. *Writing: Teachers & Children at Work*. Portsmouth, NH: Heinemann.

Poplin, M. S. 1983. *Learning Disabilities at the Crossroad*. Paper presented at the annual meeting of the Claremont Reading Conference. ERIC reproduction number Ed 229 958.

# literature circles and literature response activities

JEROME HARSTE AND
KATHY G. SHORT

### LITERATURE CIRCLES

Readers need time to read both extensively for enjoyment and information and intensively to deepen and enrich a reading experience. When readers are given time to respond to a book, they make the ideas encountered in the literature personally meaningful and are able to extend those ideas in a variety of ways. Through talking about books with others, readers are given the time they need to absorb and savor a book so that the book becomes a significant part of their life experiences.

Talking about a piece of literature with others gives readers time to explore half-formed ideas, to expand their understandings of literature through hearing others' interpretations, and to become readers who think critically and deeply about what they read. Readers need to understand that a variety of interpretations exist for any piece of literature and that they can collaboratively explore their interpretations with one another to reach new understandings. Literature Circles help readers become literate.

Literature provides readers with an important way of learning about the world. Literature combines both knowing and feeling. Literature educates and entertains. It stretches the imagination, allowing readers to see their world in a new way and to imagine other possible worlds. The stories we create from our experiences allow us to bring meaning to those experiences and to understand how our world works. Literature, however, is just one kind of literacy that students need to become proficient readers. There are many different kinds of reading materials in addition to literature that students should be reading, such as magazines, newspapers, directions, maps, and so on. The following resources and activities will help you assist students in connecting literature to their world and the world of your classroom.

Reprinted with permission from *Creating Classrooms for Authors: The Reading-Writing Connection* by Jerome Harste and Kathy G. Short, with Carolyn Burke. Copyright © 1988 by Jerome Harste and Kathy G. Short; published by Heinemann Educational Books, Inc.

**Materials/Procedures**

\*   Multiple copies of good literature that will support intensive discussion

1.  Several pieces of literature should be selected by the teacher, the students, or both. These are introduced to the class by giving short book talks and then making the books available for the students to browse through. For young children, the teacher may read each choice aloud to the class.

2.  Students must then decide whether they want to sign up for a Literature Circle and which one they want to join. This choice can be indicated either by signing up on a chart for a certain piece of literature or by having students mark their first and second choices on a piece of paper that they give to the teacher, who then forms the groups. These groups should have four or five members.

3.  Students read the piece of literature and meet in Literature Circles to discuss the book. There are several variations depending on whether students read the book before beginning the discussion.

    a.  Students must read the piece of literature before coming to the circle. Students reading longer chapter books can read these the preceding week, either as homework or during their extensive reading time. For young children who cannot read the literature independently, teachers can read the literature to them and then place the literature with a tape in the listening center.

    b.  Students read the literature as they discuss it. Each day, the group meets to discuss briefly the part of the literature they read the previous day and to decide as a group what they will read for the next day. Once the book is finished, the group meets for more intensive discussion of the entire book.

4.  Literature Circles usually last anywhere from two days to a week, depending on the length of the book and the depth of the discussion about the book. Often only half the class is involved in Literature Circles at any one time, and the others are doing extensive reading. Literature Response Activities, writing, and so on.

5.  The Literature Circle discussions are open-ended, focusing on bringing the literature and the reader together. The following are some variations in how these discussions can be conducted:

    a.  The teacher begins the discussion on the first day by asking a broad question, such as "What was this story about?" or by asking students to "Talk about this book while I listen." From this initial discussion, the teacher gets an idea of which aspects of the book the students find the most interesting. The teacher participates as a member of the group, contributing comments and asking open-ended questions. The direction of the discussion in the Literature Circle and the types of questions asked depend on what the readers are most interested in and on which aspects of the book are most outstanding. For example, if the book is an excellent example of character development or description of setting, then this as well as the students' interests would influence the focus of discussion. Group members should be encouraged to make links between the book and their life experiences as well as other pieces of literature. This should be done in a way that deepens and extends their understanding of the literature without taking them away from the story.

b. The group can begin by discussing reactions to the book, sharing favorite parts, and raising questions about parts that they did not understand or that surprised them. The group then makes a list of issues or questions they want to discuss. They use this list to guide their discussion over the next few days.

6. At the end of each day's discussion, the group should decide on what they want to talk about the next time they meet. This gives students time to reread certain sections of the book and to think about the topic or question so they are more prepared to talk the next time. Some teachers give students the option of writing their ideas in Literature Logs. The Literature Circle then begins by having students share from their logs.

7. Although the teacher will often begin as the leader of Literature Circles, once the students understand how these groups operate, the teacher should not always be involved as a member or leader. The section on the teacher's role discusses a variety of ways to involve teachers and students in the circles.

8. At the conclusion of a Literature Circle, the members of that circle can be asked to present the book to the rest of the class or to write personal responses to the book in Literature Logs.

## Teacher's Role

For Literature Circles to be successful, there needs to be a classroom environment already established that supports risk taking and varied contructions of meaning from reading. If the students feel that they must reproduce what the teacher thinks is *the* meaning of a piece of literature, the Literature Circles will not be productive. Students who have a long literacy history of basal reading groups may initially treat Literature Circles as basal reader discussions and focus on the text to come up with the "right" interpretation. They will be used to sitting back and answering the teacher's questions and may not know how to talk and work collaboratively with other students. The teacher will need to provide other kinds of curricular strategies to establish a learning environment that supports Literature Circles and should not be discouraged if students say little when they first become involved in these discussions.

It is essential that students have time daily to read widely from many different kinds of reading materials. They also need to be authors who have published their own writing and participated in Authors' Circles. The discussions in Authors' Circles have a major impact on Literature Circles. The teacher should be reading aloud to the class and using the whole-class discussions after reading aloud to demonstrate the types of questions and topics that the students can focus on in Literature Circles. In addition, students should be involved in responding over time in a variety of ways to literature including art, music, drama, writing, and so on.

Literature Circles should be connected to other parts of the curriculum. If students are focusing on a study of families or different cultures, then literature can be chosen that deals with family situations or the clash of cultures. If students are reading a particular genre, such as folktales, they should be invited to try writing their own folktales; or if students are going to be writing some type of nonfiction report, Literature Circles can focus on nonfiction.

The depth of discussion in Literature Circles depends on the rich history of stories to which the pieces of literature being discussed are connected. There are various ways that this rich history can be built: use of familiar stories that students have heard over and over, multiple readings of the same story in the classroom, relating the book to other books read previously in the classroom through topic, genre, theme, author, and so on, or relating the literature to themes or topics being discussed in the classroom.

During the initial circles, the teacher should demonstrate the types of questions and discussion behaviors that are appropriate to establish a supportive context for sharing and constructing interpretations of literature. Varied interpretations are accepted as long as the reader can support them. Readers are asked to support and explain what they say, rather than simply making statements about their reading experience with a particular book. The teacher also encourages readers to explore each others' interpretations and collaboratively to build new understandings of the literature during the Literature Circle. Literature Circles are a time of exploration with one another, not a time to present a formal or final interpretation of a particular piece of literature. Readers need to listen to each other (that includes the teacher) and to build off of each others' comments. Both the students and the teacher should reply to one another rather than assess, to avoid cutting off discussion.

Literature Circles can be organized in a variety of ways so that teachers and students share in the control of these groups. Although the groups will probably begin with the teacher taking an active role as the group leader, the teacher needs to allow students to take over and direct the discussion. Because of the teacher's greater experience and knowledge, the teacher's presence in Literature Circles influences the dynamics of the group. Teachers can change their role from leader to member by waiting for student responses rather than dominating the discussion and by occasionally offering their own opinions about what is being discussed rather than asking questions. Teachers can offer differing amounts of support and share control with students by trying different variations of the circles in which they are sometimes present and at other times circulate from group to group, or not join the group at all. Instead of the teacher serving as the source of open-ended questions or of a broad focus for the discussion, students can come to the circle with their own questions or focus. These options ensure that the groups have a specific purpose or problem that is being discussed but vary who is establishing that purpose or problem: the teacher, the students, or teacher and students together.

The teacher needs to obtain multiple copies of books, especially if the books are chapter books. Picture books can be easily shared among the group members, but students need their own copies of the longer books. Check the libraries, other teachers, Chapter 1 and resource teacher collections, and closets. Use the bonus points from paperback book clubs to buy sets. See if the school will let you use some of your textbook or workbook money to buy sets (get several teachers to join together and share sets). See if you can get money to buy sets through the parent-teacher organization or a fundraiser. Short stories and poems can be photocopied. Remember that picture books are not just for young children but can be used productively with older readers. It is best to use a variety of literature, including fiction and nonfiction, poetry, short stories, picture books, and chapter books.

## Follow-up

1. Students may discuss one piece of literature that everyone has read.
2. Students may discuss a variety of texts that are related in some way.
3. The circle may focus on literature by a particular author or poet.
4. Students may discuss literature by a local author who can then visit the group.
5. By discussing literature written by class members, Literature Circles may recognize the authorship of children within the room which can lead to interesting and insightful discussions. The group first meets and discusses the book without the author present and then invites the author to join the group.
6. Any of the discussions described can occur in groups that cut across grade levels.
7. Calkins (1986) describes literature groups in which the teacher had the entire class reading the same genre. Each day, the teacher had a secret question for the students to discuss. After discussing the question in small groups, the class then came together as a whole to discuss the question. Sometimes the small groups had read the same book and, at other times, each child had read a different book. However, because the books came from the same genre (mystery stories), the students were able to discuss the questions productively with one another.
8. Karen Smith uses read-aloud time to help students listen and build their comments off of each other. After reading aloud, she steps outside the group and asks them to discuss the chapter while she takes notes. At the end of the discussion, she shares her observations

with the students, particularly noting any comments that students made that built off of what someone else had said.

## LITERATURE RESPONSE ACTIVITIES

Readers deepen and extend their interpretations of literature when they respond to that literature in a variety of ways. Involving readers in response activities allows language users to savor and asborb books and gives them time for reflection. Both verbal and nonverbal responses should be encouraged. When readers move from reading to writing or from reading to art or drama, they take a new perspective on the piece of literature. In the process of trying to express their interpretation of the literature through various sign systems, they discover new meanings and expand their understandings of what they had earlier read. Students need the chance to respond to literature in a variety of ways over time. Their responses become more complex and reflective when response is not seen as a one-shot affair. The following resources and activities will help you assist students as they learn to respond within a community of readers and writers.

### Materials/Procedures

* Literature.
* Supplies needed for responses through talking, writing, art, drama, movement, music, and so on.

1. A piece of literature should be read individually, in small groups, or as a whole class.
2. Students should have time to share their responses to a particular book informally with one another.
3. The teacher should invite students to explore the variety of ways in which they can respond to a piece of literature. Supplies for the various kinds of responses should be located in a center for easy access by students. A brainstormed list of possible ways to respond to a book should also be in the center.
   The following is a list of some types of response activities:
   a. Book Sales involve students in creating a commercial to sell a favorite book to the class.
   b. Students can create murals, dioramas, roller TV shows, pictures, paintings, papier-mâché, collage, sculpture, mobiles, and posters.
   c. Students can perform dramatized versions of the literature or create a puppet show.
   d. Writing or dramatizing a story can involve students in building off of the literature. For example, children can create a new ending, write a different story with the same theme or characters, or tell the story from a different character's point of view.
   e. Journals or letters can be written from the point of view of characters in the book, or students can create a newspaper based on the time period and events in the book.

f. Students may write about their responses to the literature in Literature Logs.

g. Readers may meet to discuss and explore their interpretations of literature in Literature Circles.

h. Children may use Sketch to Stretch, in which readers sketch the meaning of the story and share their sketches with each other.

i. A Readers' Theatre may be developed from the literature.

j. A game from the book for others to play can be created. Games can be board games or be based on TV game shows.

k. Displays or learning centers related to the literature may be set up.

l. Cooking experiences may be used to extend learning.

m. Informal Author Sharing Times allow students to talk with one another about the literature they are reading.

n. Students may interview one another about their response to the book or simulate an interview with the author.

o. Students may research the setting of the book or the life of the author.

p. Comparison charts or webs of related books or topics may be developed.

q. Children may participate in a book party, dressing up as book characters.

r. Children may create a tableau, a living picture of an action or scene frozen in time, arranged on stage.

**4.** Students need the opportunity to respond to literature in a variety of ways over a period of time.

**5.** Students should be encouraged to share their responses with one another as well as with other audiences when appropriate. These Literature Response Activities should be received by the group just as pieces of writing are received. The audience tells what they liked about the response and has a chance to ask questions.

### Teacher's Role

At the beginning of the year, the teacher needs to spend some time with students exploring the variety of ways in which they can respond to literature. This exploration can take the form of brainstorming as well as the actual involvement of students in a variety of types of responses. The teacher can create a center that lists the types of responses students can make and contains the supplies they are most likely to need for these responses. The teacher can also offer specific invitations of ways students can respond to books read aloud to the class.

### Follow-up

**1.** Related activities include Literature Circles, Say Something, Learning Log, Sketch to Stretch, Cloning an Author, and Save the Last Word for Me.

2. Instead of asking students to retell a story, the teacher can ask them to talk about how they have changed as a result of reading the book or what they know now that they didn't know before.

## APPENDIX A: EXAMPLES OF OPEN-ENDED QUESTIONS (LITERATURE CIRCLES)

The following questions are taken from *The Child as Critic*, 2d ed., by Glenna Davis Sloan. New York: Teachers College Press, 1984.

1. Where and when does the story take place? How do you know? If the story took place somewhere else or in a different time, how would it be changed?
2. What incident, problem, conflict, or situation does the author use to get the story started?
3. What does the author do to create suspense, to make you want to read on to find out what happens?
4. Trace the main events of the story. Could you change their order or leave any of them out? Why or why not?
5. Think of a different ending to the story. How would the rest of the story have to be changed to fit the new ending?
6. Did the story end the way you expected it to? What clues did the author offer to prepare you to expect this ending? Did you recognize these clues as important to the story as you were first reading/hearing it?
7. Who is the main character of the story? What kind of person is the character? How do you know?
8. Are any characters changed during the story? If they are, how are they different? What changed them? Did it seem believable?
9. Some characters play small but important roles in a story. Name such a character. Why is this character necessary for the story?
10. Who is the teller of the story? How would the story change if someone else in the book or an outside narrator told the story?
11. Does the story as a whole create a certain mood or feeling? What is the mood? How is it created?
12. Did you have strong feelings as you read the story? What did the author do to make you feel strongly?
13. What are the main ideas behind the story? What makes you think of them as you read the story?
14. Is this story like any other story you have read or watched?
15. Think about the characters in the story. Are any of them the same type of character that you have met in other stories?

The following questions are taken from *Child and Story*, by Kay Vandergrift. New York: Neal-Schuman Publishers, 1980.

1. What idea or ideas does this story make you think about? How does the author get you to think about this?
2. Do any particular feelings come across in this story? Does the story actually make you feel in a certain way or does it make you

think about what it's like to feel that way? How does the author do this?

3. Is there one character that you know more about than any of the others? Who is this character and what kind of person is he/she? How does the author reveal the character to you? What words would you use to describe the main character's feelings in this book?

4. Are there other characters important to the story? Who are they? Why are they important?

5. Is there anything that seems to make this particular author's work unique? If so, what?

6. Did you notice any particular patterns in the form of this book? If you are reading this book in more than one sitting, are there natural points at which to break off your reading? If so, what are these?

7. Were there any clues that the author built into the story that helped you to anticipate the outcome? If so, what were they? Did you think these clues were important when you read them?

8. Does the story language seem natural for the intent of the story and for the various speakers?

9. Every writer creates a make-believe work and peoples it with characters. Even where the world is far different from your own, how does the author make the story seem possible or probable?

10. What questions would you ask if the author were here? Which would be the most important question? How might the author answer it?

## APPENDIX B: LITERATURE TO EXPLORE
## (LITERATURE CIRCLES)

### Picture Books

Aardema, V. 1975. *Why mosquitoes buzz in people's ears*. New York: Dial.

Anderson, H. C. 1979. *The ugly duckling*. New York: Harcourt Brace Jovanovich.

Bulla, R. 1955. *The poppy seeds*. New York: Crowell.

Carle, E. 1977. *The grouchy ladybug*. New York: Crowell.

Carrick, C. 1976. *The accident*. New York: Clarion.

Cooney, B. 1982. *Miss Rumphius*. New York: Viking.

de Paola, T. 1978. *The clown of God*. New York: Harcourt Brace Jovanovich.

Freschet, B. 1973. *Bear mouse*. New York: Scribner.

Galdone, P. 1970. *The three little pigs*. New York: Clarion.

Hazen, B. 1979. *Tight times*. New York: Viking.

Hodges, M. 1984. *Saint George and the dragon*. Boston: Little, Brown.

Innocenti, R. 1985. *Rose Blanche*. Mankato, MN: Creative Education.

Keats, E. J. 1967. *Peter's chair*. New York: Harper & Row.

————. 1968. *A letter to Amy*. New York: Harper & Row.

Lionni, L. 1963. *Swimmy*. New York: Pantheon.

————. 1967. *Frederick*. New York: Pantheon.

Lobel, A. 1967. *Potatoes, potatoes*. New York: Harper & Row.

————. 1972. *Frog and toad together*. New York: Harper & Row.

————. 1982. *Ming Lo moves the mountain*. New York: Greenwillow.

Luenn, N. 1982. *The dragon kite*. New York: Harcourt Brace Jovanovich.

Maruki, T. 1980. *Hiroshima no pika*. New York: Lothrop, Lee, and Shepard.

Mayer, M. 1968. *There's a nightmare in my closet*. New York: Dial.

————. 1976. *Everyone knows what a dragon looks like*. New York: Four Winds.

Miles, M. 1979. *Annie and the old one*. Boston: Little, Brown.

Ness, E. 1967. *Sam, bangs and moonshine*. New York: Holt, Rinehart & Winston.

Perrault, C. 1954. *Cinderella*. Illustrated by M. Brown. New York: Scribner.

Sendak, M. 1963. *Where the wild things are*. New York: Harper & Row.

————. 1981. *Outside over there*. New York: Harper & Row.

Spier, P. 1977. *Noah's ark*. Garden City, NY: Doubleday.

Steig, W. 1977. *Caleb and Kate*. New York: Farrar Straus Giroux.

————. 1979. *Sylvester and the magic pebble*. New York: Windmill.

Steptoe, J. 1969. *Stevie*. New York: Harper & Row.

————. 1984. *The story of the jumping mouse*. New York: Lothrop, Lee, and Shepard.

Van Allsburg, C. 1981. *Jumanji*. Boston: Houghton Mifflin.

————. 1984. *The mysteries of Harris Burdick*. Boston: Houghton Mifflin.

Waber, B. 1972. *Ira sleeps over*. Boston: Houghton Mifflin.

Ward, L. 1952. *The biggest bear*. Boston: Hougton Mifflin.

Wilde, O. 1984. *The selfish giant*. Natick, MA: Picture Book Studio.

Yashima, T. 1955. *Crow boy*. New York: Viking.

Yolen, J. 1977. *The seeing stick*. New York: Crowell.

Zolotow, C. 1972. *William wants a doll*. New York: Harper & Row.

**Chapter Books**

Alexander, L. 1965. *The black cauldron*. New York: Holt, Rinehart & Winston (Also other Prydain Books).

————. 1981. *Westmark*. New York: Dutton.

Armstrong, W. 1969. *Sounder*. New York: Harper & Row.

Babbit, N. 1975. *Tuck everlasting*. New York: Farrar Straus Giroux.

Banks, L. R. 1981. *The Indian in the cupboard*. Garden City, NY: Doubleday.

Bishop, C. 1964. *Twenty and ten*. New York: Viking.

Burnett, F. [1910] 1962. *The secret garden*. New York: Lippincott.

Byars, B. 1970. *Summer of the swans*. New York: Viking.

————. 1977. *The pinballs*. New York: Harper & Row.

Cleary, B. 1983. *Dear Mr. Henshaw*. New York: Morrow.

Collier, J., & Collier, C. 1974. *My brother Sam is dead*. New York: Four Winds.

Coerr, E. 1977. *Sadako and the thousand paper cranes*. New York: Putnam.

Estes, E. 1944. *The hundred dresses*. New York: Harcourt Brace World.

Fox, P. 1984. *One-eyed cat*. New York: Bradbury.

Fritz, J. 1982. *Homesick: My own story*. New York: Putnam.

George, J. 1972. *Julie of the wolves*. New York: Harper & Row.

Hunter, M. 1975. *A stranger came ashore*. New York: Harper & Row

Juster, N. 1961. *The phantom tollbooth*. New York: Random House.

L'Engle, M. 1962. *Wrinkle in time*. New York: Farrar Straus Giroux.

————. 1981. *Ring of endless night*. New York: Farrar Straus Giroux.

LeGuin, U. 1968. *Wizard of Earthsea*. Emeryville, CA: Parnassus.

Lewis, C. S. 1961. *The lion, the witch, and the wardrobe*. New York: Macmillan.

Lowry, L. 1977. *A summer to die*. Boston: Houhgton Mifflin.

MacLachlan, P. 1985. *Sarah plain and tall*. New York: Harper & Row.

————. *Seven kisses in a row*. New York: Harper & Row.

McKinley, R. 1978. *Beauty*. New York: Harper & Row.

————. 1982. *The blue sword*. New York: Greenwillow.

O'Brien, R. 1971. *Mrs. Frisby and the rats of NIMH*. New York: Atheneum.

O'Dell, S. 1960. *Island of the blue dolphins*. Boston: Houghton Mifflin.

————. 1970. *Sing down the moon*. Boston: Houghton Mifflin.

Paterson, K. 1977. *Bridge to Terabithia*. New York: Crowell.

————. 1978. *The great Gilly Hopkins*. New York: Crowell.

————. 1980. *Jacob have I loved*. New York: Crowell.

Raskin, E. 1978. *The Westing game*. New York: Dutton.

Rawls, W. 1961. *Where the red fern grows*. Garden City, NY: Doubleday.

Rylant, C. 1986. *Every living thing*, New York: Bradbury.

Smith, D. B. 1973. *A taste of blackberries*. New York: Crowell.

————. 1975. *Kelly's creek*. New York: Crowell.

Smith, R. 1984. *The war with grandpa*. New York: Delacorte.

Speare, E. 1983. *Sign of the beaver*. Boston: Houghton Mifflin.

Taylor, M. 1976. *Roll of thunder, hear my cry*. New York: Dial.

————. 1981. *Let the circle be unbroken*. New York: Dial.

————. 1987. *The gold cadillac*. New York: Dial.

Taylor, T. 1969. *The cay*. Garden City, NY: Doubleday.

————. 1981. *The trouble with Tuck*. Garden City, NY: Doubleday.

Voight, C. 1982. *Dicey's song*. New York: Atheneum.

————. 1984. *Solitary blue*. New York: Atheneum.

————. 1987. *Comes a stranger*. New York: Atheneum.

Yolen, J. 1974. *The girl who cried flowers*. New York: Schocken.

————. 1977. *The hundredth dove*. New York: Schocken.

**Poetry**

Greenfield, E. 1978. *Honey, I love*. New York: Crowell.

Livingston, M. 1958. *Whispers and other poems*. New York: Harcourt Brace World.

McCord, D. 1977. *One at a time*. Boston: Little, Brown.

Merriam, E. 1984. *Jamboree*. New York: Dell.

————. 1986. *A sky full of poems*. New York: Dell.

Prelutsky, J. 1984. *The new kid on the block*. New York: Greenwillow.

**REFERENCES**

The concept of Literature Circles was developed by Kathy Short and Gloria Kauffman, based on Karen Smith's work with literature studies. Their initial exploration of this curricular therapy is discussed in:

Short, K. G. 1986. *Literacy as a collaborative experience*. Ph.D. diss., Indiana University, Bloomington.

Other references pertaining to Literature Circles include:

Barnes, D. 1975. *From communication to curriculum*. Portsmouth, NH: Boynton/Cook.

Calkins, L. M. 1986. *The art of teaching writing*, chapters 22–24. Portsmouth, NH: Heinemann.

Hepler, S. I. 1982. *Patterns of response to literature: A one-year study of a fifth- and sixth-grade classroom*. Ph.D. diss., Ohio State University, Columbus.

Huck, C. 1977. Literature as the content of reading. *Theory into Practice* 16 (5): 363–371.

Sloan, G. 1984. *The child as critic*. 2nd ed. New York: Teachers College Press.

Vandergrift, K. 1980. *Child and story*. New York: Neal-Schuman.

The following books contain suggestions for Literature Response Activities:

Coody, B. 1983. *Using literature with young children*. 3d ed. Dubuque, IA: William C. Brown.

Cullinan, B., ed. 1987. *Children's literature in the reading program*. Newark, DE: International Reading Association.

Moss, J. 1984. *Focus units in literature*. Urbana, IL: National Council of Teachers of English.

Somers, A., & Worthington, J. 1979. *Response guides for teaching children's books*. Urbana, IL: National Council of Teachers of English.

Whitehead, R. 1968. *Children's literature: Strategies of teaching*. Englewood Cliffs, NJ: Prentice-Hall.

# student journals

TOBY FULWILER

# 21

Journal writing introduces students to expressive writing easily and systematically. In 1967, when I began teaching college English, I assigned journals in composition and literature courses, but used them sparingly in the classroom, preferring students to write on their own. Some students used them well, while most never really understood what kind of writing they were supposed to do in them. I no longer trust to chance; journals work now for most of my students because I use them actively every day to write in, read from, and talk about — in addition to whatever private writing the students do on their own. These everyday journal-writes replace other routine writing assignments, from pop quizzes to book reports. Journal writing in class stimulates classroom discussion, starts small group activity, clarifies hazy issues, reinforces learning, and stimulates imaginations.

Journal writing works because with every entry instruction is individualized; the act of silent writing, even for a few minutes, generates ideas, observations, emotions. It's hard to daydream, doze off, or fidget while one writes. Journal writing won't make passive students miraculously active learners; it does, however, make it harder for students to remain passive.

Teachers in all subject areas and grade levels find it easy to increase class writing by using journals. Regardless of class size, this kind of informal writing need not take more teacher time; journals can be spot checked, skimmed, read thoroughly, or not read at all, depending on the teacher's interest and purpose. Journals have proved to be remarkably flexible documents; some teachers call them "logs," others "commonplace books" or "day books," still others "idea notebooks." While I prefer students to keep looseleaf binders, science teachers (conscious of patent rights) often require bound notebooks. While I suggest pens (pencils smear), a forestry teacher suggests pencils (ink smears in the rain). And so on.

Reprinted with permission from *Teaching with Writing* by Toby Fulwiler. Copyright © 1987 by Boynton/Cook Publishers, Inc.

## ACADEMIC JOURNALS

What does a journal look like? How often should people write in them? What kinds of writing should they do on their own? How should I grade them? These questions often occur to the teacher who has not used or kept journals before. Following are some possible answers.

Journals might be looked at as part diary and part class notebook: while diaries record the private thought and experience of the writer, class notebooks record the public thought and presentation of the teacher. The journal is somewhere between the two. Like the diary, the journal is written in the first person about ideas important to the writer; like the class notebook, the journal may focus on academic subjects the writer wishes to examine.

*Diary* ————————→ Journal ←———————— *Class notebook*
*(Subjective expression)*      (I/it)          *(Objective topics)*

Journals may be focused narrowly on the subject matter of one discipline, or broadly on the whole range of a person's academic and personal experience. Each journal entry is a deliberate exercise in expansion: "How far can I take this idea? How accurately can I describe or explain it? How can I make it make sense to me?" The journal encourages writers to become conscious, through language, of what is happening to them, both personally and academically.

Student writers should be encouraged to experiment with their journals, to write often and regularly on a wide variety of topics, to take some risks with form, style, and voice. Students should notice how writing in the early morning differs from writing late at night. They might also experience how writing at the same time every day, regardless of inclination or mood, often produces surprising results. Above all else, journals are places where students can try out their expressive voices freely, without fear of evaluation. Students can write about academic problems and progress to sort out where they are, how they're doing and perhaps discuss what to do next. Teachers can ask students to engage in certain kinds of speculation in their journals and so plant seeds for class discussion and more formal writing projects.

## JOURNAL ASSIGNMENTS

Journals record each student's personal, individual travel through the academic world and also serve as springboards for formal writing assignments; they generate life and independent thought in a some-times over-formal classroom atmosphere. *Any* assignment can be made richer by adding a written dimension which encourages personal reflection and observation. Field notes jotted in a biology notebook become an extended observation written in a biology journal; this entry, in turn, might well become the basis for a major research project. Personal reflections recorded in a history journal can help the student identify with, and perhaps make sense of, the otherwise distant and confusing past. Trial hypotheses might find first articulation in social science journals; continued writing about strong ideas can develop those ideas into full-fledged research designs and experiments. The suggestions which follow might be useful in some of your classes:

## Starting Class

Introduce a class with a five-minute journal-write. Any class. Any subject. In a discussion class, suggest a topic related to the day's lesson (a quote from the reading assignment, for instance), and allow those first few minutes for students to compose (literally) their thoughts and focus them in a public direction; without that time, the initial discussion is often halting and groping. After such a journal entry, the teacher may ask someone to read an entry aloud to start people talking. It is hard sometimes to read rapidly written words in public, but also rewarding when the language generates a response from classmates. I often read my own entry first to put students at ease, for my sentences may be awkward, halting, and fragmentary just as theirs sometimes are. Repeated periodically, this exercise provides students with a structured oral entry into the difficult public arena of the classroom and helps affirm the value of their personal voice.

Like the discussion class, the lecture also benefits from a transition exercise which starts students thinking about the scheduled topic. For example, prior to beginning a lecture in a nineteenth-century American literature class studying Transcendentalism, I often ask students to define their concept of romanticism in their journals. I might then commence lecturing directly, using the brief writing time to set the scene or mood for the lecture; or I might start a short discussion based on the student writing as a lead into the lecture. Either way, the students involve themselves with the material because they have committed themselves, through their own language, to at least a tentative exploration of an idea.

## Summarizing

End a class with a journal-write. This exercise asks students to summarize information or ideas they have learned during class. The summary entry serves several purposes: to find out what, if anything was learned today, and to find out what questions are still unanswered. These issues can be handled orally, of course, without a journal, but writing loose thoughts onto paper often generates tighter thinking. And again, private writing in a noisy, busy public forum allows the learner to collect thoughts otherwise lost in the push-and-shove hurry to leave class. Too often instructors lecture right to the bell, still trying to make one last point, while at the same time realizing by the rustle in the room that the students are already mentally on their way to lunch. Better, perhaps, to cover less lecture territory and to end class with students' own observations and summary in journals. That final act of writing/thinking helps students synthesize material for themselves and so increases its value.

Gary Johnson (1981), a teacher in the Fine Arts Department of Northern Kentucky University, uses journals at summary points in his music appreciation class. In describing how journals help his music students, Johnson makes a good case for students in all subject areas:

*In Music Appreciation, I found students were able to remember material presented in a lecture format if I assigned a timed write at the conclusion of an important articulation point in the lecture. In reading student-writes, it became evident that they were going far beyond the "lesson summary" use of the journal. The journal-write itself seemed to be an aid to comprehension. Students would often begin with "I really don't understand (such and such)" then, at some point, add, "I guess it means that . . ." or "It has something to do with . . ." Then the writes tended to step logically through the subject, ending with either a well-defined question for the instructor, or a comment that took the subject one step beyond the lecture. The journal-write seemed to force students to think through a topic and synthesize discrete facts into a logical framework for retention.*

Teachers may also ask their students to summarize a given unit in a course, or the meaning of the whole course itself. Following is a journal entry written by a student at the end of a college American literature class:

*I suppose this will be the last entry I make in this journal, so I would like to sort of use this time to sum up my thoughts I have up to this point. So far, at least the first two authors we have to read have led tragic, unhappy lives. I wonder if this is just a coincidence or if it has something to do with the personality of a successful writer. I feel that through the use of this journal over the weeks I have been able better to understand certain aspects of each story by actually writing down what's bothering me, what I like, and what I don't. A lot of thought has gone into the past pages, and that thought has really contributed to making the class better. Many times I didn't even realize that something bothered me about a story until I put down my feelings in words. I wasn't even sure how I even felt about The Sun Also Rises until I kicked a few ideas around on paper. In short, this journal has been a useful tool in my understanding and appreciating this class.*

[TOM K.]

Even as he writes about the value of the journal, Tom shows us his speculative personal style with phrases like "I suppose" and "I wonder." Reviewing his journal, the writer notes that his written observations about "what's bothering me" have helped him see larger patterns. The very structure of the journal — sequential, chronological, personal — provides the material from which generalizations and hypotheses can be made. The journal leads this student to wonder about the relationship between good writing and "tragic, unhappy lives." In this manner, each individual act of summary is potentially a discovery.

**Focusing**

Structure a class through a journal-write. Plan a five-minute writing task in the midst of the 50-minute class to give focus to an idea or problem. Listening becomes passive and notetaking often mechanical; even the best students drift into daydreams from time to time. A journal-write gives students a chance to re-engage themselves personally with the class topic. Writing changes the pace of the class; it shifts the learners into a participant role and sometimes forces clarity from confusion simply by demanding that pen be put to paper. Writing clears out a little space for students to interact with the ideas thrown at them and allows them to focus problems while the stimulus is still fresh. "Reflect on the notion that Karl Marx is a philosopher rather than a scientist," or "Explain the phrase 'How do I know what I think until I see what I say?' in your own language and make sense of it." If planned in advance, these pauses can be both welcome breaks and fruitful exercises.

In the middle of a class studying "scientific and technical writing," I discovered a number of students who questioned the idea that even technical writing was persuasive, depending on how facts and information were presented, phrased or formatted. I gave the class an impromptu journal assignment, asking them to write for five minutes on the thesis that "all writing is persuasive." Following is a sample response:

*"All Writing is Persuasive"—It's hard to write on my understanding of this quote because I don't think that all writing is persuasive. What about assemblies for models and cookbook recipes. I realize that for stories, newspaper articles, novels and so forth that they are persuasive. But is all writing persuasive? I imagine that for assemblies and so forth that they are persuading a person to do something a particular way. But is this really persuasive writing?*

*[JIM S.]*

By writing about their understanding of this idea, rather than just arguing back and forth in class, students were forced into a deeper, more thoughtful consideration of the proposition. Writing allowed them to test the idea in private, in conversations with themselves, and so made the ensuing public discussion more careful. This student, for example, begins by writing, "I don't think that all writing is persuasive," and concludes by recognizing that even in assembly instructions "they are persuading a person to do something a particular way." The writing has sharpened the focus of the learning.

A variation on the planned writing pause is the spontaneous one, where the teacher senses misunderstanding in the audience or where the teacher even loses track of an idea. While writing in journals, both teachers and students may refocus the problem and so make the next 15 or 20 minutes more profitable.

A digressive or rambling discussion may be refocused by simply calling time out and asking students to write for a few minutes in their journals: "What are we trying to explain?" or "Restate the argument in your own words; then let's start again." Pauses in a discussion change the class pace and allow quiet, personal reflection. Teachers can all use a little time out in some classes, yet seldom find a pedagogical justification for it. The journal-write is a good solution. In one-sided discussions, where a few students dominate and others can't participate, interrupt with a short writing task and sometimes the situation reverses itself, as the quiet ones find their voices while the loud ones cool off. The group also can become more conscious of the roles people play in class by asking questions like: "What is your part in this discussion?" or "Try to trace how we got from molecules to men in the last 15 minutes," or "Why do you think Sarah just said what she did?" Writing about talking provides distance and helps generate thoughts we didn't have before.

## Problem Solving

Use journals as a vehicle for posing and solving problems. In a class on modern literature, ask students to write about the lines in an E. E. Cummings poem which they don't understand; the following day many students will have written their way to understanding by forcing their confusion into sentences. What better way to make sense out of "what if a much of a which of a wind" or "my father moved through dooms of love"? Math or science teachers might ask their students to solve difficult equations by using j-writes when they are confused. For example, Margaret Watson (1980), a high school teacher from Oklahoma, reports that using journals in her mathematics classes has improved her students' ability to solve math problems. She asks students questions such as: "The problem I had completing a square was . . ." and "This is how to . . ." Watson reads the journals and comments to each student individually about his or her feelings about mathematics: "This two-way conversation has been beneficial to the class. The students realize I hear them and care. They seem to have looked inside themselves and to have seen what they could do to help their mathematical problems. Many of their grades improved."

The journal could become a regular tool in any subject area to assist students in solving problems since the act of writing out the problem is, itself, a clarifying experience. Switching from number symbols to word symbols sometimes makes a difference; putting someone else's problem into your own language makes it *your* problem and so leads you one step further toward solution. The key, in other words, is articulating to yourself what the problem is and what you might do about it. Following is a brief example of a student talking to himself about a writing block:

*I'm making this report a hell of a lot harder than it should be. I think my problem is I try to edit as I write. I think what I need to do is first get a basic outline of what I want to write then just write whatever I want. After I'm through, then edit and organize. It's hard for me though.*

*[BRUCE M.]*

### Responding

Use journals to sharpen student responses to their academic experience. Class discussions, teacher questions, books, movies, TV and music all provide material to be written about. Using the journal as the place to write their reactions to class material asks the students to go one step beyond vaguely thinking about their responses—but stays short of making a formal written assignment which might cause unproductive anxiety over form or style. In some disciplines, like engineering, math, or physics, such questions might be less "open-ended" than ones asked in liberal arts courses, but even in the most specialized fields some free, imaginative speculation helps—and when that speculation is recorded in the journal, students have a record to look at later to show where they've been and perhaps suggest where to go next.

Science and social science teachers might ask students to keep a "lab journal" in addition to a lab notebook to record responses to their experiments. This adds a personal dimension to keeping records and also provides a place to make connections between one observation and the next. Perhaps journal entries should be interleafed next to the recorded data. The same may be done with a "field notebook" in biology or forestry: to the objective data add each student's own thoughts about that data. Such personal observations might prove useful in writing a report or suggest the germ for another paper or project.

A college political science professor uses journals for a variety of homework assignments in his course, American Government and Politics. He asks students to record frequently their opinions about current events; he also requests them to write short personal summaries of articles in their journals, thereby creating a sequential critical record of readings accomplished during the term. While both of these activities may be conducted through other written forms, using the journal is simple and economical for both students and teacher. In like manner, a high school teacher of remedial English asks his students to practice writing about movies he shows in class. The following entry was written in response to a science fiction film:

*The movie was pretty good. It's weird how they could make a human out of that stuff and say they're a Robot. If people could change color I sure as hell wouldn't want to change. The movie was pretty shocking to me. I hope it really doesn't happen in the future. I really don't know how people could plug themselves in just to wake up, that's pretty dumb. It would be pretty decent to see Robots looking just like all of us though.*

*[ANDREW M.]*

This entry has the characteristic misspellings and awkward punctuation of a remedial tenth-grade writer; it also reveals some interesting thoughts which could contribute to both class discussion and a future writing assignment. Here we have material to talk and write about further; the act of writing the response to the movie preserved and maybe even generated the thought.

In addition to responding to readings and movies, journals prove useful for highly subjective experiences such as listening to music. One of music teacher Gary Johnson's (1981) students, a physical education major, put it this way:

*There are times, when listening to a piece of music, that it "does something" to you. Music plays on your emotions. Many times it's difficult to interpret your emotions. It seems the easiest way would be writing them down.*

*I find it helpful — because sometimes a work is so good (or so bad) — you have to get it out of your system. I also find journal writes helpful when I study for a test. At that moment you do a write you have more insight into it than you will a week later. A week later you may understand it better — but you won't have the initial insight you did at first.*

[SHARON L.]

Another music teacher asked her students to keep "listening journals" to record their daily experience of hearing music. Periodically, she conducted discussion classes which relied heavily on the subjective content of the journals and so involved the students both personally and critically in her course content. In similar fashion, a drama teacher currently asks his actors to keep a journal to develop more fully their awareness of a character or scene. He has found that his student actors work their way into their characters by writing out responses to various scenes, dialogues and dramatic events within the play.

**Progress Reports**

Use journals to monitor student progress through the class. Richard Heckel, a Michigan Tech metallurgy professor, has prepared a full-page handout with suggestions to students about using journals in Introduction to Materials Science. He uses journals to encourage thoughtful reflection upon important topics, to practice writing answers to possible exam questions, and to improve writing fluency. Specifically, he asks students to write about each day's lecture topic prior to attending class; after class, they are asked to write a summary or write questions about the lecture. Periodically, these journals are checked to monitor student progress through the course, but they are not graded. Heckel also monitors his own teaching through journals. In reading his first batch of 100 journals, he was surprised to discover few charts, diagrams or drawings among the student writing. Believing that metallurgical engineers must develop visualization skills to a high degree, he introduced a unit on visual thinking into his course. Here the journal indicated to him what was missing in the thinking processes of his students and so changed a part of his pedagogical approach.

Robert Stinson (1980), geography professor at Michigan Tech, has used journals for 10 years in large lecture classes. In Recreational Geography, he asks students to keep journals to stimulate their powers of observation. By requiring students to write down what they see, he finds that they look more closely and carefully and, hence, begin to acquire the rudimentary techniques of scientific observation. He also requires students in Conservation to keep journals; specifically, at the beginning of new course topics, he asks them to write definitions of terms or concepts which they misuse or misunderstand. At the conclusion of each topic, he requests another written definition to compare how their initial perceptions have changed. During the final week of the 10-week course, he asks students to compose an essay about their attitude changes toward conservation as a result of the course. The journal is the primary resource for this last assignment, revealing to both instructor and student what has been learned, what not.

I often ask students to make informal progress reports to themselves about what they are learning in class. I'm interested in having students share these thoughts with me and/or the class — volunteers often read passages aloud after such an assignment. But more important, I think, are the observations students make to themselves about what they are learning. My question is the catalyst, but the insights are only of real value if they are self-initiated. Following is a sample response from a student studying technical writing; he refers to an exercise in which the entire class "agreed" that one piece of writing was better than another:

*After, we took a vote and decided which proposal letter we liked the best — it really made me wonder. I hadn't realized it but we've been conditioned to look for certain things in this class. I guess that's the purpose of any class, strange how you don't notice it happening though.*

[ARNOLD S.]

## Class Texts

Ask students to write to each other, informally, about concerns and questions raised in the class. By reading passages aloud, or reproducing passages to share with the class, students become more conscious of how their language affects people. First-year humanities students actually suggested that duplicated journal passages should become a part of the humanistic content of the course; we mimeographed selected journal entries, shared them for a week and all learned more about each other. Passing these journal-writes around class suggested new writing possibilities to the students; in this case, the stimulus to experiment came from classmates rather than teacher and so had the strong validity of peer education.

An entry such as the following, written about a geography class, can go a long way toward provoking classmates into a discussion of topical issues:

*I don't know if I'm just over-reacting to my Conservation class or not, but lately I've become suspicious of the air, water, and food around me. First we're taught about water pollution, and I find out that the Portage Canal merrily flowing right in front of my house is unfit for human contact because of the sewage treatment plant and how it overflows with every hard rain. Worse yet, I'm told raw sewage flows next to Bridge Street. I used to admire Douglas Houghton Falls for its natural beauty, now all I think of is, "That's raw untreated sewage flowing there."*

*Our next topic was air pollution. Today I was informed that the rain here in the U.P. has acid levels ten times what it should, thanks to sulfur oxide pollution originating in Minneapolis and Duluth. I'm quite familiar back home in Ishpeming with orange birch trees due to iron ore pelletizing plants.*

*Is there any escaping this all encompassing wave of pollution? I had thought the Copper Country was a refuge from the poisonous fact of pollution, but I guess its not just Detroit's problem anymore. As I write these words, in countless places around the globe, old Mother Nature is being raped in the foulest way. I get the feeling someday she'll retaliate and we'll deserve it. Every bit of it.*

*[BILL W.]*

An additional note about this entry: notice the number of references to local places (Portage Canal, Bridge Street, Douglas Houghton Falls); Bill doesn't bother to explain or identify these references because his writing is aimed at an audience familiar with the area about which he writes. Initially he writes to himself, but if he chooses later to share an entry with classmates, he can assume that they know the local areas as well as he does. Journal writing is characterized by this limited, closed context, in which the writer assumes his writing will not go far from his own person. To shape this piece for a larger audience would require explaining that these geographic sites are in and around Houghton, Michigan in the Upper Peninsula, etc. A beneficial corollary of writing to a limited audience is more frank, honest, and vulnerable writing; Bill trusts that this writing won't see large circulation and so feels freer to say more, take some risks, and write about what's really on his mind.

### Records of Intellectual Growth

Journals have a signal value in preserving early thought and, at the same time, encouraging that thought to develop and change as the writer develops and changes. Consider the following fragments from Joan's journal, which show her progress through a summer course, Introduction to Philosophy. Joan, a senior, was required by her instructor to keep a journal and record her reactions to the class and to new ideas that she encountered during this five-week course. Here is an entry from early in her first week of class:

*This philosophy stuff is weird! Hard to conceptualize. You try to explain it to someone and just can't. Like taking 3 pages of the book to decide whether or not a bookcase is there. Someone asked me if you really learn anything from it. I didn't think so but I finally had to say yes. I really never realized how we speak without really knowing (??!) what we are saying. Like I told her, the class is interesting and time goes by fast in it but you have to concentrate and sort of "shift" your mind when you are in class. You have to really think and work hard at keeping everything tied in together—it's like a chain where you have to retain one thing to get the next. I also told her that if you really do think and concentrate you begin to agree with this guy on skepticism, etc. and that's really scary—you think at the end of that book will be this little paragraph saying how everything really does exist as we see it and we really do "know" things, they were just kidding!*

At the beginning she wonders about the nature of her new course of study: "weird." She encounters Descartes for the first time and openly explores her thoughts on paper, hoping that his ideas are essentially a joke and that Descartes is "just kidding." Near the end of the course a month later, after much debate in her journal about her religious beliefs, she writes:

*You know, as the term is coming to a close I am tempted to sit back and think if I really mastered any skills in philosophy. Sometimes when I come up with arguments for something I feel like I am just talking in circles. Or "begging the question" as it's been put. One thing I can say is that Philosophy has made somewhat of a skeptic out of me. We are presented with so many things that we take for granted as being there and being right—we were shown evidence and proofs that maybe they really aren't there and aren't true. You know, I still feel like I did the first entry I put in this journal—maybe the last day of class you will say—"I was just kidding about all this stuff—the world really is as you imagine it—there are material things, God does exist with evil, etc." But I realize these arguments are valid and do have their points—they are just points we never considered. I can see I will not take much more for granted anymore—I will try to form an argument in my mind (not brain!).*

At this point we see her reflecting on her course of study, on her journal, and on how she has possibly changed. Joan remains a Christian—a belief she has asserted several times in her journal—but she now also calls herself "somewhat of a skeptic," as she writes about her own changing perceptions. Again, this is informal writing, not meant to be graded—or necessarily ever read by someone else. But the journal writing assignment encourages her to explore and develop her ideas by forcing her still-liquid thought into concrete language.

Joan's final entry, a few days later, reflects on the value of this expressive assignment:

*Before I hand this in, I have to write a short blurb on what I thought of this journal idea. I have to admit, at first I wasn't too fired up about it—I thought "what I am going to find to write about?" The first few*

*entries were hard to write. But, as time went on I grew to enjoy it*
*more and more. I actually found out some things about myself too.*
*Anyway I did enjoy this and feel I like would be giving up a good*
*friend if I quit writing in it!*

*The*
*End*
*(for now!)*

Personal writing, in other words, can help students individualize and
expand their learning by encouraging them to force the shadows in
their mind—as Vygotsky says—into articulate thought. Art Young
(1983), in studying both expressive and poetic writing, argues that
such writing not only encourages students to learn about certain
subjects and express themselves, but also that it gives them the time
"to assess values in relation to the material they are studying."
Certainly we witness our philosophy student using her journal to
mediate between her personal values when she enrolled in class and
the somewhat different ones presented by the professor during the
course. The key, of course, is that the journal provides for the capture
of these shifting, sometimes colliding, continually developing thoughts.
Other academic documents dwell primarily on final, finished versions
of thought and do not reveal the process by which these final thoughts
were achieved.

## READING AND EVALUATING STUDENT JOURNALS

Reading student journals keeps teachers in touch with student
experiences—frustrations, anxieties, problems, joys, excitements.
Teachers who understand the everyday realities—both mental and
physical—of student life can be better teachers because they can
tailor assignments and tests more precisely to student needs. In other
words, reading student journals humanizes teachers.

Some teachers insist on not reading student journals, arguing they
have no right to pry in these private academic documents. It is a
good point. However, there are important reasons why the teacher
ought to look at the journals—and precautions which can eliminate
prying. First, for students just beginning to keep journals, a reading
by a teacher can help them to expand their journals and make them
more useful. Sometimes first journals have too many short entries; a
teacher who notices this can suggest trying full-page exercises to
allow writers more space to develop an idea. Second, some students
believe that if an assignment isn't seen by a teacher, it has no worth.
Thus, the teacher may decide at the outset that looking at the journals
will add needed credibility to the assignment. Third, students feel
that journals must "count for something," as must every requirement
in a high school or college setting. And, "If teachers don't look at
these things, how can they count 'em?"

One way to count a journal as part of the student's grade is to
count pages. Some teachers grade according to the quantity of writing:

100 pages equals an 'A'; 75 a 'B'; 50 a 'C'; etc. Other teachers attempt to grade on the quality of insight or evidence of personal growth. Still other teachers prefer a credit/no credit arrangement: to complete the requirements for the course, students must show evidence that they have kept a journal. Teachers need only see that pages of journal writing exist; they don't need to read the entries. While fair, this method precludes the teacher from learning through students' writing.

To resolve this apparent paradox between the students' need for a private place to write and the benefit to both student and teacher from a public reading, I ask students to keep their journals in a looseleaf format and to provide cardboard dividers to separate sections of the journal. Thus, I am able to look at sections dealing with my course, but not to see sections more personal or concerned with other courses. And if portions of the student's commentary about a particular class would prove embarrassing, the looseleaf allows removal of that entry prior to my perusal. I may ask for the pages concerning American literature, for example, skim them quickly, and hand them back with suggestions only for those students who aren't gaining much from the experience. At the end of the course, I may check the journals again and assign a credit/no credit mark. Or I may raise student grades for good journals (lots of writing) but not penalize students for mediocre ones. Such informal evaluation doesn't take much time, but the benefits to both students and teacher are obvious.

Near the end of the term, I usually ask students to prepare their journals for a "public" reading, to delete any entries too personal to share, and then to add page numbers, a table of contents for major entries, and an introduction. Finally, students write an entry in which they formally evaluate their own journal: "Which entries make the greatest impact on you now? Which seem least worthwhile? What patterns do you find from entry to entry?" For some students, this proves to be the clarifying activity of the term, the action which finally defines the journals. In other words, students use their journals to reflect on the value of journals. For many, this informal, non-graded writing is a new and pleasant experience. In the words of one student:

*The journal to me has been like a one-man debate, where I could write thoughts down and then later read them, this seemed to help clarify many of my ideas. To be honest there is probably fifty percent of the journal that is nothing but B.S. and ramblings to fulfill assignments, but, that still leaves fifty percent that I think is of importance. The journal is also a time capsule. I want to put it away and not look at it for ten or twenty years and let it recall for me this period of my life. In the journal are many other things besides the writings, such as drawings and pages from this years calendar. It is like a picture of this period of my life. When I continue writing a journal it will be of another portion of my life.*

*[KEN M.]*

## TEACHER JOURNALS

Teachers who have not done so should try keeping a journal along with their students. Journals don't work for everyone; however, the experience of keeping one may be the only way to find out. Teachers, especially, can profit from the regular introspection and self-examination forced by the process of journal writing. The journal allows sequential planning within the context of a course. Its pages become a record of what has worked, what hasn't, and suggestions for what might work next time. Teachers can use journals for lesson plans, to work out practice exercises, and to conduct an on-going class evaluation. The journal may become a teaching workshop and a catalyst to generate new research ideas as well as a record of pedagogical growth.

Teachers should consider writing daily, in class, along with their students. Teachers who write with their students and read entries aloud lend credibility to the assignments. Doing the writing also tests the validity of the writing task; if the instructor has a hard time with a given topic, it provides an insight into the difficulties students may encounter and so makes for a better assignment next time.

The journal provides an easy means to evaluate each class session; the journal is not the only way to do this, of course, but it proves a handy place to keep these records, alongside the planning sessions and the in-class journal writes. One of my own entries, for example, written 10 minutes after class, reads like this:

*Class went well today—but much slower than I expected. I worked on "paper topics" with people—first privately in their journals, next in small groups, finally on the blackboard for the whole class to talk about. All were too broad and general—so I asked people to rewrite and redefine and refocus—in fact, I badgered people out loud to limit their topics. Badgered too much?*

Jottings like this may help teachers understand better their own teaching process and sometimes result in useful insights about what should or shouldn't have been done. These evaluations also act as prefaces for the next planning session, pointing toward more structure or less. And when a class, for one reason or another, has been a complete failure, writing about it can be therapeutic; I try, at least, to objectify what went wrong and so create the illusion of being able to control it the next time.

Journals are interdisciplinary and developmental by nature; it would be hard for writers who use them regularly and seriously not to witness growth. Journals belong at the heart of any writing-across-the-cirriculum program. They promote self-examination on the one hand and speculation about ideas on the other; as such, they are as valuable to teachers in the hard sciences as to those in the humanities. To be effective, however, journal use in one class should be reinforced by similar use in another class. Of course, for teachers in some disciplines the personal nature of journals may be of secondary importance, with the primary focus remaining the student's grasp of specialized knowledge. However, the importance of coupling personal with academic learning should not be overlooked; self-knowledge provides the motivation for whatever other knowledge an individual learns and absorbs. Without an understanding of who we are, we are not likely to understand fully why we study biology rather than forestry, literature rather than philosophy. In the end, all knowledge *is* related; the journal helps clarify the relationships.

## WORKSHOP ACTIVITIES

### Pre-Chapter Journal Writing

Write for five minutes about one of the following topics:

1. What are your prior associations with journals? Do you keep one? Have you ever kept one? Do you know someone who has or does? Have you ever assigned one to students? With what results?
2. Can you imagine any reasons why students might benefit from keeping a journal in your subject area?
3. What problems have you had—or would you anticipate—when students keep journals in school?

### Post-Chapter Journal Writing

Use your own journal to develop a plan for assigning journals in one of your own courses:

1. Which class that you currently teach would lend itself to journal assignments? Why do you think so?
2. Can you think of five specific journal assigments to ask your students to write during the first week of class next term?
3. What objections to assigning journals do you anticipate from colleagues? How might you answer them?

### Workshop Exercise

DOUBLE-ENTRY JOURNAL

One idea suggested by Ann Berthoff (1978) requires students to write regular entries on the right-hand notebook page and leave the left-hand page blank so the writer may add further thoughts about modifications of the ideas written on the right-hand page.

To explore this idea in one of your classes which is already keeping journals, start each Monday (or Tuesday) by asking students to return to one entry written the previous week (or weeks) and write their thoughts about the earlier thoughts. (10 minutes)

Ask for volunteers to read their revised entries aloud, including the original entry if necessary.

Repeat regularly in subsequent classes or make this a homework requirement for the remainder of the course.

### Classroom Handout

SUGGESTIONS FOR USING ACADEMIC JOURNALS

*What Is a Journal?* A journal is a place to practice writing and thinking. It differs from a diary in that it should not be merely a personal recording of the day's events. It differs from your class notebook in that it should not be merely an objective recording of academic data. Think of your journal rather as a personal record of your educational experience, including this class, other classes, and your current extracurricular life.

*What to Write.* Use your journal to record personal reactions to class, students, teachers. Make notes to yourself about ideas, theories, concepts, problems. Record your thoughts, feelings, moods, experiences. Use your journal to argue with the ideas and readings in the course and to argue with me, express confusion, and explore possible approaches to problems in the course.

*When to Write.* Try to write in your journal at least three or four times a week (aside from your classroom entries). It is important to develop the *habit* of using your journal even when you are not in an academic environment. Good ideas, questions, etc., don't always wait for convenient times for you to record them.

*How to Write.* You should write however you feel like writing. The point is to think on paper without worrying about the mechanics of writing. The quantity you write is as important as the quality. Use language that expresses your personal voice — language that comes natural to you.

SUGGESTIONS
1. Choose a notebook you are comfortable with; I recommend a small (6″ × 9″) looseleaf.
2. Date each entry; include time of day.
3. Write long entries; develop your thoughts as fully as possible.
4. Use a pen (pencils smear).
5. Use a new page for each new entry.
6. Include both "academic" and "personal" entries; mix or separate as you like.

INTERACTION
I'll ask to see your journal several times during the term: I'll read selected entries and, upon occasion, argue with you or comment on your comments. None of the dialogue with you will affect how much your journal is "worth." A *good* journal will be full of lots of long entries and reflect active, regular use.

CONCLUSION
At the end of the term please (1) put page numbers in your journal, (2) make a table of contents for significant entries, (3) write an introduction to the journal, and (4) an evaluation of its worth to you.

## Teachers and Students Respond

KEEPING JOURNALS
1. The journal is useful to me because it forces me to think and forces out thoughts that otherwise might not come out. It disciplines the mind. It gets me thinking early in the morning. It forces me to appreciate the fact that listening and reading are active enterprises

and that unless one reflects upon what one has heard and read it will not become part of one. I am reminded of a paradox. Homer, Socrates, and Milton (after his blindness) did not write; yet all three were brilliant thinkers. The key to understanding their brilliance is that they reflected on what they heard and read and what they thought. Writing a journal is not a substitute for thought or thinking itself; it is a tool that is useful in stimulating thought. Great minds can think without writing.

2. This term was the first term that I did not find writing in a journal to be a tedious and hard process. I think one reason for this is that you never specified the number of journal entries we were required to write per week. I had the freedom to choose what and when I wanted to write.

I found the journal very helpful in analyzing pieces of writing. It seems that whenever I had read something now I must have a piece of paper handy to make notes and write questions. I find myself doing this for readings in my other classes so I must say that this journal has helped improve my study habits.

My journal entries were also helpful/useful when it came to writing my papers because I had written down some notes and ideas while the story was fresh in my mind and I could take these ideas and further develop them.

Finally, I found the journal helpful in my personal life. Like when I had trouble with a story. I would try to work out my personal problems on paper. All those journals have been destroyed by my choice, though.

I think I will probably continue to keep a journal from now on. It will probably be more on a personal level than "scholarly" level because I use my class notebooks for that type of writing. I would almost feel lost without having a journal around in which I know I could write when I wanted to put my thoughts down on paper.

3. When I made up my table of contents I was forced to go back and reread practically all of my entries. For this entire term I was convinced I had no ideas of value in the journal. I repeated this belief in class several times. But now I find this isn't the truth. I was surprised to see how little I wrote about the dorm and my family and how many times I led up to full fledged ideas. They often were not fully developed. My entries served as jumping off points.

Before the Table of Contents I was unhappy with this journal. Now I am satisfied and can say it is finished.

## REFERENCES

Berthoff, A. E. (1978). *Forming/Thinking/Writing: The Composing Imagination*. Portsmouth, NH: Boyton/Cook.

Johnson, G. (1981, September). *Writing Across the Disciplines Newsletter, 1* (1).

Stinson, R. (1980, Spring). Journals in the Geography Class. *WLA Newsletter*, 15.

Watson, M. (1980, October). Writing in Math Class. *Mathematics Teacher*, 518–519.

Young, A. (1983). Value and Purpose in Writing. In P. L. Stock (Ed.), *Fforum: Essays in Theory and Practice in the Teaching of Writing*. Portsmouth, NH: Boynton/Cook.

# living an involvement with literacy
## an interview with yetta goodman

RUTH HUBBARD

**Ruth Hubbard**: I'd like to start by asking you what you're reading now.

**Yetta Goodman**: I've been dipping into so many things, but the most important book recently is a biography of a woman named Lucy Sprague Mitchell. She founded Bank Street College and was probably *the* most important female in the Progressive Education Movement. And what's concerning me about it is most people know John Dewey, they've heard of William Kilpatrick, they've heard of accounts of the men of the progressive movement. But they don't know about Lucy Sprague Mitchell.

**RH**: What kinds of work was she doing?

**YG**: Basically, she was doing what a number of us in whole language are involved in today. She was doing research; she was in teacher education because Bank Street College came out of an experiment in teacher education, and then she was doing work with kids in classrooms herself, and she was writing a lot.

**RH**: So there are books and article that she's written?

**YG**: Oh, yes. I've been reading her work as well as wonderful biography of her by Joyce Antler. I like biographies very much, and I was reading and enjoying this book, then all of a sudden I began to realize the impact that this woman had on progressive education. But it's not only her, there must have been about a dozen strong women involved in the whole response to immigrant education in the twenties and thirties, and they were all involved in progressive education.

**RH**: And they've been left out of the history?

**YG**: Well, if you look into the Progressive Education Movement, you'll find reference to Lucy Sprague Mitchell, but the references are not as obvious as the references to the men. And I think part of it is related to sexism, but probably an important part is the fact that the women were the practitioners — or seemed to be the practitioners because actually, they really were all involved in research. But because they were dirtying their hands working with kids, they were the low-status fold. And the philosophers and the people who spent their time at the universities were the high-status people, so they're the ones who got the credit for the movement. Their names become more known historically while the real practitioners got sort of lost in the shuffle. In a short piece I wrote about Lucy Sprague Mitchell, I raise the question, is that going to happen now, too? Teachers are involved in writing now, and they're involved in doing classroom research, and they're much more involved in inquiry. Will their voices get lost because they're practitioners . . . and they're women?

**RH**: I think that's an important concern because I do hear that debate—some people asking, "Can teachers be real researchers?"

**YG**: Right. That's a significant issue—Jerry Harste and Carolyn Burke and Dorothy Watson have just addressed that in a little book that came out of Canada called *Whole Language: Inquiring Voices.* Jerry, Carolyn, and Dorothy feel, as I do, that good teaching *is* research. It may be that people want to differentiate the term *inquiry* from *research*. And I don't have any problem with some researchers saying "I do a different type of work than teachers do." That's okay, but what I'm bothered about is when they denigrate the inquiry of teachers because somehow it's not as good as theirs. That's an elitist position.

**RH**: And I've also heard university researchers who say, "Well, I don't do research on my teaching so why should I expect teachers to?"

**YG**: When someone says, "I don't do any research on my teaching," I wonder if they have any sense of what they're really saying. Because what they're saying to me is that they don't reflect on their own practice. What an indictment against what they believe about self-evaluation, about critical thinking, about reflective thinking, and how important it is! John Dewey talks about how essential it is to all teachers and to all scholars. If you feel you have the right to tell teachers what to do in their teaching, the least you can do is evaluate your own teaching. I think that's one of the problems of teacher education: There are too many people in colleges of education who somehow feel that they have a right to tell other people how to teach and yet they never reflect on their own teaching. That's another little project that some of us are trying to organize—to begin to look at how we can bring the concept of whole language into teacher education. And not just into teacher education as an abstract kind of idea, but truly within our own teaching personally.

**RH**: . . . So that teachers are seeing it demonstrated as they're learning about it?

**YG**: Right. But also if you believe that that's how learning takes place. It's not just an issue of demonstration; it's an issue of living a particular kind of learning involvement. And the whole notion of building an academic *community*, that people talk about.

**RH**: It's such a rich and important area to explore!

**YG**: I try to get my students to realize that what we believe today isn't just out of whole cloth, but builds on a tradition of humanistic, holistic, education that goes back for centuries. If we are really going to make this view of learning and teaching significant, we've got to understand that these aren't just fads or flashes in the pan, but that indeed their roots are well-established, theoretically. When teachers respond to issues, it's important that they're not just responding with, "Well, I think it's good," "The kids like it," or "It's fun." Instead, they're responding from the point of view that they know it has an incredible and powerful history. Sometimes I almost get discouraged because I go back and I find everything that I think I invented myself is right there!

**RH**: And perhaps the climate wasn't ripe for it?

**YG**: The climate *was* ripe for it. It's just that forces in education are dynamic. When certain things begin to happen, and political forces get worried that maybe things are going too far in one direction, the response is political, not educational. Right now, I think, the "back to basics" movement is a response—not to the sixties, as some people say—but to the twenties, thirties, forties, fifties and sixties, where we were really trying to open up education for all kinds of people. Even when you go back to Lucy Sprague Mitchell, the whole focus on public education in the twenties was to bring education to the immigrant poor, providing opportunities and experiences for them so they could grow. The language is the same; it sounds like the things we talk about today.

**RH**: What is going on now in the field of literacy that you find exciting?

**YG**: Well, one major excitement is the whole focus on literature. And in a sense I feel the excitement more from the publishers and whole language teachers than I do from the academic area. I don't know if you realize that children's books sales have doubled in the last five years?.

**RH**: No, I didn't know that.

**YG**: There was an article in the *Smithsonian* stating that they don't know how to explain it. But I think that what's happening has a lot to do with whole language classrooms, with the literacy initiative in California, and now, of course, Bea Cullinan's involvement in a national literacy initiative. With all this new focus on children's literature, the market is growing. And so more people are writing for it. The interesting thing is that not only are there more books, but the new books coming out are so *exciting*. The kinds of things that Eric Carle does when he goes beyond the pages of the book, for example. And then, Joanne Cole who has developed the Magic Schoolbus books. She's developed a new genre. I invited a ten-year-old to come into our class and read the *Magic Schoolbus* book; I wanted to see if he understood that it was both fantasy and fact. And he did!

I asked him, "Why do you suppose the author would want to write something like this?" and he said, "Well, you know, lots of times if you're going to study the waterworks at your school, it would be boring if it was just nonfiction, so she put a funny teacher in, and I had a teacher like this once and she was really nutty, too." So he really did have a sense that the author was using fiction to get across the knowledge base that she was presenting. I think we'll have a whole new focus on science, math, and social studies.

**RH**: It's wonderful to begin to see literature as an integral part of the curriculum. But I don't mean that it's good to see it "used" to teach something—it needs to be enjoyed in its own right.

**YG**: Yes. We don't want to "basalize" it. That's one of the things I'm a little disappointed in—that there's so much basalizing of literature. But I think all that points to the fact that teacher education has done a poor job of helping teachers become acquainted with children's books. Reading departments are especially to blame for that: you can get a masters and doctorate in reading at many institutions in this country and never take one course in children's literature! That should be an indictment against every reading department that allows that to occur. So I'm excited about focus on children's literature: the growing awareness of expanding literature for kids and using real books as part of the reading program.

The other area I'm fascinated with is the development of the concept of the roots of literacy. That's now become an international movement. This past October 1 was in Rome as part of the development of an international center for the study of literacy processes. More and more people worldwide are beginning to see that kids don't wait to learn literacy in school but it's really part of a cultural process that begins as kids transact with print in their environment and with written language in the homes and communities. So that's something else I'm excited about.

**RH**: On the other hand, what are some current research trends that you find disturbing?

**YG**: I guess I don't find research trends disturbing; it's how people might make use of it. People have a right to research what they want to research. It's when we take that research and impose it on others. In a sense, almost any of the research that we're talking about can become something negative.

I was just in Argentina at a literacy conference. Emelia Ferreiro has become a major focus; she's really a heroine in South America. But what's happening is that people are trying to take what she's talking about and teach kids her stages. So what concerns me is not the research itself, but the notion that somehow, a research study should be immediately applied to the classroom without putting it to important questions: In what way does this relate to curriculum? What way does this relate to teaching and what we know about classrooms? That's what's terrible about the arrogance of all researchers; they think they have a right to go in and tell teachers what to do after they've done some research. They may say teachers haven't done their homework in the field of research, but most researchers haven't done their homework in the field of teaching in the classroom and kids and learning. And I find that that's a terrible problem. I don't think all the answers are in the research; research is simply another way of informing ourselves. The answers are in teachers working together—raising issues, discussing them, planning for them, and self-evaluating throughout the process.

Emelia said in her speech in Argentina, "Research can never keep up with practice." Teachers can't wait for researchers to give them answers, because they're [teachers] working in the whole context of the classroom. They can't wait and say, "Okay, Emelia, we have to wait for you to tell us that kids knows that three letters are words." You know, that's ridiculous thing, and yet there are a lot of researchers who believe that. "Once I've done research, then tomorrow, I'll be able to take this in the classroom." I have to be careful about this myself! It would be easy for me to say that every teacher should do miscue analysis on every kid in their classroom. Well, my God! Any teacher who did that would drive herself crazy! I mean, miscue analysis is a tool to inform yourself, to become aware how much information you can gather using miscue analysis. But teachers have to make some decisions as to when they want to use it, which kids they should do it with, what information they need, and when to get it because there's just too much there. So I think that we've got to be very careful.

**RH**: Who would you say was an influential teacher in your life?

**YG**: I think about that a lot because as I'm trying to understand the history of education, I'm also trying to understand my own educational history. I have memories of teachers in elementary and secondary—but I don't have one teacher I can point to and say, "Boy, this teacher changed my life." I think my main awareness of teachers came in graduate school. E. Brooks Smith was department chair of the Elementary Education Department at Wayne State University. In the late fifties and early sixties the school had a strong group of progressive educators there. Wonderful humanistic people. Brooks was my major professor there, and a woman by the name of Marian Edmond was also on my committee. If I think of two teachers who've influenced me, those are the two people I always want to thank. Brooks awakened in me that teachers are researchers; I had no sense of that at all before. My background is working-class and I came from a bilingual home, so my first language was not English. Teachers always reminded me of that all through school. Even going to college was just what I did as something to fall back on—and teaching was something a woman could do....

**RH**: But you didn't necessarily feel a calling to teach in the beginning?

**YG**: I think my calling to teaching was part of being in an upwardly-mobile immigrant family, where teaching is what girls do. I always liked kids, and I knew I was good with kids. But it wasn't until I got into this community of scholars in my doctoral program that people

began to pay attention to what I was saying as well as how I
worked with kids. So Brooks Smith really awakened that intellec-
tualism in me. And then Marian Edmond is an incredible lady.
She's eighty-eight years old right now and she's retired.

**RH**: It sounds like you still keep in touch with her?

**YG**: Oh, yes. In fact, I just got a letter from her yesterday. Let me see
if I can pull this out. You might be interested in this. She sent me a
card that she got: It reads "Members of the St. Peter's High School
Class of 1929, meeting to celebrate their sixtieth anniversary, send
you greetings and sincere expressions of gratitude for the time you
spent with us as a teacher and class advisor." So this is the class of
'29, on their sixtieth anniversary, sending Marian Edmond a card!

And she writes, "Teaching is indeed a marvelous profession. The
enclosed card received the other day gave me great satisfaction.
Twenty-one persons showed up out of a class of sixty-six—that
speaks well for longevity in Minnesota." She finishes her letter
telling me "I have also embarked on a big project of researching
and writing my mother's history."

Vibrant woman! When she was sixty, she was involved in the
peace movement at Wayne State. I remember her when we had all
those activities on campus. She was always there, white haired,
addressing people about the horrors of the Vietnam War. Now,
she's working with Amnesty International and has an interesting
group she meets with writing monthly letters.

**RH**: That's inspiring!

**YG**: Marian is my mentor. She gave me a sense of humanism and
Brooks Smith gave a sense of scholarship. And, of course, the
marvelous group of people at Wayne State at that time—a whole
group of students with whom I've developed a camaraderie, such
as Carolyn Burke, Bill Page, and Dorothy Watson. It's lasted
till this day. And my partnership with Ken is another important
element—that totally immersed living experience.

**RH**: It sounds a little like a modern-day educational Bloomsbury
Group.

**YG**: Well, it's an incredible group of people. We respect and love
each other. We fight a lot. And we keep in touch with each other. I
think it may be one of the things that has launched the whole
language teacher-support groups. We realized that here we were, a
group of academics teaching at the university level, working with
teachers, and how that support group we had kept us going. And
we've broadened out to others who were like-minded. "Look what
we got from this group—look what we get from each other." And
other teachers need this, too. We all need to sit down with each
other and share and talk and complain. Yes, and argue and inquire
and research.

# writing and reading from the inside out

NANCIE ATWELL

23

I'm an English teacher, certified to teach grades seven through twelve, and currently teaching grade eight. I go to a party. I'm introduced to a stranger. He says, "What do you do?" I say, "I'm an English teacher." He says, "Oh. Then I guess I'd better watch my grammar."

This conversation occurs often enough—even at faculty parties—for me to realize I'm a stereotype. Like all stereotypes, I'm one I don't like a whole lot. Fueled by red ink, I'm the self-appointed guardian of your language—somebody so obsessed and narrow it's not outside the realm of possibility that I'd critique your sentence constructions at a cocktail party.

I'm the doorman at what Frank Smith (1983) calls "the club." And there's no access to anyone who can't name and define the parts of speech; who doesn't know George Eliot's real name; who won't appreciate the stories and poetry in some publisher's latest version of a literature anthology; who can't name the Roman equivalents of the Greek deities; whose paragraphs don't conform to Warriner's models.

It's like Ken Kesey said: you're either on the bus, or you're off the bus.

For a long time, I was virtually alone inside the bus. Other adults—including most of my elementary school colleagues—were on the outside. They were generalists; I was the expert. English was my field. I read Literature and subscribed to *The New York Review of Books*.

My students were outsiders too—although every year I'd let a few aboard. The gifted ones, right? whom I'd recognize and elevate, loaning them my own books and responding to their writing in private meetings after school.

I reinforced the stereotype. I taught English as a body of knowledge a few would "get." The rest would never "get" it. (These were the ones I'd intimidate at cocktail parties.)

But sometime over the last three years, when I wasn't watching,

Reprinted with permission from *Breaking Ground: Teachers Relate Reading and Writing in the Elementary School*, edited by Jane Hansen, Thomas Newkirk, and Donald Graves. Copyright © 1985 by Nancie Atwell; published by Helnemann Educational Books, Inc.

the bus filled to its limits, and the walls dissolved. The metaphor became irrelevant because suddenly everyone was inside the bus— *inside written language.* I was there; my colleagues and principal were there; all my students were there.

Let me illustrate.

One afternoon last September five things happened within one fifteen minute period that put a serious crimp in my cocktail party stereotype.

Bob Dyer, the principal at my school, put a Bette Lord novel in my mailbox with the note, "I think you and your kids might enjoy this."

Underneath Lord's book was my copy of Francine Du Plessix-Gray's *Lovers and Tyrants.* Susan Stires, our resource room teacher, had returned it with the note, "God, can she write. Thank you for this."

Under Francine was a message from Nancy Tindal, a kindergarten teacher: "Do you have time some afternoon this week to respond to my Open House speech?"

When I went back to my classroom, I found a note on the chalkboard from a former student who'd borrowed a novel the week before: "Hi. I was here but you weren't. I love *Portrait of Jenny.* Who *is* Robert Nathan? Your favorite freshperson, Amanda."

And finally Andy, another freshperson, came by with a copy of an interview with author Douglas Adams that he'd promised me over the summer.

It was only because these things happened one on top of another that I noticed and considered what was going on. These teachers and students and I are in on something together. I'm going to call what I have around me, what we have together, a literate environment. By literate environment I mean a place where people read, write, and talk about reading and writing; where everybody can be student and teacher; where everybody can come inside.

This chapter is about how we teachers can get our classrooms and schools to become literate environments, how we can help everyone approach written language from the perspective of "insider." I'm grateful to Tom Newkirk in his article "Young Writers as Critical Readers" (1982) for that notion of bringing students inside written language, as critics, as enthusiasts, as participants.

It's as participants in the processes of writing and reading that students—and teachers—become insiders. We become participants when we open up our classrooms and establish workshops where students and teachers write, read and talk about writing and reading. I'm going to separate writing and reading for a while and talk about them one at a time, So I can more effectively talk about them together later on. And I'll start with writing, because that's where I started in my own classroom and school, my own literate environment.

## WRITING WORKSHOP

I teach writing and reading, as two separate courses each day, to three heterogeneous groups of eighth graders. These groups include special education students. All my students write every day. And every day, almost everybody is doing something different. These are some of the things you'd see them doing if you visited writing workshop.

As insiders, these writers have intentions: things they decide they want to use written language to do. They find their own topics and purposes for writing.

Using insiders' jargon, they call their writing a draft. When drafting, they try to get down on the page what they know and think, to see what they know and think.

They read drafts of their writing—to themselves, and aloud to each other and me—in conferences. We listeners tell writers what we hear and don't hear. We ask questions to help writers think about what's on the page. Sometimes we offer, from our own experiences as writers, alternative approaches or solutions. But we can only offer. Writers who are insiders may reject our advice.

As fellow insiders, we applaud when writers find ways to accomplish what they hoped to accomplish—as they shape the content of their writing, making graceful meanings. Sometimes we suffer all the heart-aches and headaches of insiders in the process.

All this thinking, writing, and talking take time. Writers in a workshop take all the time they need to make the writing good. And I haven't touched on the most time-consuming and least visible insiders' activity: all the writing that happens in the heads of people who write. Donald graves calls this planning "offstage rehearsal": "I wrote this poem in my head, lying in bed this morning" or "On our way home, I knew I wanted to write about what had just happened."

Finally, with pieces that are going public, writers clean up. They put their writing in the forms and formats their readers will need. They edit. Their teachers help, talking with them about new skills and rules, always in one context: how to get this piece to read as the writer wants it to. With their own intentions at stake, insiders take rules seriously. They use the rules and conventions; the rules and conventions don't use them. These writers will never be intimidated by English teachers at cocktail parties.

It sounds nice, doesn't it? Well, getting it to happen is one of the hardest things I've ever done.

Up until three years ago, nobody wrote much of anything at my school. Nobody wrote because nobody taught writing. Nobody taught writing because nobody was trained to teach writing.

Then, with the help of my teacher, Dixie Goswami of Middlebury's Bread Loaf School of English, fifteen teachers established our own, home-grown, in-service program. Its goal was a K-8 writing curriculum. To get there, we *together* got inside writing. We became writers and researchers and started looking at how people write, and why, and the conditions in which people get good at writing (Atwell, 1982). The Atkinson Academy reports of Donald Graves, Lucy Calkins, and Susan Sowers (1978—81) were our research models as we looked at ourselves and our students as writers.

In the end, the writing program we'd sought to develop was much bigger than a program. It's become a way of life. Writing workshop is perpetual—day in, year out—like breathing, but sometimes much, much harder. We're constantly gathering ideas for writing, planning, writing, conferring, and seeing our writing get things done for us in our real worlds.

Mary Ellen Giacobbe (1983) provides a helpful summary of the multitude of qualities characterizing a writing process workshop. She brings it down to three: time, conferences, and responsibility.

Writers need time—to think, write, confer, write, read, write, change our minds, and write some more. Writers need regular time that we can count on, so that even when we aren't writing we're anticipating the time we will be. And we need lots of time—to grow, to see what we think, to shape what we know, to get help where and when we need it.

This help comes during conferences. In conferences, we describe or share what we've written. Others read or listen to our voices, tell us what they hear, and help us reflect on our information, style, and intentions.

Discovering our intentions is what responsibility is all about: As a writer, what do I want to do, need to do? Does this piece of writing, as it stands, do what I want it to? If not, how might I change it?

As young writers work with these questions, other writers work with them, some of them teachers. We teachers respect a writer's final say but, along the way, describe the options we've gleaned from our own experiences as writers collaborating with other writers. Mary Ellen Giacobbe calls this "nudging." We nudge by sharing what we know; we acknowledge the writer's ultimate responsibility by accepting it when our nudges are ignored. But next time around, we nudge again.

When we allow time, conferences, and responsibility, we create contexts in which writers write and get good at writing. We expect students to participate in written language as writers do. And their efforts exceed our expectations as they make written language their business. At our school, over ninety percent of our K−8 students specifically identify themselves as writers.

I know these same principles of writing are at work in many schools and classrooms. Occasionally, I'll become really naive and complacent and imagine that we're on the cutting edge of a trend sweeping the nation, that the U.S.A. is one, big, happy busful of insiders. And just as soon as I start feeling smug, something comes along to take the stars out of my eyes. More often than not, the "something" is a realization about my own teaching. My most recent encounter with reality concerns the teaching of reading.

## READING WORKSHOP

At my level, junior high, there seem to be two ways a reading course can go: either a skills/drills/basal textbook approach—essentially an extension of elementary programs—or a watered-down lit. crit.

approach of the type found in many high school English classes. Until two years ago, my approach to reading was the latter: pass out the anthologies, introduce the vocabulary, lecture about genre or theme, assign the story or parts of the story, give a quiz on comprehension and vocabulary, conduct a whole-class post mortem, and sometimes assign an essay. Students also had two periods each week of sustained silent reading.

A little over two years ago, I began to be aware of the contradictions between my beliefs about writing and my instruction in reading. I confronted a situation Tom Newkirk calls "the writing ghetto — this one period each day when students climbed aboard the written language bus, sat behind the wheel, and drove. What they and I did as writers in our writing workshop, and what they and I do as readers, had little to do with what went on in the reading course.

A personal digression: what I do as a reader.

As a reader, I usually decide what I'll read. But I get help — recommendations — from my husband and friends, with whom I talk a lot about books, and from reviews. I also draw on my prior experiences as a reader. I like John Updike's novels; chances are, I'm going to like *The Witches of Eastwick*. And I go back to books I've read, reentering and reconsidering the writing.

Sometimes I engage in activities that involve reading and I can't decide what I'll read. For example, the text is required for the course; the application has to be correctly filled out; I want to serve an interesting edible dinner. But nobody had better do anything so outright silly as give me a vocabulary quiz, a comprehension test, or a chance to respond that's limited to the kinds of questions found in teachers' guides or high school essay tests.

I read a lot, at least a couple of books a week. And I have routines, times I know I'll read and count on reading — before I go to sleep at night; in the morning when Toby, my husband, is in the bath; at the breakfast table on weekend mornings. Some of my reading happens away from books. I think about characters, plot twists, and turns of phrase. I playback lines of poetry. I suddenly see, in something that happens in my real world, what an author was getting at.

Do you see what I'm getting at?

The same elements that characterize writing workshop characterize my behavior as a reader. I exercise *responsibility*, deciding what and why — or at the very least, how — I'll read. I spend regular, frequent *time* reading and thinking about other's writing. I *confer* with other readers, talking about books naturally as an extension of my life as a reader.

And much of this talk takes place between Toby and me at the dining room table, talk about novels, poems, articles, and editorials, and general literary gossip. That dining room table is a literate environment where we analyze, criticize, interpret, compare, link books with our own knowledge and experiences, and go inside written language.

I'm dwelling on my dining room table because it's become the metaphor I use whenever I think or talk about what I want my reading course to be. As my teaching of writing was transformed by my getting inside writing, so my teaching of reading is changing as my students and I get inside others' writing; in short, as we *read writing* just as we *write reading*.

To get my dining room table into my classroom, I started with the issue of time, expanding independent reading to four class periods per week. In addition to having lots of regular time for reading, kids are deciding what books they'll read and at what pace they'll read them: again, issues of responsibility. They mostly read books that tell stories — fiction, autobiographies and biographies — and poetry. I added titles to the classroom paperback library and included collections of my students' writing as we published magazines through the school year.

Last year's eighth graders, including eight special education students, read an average of thirty-five full-length works, form Blume to Brontë to Verne to Vonnegut to Irving — Washington and John.

The remaining issue, of reading conferences, is one I had to work with. I have seventy students for reading. I needed a practical way to initiate and sustain good, rich, dining room table talk with each of them.

In September, each eighth grader received a folder with a sheaf of notebook paper clipped inside and a letter from me that included these instructions:

*This folder is a place for you and me to talk about books, reading, authors and writing. You're to write letters to me, and I'll write letters back to you.*

*In your letters, talk with me about what you've read. Tell me what you thought and felt and why. Tell me what you liked and didn't like and why. Tell me what these books meant to you and said to you. Ask me questions or for help. And write back to me about my ideas, feelings and questions.*

The use of letters was inspired by the dialogue journals kept by sixth-grade teacher Leslee Reed and her students (Staton, 1980). I reasoned, why not use writing to extend kids' thinking about books — to go inside others' written language in written conferences? My hunch was that, since writing allows for a kind of reflection not generally possible with speech, our written talk about books would be more sustained and considered than oral conferences. Another consideration was the possible connections students might make between what they read and wrote. As a researcher, I wondered if their own writing and the writing they read would intersect.

Each year, my students and I have written back and forth almost three thousand pages of letters. For the remainder of this article, I'll take you inside two of these sets of correspondence, showing how two eighth graders got thoroughly inside reading and writing through participating with me and their peers as readers and writers. And, most remarkable to me, I chose these two because I thought they were fairly ordinary. As I looked closer, as always happens with research, I discovered how extraordinary they are.

### DANIEL

I'll start with Daniel. You probably already know him. He always wears this outfit: blue jeans, duck boots, and a chamois shirt over a T-shirt. He owns a dirt bike, a .22, and twenty lobster traps. Daniel wants to be a lobsterman full time when he finishes school.

At the beginning of grade eight, students answered questions about themselves as readers and writers. Daniel estimated, "I've read maybe one or two whole novels in my whole life." He'd never bought a book or borrowed one from the town library, and read one magazine, *Dirt Bike*. He could name one book he'd enjoyed reading, Beverly Cleary's *Runaway Ralph*, and he said his ideal novel would be about motorcycles and races. In answer to the question, "Are you a writer?" Daniel was one of that ten percent who said no. He also said, 'I don't like what I write. I never like it."

The first week of school I gave Daniel a new novel and told him I hadn't read it yet but knew that the author, Susan Beth Pfeffer, wrote well for kids. I invited Daniel inside. He took *About David*, read it, and at the end of September told me what he thought.

*9/30*

*Dear Miss Atwell,*
    About David
    *I liked it because it made me feil it happened to me. it was one of the first books I read that I enjoyed. Because I don't read much. I liked it when they talked about David and the feilings his friend and family (or lyns parents) felt.*

*10/1*

*Dear Daniel,*
    *Do you think you'd read more if you could find more really good books? Your note about* About David *made me sad. It seems like you haven't found many books you've enjoyed. There are so many novelists who describe people's feelings as well as Pfeffer does.*
    *For example, I think you'd like* Tex, *by S. E. Hinton. Have you read it?*
    *Write back*

*Ms. Atwell*

*Dear Miss Atwell,*
    *I dont think I would read more because I an too bissee. did you ever read About David? no I have never read this book*

When I got around to reading *About David*, I wrote to Daniel about Pfeffer's intentions:

*10/25*

*Dear Daniel,*

*I read* About David *on Wednesday. You're right: it's definitely a book about feelings. I cound't imagine, where Pfeffer could possibly go after opening her novel with a suicide/double murder. But the way she slowly develops the aftermath—focusing on the effects of David's actions on the people who are left—just knocked me out. Thanks for recommending it.*

*Ms. Atwell*

Our correspondence continued. Then, at the end of October, I panicked about grades—about how to evaluate independent reading—and placed myself squarely between Daniel and books. I set a minimum number of novels to be read each grading period. Daniel, who had finished three novels by this time, revolted.

*Dear Ms. Atwell,*

*Why should people get bad grades because they don't like to read or are slow?! In my case I can't find books I like. All the books I've tried to read I dont like but the 3 I read. I am just saying it's not fair!*

*Daniel*

*11/3*

*Dear Daniel,*

*I won't give bad grades to people who read slowly. If you put in the time and use it well, you'll get a good grade.*

*I also won't give the bad grades to people who don't like to read. It depresses me that people sometimes feel that way, but I won't give someone a bad grade for an opinion different from mine.*

*I do give bad grades to people who don't read or don't use reading time well. In this class, which is called reading, I'm expecting my students will read.*

*I know hundreds of good books, as good as the ones you've read this year and liked. Mrs. Fossett does, too.*

*Ms. A*

Daniel responded: "Thanks for explaining the situation. I will see Mrs. Fossett. And find more books. I'm going to the town library with some friends on Friday and I'll look for some books."

I received a quick note the following Monday: "I did not have good luck at the library and I will have to go out of town to find a good set of books."

That Daniel and his friends were going to the town library as a social occasion was one of many first signs that a literate environment was emerging among eighth graders. In fact, through the rest of the school year, Daniel referred to David, Lance, Amanda, Jenny and other kids in the class, and conversations they'd had about particular novels and authors. Another small sign was Daniel's plan—to look for books to buy, to own.

Other signs appeared. In the spring, Daniel started taking books home to read. I asked why. He responded, "I took it home because it was getting interesting and I just, simply, liked it."

In December, I gave Daniel a copy of *Tex*, and he discovered S. E. Hinton. After that he was independent of me as a reader. With a few exceptions we spent the rest of the school year talking about books Daniel discovered. The motivation to find writers he wanted to read was inside him.

*12/22*

*Ms A. I found That Was Then This Is Now and it is a very good book. I put E.T. back, I'll try it after I finish this one. Or I will find one more of S. E. Hinton's books like the Outsiders.*

*Capt. Daniel Alley*

Daniel finished *That Was Then, This Is Now* on January 6 and wanted more Hinton.

*Ms. A.*
*Now I wont have to get that book and read it. Thanks. Do you know any other good books that are by S. E. Hinton? That Was Then This is Now was a real good book but I wish it could have ended a lot more happy than it did. It was so sad because you could see Bryen loosing his brother or best friend and it changed his hole life from good to bad.*

*Daniel*

Daniel was one of a number of readers who'd begun to suggest revisions in what they read. For example: "I wish Paula Danziger had made the father less like a cartoon character." "This book got good as I got into it, but I think the author should have tried a different lead." "Parts of this book make no sense and the author should change them."

I think this kind of criticism reflects what students were doing as writers, in writing workshop, at the same time they were reading these novels. In writing workshop they analyzed what they wrote for strengths and weaknesses. They went after effects, playing with the sound of their writing. They worked on providing sufficient detail, on recreating reality for their readers. They experimented with technique—different kinds of leads, ways of using dialogue. They shifted focus by deleting and expanding content. And they talked with me and other writers about what they were doing. I think printed texts stopped seeming sacred to these authors: everybody's writing became fair game.

Daniel started the year by writing a series of one or two paragraph business letters—to Honda, Hubba Bubba Bubble Gum Company (he'd found a piece of strawberry in his pack of raspberry) and actresses Loni Anderson and Valerie Bertinelli, among others. He churned these out. I worried that none of this writing meant much to him. I suggested topics and other modes—I nudged. And I waited.

Then, in December, Daniel started a series of long narratives describing the nonfiction adventures of Daniel and his friends Tyler and Gary and their boats, motorcycles, and bicycles. It's my theory that these emerging topics reflected the writing Daniel was reading: stories about boys on their own without adults, loyal to each other, told with humor and occasional lyricism. In December, Daniel was reading S. E. Hinton *and writing* S. E. Hinton. He published all of these stories as photocopies for Tyler and Gary.

This is a one-page excerpt from "Camping," a five-pager and the very first piece in the Daniel-Tyler-Gary series, which he completed the first week in January.

*We were on a ledge so we put the tent so it was half on the rock and half on the dirt. We sat back and looked off. We could see out over the harbor about four miles. "I'm hungry. Let's eat," Tyler demanded.*

*"Not yet. We only have a little food," I said, taking charge.*

*"I'll starve!" he said sarcastically.*

*"Let's do something before dark," Gary said.*

*"Like what?" I said, like there was nothing to do. We sat thinking for a while.*

*"Let's go for a ride," Tyler suggested.*

*"Yeah, to Alfred's store to get some cigars!" We grabbed our helmets and took off, down the trail. The lady working at Alfred's knew their parents, so I had to go in!*

*"Let's not bother with cigars," I pleaded.*

*"Don't worry about it; it's going to be easy," Tyler said casually.*

*"Easy for you to say. You're not going in!"*

*"Don't be a pup! Just go," Gary laughed.*

*"I'm goin'; I'm goin'! Don't rush me!" I said, as they rushed me. I had on a felt hat, down touching my sunglasses to hide my face. I also had my collar turned up and stood on tiptoe so I looked bigger. I walked in with a piece of paper, like a shopping list. I looked around like I'd never been in before. I asked for William Penn Braves, like I did not know what they were.*

*"How many?" the lady asked.*

*"Five please."*

*When I got outside, I sighed with relief. (I did not tell them, but I was kind of scared.)*

In the spring, Daniel started reading a new genre, survival-in-the-wilderness novels. He started with Arthur Roth's *Two for Survival*, about two boys trying to make it out of the woods to civilization after their plane crashes in a snowstorm. At the same time, Daniel started "Trapped," his own first piece of fiction, about two boys trying to make it out of the woods to civilization after their motorcycle fails in a snowstorm. As Daniel put it, "*Two for Survival* is getting to sound like my piece in parts."

Daniel worked on "Trapped" for five weeks, writing it in two parts. He wrote one draft and made only minor revisions on the page. Most of the exploring for this piece went on in Daniel's head. He spent time sitting thinking before almost every word he wrote. He talked a lot about this piece with other writers. He worried about the credibility of Mike, his narrator and main character. He wondered whether he had enough detail "so readers could see it happening," something he'd noted twice in his letters about Hinton's writing. Daniel also consulted a Boy Scout manual to find out about frostbite symptoms and treatment.

I'll share just the conclusion of "Trapped." In the story so far, Chris and Mike, out motorcycling on a springlike day in February, get caught in a snowstorm and pitch camp. When the temperature drops quickly, Chris suffers frostbite, which Mike treats. Mike makes various attempts to get them both rescued. His plan to tie Chris on the motorcycle and bull their way through the snow has just failed:

*I felt the cold again as if I were coming out of an invisible shell. What could I do? Darkness had begun, and I felt like falling into a deep sleep. I was so tired I didn't feel the cold, and I felt weak and limp. I untied Chris, which wasn't easy in my condition. I knew now the snow was too deep to travel in. I grabbed his shoulders and slid him off the seat. His foot got caught on the foot peg. I pulled and the bike came flying over and we went down, too. I felt my back hit the snow, and I lay there silently. How long could this last? It was then I remembered my grandfather telling me all those stories about storms that had lasted for five or ten days. This brought the little hope I'd held down to almost nothing.*

*Suddenly I heard a low, muffled rumble. I sat up and strained to listen. I heard nothing but the rustle of the trees in the wind. After about five minutes, I heard it again, and it hit me like a bolt of lightning: it was the plow truck doing the road!*

*I stood up and mindlessly ran toward the faint sound. I only made it a few feet before I collapsed in the knee-deep snow. I again frantically tried to run, but felt dead. I looked toward the sound and saw a yellow, flashing tint through the black, frozen night.*

*It came closer; I could hardly think. I was warmed by the thought of being saved as the headlights came into sight. With my last remaining strength I stumbled toward Chris. I stood towering above him and screamed, "We're saved! We're saved!" There was no reaction.*

*"Get up, Chris! Someone is here to pick us up." Still he didn't move. I panicked, not knowing what to do. I was really scared now, that the truck would go by and we'd be lost forever. I blindly wobbled about fifty feet in front of the truck . . . and it stopped.*

Daniel loved "Trapped." His letters to me consistently included his opinions on how authors were concluding their novels; he loved his conclusion. He said, "I wanted to give the feeling of being trapped and then, at the end, just spring the trap and stop the piece there; like, you're *free*."

At the end of the eighth grade Daniel wrote, "I have said all along that to write well you have to like it. Well, I like it. Yes, I am a writer. I learned to write by gradually writing and getting better . . . I used to say I wasn't a writer. But I didn't know that even if I'm writing in school, I am still a writer. My best pieces are the ones that sound like a professional writer wrote it."

Over his eighth grade year, Daniel read twelve novels and wrote me thirty-five letters. He used this year to get inside professional writers' prose and to write reading. And he did this because he had time to read and write his choice of books and topics, and chances to talk with other readers and writers about good writing.

## TARA

The gains students like Daniel made thrilled me. This pleasure was compounded by the equally impressive growth of other students, some of them already dedicated readers at the beginning of eighth grade. Tara, Daniel's classmate, falls into this category.

In September Tara said, "I love to read because I love to travel, and good books make me feel like I'm living in the story." She regularly bought books and could name half a dozen novels she'd read over the summer. Tara named her favorite books by listing their authors — Judy Blume, Lois Lowry, and Laura Ingalls Wilder. Books she didn't enjoy reading were textbook anthologies: ". . . books like *Thrust* and *To Turn a Stone*, because the stories are boring and because I didn't like the questions after."

During her eighth-grade year, Tara continued to love books. She read fifty-one novels, September to June.

In September, like Daniel, Tara also provided some information about herself as a writer. And she, like Daniel, said, "No — I'm not a writer. A good writer needs a good imagination. That's not me."

Tara did not connect the writing she read and the writing she wrote. Although, unlike Daniel, she loved to read, the stories she read were someone else's domain — someone, somewhere, graced with a good imagination. Staying on the outside of written language, Tara read *reading*. And in writing class I fought with her for months as she accomplished little of her own, convinced she had no imagination and nothing to say. The little she wrote she didn't like: a long, unfocused piece about the first day of school that she abandoned, a couple of letters to the principal about school policies, a report for science class, a narrative about a babysitting experience that consumed pages, came to no point, and was eventually abandoned, too. I lost sleep over Tara.

But in reading class, Tara wrote — pages and pages and pages of letters. She was fascinated with what she did as a reader and how it compared with what I did as a reader.

*9/27*

*When I read, it's a special time for me to be alone. I sit on my bed with a pillow leaning against the wall and another one on my lap so*

*I don't have to hold my arms up. I get completely relaxed. Also, after I finish reading, I just sit for a while thinking about the book. So by the time I see anyone, the feeling is gone. The only thing that bothers me is when I get a phone call or if it's time for dinner and I'm right in the middle of a good book. I try to get the interruption over with so I can get back to reading. How about you?*

*When you read, do you do it to take your mind off your problems and to go into a different world, or just for pleasure, or both? I think I do it for both.*

*Also, if you have your mind on a problem and then try to read, do you have to concentrate a little bit in the beginning to set your mind on the book? I'm just wondering because this happens to me.*

Someday I'll write about students' reading processes as they describe them. For example, Tara articulates nicely how she plans ("Now I have about six books lined up to read but I think I'll read *A Wrinkle in Time* next") and how she revises; how she reseeks meaning ("I finished *Waiting Games* . . . I had to reread the ending a few times before I understood it"; "The ending of *The Outsiders* works so well I feel like starting over and reading it again.")

Tara also wrote and talked a lot about how what she read made her feel. She cried when Paul died in *P.S., I Love You*; when a boy character behaved badly in another novel she wrote, "I don't know any boys like Danny, but if I did I'd want someone to dump him, just to show him how it feels"; she said, "*A Ring of Endless Light* gave me this wonderful feeling inside I just can't explain."

At the end of December Tara and I started talking about what authors were doing to give her those feelings, as in this exchange about L'Engle's *Ring of Endless Light*.

*. . . I think this book is a good example of describing your surroundings and your thoughts and feelings. What I mean is: I can think back to parts of the story and see pictures of what it looked like. It's great to be able to do that! I really love this book! It's one of the best I've ever read!*

*Tara*

*12/20*

*Dear Tara,*
*I know exactly what you mean. And the feeling you carry with you is a warm one, a contented one, right? I just reread the novel* The French Lieutenant's Woman, *and I'm carrying its "feeling" with me today. I suspect I'll go home tonight and reread its first ending (it has two) as a way to extend the feeling.*

*What is it about good writing that allows us to do this; what makes good books have this effect?*

*NA*

*12/20*

*You're right about my feeling—that's what it's like. I sometimes reread parts of books just like you might do. I think it is because the authors include so many thoughts, feeling and descriptions that we can "lose" ourselves in the books, in the writing.*

*Tara*

From January on, Tara wrote letters about authors as people making decisions — choosing how they'll present information; controlling tone, voice and style; doing specific things to give her her reading feelings. Her new vocabulary and perspective came from two sources: the way I talked with her about books and the way students and I talked about their writing in writing workshop.

For example, she wrote, "I like *My Darling, My Hamburger*. I like the technique of the letters. I also like the way the boy's feelings are told — in most novels boys are only objects that talk." "In *And You Give Me a Pain, Elaine*, I like the way the author brings everything together. The small episodes are so different — it's almost like the author wrote many short stories and put them together. Yet they all fit. Like a puzzle!"

And of *Where the Red Fern Grows*, Tara said, "I love the descriptive words, the detail, and the way everything ties in. . . . This book shows a new way to begin a piece — going back in time through thoughts. . . . About *Red Fern*: I pictured the boy as Daniel. I don't know why. Maybe because he's that type."

Like Daniel, Tara's major literary influence in eighth grade was S. E. Hinton, who wrote her first novel, *The Outsiders*, at her dining room table when she was fifteen. Tara, too, started modeling her writing on Hinton's. This excerpt is from March.

*I loved* The Outsiders! *I can't believe Hinton was only 15! It's really interesting the way she asked her friends for help . . . My latest poem ("Sleep") I thought of on the way to Sugarloaf. I planned out just what I wanted to say. In the part where I repeat myself I did that because of* The Outsiders. *The only reason I thought of doing it this way was because of this book.*

I asked Tara if she were noticing herself reading differently, coming at others' writing as someone who's a writer herself. She replied:

*What you said about reading like a writer — I never used to do that. Last year I wouldn't have known what you meant. I guess I really do read books differently now. It's interesting because lots of times I don't realize it when I learn things, but this is something I'm aware of.*

Once Tara named it, she knew it. From this point on, she refined and refined her theory:

*I just realized I'm starting to like books with points: books that make me think, that have meaning. . . . One of the best things you've done for me is you've opened books up, almost like dissecting something in science. I think I enjoy them more now that I can understand and appreciate what the authors have done.*

*For me, writing and reading are starting to combine. The other night my dad and I were talking about me and why I love to read but don't enjoy writing. "I think it's because I can't write the kinds of things I like to read." This was the night before I wrote "Beautiful Mountains."*

"Beautiful Mountains," written at the end of March, was the first piece Tara wrote she thought was good. It was a breakthrough for her as a writer.

*3/20*

BEAUTIFUL MOUNTAINS

*"This is so fun, and it's beautiful!" was all I could think as Justine and I skied down Lower Winter's Way. We were at Sugarloaf, and this was our first run down. Justine was a little ways ahead of me, but I was too involved in making sure I didn't fall to watch her. This entire slope was covered with moguls so I had to pay attention. Every so often we would stop to look around. It really was beautiful! There were mountains all around, and the trees were so weighted down with snow most were bent over. The mountains were bluish with lots of white patches. There were clouds covering the peaks. I had never seen anything that looked like this, so as we skied down, my mind was filled with beautiful pictures.*

*All of a sudden, Justine's voice interrupted my thoughts. "Tara!" she yelled in a horrified voice. "Look!" My eyes focused on where she was pointing. Two ski patrolmen were dragging a rescue sled about fifteen feet away from us. The only part of the person that we could see was the face. It was a woman; she reminded me of a mannequin. Her eyes were closed, and even though I've never seen a dead person, that is what I think one would look like. She had fair skin, but underneath it was very dark. She looked so cold. She also looked like she was in pain—tensed up, I guess . . . dead; that's the best word to describe how she looked.*

*The sled passed by in a matter of seconds, but it was long enough to get a picture of her fixed in my mind. I looked again at the once-beautiful mountains. All I could see was her. I'll never know if she was dead, but beautiful mountains will never look the same.*

Tara's comments about "Beautiful Mountains," her writing, and her reading were the germs of a report she wrote in May. I gave her a nudge, asking if she'd be interested in studying our letters and describing what had happened to her as a reader and writer. She was interested. In her lead, Tara lays claim to the title she'd refused before: writer.

MY THOUGHTS ABOUT READING AND WRITING
(HOW THEY HELP EACH OTHER TO HELP ME)

*By Tara*

*I, as a writer, learned to write by reading, writing, listening to other people's writing, and discussing my writing.*

*The way reading helps me is when I "open up" a book I've read. To do this I sort out the parts I like and don't like and decide why. I notice how the author started, ended, and tied the middle together. Then, I look for good describing words and the way thoughts and feelings are used.*

*I try to decide whether or not the book is "good." For me a "good" book is one that I enjoy, one that fully takes me into another world, one that is believable, one that I get so caught up in I want to finish it, and one that I can picture in my mind.*

*When I finish a book, if I can go back and picture different parts, I know the author added many details and descriptions. This is something I try to do with my own writing.*

*Madeleine L'Engle's books (*A Wrinkle in Time *and* A Ring of Endless Light*),* Where the Red Fern Grows *by Wilson Rawls, and* Find a Stranger, Say Goodbye *by Lois Lowry are all good examples of this kind of vivid writing.*

*Learning to write well also takes a lot of practice. In the two years I've been writing, I've only written one piece I would consider "good." But I've learned from all the mistakes in my other pieces.*

*I also learn from other people's work. My one "good" piece ("Beautiful Mountains") was written the way it was because of a few, very good stories by other authors.*

*I kept "Beautiful Mountains" in my head (without much conversation) because of a piece I really liked by Justine Dymond, entitled "A Night in the Life." I made a point with my piece because of* The Outsiders *by S. E. Hinton. I added and took out certain details because of other students' stories I've heard that have too many, not enough, or the wrong details.*

*Also, when I finish a good book I like to sit and think about it for a few minutes. When I read "Beautiful Mountains" to my class, there was a few-second silence at the end. I could tell people were thinking about it. This is the kind of response I wanted, and it made me feel good about my piece.*

*My reading log has also been a big help. Talking (writing) has helped me to understand reading and writing much more than I used to.*

*All these factors, combined as one, have helped me in gaining knowledge about reading and writing. I read and write differently now and, I would say, better.*

## CONCLUSION

All these factors are combined as one in one place: a literate environment.

I've used various metaphors to characterize this environment. It's Frank Smith's reading and writing club. It's the Merry Pranksters' bus that holds everyone. It's a dining room table with seventy chairs around it.

A literate environment is not a reading and writing program — a monolithic Writing Process featuring prewriting, writing and rewriting, or some other combination of lock-steps. It isn't even teachers and students corresponding about books. In schools, a literate environment is wherever written language is the natural domain of the children and adults who work and play there.

I've described my own attempts at establishing a literate environment, my own particular methods. But it's beyond specific teaching methodologies that Daniel and Tara point me. They — and all the other eighth grade readers and writers — leave me with a fellow feeling I haven't known before as a teacher. Now that I'm off my English teacher pedestal, I want to deepen and extend this feeling the rest of my years in the classroom.

I think my students and I will find our way together. We're partners in this enterprise, all of us moving together *inside* writing and reading.

## REFERENCES

Atwell, Nancie, "Class-Based Writing Research: Teachers Learn from Students." *English Journal* 70 (1982): 84–87.

Giacobbe, Mary Ellen, Classroom Presentation at Northeastern University Writing Workshop, Martha's Vineyard, MA: July, 1983.

Graves, Donald, Lucy Calkins and Susan Sowers, Durham, N.H.: Papers and articles initiated at the Writing Process Laboratory, University of New Hampshire: 1978–81.

Newkirk, Thomas, "Young Writers as Critical Readers." In *Understanding Writing*, edited by T. Newkirk and N. Atwell. Chelmsford, MA: Northeast Regional Exchange, 1982.

Smith, Frank, "Reading and Writing Club," presented in an address at the Maine Reading Association Conference, Bangor, Maine, October 1983.

Staton, Jana, "Writing and Counseling: Using a Dialogue Journal." *Language Arts* 57 (1980): 514–18.

# 24

# why can't we live like the monarch butterfly?

LINDA RIEF

LOG ENTRY—JANUARY 4, 1984:

*If this is really what old is all about, I don't want to grow old. I'm not scared of being old. I'm scared of growing out of being young. Why can't we live like the monarch butterflies? They are ugly when they are young. Then when they spread their wings they soar and the world stands and watches this lovely butterfly.*

*Alison*

I designed a unit entitled "Generations" because I want my students to see learning as connected to situations beyond our classroom walls. I want them to listen to, think about, and interact with people outside the classroom about real issues.

Alison, a student in my eighth-grade English class, was responding in her log to what was on her mind. Our earlier reading and writing about relationships between generations were still fresh in her thoughts. What I intended with the unit seemed to be working.

After reading *How Does It Feel to Be Old?* by Norma Farber, aloud to the students, I said, "This book reminds me of the time my grandmother said she had something special in her top bureau drawer to show me. The smell of April Violets powder permeated the room as she took out a pink-flowered satin case. Inside, rolled in tight coils, were two yard-long braids of jet black hair. It stunned me to think the braids had been cut from my grandmother's hair when she was a teenager. I couldn't imagine her as being someone other than my white-haired, soft-spoken, smooth-skinned grandmother. She began to tell me about the beach trips to Manomet in Grampa's Model-T Ford. It was a wonderful afternoon."

I asked my students, "How often do you speak to your grandparents or parents long enough to find out what memories they hold dear? What life was like for them as teenagers? What life is like for them now? How they feel about growing older?"

Silence.

"How would you find out?" I asked.

"Ask them!" the students replied.

"What kinds of questions would you ask them?"

We brainstormed and came up with all kinds of questions, such as:

*What kind of relationship did you have with your parents?*
*What was expected of you as a member of a family?*
*What were the latest fads when you were a teenager?*
*Did friends ever talk you into doing something you thought was wrong? How did you feel?*
*What concerned or worried you the most as a teenager—in your personal life? in the world around you?*
*In what ways is life better now than when you were a young person?*
*In what ways was life better when you were young?*
*What does old mean to you? What does young mean to you?*
*How would you describe "growing old"?*
*What don't you want to happen to you when you get old?*
*What worries you the most about growing old?*
*What are you afraid of? What makes you happy?*
*If you could give any advice to young people, what would it be?*

We then talked about interviewing.

## INTERVIEWING

Few opportunities exist in schools for students to gather information from primary sources. Students don't realize that people often give them more useful information for writing than books or encyclopedias. Not only is the information more valuable, but the process involved in using the gathered material is invaluable to students as writers. In order for students to use the information they gather during an interview for various kinds of writing they must think out their own arrangements of words and synthesize this information with their own perceptions.

Students need guidelines for conducting an interview. For example: Ask the right questions, those which seem to be getting the most information, not just yes or no answers. Ask follow-up questions to preliminary information—things you want to know more about, or you are still wondering about. Use questions that ask how? why? tell me more about that. . . .

Show the students a good interview with follow-up questions and a poor interview that elicits little information, only yes or no answers.

POOR INTERVIEW

*Did you like school as a teenager?*
*No.*

*What was life like when you were young?*
  *Not bad. Not good.*
*What kind of relationship did you have with your family?*
  *Good.*
*Did you like your parents?*
  *Yes.*

GOOD INTERVIEWS

*In what ways was life better when you were a teenager than now?*
  *The world was a better place to live thirty years ago as far as I'm concerned.*
*In what way?*
  *If you wanted something you had to work and save for it. But not anymore.*
*How's that different from now?*
  *Now, you just hold a plastic card and you can have it. Kids ask and they get. They don't know the value of hard work and don't have any appreciation of what it takes to earn a living.*
*Whose fault is that?*
  *I'm not saying it's the kids' fault. It's the fault of the parents and our society.*
                                                            *—Charlie, age seventy*

*What was school like when you were a teenager?*
  *Teachers made school humiliating.*
*What do you mean by "humiliating"?*
  *Sometimes I got in trouble in school. I skipped school once and had to sit in the corridor all day with a dunce cap on my head.*
*What else did they do?*
  *Once I got caught chewing gum and had to put it on the end of my nose all day. They also made bad grades public.*
*How did they do that?*
  *By announcing to the whole class what you got or posting your bad grade as an example to others.*
                                                            *—Elaine, age sixty-two*

Like William Zinsser (1980), I advise:

DON'T USE TAPE RECORDERS! Recording is not writing. Equipment can malfunction, it takes hours to transcribe the words, and there is no longer any involvement in the writing process.

BE EXTREMELY OBSERVANT WITH HAND, HEART AND EYES. Take down as many exact quotes as possible from the person being interviewed to make the story alive. Try to capture the feelings behind the words—note any sadness, delight, enthusiasm, confusion, etc. Note what people look like—a physical description, especially of their faces—and note what they do as they talk or react to you—fidget, lean forward, wring their hands, whisper, yell, watch you, or look away. For example:

Pieter B. wrote of Charlie, age seventy: *Charlie is a man of average height, with a kind and caring face that seems fatigued from years of hard work. His hands are worn and slightly wrinkled and his face is permanently darkened from long endless days of working under the hot summer sun.*

Becky B. wrote of Elsie: *Elsie, a small, frail, white-haired lady in her mid-seventies, sits sleepily in an overstuffed chair, occasionally dozing off.*

Seth wrote of Charlie, age eighty-nine: *Tall and heavyset, Charlie sits in his room at the nursing home, staring out the window, longing for the family that isn't there. In very good health, except for eyes stricken with cataracts, he enjoys walking, although it is getting increasingly difficult.*

TRANSCRIBE NOTES TO A FINISHED COMPLETE SENTENCE FORMAT. *Try for a balance between what the person is saying in his own words (through selective quotes that show the person) and what you write to explain and connect what the person is saying.*

The students set up interviews with parents and grandparents. We talked about using nursing home patients to interview in place of, or in addition to, a grandparent. I agreed with the students that sometimes the patients are not the most cooperative or easy to talk to, and questions should therefore be asked selectively.

Before the students left for the nursing home, I read the poem, "The Little Boy and the Old Man" from *A Light in the Attic* by Shel Silverstein, because it shows so succinctly how a small child and an old man share similar problems and feelings. Only years separate people.

*The Little Boy and the Old Man*
*Said the little boy, "Sometimes I drop my spoon."*
*Said the little old man, "I do that too."*
*The little boy whispered, "I wet my pants."*
*"I do that too," laughed the little old man.*
*Said the little boy, "I often cry."*
*The old man nodded, "So do I."*
*"But worst of all," said the boy, "it seems*
*Grown-ups don't pay attention to me."*
*And he felt the warmth of a wrinkled old hand.*
*"I know what you mean," said the little old man.*

When the students returned from the nursing home, we began reading and writing about the relationship of generations.

## READING

In a literate environment (see Atwell's chapter in this volume), reading and writing cannot be separated. I chose books, poems, essays, and short stories as models for the writing I hoped the students could accomplish.

I had three ways of getting at reading, all designed around writing.

### Literature I Read to the Students

I read poems, short stories, or selected sections of books to the class. They simply listened. Sometimes I asked them to share a response or personal reaction to the piece, but only if they chose to share their response. Sometimes I asked them to share a response in their logs.

### Literature I Read with the Students

We read selected stories, poems, or essays together as the various pieces of writing were being drafted. In addition to modeling good literature, I think students learn to read better if they see words as they listen to someone reading.

Vocabulary work was built into this kind of reading, perhaps in response to parents questioning, "What *are* you doing with vocabulary?" or perhaps because vocabulary in content is far more palatable and worthwhile than through lists of isolated words. However, I'm still not sure my way is the best way, especially after David, bending over a dictionary, told me, "Boy, you sure know how to ruin a good piece of literature!"

In response to these poems and stories, students drafted, revised, and wrote responses such as the following:

*My father said, when I was six years old, that my mother went on a long trip. What I finally found out was, she had run out on us. I still miss her, but I try not to think about it much.*

— *Richard, in response to "The Colt" by Wallace Stegner*

*The poem "Meditation on His Ninety-First Year," by John Haag, puzzled me, for the man accepted death so calmly. How can anyone sit there and wait until it happens. Death scares me, but puzzles me. I wonder how I will accept death? The poem reminds me of my grandmother. Recently my grandmother went to the hospital. She had a stroke. It was hard for me because nobody would tell me her condition and I couldn't go see her because I was sick. She told me later she wasn't sure if she would live or die. She expected to die, but she didn't.*

*As soon as she got out of the hospital, I rode my bike straight to her house. She told me she had a stroke and thought she might not live. But she said she had too many things to do and lots left to accomplish. Summer was coming and she had to open up the camp. She said she didn't want anyone to miss her when she was gone, so she said, "I decided. I'm not going!"*

*"Not only that," she said, "but who would take care of Grampa, and the house?"*

*And I said, "And what would I do without your love and understanding?"*

— *Steve*

### Literature the Students Read on their Own

From a recommended list of books, which included a free choice, the students had eight weeks to read two stories, one specifically on the elderly, the other on family relationships. I asked them to relate their immediate response and feelings to the books, to relate the stories to their own experiences, to talk about the main characters and how they changed, and to talk about what they would have done differently if they had written the book.

Lisa B. wrote:

*In the story* Getting Nowhere *by Constance Greene, I liked the phrase, "The day dragged on like a turtle out for a walk." It describes a boring day excellently. I disliked the phrase, "That's some piece!" I've never heard a reference to a female that's so crude. It's as if she was a new Porsche or something. If I had written this story, I would have put less emphasis on the stepmother and more on the stepson's problems facing reality.*

While we were reading, we were writing.

### WRITING

All writing in the unit came from the interview as a primary source of information, in bits and pieces, or simply as stimulation, the stirring of memories.

We talked about good writing. The students feel that good writing pulls a reader in, and keeps her reading. It causes some reaction in a reader and the reader can usually identify with the writing. Because middle-school students are still imitating styles, they need *models* of all kinds of good writing of the type or kind they are asked to do.

At middle-school level students need to write more than personal narrative. I asked the students to attempt several kinds of writing: impression, a personality portrait, and an experience, in addition to writing responses to numerous pieces of literature as they wrote.

### Impression

I wanted the students to see the impressions left on others by older people and grandparents, especially those in nursing homes. I include the two following pieces of writing because they are good examples of impressions from a teenager's point of view. I read the poem "Old People" by Fay Longshaw to the class. The poem describes old people as neglected "like an unwanted toy put down and then forgotten." Together we read the short story "The Moustache" by Robert Cormier. The story is about a teenage boy who visits his grandmother in a nursing home. He feels guilty because he hasn't seen her in so long. At the nursing home, he discovers she is not just his grandmother, but a real person, with guilt feelings of her own.

*"I sit here these days, Mike," she said, her voice a lullaby, her hand still holding mine, "and I drift and dream. The days are fuzzy*

*sometimes, merging together. Sometimes it's like I'm not here at all
but somewhere else altogether. And I always think of you. Those
years we had. Not enough years, Mike, not enough . . ."*

*. . . "And I think of that terrible night, Mike, that terrible night.
Have you ever really forgiven me for that night?"*

*"Listen . . ." I began. I wanted to say: "Nana, this is Mike your
grandson, not Mike your husband."*

*"Sh . . . Sh . . ." she whispered, placing a finger as long and cold
as a candle against my lips. "Don't say anything. I've waited so long
for this moment. To be here. With you. I wondered what I would say
if suddenly you walked in that door like other people have done. I've
thought and thought about it. And I finally made up my mind — I'd
ask you to forgive me. I was too proud to ask before."*

*. . . "Nana," I said. I couldn't keep up the pretense any longer,
adding one more burden to my load of guilt, leading her on this way,
playing a pathetic game of make-believe with an old woman clinging
to memories. She didn't seem to hear me. (pp. 207−208)*

After reading this passage, I asked the students to close their eyes:
What words come to mind about the nursing home? What's the one
dominant feeling or impression you had? What stands out still in your
mind?

The students drafted, revised and wrote.

*The nursing home*
*was a series of small,*
*cramped,*
*cubicles,*
*which granted one*
*just barely enough room*
*to exist within.*
*In one such cubicle*
*sat an elder woman*
*shying from*
*any outer form*
*of activity.*
*"I'm old now. I'm unable to do that anymore,"*
*was her excuse*
*for not playing any games,*
*not taking walks,*
*not staying to socialize when a room fills,*
*and many other pleasurable pastimes.*
*So she sat*
*silently,*
*alone,*
*in front of her window,*
*looking out*
*upon a world*
*of fluttering autumn leaves*

*framed*
*against a seemingly never-ending,*
*bright-blue sky.*                                                    — *Lisa*

I walked into Oceanside Nursing Home feeling very inferior and small. My assigned elder, Ethel, didn't help. Her attitude made me feel obligated to impress her. Her hearing problem and her soft voice only made matters worse.

"Ethel, how long have you been here?" I yelled, so she would hear me.

She mumbled, as though she didn't want to answer at all.

"What?" I yelled, trying to keep the one-sided conversation going. I tried to be polite.

"Too long!" she grunted, and sighed a disgusted "Pffah!"

I thought the whole room of elderly patients and classmates was staring at me. But they were having the same kind of problems.

"Would you like to play a card game?" I suggested.

"I already told you my name — Ethel. Didn't you read my letter?"

"No, no . . . would . . . you . . . like . . . to . . . play . . . a . . . card . . . game?" I said again, slowly, loudly, and clearly, trying not to show my frustration.

"Okay," she replied.

We played the most unexciting game of "Crazy Eights" I have ever played. I not only made my moves, but I made hers as well. To make her happy I fixed it so that she won every game. At least that put some oomph into the afternoon.

However, the game brought boredom to Ethel. I suspected such when she said, "Is this all you kids do for fun?"

"No," I mumbled. "Would you like to play . . ." I began. But I noticed my class was leaving.

"It was really nice to meet you, Ethel." I moved toward her to give her a hug, but she turned the wheelchair so that her back was facing me.

Maybe she's just frustrated at being alone so much. I hope it wasn't me.

— *Ben*

**Personality Portrait**

Together we read the personality portrait of "Annie Lane" from the book *don't send me flowers when I'm dead* by Eva J. Salber. I wanted the students to read a good example of writing that revealed a character in several ways through an interview.

ANNIE LANE — *71* — *"Don't send me flowers when I'm dead. I want them now."*

*Annie Lane, tall and sturdy, her fair complexion shielded from the sun by an old-fashioned sunbonnet, works her land and is proud of it. In very good health, except for deafness, she wears a large hearing aid pinned to her dress.*

*I was next to the baby in my family. I had to work hard—I was a widow woman's child. I was raised to work. We had to dig our living out of the ground. I quit school when I was in the seventh grade and got married ... My husband was a farmer, too, so I went right on helping him with the farm. We both worked hard. A farmer never gets rich but we lived a happy life ...*

*I was raised to work and I still enjoy it. I'll go on working as long as I'm able. When I'm not able, when I get to that, I hope I'll do a big day's work and lay down at night and go to sleep and not wake up.*

*I tell people, "Don't send me flowers when I'm dead. I want them now." It wouldn't do me two cents worth of good after I'm dead to put me in my grave and put a pile of flowers on me as big as this house. If you've got a flower you want me to have, give it to me while I'm living. (pp. 20−21)*

We talked about how a writer reveals a character's personality by describing his or her physical appearance, what the person says or does, the person's thoughts or feelings, and the person's effect on other people. I asked the students to try to describe the person they interviewed—a grandparent or the person at the nursing home.

The students drafted, revised and wrote.

*Nana is the kind of person who would give you the shirt off her back, but then complain about how cold she is.*

*—Ann*

*Marjorie H., age 68: "Old is older than me. It isn't how you feel, it's how you think."*

*Marjorie sits down, sliding a pillow behind her somewhat disfigured back. She lowers her cigarette, takes up her beer, and picks a white hair off her stylish knit sweater. She is back from her job at a dry cleaners, where she does specialty sewing jobs.*

*The atmosphere is a comfortable one. The room is clean, although small and cluttered. Her well-favored Welsh Terrier wanders about in search of extra attention from her guests. As Marjorie talks, her eyes reflect the light of knowledge, knowledge of things past and present.*

*"I went to Newton schools, which, according to the census, were some of the best. I didn't like them. They were large schools with forty in a class. My graduating class was one of seven hundred. They weren't intimate, and the social life was a small clique excluding most of us.*

*"If I ever had a chance to live my life over though, I would choose to skip my teen years. I was constantly worried about little things like deadlines on homework. I can't remember ever being that happy during those years.*

*"If I could give any advice to a young person it would be, 'Keep your cool and you'll live longer.' I think kids today still worry too much."*
— *Lisa*

### Experience

I wanted the students to hear how other writers tell of their experiences with grandparents—to realize that what students might think of as trivial is what is really important in the experience.

   While writing an experience piece, we read together the poem "Grandfather" by James K. Cazalas, the essay "On Being a Grand-daughter" by Margaret Mead, and the short story "Good-bye, Grand-ma" by Ray Bradbury. In the short story by Bradbury, great-grandma, at age ninety, has lain down in her bed knowing it is time to die. Her family tries to tell her it is not the time.

*"Grandma! Great-grandma!"*
*The rumor of what she was doing dropped down the stairwell, hit, and spread ripples through the rooms, out doors and windows, and along the street of elms to the edge of the green ravine.*
*"Here now, here!"*
*The family surrounded her bed.*
*"Just let me lie," she whispered.*
*Her ailment could not be seen in any microscope; it was a mild but ever-deepening tiredness, a dim weighting of her sparrow body; sleepy, sleepier, sleepiest.*
*As for her children and her children's children—it seemed impossible that with such a simple act, the most leisurely act in the world, she could cause such apprehension.*
*"Great-grandma, now listen—what you're doing is no better than breaking a lease. This house will fall down without you. You must give us at least a year's notice!"*
*... "Grandma, who'll shingle the roof next spring?"*
*Every April for as far back as there were calendars, you thought you heard woodpeckers tapping the housetop. But no, it was Great-grandma somehow transported, single, pounding nails, replacing shingles, high in the sky!*
*"Douglas," she whispered, "don't ever let anyone do the shingles unless it's fun for them."*
*"Yes'm."*
*"Look around come April, and say, 'Who'd like to fix the roof?' And whichever face lights up is the face you want, Douglas. Because up there on that roof you can see the whole town going toward the edge of the earth ..." (pp. 92–93)*

We each wrote about an experience with a grandparent or an elderly person in an attempt to show the kind of relationship we have with that person.

*Grandma's chubby body slouches over the stove, waving her hands like a magician, trying to get her meat to cook. I watch her, thinking back ...*

*She's a funny lady, but she lost a lot of her sense of humor when she became sick. I think back to the first time I spent the night here . . .*

*Grandma looked weak. She had just gotten out of the hospital for a kidney ailment. She wasn't peppy and perked up as usual. We played "Kings to the Corner," her favorite card game.*

*In the middle of the game she sat back. The room was quiet except for the sound of buses and cars passing below. The smell of her apartment was suddenly swept away in a fraction of a second as a breeze blew at the curtains. The moon glistened through my ginger ale.*

*Grandma sat like that for a couple of minutes. She looked lost. Her expression was blank . . . and something . . . just looked wrong, out of place. A tear rolled down her cheek. Just the thought of Grandma being sad dampened my spirits.*

*Her words came out cold and uncaring. "I'm old!" She brought her hands to her face and examined her wrinkled skin. "I've lost the freedom of myself. They want to put me in a nursing home. You—you have qualities, qualities I'll never have again. Use them. You'll only be cheating yourself if you don't."*

*I didn't understand her then. I was only ten years old. She was sent to a nursing home, but she got better and returned to her apartment. She's helped me through a lot and I know I'd hate to lose her.*

*Grandma turns from the stove and sits at the table. She gets so wrapped up in the interview, she forgets the meat and it burns. But it doesn't matter. Before I leave, Grandma smiles, gives me a kiss and her eyes glisten. Now I know what she meant.*

*—Diana*
*Based on a true incident.*

## PUBLICATION

Publication is important to students. They need to see their own words in print. They become *real* writers.

The students compiled the final drafts of their writing into individual booklets, made a cover, and chose one sentence (a quote of their own) that showed what they thought about the relationship of generations.

The students wrote:

*Older generations have more experience and reverence for life than younger generations.*
*The young and the old need love, attention and confidence in themselves.*
*If parents don't show love for their children, the children will not learn to love.*
*Older generations don't want to be a burden on anyone.*

Students indicated the three best pieces of writing on their booklets, which were to be graded and submitted for consideration for publication in the class anthology. Every student had at least one piece of writing in our magazine — "Generations — A Literary Experience."

Since our publication came out, Joey, who told me in September that he really didn't like to write and wasn't very good at it, has asked me if I know of any other publications, other than ours, that might like to print his piece on his grandmother. Joey's self-confidence has improved so much, he readily admits he enjoys writing and sharing that writing now. He reads his own pieces over and over, and reads his peers' writing in the same booklet. Students need to feel not only pride in their own words, but they need to see good examples of what other classmates write.

When I handed out the ivory-colored magazines, I watched as the students marveled at the professional printing, then quickly turned to the "Index of Writers," ran their fingers down to their names, mouthed their page and turned to read. I noticed Kristi as she read. I knew which piece she was reading and my eyes filled with tears — again.

*It was a dreary evening. I decided to go to bed early. As I was falling asleep, I thought about how sick my grandfather was and how I hadn't seen him today. Maybe there was a reason I didn't go to see him. Maybe because he was looking worse each day. The cancer was eating away at him. Maybe when I saw him all I thought about was how awful it would be if he died. Maybe I already missed all the great times we used to have that we couldn't now. Maybe . . .*

*I remember my mom coming in to shut off the light.*

*I tossed all night long. A ringing telephone startled me. I hoped maybe it was just a dream, but it kept ringing.*

*"Hello," I said with hesitation. I knew it was about my grandfather. Why else would anyone be calling at one in the morning?*

*"Hi Kris," my aunt replied. "Is your mom there?"*

*When my mom got off the phone, she looked at me, then at the ground.*

*"Kris, Bampa died."*

*I went to school the next day, although I really couldn't concentrate on school work. When I got home I gave my mom a hug and started to cry. She looked at me and said, "I have something for you."*

*She handed me an envelope. "It's from Bampa," she explained. "He wrote you a letter a few months ago and asked your grandmother not to give it to you until after he passed away."*

*I took the letter into my room and sat on my bed. I opened the letter, reading it slowly, taking in every word.*

> *Kristi,*
> *I guess you always knew how much I really loved you. You brought much joy into my life. You'll always be my little girl . . .*
> *. . . Remember Kristi, I don't want any tears shed over this.*
>
> *— Kristi*

## REFERENCES

Christensen, Jane. *Your Reading — A Booklist for Jr. High and Middle School Students*. Urbana, Ill.: National Council of Teachers of English, 1983.

Cormier, Robert. *Eight Plus One*. New York: Bantam Books, 1982.

dePaola, Tomie. *Nana Upstairs and Nana Downstairs*. New York: G.P. Putnam's Sons, 1973.

Donelson, Kenneth and Nilsen, Alleen. *Literature for Today's Young Adults*. Glenview, Ill.: Scott, Foresman, 1980.

Farber, Norma. *How Does It Feel to Be Old?* New York: E. P. Dutton, 1979.

Huck, Charlotte S. *Children's Literature in the Elementary School*. New York: Holt, Rinehart and Winston, 1979.

McDonnell, H., Cohen, R. Gage, T. and Madsen, A. *Literature and Life*. Glenview, Ill.: Scott, Foresman, 1979.

Pooley, Robert C. *Counterpoint in Literature*. Glenview, Ill.: Scott, Foresman, 1967.

Salber, Eva J. *don't send me flowers when I'm dead*. Durham, N.C.: Duke University Press, 1983.

Shanks, Ann Zane. *Old Is What You Get: Dialogues on Aging by the Old and Young*. New York: Viking Press, 1976.

Silverstein, Shel. *A Light in the Attic*. New York: Harper and Row, 1981.

Tway, Eileen. *Reading Ladders for Human Relations*. American Council on Education, Washington, D.C.: 1981.

Welch, B., Eller, W. and Gordon, E. *Introduction to Literature*. Lexington, Mass.: Ginn and Company, 1975.

Zinsser, William. *On Writing Well*. New York: Harper and Row, 1980.

# mark shared
# with the class today

PAT MCLURE

In our first-grade classroom the children have some time each day to work on their writing. They write about their experiences and interests, share their writing with their friends through informal conversations and spontaneous peer conferences, and they have conferences with me. Each morning two or three children sign up to share some of their writing with the whole class. It may be a piece they are working on, or it may be a finished piece that has been typed and bound in a hard cover. We started writing on the first day of school, and children have been sharing writing with the class almost every day since.

Mark shared some of his writing for the first time on February 23. He had worked on pieces during the fall, including a published book with pictures and labels of all the rides he had been on at Disney World. Sharing with the entire class was a big step for Mark to take. He had listened to his peers share, and he had contributed a few questions and comments, but it wasn't until he published a book about his parrot that he had a piece of writing that he was willing to share.

Holly, the parrot, was a Christmas present to his family. He began the piece about the parrot in January. Mark had spent many writing sessions working first on illustrations using one of the basal readers to help him draw a parrot, as well as spell the word. Gradually Mark started writing some phrases and short sentences to go with his pictures. He needed a lot of encouragement to stay with his piece. He and I had several short conferences about it during January and early February. During these conferences Mark would read his piece aloud, and I would note each time that he was including more information. One such conference in February went something like this:

**Mark**: "He can do this."
**Me**: What can he do?
**Mark**: He tries to crack nuts.
**Me**: What kinds?
**Mark**: Peanuts.
**Me**: So what will this be about?

**Mark**: He can crack peanuts.
**Me**: That would be interesting.

Mark writes.

His page now has: HE KeN. bo Thesi Kicg Nites [He can do this: crack nuts.]
The more Mark learned about his bird, the more he would include in his piece.

Around the middle of February Mark said the piece was finished and he would like to publish. I typed it for him as he read it to me, and then he spent several more days illustrating the typed pages. He even took great pains with the binding of his book, looking over several of our wallpaper covers before making his choice for cover material. He then compared his cover print with different colors of paper for his endpapers and different colors of tape for the spine. The decisions made, the book was finally assembled. I asked Mark if he would like to share his book with the class. At other times when I had asked him about sharing, he would tell me that he would "think about it," but the final answer had always been no. I always accepted this answer, because I felt that the decision was his to make.

This time, however, the answer was yes. He felt he was ready. A half-hour later he was sitting in the "Author's Chair" reading his book to his peers.

MY PARROT BOOK

*My parrot likes the cage.*
*My parrot said, "Hi."*
*My parrot likes mirrors.*
*He can do this: crack nuts.*
*My parrot likes honey sticks.*
*My parrot likes to play.*
*He is Holly.*
THE END

Mark's book was well received. The children were interested in what he had written about Holly, and they wanted to know all about the parrot. He answered some of their questions by pointing out details in his illustrations, and he told them little stories about the way Holly acted. They were delighted by his anecdote of how Holly sings himself to sleep. Mark even imitated the sounds. The sharing session went on for over twenty minutes and ended in applause for Mark. The other children in the class had shared pieces of writing, and they knew how proud an author can feel about his published book. They had also learned some things about Mark's interesting pet.

Just before going home that day, Mark asked me how he might add more pages to his book. He wanted to write more about Holly, since everyone wanted to know more. I told him that some authors accomplish this by writing a sequel. He was excited by his sharing experience, and he was talking about ideas for the new Holly book as he went out the door that afternoon.

During our next morning's writing session, I was busy with other children, and I didn't have time to talk to Mark about his writing. Just before the end of the session, Mark presented me with the second Holly book and announced that it was ready for typing. Apparently, the ideas had rushed on to the paper for him. No one else in the class had ever completed a story so quickly. This time the illustrations were not as important. Only two pencil drawings accompanied the test in his folded-paper booklet.

Mark and I had a chance to have a conference later in the day. By that time he had written two more pages. We typed his book before the end of the afternoon, and he worked on illustrating his published pages the next morning. He signed up to share this book with the class as soon as it was bound.

MY BOOK, HOLLY

*He flies.*
*He can come on your shoulder.*
*He can come on your arm.*
*He eats his vitamins in his water.*
*Holly is green with red around his eyes*
*and he has yellow on him.*
*He can sing himself asleep.*
*He sleeps on his bar.*
THE END

Mark was now seen by his peers as our parrot expert.

Despite his initial reluctance, sharing his writing with the class has been a positive experience for Mark. I feel there is a strong sense of community in our classroom, one that is heightened by the sharing experience of the writing process. Mark definitely felt and benefited from the support and interest of his peers. His creative efforts were recognized and accepted by his peers just as each of them had been accepted for their efforts when they shared their writing with the group.

Mark has gone on to share many other pieces at various stages of completion with the class. His subjects have included soccer, his friends, and his dog. Now he is even experimenting with different forms of writing by trying to write some poetry about Popeye.

The experience Mark had with sharing is not so unlike my own recent experience. Many of the teachers in our school have been meeting once a week to work on our own writing. This has come about as a part of a research project conducted in our school by Don Graves and Jane Hansen from the University of New Hampshire.

Like Mark, my first time to share with the whole group came in

February. I remember how nervous I felt about reading my piece to a group of peers. The first draft had been written in the fall. I had some opportunities to share a draft with the whole group but had not volunteered. I preferred to have conferences with one or two peers in a small group. Each conference prompted some revisions. I even contacted an antique dealer specializing in Shaker furniture to be sure that my information was accurate. Through this interview I gained more information. As with Mark, the more I learned about my topic, the more I could write, so I added some of the interview to my piece.

The binding was also important to me — I wanted it to look finished. I decided to use a side-sewn cover, and I chose a dark calico that was in keeping with the period of furniture I had written about. For me, and apparently for Mark, the appearance of the final product mattered. There is a sense of satisfaction that comes when you complete a project that you have labored on for some time.

My work was well received and accepted by the adult group and I felt encouraged to attempt more writing. I can't say that I sat down the next day and dashed off another story as Mark had done; however, here I am at the typewriter.

As Mark's story and my story show, the sharing of one's writing is an important element of the writing process. It has a very practical side in that through the questions and comments following a reading, the writer is helped to see how the audience understands the piece. It is also through the sharing that the student who is sharing really begins to perceive himself as a writer, and his peers accept him as one.

In order to take the risk of sharing a piece of writing, the writer has to trust his peers. The writers in our class know and trust their audience. They feel accepted by their peers for their efforts in all areas over the course of the year. They have been recognized as experts in certain areas because of the published works they have shared with the group.

# fifth graders respond to a changed reading program

CORA LEE FIVE

26

How can teachers continue to learn about teaching? This question receives much attention in the current discussion about improving schools. Throughout my teaching career I have attended many university courses and inservice workshops. Usually these are opportunities for teachers to learn about new curricula and teaching approaches. Although these sessions have introduced me to many ideas I would not have come across on my own, I have had to find my own ways to make new ideas work in my classroom.

My own classroom research has helped me understand the impact new approaches have in my own classroom. As a teacher-researcher I welcome the opportunity to test hypotheses and pay attention to what my experiences teach me. Observing, listening, and questioning keep me alert to my students' needs and help me find ways to improve my instruction. Often this means involving the students in the research. I do this by telling them that I, too, want to learn, and by explaining what it is I want to learn. As my students become an active part of my research, we become a community of learners, rather than a teacher-centered classroom. The result is reciprocity in our learning: I learn from my students as they learn from me.

Classroom research helped me improve the way I teach reading. What follows is an account of my efforts to adapt and try out a new reading program with my fifth graders. I will acknowledge the ideas I received from other people who inspired the various changes I attempted. But I will concentrate on what I learned as I made these program changes and how my research enabled me to figure some things out for myself.

Over the past few years, the work of three people — Nancie Atwell, Mary Ellen Giacobbe, and Jerome Harste — has profoundly influenced my teaching of reading. Atwell's (1984, 1985) description of how her eighth graders responded to their reading by writing letters to her in dialogue journals stimulated my own thinking. She became involved in students' reactions to books by writing letters back to them.

Giacobbe (1985) made me realize that teachers must be responsive to children and their reading. She described ways to hold a quick reading conference with each child every day. Harste (1984, 1985) interested me in viewing children as informants and learning from them. His ideas helped me recognize the benefits of encouraging children to use many strategies to make meaning and of allowing time for collaborative learning—time for students to talk, time for them to think and respond.

Inspired by the insights of these three people, I embarked on a new venture two years ago—the creation of a reading program that would give children time to read and time to make meaning through writing and talking about books. The twenty-five students in my self-contained classroom had a wide range of abilities. The class included children who had learning disabilities and children who spoke English as a second language. I hoped all of these students would turn into readers who loved reading, and I hoped research would help me recognize how that happened.

The first thing I did was the most difficult: With much trepidation, I gave up the reading workbooks. As an alternative, I set up a reading program based primarily on Atwell's approach using dialogue journals. It had worked with her eighth graders; would it work with my ten-year-olds? The answer turned out to be, "Yes." My students became immersed in books—they began to talk books, authors, reading, and writing. And so did I.

As I considered how I wanted to use the ideas of Atwell, Giacobbe, and Harste, I noticed that three crucial elements—time, ownership, and response—made my new approach to teaching reading similar to the process approach to teaching writing. It was essential to increase the amount of school time children had for reading. Each forty-five minute reading period began with a mini-lesson during which the class and I discussed character development, setting, titles, different genres, or various aspects of the reading process. Following this lesson students read books of their own choosing. During this reading time I spoke briefly with each child about his or her book, and then I spent the remainder of the period reading a book of my own choice. We ended the period with either a group sharing-time, often related to the mini-lesson, or discussions among two or three students who talked about some aspect of their books.

The children maintained ownership in this process because they decided what to read. Books from home, from the public and school libraries, and from the classroom all became texts for our reading period. Children read the books they selected, not those assigned by me.

The third element, response, became the focus of my research. Discussions during the reading period were not the only way the students communicated about what they read; they also responded to their reading in a variety of ways in their literature journals. The primary way of responding was a letter to me when they finished a book. I read their journals and wrote letters back to them. They also wrote several letters each month about their books to a friend or partner in the classroom. This written communication following the completion of a book or the arrival of a partner's letter was completed during the reading period.

One of my first observations was of the difference between the oral and written responses. When the students talked to each other, they usually retold the literal details of the story. When they wrote, they apparently used time to reflect, to think. The letters, in particular, fascinated me because I could return to them and read them again. As each child's work accumulated, I could more easily follow the changes and development in their thinking about literature. At the beginning of the year the journal responses resembled the book reports which the students had prepared in their earlier grades. The children summarized plots and offered recommendations about their books. Gradually, the topics addressed in the mini-lessons and in our discussions of the books I read aloud began to appear in the children's journal entries. Their letters to me and to each other eventually included discussions of the following:

- the characters, often making personal connections to them
- the main idea or focus of the book
- the tone or mood
- characteristics of a particular author or techniques used by the author that they wished to apply to their own writing
- the way a certain lead, ending, image or a particular voice or feeling contributed to a story
- their predictions, inferences, and questions based on the books
- their own interpretations of their reading
- their own reading process, and of how they learned to read.

As I collected and compared students' responses and asked myself new questions about how students handled this task and became more involved in their reading, I learned much from Danny. Danny, who did not like reading at the beginning of the year, used one of his journal entries to describe his experience of learning to read.

*Dear Miss Five*
*when I was 4 years old my mom ust to read to me. some times she would let me try. I was pretty pitifull. then in kindergarten I always acted like I was reading and never raised my hand to read out loud. then in first grade we had a reading period and I sat and turned the pages. by this time I was a pro at turning the pages. when the teacher came over I don't know how she noticed but she did and she knew I didn't know how to read and she taught me how to read. Also the new kid on the block was danish and he didn't know any english so as I taught him I taught my self in a way. . . .*

After two months of the school year there were signs of Danny's increasing involvement with books. Here is how he responded at that time to Okimoto's (1982) *Norman Schnurman, Average Person.*

*November 27*

*Dear Miss Five,*

*This letter is about Norman Schurnman—"Average Person". The things I liked best about this book were, feeling and comedy. Especially feeling. Because when I read the part when he told his Dad he didn't want to play football. I think he deserved "Ten Medals"! Because if I had a Dad like that I would have probably played the whole season even if I was that bad and got hurt alot. because I wouldn't have the heart to watch him put his head down in dissapointment. And if he did put his head down, I would have felt so guilty I would have came back ten minutes later and said Dad I'll play, No matter how bad it felt. But I guess me and norman are different people. And I thought the author had a good ending because it made you in a way forget about the incident with his Dad.*

*Truly Yours,*
*Danny*

In my letter back to Danny I commented on the personal connections he was beginning to make with the characters.

*November 27*

*Dear Danny,*

*I could tell you were really involved with the characters in this book. I agree with you that Norman had a difficult decision to make. It must have been very hard for him to tell his dad, but I imagine it was also very hard for Norman to keep playing on the team. I guess Norman felt he did the best he could do and had to make his own decision.*

*You made a good point about the ending. Perhaps the author wanted a happy ending, and the ending in the book does make you forget about the situation with his father.*

*Sincerely,*
*Miss Five*

Four months later Danny loved to read and write and developed an interest in the authors of the books he was reading. He discovered the writer Byars through *Good-bye, Chicken Little* (1979) and began to wonder about the basis for her story.

*. . . I thought that this book was so true and this may have happened to a kid. I think I might send a letter to Betsy Byars to see if this book was based on experience. I thought his biggest mistake was fighting with conrad. this book was so good I wish I could read it forever.*

That discovery was important to Danny in several ways. He wrote to Byars and treasured the letter he received in return, stapling it into his literature journal. He read all the rest of her books. He also decided to write in his personal journal every night because, as he explained it, "In case I really do become an author, I want to remember all my experiences so I can put them in books for kids my age."

As the year progressed, many students began to experiment, struggling to interpret the ideas in the books they read. Josh described the character Jess in Paterson's (1977) *Bridge to Terabithia*.

*Dear Miss Five,*

*Jess has so many feelings its hard to discribe him. Let's say he had three stages. First, a normal, hardworking stage at the beginning, and feelings, if he had any, would never be shared with anyone else. The second stage, when Leslie came into his life, tured into a kind of magical stage in a way for him. The third stage, when Leslie died, he began to relate to adults. These three stages make him real.*

*Sincirly,*
*Josh*

John, a less able reader, responded to the same book.

*Dear Miss Five,*

*I think that Jess is changing on the inside because of lesslys death. He is starting to understand not only his father but all gronups and I think that he likes his sister better.*

Etay began to interpret and extend his ideas after only a few weeks. His response to Byar's (1974) *After the Goatman* and his other letters showed his developing ability to look beyond the story line.

*Oct. 21*

*Dear Miss Five,*

*On Thursday I finished* After the Goat Man. *I thought it was better than all the other books I read by Betsy Byars. I think she got the idea of the goat from as goats are supposed to be stubborn and the character is stubborn. I think thats her symbol for the character. I also like the way she puts Harold as a kid still in his fantasys and still dreaming about himself. I like the way she put her characters. There is also something that I liked about an anology about life. Figgy puts life as a spider-web and everybody's all tied up except for him, and he's only tied up by one string which is his grandfather (the Goat Man.)*

*Etay*

Etay found a connection between *The Night Swimmers*, also by Byars (1980), and Paterson's (1977) *Bridge to Terabithia*.

*... In the end of the book Roy asked his oldest sister "is the Bowlwater plant really a big gigantic plant with bedspreads for flowers" and he went on explaining his fantasy. His oldest sister answered "no." At that moment I thought about the book. I thought maybe that was Roy's bridge (like Bridge to Terabithia) from his fantasy world to reallity world.*

*Etay*

The development of the comments in the letters suggested to me that students become better readers when their early, and perhaps less successful, attempts to search for greater depth in their books are not treated as comprehension problems. Just as experimenting and risk-taking are important in learning to write, they are also important in learning to read. I began to pay more attention to how students found ways to express what certain books meant to them.

In the winter Etay discovered Alexander's (1981) *Westmark* trilogy. When he finished the last of the three books, he wrote a long letter relating the ideas throughout the trilogy. The conclusion of the letter summarized his thoughts.

> ... *In the end it wasn't the monarchy that won the war but the people. And the people are the ones who took over everything. I think in this triology Lloyd Alexander shows what happened in England. In the start England's monarchy had power over everything, like in the first book (Westmark). Slowly the power of the monarchy lessened, until now the monarchy has probably no power at all. In the Beggar Queen, in the end, the monarchy was overthrown by the people.*
>
> *Etay*

Many students, including David, used their letters to express the joy of finding a wonderful book.

> *Dec. 17*
>
> *Dear Miss Five,*
> *Yesterday I finished the best book, called,* The Green Futures of Tycho. *As soon as I read the back of it at the book fair I knew it was the book for me. And I was right, it felt as though it was made especially for me. . . . Ever since I was a little kid, I loved the thought of going into the past & the future, & telling my future, & thinking about all of it.*

But David's response was not limited to this personal interest in the book's topic. He also commented on the author's craft.

> ... *I like how the author kept changing & making the future & past more exciting. Like in the future he invented things, but didn't tell what they did, he let you figure it out. You should definitely read it to the class.*
>
> *From*
> *David*

The letters to partners raised some new questions about children as responders to literature. Three or four times a month each child would write about his or her book to another child in the class. The understanding was that if they received a letter, they were required to write back. Their letters to each other often differed from the ones they wrote to me; they struck me as having a more casual tone, and the writers seemed less concerned with what they thought I expected them to say in their response. Early in the school year David and Etay started to write to each other.

> *Oct. 8*
>
> *Dear Etay,*
> *I just finished* A Wrinkle in Time. *It is great book. I think you*

*should read it again. Some parts of the book are pretty confusing though.*

*From,*
*David*

*Dear David,*
*I hate science fiction!!!*

*Etay*

By November more of an exchange of ideas appeared.

*November 14*

*Dear Etay,*
*I am reading a book called* Alice's Adventures in Wonderland. *I don't like it very much. I think it is to boring! It seems that it takes forever. I have always liked Alice in Wonderland, but I don't like this one. Even though it is by the original author, Lewis Carrol. I am up to The Mock turtle's story. My favorite parts so far is when she was playing croquet & when she kept growing & shrinking when she ate the mushroom, even though those parts are not so good. I am not going to read,* Trough the Looking Glass.

*David*

*Dear David,*
*I can see that you didn't like this book. I didn't like it either. I thought it was just an adventure after an adventure and then all it lead to was a dream. It was written the best way it could but I don't think it was made for our age. I think it was made for smaller kids (who see it as a cute little fantasy) or for grownups (who see it with some meaning). We're in the middle because we're too big to see it as a cute fantasy and we're too small to see it with some meaning.*

*Etay*

The letters my students wrote to me and to each other also made me think about the classroom context needed to support their reading. I realized that they read with greater depth when they selected their own books, ones that appealed to them rather than those that I thought they "should" read. I also realized that they probably took risks to find ways to express themselves because I did not label their comments as "correct" or "incorrect." A classroom environment that accepted and respected what children said about books was necessary for these journal entries and their increased interest in reading. Furthermore, the example of the peer correspondence shows that the acceptance from other students can be as important as the teacher's.

Writing letters was not the only way my students responded to literature. "Mapping" is another strategy. Krim (1985, 1986) uses mapping with her senior high school students. Intrigued with her concept, I decided to try it with my fifth graders. I asked some students to map Paterson's (1977) *Bridge to Terabithia*. Some of their drawings appear in Figures 26–1 and 26–2.

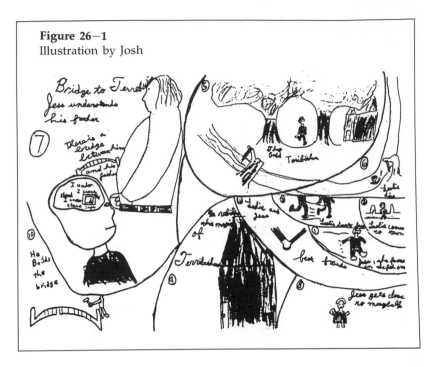

**Figure 26—1**
Illustration by Josh

*Bridge to Terabithia* is a story about a fifth-grade boy, Jess, who has difficulty relating to other people. He has no friends until Leslie moves near his home. Together they create Terabithia, a kingdom where Jess is king and Leslie queen. Jess loses his friend when Leslie has a fatal accident in Terabithia. As he tries to adjust to her death, Jess grows and begins to build a closer relationship with his father and others. In the end, Jess is able to give the magic of Terabithia to his younger sister Maybelle.

In his map see (Figure 26—1) Josh used lines and numbers to connect his drawings of important events. Although most of the events appear in comparatively small drawings, Josh represented two key points of the story with larger drawings. In one he made a bridge between Jess and his father; in the other he showed Jess rebuilding the magic of Terabithia for his sister Maybelle.

Amy mapped the story in a different way (see Figure 26—2). She saw the book in terms of feelings and made a flow chart with the characters Jess and Leslie at the top. They come together at school, where Jess is at first "anxious" and Leslie feels "different and out of place." "Proud but mad" are Jess's feelings after a specific school experience that made Leslie feel "happy." As their friendship progresses, they are both happy but, as Amy notes, in different ways. Amy follows with other feelings that describe the characters until Leslie's death. Then she continues with the range of emotions Jess experiences as he tries to deal with and accept the loss of his best friend.

Another strategy I used is one suggested by Harste (1985) called Sketch to Stretch. In this approach, as in mapping, the students pick out the most important ideas in their books and combine them in a

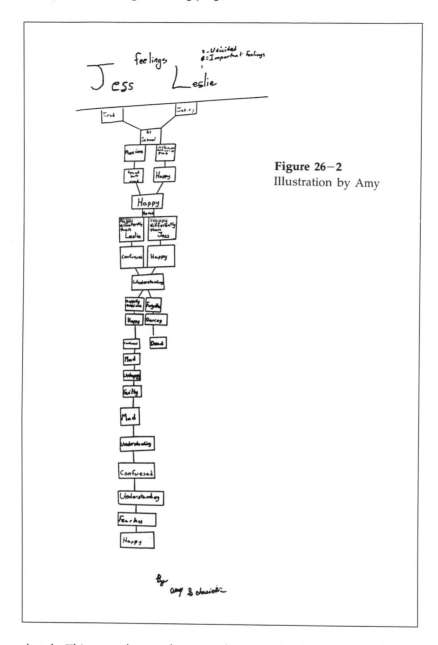

**Figure 26–2**
Illustration by Amy

sketch. This turned out to be a good way to develop sequencing skills as students connected events in a logical order to make a meaningful whole.

David has sketched the important parts of *Good-bye, Chicken Little* (see Figure 26–3) and has numbered his sketches to show the order in which they occur: the uncle drowns, Jimmy feels guilty and responsible, he fights with Conrad, they become friends again, and in the last picture David wrote that Jimmy "almost" forgets, and "everything turns out almost perfect."

The effect this kind of reading program had on both my students

**Figure 26-3**
Illustration by David

and me continues to amaze and excite me. By the fourth month of the program I could see children listening to each other and seeking recommendations for their next selections. They wondered about authors and tried to imitate authors' techniques in their own writing. They looked for feelings, for believable characters, and for interesting words, and they were delighted with effective dialogue.

Another indication of students' interest and joy in reading was the number of books they read during the year. The less able readers, including students with learning disabilities and those for whom English is a second language, read between 25 and 42 books each; the average readers read about 47; and the top readers between 47 and 144 books.

And the new approach had an effect on me. My students and I began to talk books before school, at recess, and at lunchtime; their reading period never seemed to end at twelve, even though the bell had rung. Their enthusiasm was infectious. I was constantly drawn into their discussions and especially their thinking, as I became more and more involved in their reading and their responses. This approach and my researcher's role helped me continue to learn more about these students, their reading processes, and their attitudes. Again and again, I saw the importance of giving them freedom to read and opportunities to experiment with and to explore their own ideas.

By collecting, sorting, reading and rereading their letters, maps, and sketches, I found for myself a much closer view of how children struggle and then succeed to find meaning in books. The process also kept me engaged in learning because it led me to new questions. What do children learn from my mini-lessons? In what situations will children take more risks with interpreting what they read? These new questions might be ones that help me reach more children in the way I reached John.

John, a real hold-out in terms of reading and loving books, a boy who completed reading few books in the fourth grade, could not have given me a greater gift. One day, I found him at his desk when everyone else had gone to lunch. He was reading. When I walked in he looked up and smiled, saying, "I love this book. I just have to finish this chapter before I go out."

## REFERENCES

Alexander, L. (1981). *Westmark*. New York: Dutton.

Alexander, L. (1982). *The kestrel*. New York: Dutton.

Alexander, L. (1984). *The beggar queen*. New York: Dutton.

Atwell, N. (1984). Writing and reading literature from the inside out. *Language Arts*, *61*, 240–252.

Atwell, N. (July, 1985). *Reading, writing, thinking, learning* [course]. Institute on Writing, sponsored by Northeastern University. Martha's Vineyard, MA.

Byars, B. (1974). *After the goatman*. New York: Viking.

Byars, B. (1979). *Good-bye, Chicken Little*. New York: Harper & Row.

Byars, B. (1982). *The night swimmers*. New York: Delacorte.

Giacobbe, M. E. (July, 1985). *Reading, writing, thinking, learning* [course]. Institute on Writing, sponsored by Northeastern University. Martha's Vineyard, MA.

Harste, J. C., V. A. Woodward & C. L. Burke. (1984). *Language stories and literacy lessons*. Portsmouth, NH: Heinemann Educational Books.

Harste, J. C. (July, 1985). *Creativity and intentionality* [course]. Institute on Writing, sponsored by Northeastern University. Martha's Vineyard, MA.

Krim, N. (1986). Where do we go from here? Try mapping. Unpublished manuscript.

Krim, N. (March, 1985). *Integrating reading, writing and critical thinking skills in the teaching of literature: Focus, mapping, and sequencing strategies*. Presentation at the annual spring conference of the National Council of Teachers of English.

Okimoto, J. D. (1982). *Norman Schnurman, average person*. New York: Putnam.

Paterson, K. (1977). *Bridge to Terabithia*. New York: Crowell.

Sleator, W. (1981). *The green futures of Tycho*. New York: Dutton.

# 27

## beyond basal reading
## a district's commitment
## to change

LINDA HENKE

Our conference room was ringed by tidy cellophaned samples of basal readers. The seventeen members of the reading committee sat in the midst of all that polished organization feeling more than a little disorganized. It was mid-December, and we'd been meeting twice a month in half-day sessions since school started. It had been a comfortable process thus far for most of the committee, veteran teachers who had been involved in similar program reviews and basal adoptions in the past. We'd moved through the needs assessment and review of the research with purposefulness and enthusiasm. We'd gone on to draft a belief statement and revised program goals.

Now, suddenly, unexpectedly, we were stuck. I glanced around the room at the anxious faces. Lola, a fourth grade teacher who was well-respected by her peers, had placed the issue squarely on the table. "I wonder," she said in a quiet voice, "if adopting a new basal reading program is going to make things better."

Lola was referring to four major issues which had surfaced as we attempted to match materials and methodology to our beliefs about learning to read.

### REALLOCATING THE TIME

Committee members were aghast at research findings (Anderson, et al., 1985) that an average of only seven minutes during the reading class was spent reading. As we examined our own classrooms, however, we found that workbooks, worksheets, and skills testing were eating up most of the reading block. Even the authors of our basal recommended spending no more than 60% of the time in the series; but because of our commitment to the program, we were scheduling time to read when all else was done. The committee recognized this practice stood in marked contrast to the growing body of research emphasizing the importance of extended silent

Reprinted with permission of the author. This chapter first appeared in *The New Advocate*.

reading to reading achievement, vocabulary development, and reading fluency (Anderson, et al., 1985).

## EXPANDING OUR READING OPTIONS

Robert Frost suggested that we "surround youngsters with so many books they stumble on them." We counted on the media centers as key resources in our quest to accomplish that end, but they alone could not meet the demands of the literary communities we wanted to see thriving in our schools. While we dreamt about classroom libraries with multiple copies of all kinds of trade books, we also knew that the purchase of a new basal series would exhaust the funds available for a reading adoption. We were left with an emphasis on basal readers, most with controlled vocabularies and too many excerpts for us to feel very comfortable about recommending them.

The reality seemed simple enough: if we adopted a new basal, it would become the reading program. But realistically, did we have any alternatives to basal-driven instruction?

## CHANGING ATTITUDES ABOUT READING

West Des Moines had always scored well on state and national achievement tests, so we didn't have to confront poor test scores. What we did find recurring in committee discussion was concern about "aliteracy." Our students were choosing not to read. Despite those high scores, they didn't think of themselves as readers. This fit all too well with studies finding children spending less than one percent of their free time reading (Anderson, et al., 1985).

Several of our reading resource teachers who worked with remedial students also voiced concern about "low group syndrome." Because most of our classroom reading instruction was organized into traditional ability groups, they worried about the impact of membership in the low group on children's visions of themselves as readers. Mary Ann, our newest Reading Resource teacher, commented "Despite our best efforts, some kids come to reading class with 'FAILURE' written all over their faces."

Unfortunately, it wasn't just students' attitudes that had us worried. The demands of accountability seemed to have narrowed our own vision of the teaching of reading to a skill-drill orientation which was far removed from the joyful interaction we all experienced as we talked about books with our colleagues. We wanted that same delight for our students.

## INTEGRATING THE LANGUAGE PROCESSES

Finally, our goals stressed reading and writing and speaking as mutually supportive ways of making meaning. Yet instruction organized around a language text and a basal reading series didn't come close to fostering the relationship we wanted. While most of the current basal programs incorporated writing into instructional methodology, too often it seemed "added on" rather than woven through classroom practice.

We wanted much more than that. We wanted classrooms where students were actively involved every day in reading and writing and discussion: classrooms where students exerted a good deal of control over what they read, what they wrote, and what they talked about. But how did we get there? We knew it was happening in New Zealand and Canada and in classrooms sprinkled all over the United States. But could an entire district in the heart of Iowa make such a dramatic change?

## TAKING A CHANCE

The answer was a surprising "Yes." In January, after several long and emotional meetings, the committee voted unanimously to take to the elementary teachers a much different proposal from what they had originally expected. We outlined a strategy which asked the district to:

1. Keep our current 1979 basal series, but scale back its use dramatically.
2. Develop a trade book program which would include multiple copies of selected books and skeleton teaching guides for each of the grade levels.
3. Give daily priority time to independent reading and build classroom libraries to support that emphasis.
4. Incorporate daily writing time into our reading/language block.
5. Provide intensive staff development to assist us in implementing the change.
6. Initiate a communication campaign to help parents understand the new program.

Those seventeen committee members were some of the best salespeople I have ever met. Although consensus had not come easily, each one of them now owned the proposal. In building and grade level as well as in one-on-one discussions late into the afternoons, they sold the program to their colleagues. When the district's teachers voted on January 28, only 22 of 185 voted against the proposal.

## ORGANIZATION FOR CHANGE

The first committee meeting in February was uproarious. Success had made us heady. We laughed and shared war stories about the vote. Peggy and Mary Pat chuckled over the amount of coffee cake and muffins they'd baked during the month. They were certain teachers in their building were more receptive on a full stomach. For the first hour we gloated, feeling smug in the final tally. Then, as we began to talk about our game plan, the faces grew anxious again; and not even Lola's buoyant "Everything will be wonderful" could ease the rising panic. Somehow between February and September we had to build the reading/writing program we had sold.

During the spring and summer we worked feverishly designing "Beyond the Basal." We expanded our committee and added several adjunct committees, involving many teachers in the development. In an incredible flurry of activity we sent teams to visit midwestern schools working from a whole language orientation; surveyed our own staff about books and topics their students enjoyed; spent hours in book stores; and discussed, argued, and reworked until the program began to take shape.

## BUT WHAT ABOUT THE BASAL?

One of the first items the committee tackled was a definition of the role of the basal in this new program. We recognized that it was impossible to mandate a whole language orientation, nor did we want to do that. We believed teachers needed the freedom to make professional decisions for their own classrooms. We did, however, aim for several essential commonalities in those classrooms.

So was born the great compromise. We encouraged every teacher to schedule daily priority time for independent reading and for writing workshops. Those teachers who were most comfortable with basal reading could continue to use it ... for up to fifty percent of the allocated reading time. The remainder of the block was to involve shared reading experiences drawn from our trade book program. Those who chose not to use the basal at all were free to do so ... but they consulted the basal skills taxonomy as they designed their lessons. As the program developed, we found important similarities in classroom goals and methodologies emerging but more room than ever before for individual teacher decision-making. The basal was no longer dictating the shape of our program.

Janet and Linda, first grade teachers whose classrooms were across the hall from each other successfully implemented "Beyond the Basal" the first year. Both scheduled 30 minutes daily for independent reading and 45 minutes for writing workshop. The remaining hour and 30 minutes of the reading/writing block was spent differently.

### In Janet's Room ...

a. Fifty percent of the time was spent teaching the basal; however, half of the block was also devoted to shared reading of a wide range of trade books.

b. Her instructional decisions flowed primarily from the sequence of the basal taxonomy.

c. While in the basal, students were grouped homogeneously into three reading groups: the rest of the time the students read in a variety of small groups which were generally based on interest or student choice.

The basal reader served as a useful tool for Janet, and she grew more comfortable making choices about basal stories and instructional variations as the year progressed. She talked frequently about students' enthusiasm for the trade books and was delighted with the discussion and writing generated as students read "real books."

**In Linda's Room** . . .

a. Almost all of the time was spent outside of the basal.
b. Instructional decisions flowed from students' needs to comprehend a particular text; the basal taxonomy served as a catalog of skills which she consulted as needed.
c. Grouping in the classroom was heterogenous, based on the books children chose to read.
d. Students read basal stories as they fit into a theme they were studying, but the primary reading materials were trade books and children's magazines.

Linda's classroom developed from her strong whole language philosophy. Freed from the requirement of a basal program, she created a classroom environment focusing on children's immediate attempts at meaning-making. The trade books seemed to weave themselves naturally into science and social studies, and soon it was difficult to tell when one subject area block stopped and the next began.

As the year progressed, it became clear that "Beyond the Basal" could accommodate both teachers as they modified their classroom practices to more closely align with what they believed about growing readers and writers.

## THE TRADE BOOK PROGRAM

Developing the trade book program was probably the most exciting and exhausting task we faced. At each grade level we built sets of children's books organized into thematic webs and whole class reading options. By September, shelves of colorful trade books lined the teachers' workrooms in the elementary buildings. Each teacher had at her fingertips at least five titles to offer students for whole class in-common reading and five thematic webs, all with corresponding teaching outlines.

### Whole Class Reading

We chose to organize a part of the program into whole class reading because we believe that a learning community is built on shared experiences. As children read and react to the content of a common text, they broaden their personal perspectives and become aware of other points-of-view.

Many of the books selected for whole class reading correspond with topics in science and social studies. Marguerite Henry's *Brighty of the Grand Canyon*, for example, seemed made to order for the fourth grade desert unit.

We stress that every student need *not* be able to decode every word in a whole class book, but that all can learn from listening and participating in discussions and other related activities.

The guides we developed for our whole class books include:

1. Pre-reading activities in which children explore one or more of the issues addressed in the book by relating personal experiences and offering opinions.
2. Checkpoints which provide students time to pause and reflect on what they've read.
3. Follow-up activities which frequently required the students to return to the book to locate information which would clarify, substantiate, or expand their thinking. Follow-up activities included questions, writing and drama suggestions, and occasional mini-lessons which focus on a particular reading skill readily developed in the text of the story.

Throughout the guides we stress that books should be read, discussed, and enjoyed. We encourage teachers to choose activities selectively and insure that every reading period contains a rich chunk of time devoted exclusively to reading.

### Thematic Webs

Thematic web work allows small groups of students to read and interact about books as the entire class explores a central theme such as "That Makes Me Mad," "Special Places," and "Expeditions." Around each of the themes cluster multiple copies of at least four different titles.

Judy C., a fifth grade teacher, chose the theme "Heroes and Heroines" to introduce her students to "Beyond the Basal" in the fall. The web included five books: Ann McGovern's *The Secret Soldier: the Story of Deborah Sampson*; Dorothy Sterling's *Freedom Train*; Jean Fritz's *Where Was Patrick Henry on the 29th of May*; David Adler's *Martin Luther King, Jr.*, and Roxanne Chadwick's *Anne Morrow Lindberg, Pilot and Poet*.

Judy began her web work as most teachers do . . . with a book talk about each of the titles, sharing brief excerpts, discussing the authors, and tossing in several "ticklers" to encourage children to read the books. The books were displayed in the classroom for easy browsing; and the following day, children indicated their first and second choices. With this information Judy formed the discussion groups for the two week investigation.

During web work, children read, discussed the books in their small groups and participated in large group activities exploring the heroes and heroines theme. They listed personal heroes and heroines on a large sheet of butcher paper lining the back wall, and created a time line, placing the individuals they were reading about in historical context.

As the theme continued, Judy conducted mini-lessons drawn from objectives in the basal taxonomy. During the two week study, students referred to their own trade books as they learned about such things as judging authors' qualifications, using an index, and understanding idioms.

From time to time Judy joined in the small group discussion, but most often she moved about the room, functioning as a process observer and assisting children in working out the dynamics of small group interaction. She discovered early that meaningful small group work could not be assumed; it needed to be modelled and taught. She established predictable rules and routines; defined the roles of discussion leaders, recorders, and participants; and outlined clearly for the group their tasks and time lines.

Web work was a great hit with Judy's students. Once they had a sense of how webs worked, they began to construct their own by reorganizing the multiple copies and drawing from the classroom library and the media center. It was not uncommon for the message board by the door to include notes identifying potential web topics and book titles. As the year progressed, Judy's students became increasingly confident in their ability to control their own learning.

## INDEPENDENT READING

Independent reading was certainly not a new idea in our district: most teachers sandwiched in moments for students to read from self-selected books once or twice a week. Because research tells us that the amount of independent reading children do is significantly and consistently related to gains in reading achievement, we decided to make it much more of a priority than in the past. We aimed for daily designated time beyond the optional reading of books when other work was finished. We structured the minimum of a half hour to include time for children to read the books they selected, to confer with the teacher about their reading selections, and to participate in whole class book talk.

For the first two years in the program, we offered teachers the option of using their basal workbooks or spending the equivalent funds on trade books for classroom libraries. The first year about half the teachers chose the workbook option. This year, only ten teachers out of one hundred and eighty-five in the entire district chose to use workbooks. The trade books were too exciting to pass up.

The no-workbook account involves everyone in often animated discussions of trade books. Teachers are eager to get the most for their money; they discuss, share new finds, visit bookstores, and pour through vendors' catalogs. They have become increasingly adept at matching kids and books, in part because now they have resources to purchase books when a need arises in the classroom.

At the end of the second year, workbooks will no longer be an option in our program . . . but almost all of our teachers have already discovered they don't need them anyway. The workbook money has found a new purpose and the teachers enjoy the freedom it gives them and their students to create their own reading environment.

### WRITING IN READING CLASS

It seemed to us that a reading classroom must also be a writing classroom. But rethinking our writing program and moving outside of the language text was probably the most difficult task we faced. We turned to the work of Graves (1983) and Calkins (1986) to assist us in structuring daily workshops. In the workshop setting children choose their own topics and exercise control over their writing processes. They learn to confer with each other, to revise and edit and respond to other writers appropriately.

As we explored the possibilities, teachers began to think of their language texts as resources for lessons that grew from a demonstrated need of student writing. And children began to build connections with their reading just as we had hoped. They became authors, and their work was received with the same respect as the authors of the trade books they were reading. They experimented with new devices discovered in reading, tried new genres, and reacted with so much enthusiasm that teachers were amazed. A second grade teacher commented, "These kids moan when they have to stop workshop to go to P.E. It's amazing!"

We have a way to go in those daily workshops: many of us still struggle with management problems, but I am confident our sense of experimentation will carry us through. We have decided that "work-shopping" is very similar to writing; it requires time for reflection and revision . . . and willingness to respond to the special needs of the participants involved.

### BUILDING THE SUPPORT NET

A program which urges teachers to rethink and revise their approach to literacy education must provide a support net for those willing to risk the change. At the district level we made it clear that we wanted to help with the program implementation in every way we could. We brought in nationally known speakers throughout the year and released the entire elementary staff to hear them. Jane Hansen, JoBeth Allen, Mary Ellen Giacobbe, Judith Newman, and Glenda Bissex all spent time in our district last year, addressing key issues in literacy learning.

We offered two courses each semester especially tailored to our own program implementation with university credit attached. And we paid the tuition for those teachers wishing to take any of the courses.

We scheduled monthly grade level meetings which were planned by an advisory team of teachers and dealt with successes and problems that arose in program implementation as the year progressed.

We began literacy libraries in each building which provided teachers professional literature on language learning.

We offered fireside study groups which met for three or four evenings to discuss a specific book or topic concerning whole language teaching. The district purchased multiple copies of these books, and teachers signed up for any that sounded intriguing to them.

We purchased video cassettes on language learning and conducting writing workshops with corresponding support articles and offered them to the principals for building level meetings.

Every elementary principal completed a fifteen hour course entitled "Managing and Supporting a Literacy Program," and as a result, building level support teams and coaching strategies were implemented in most buildings.

During the summers we offered the Iowa Writing Project to our teachers. The first summer 23 signed up for the three week study of writing. The second summer, 58 teachers were involved.

In August of 1986 as we were beginning our implementation, Judith Newman cautioned us that it would take five years for us to see a difference in our program . . . yet by the end of the first year, the majority of classrooms were making real strides.

## PARENT COMMUNICATION

A key strand in the support net is communication with parents. Our parent communication committee spent two weeks the first summer drafting four flyers that were sent home periodically during the year addressing issues in reading and writing.

Teachers prepared carefully for an open house in September, displaying the trade books and student writing and explaining the changes we were making. They emphasized again and again that we were not abandoning the teaching of skills; we were, however, approaching them differently.

Following the first quarter conferences, we offered a parent seminar for an evening. Ken Goodman spoke to 450 parents in a crowded gymnasium about developing literacy. His address was followed by a round of what we call "breakout" sessions in which teams of teachers explained the new program and answered questions. A final round of sessions dealt with parent involvement. The evening was a great success and parents are clamoring for more. A second seminar is planned for this fall, and we are designing classes offered through our community education program to help interested parents understand and assist in their children's literacy education.

We have made a point of being available to speak for church groups, preschool groups, PTO meetings . . . any place at all where people are interested in the literacy program.

Beyond the Basal is into its second year . . . we are still beginners at all of this. But already over 20 school districts have visited us, hungry for alternatives to traditional literacy programs. Our test scores have remained high, and parent evaluations at the end of the first year were incredibly positive. Children are reading and writing at home as they never have before.

But we also realize that there will be bumps as we continue to revise and realign what we are doing with what we believe about learning. There are still anxious faces and anxious moments. A sign in the conference room reminds us that the only person who enjoys change is a wet baby. Below it, however, a penciled addition suggests "and born again reading teachers." In some ways I think that is true. We have recovered our sense of discovery. We have become committed to the professional decision-making and development that occurs when a district moves beyond basal reading.

### REFERENCES

Anderson, R. C., E. H. Heibert, J. A. Scott, and I. Wilkinson. (1985). *Becoming a nation of readers: The report of the Commission on Reading.* Washington: National Institute of Education

Calkins, L. M. (1986). *The art of teaching writing.* Portsmouth, New Hampshire: Heinemann Educational Books.

Graves, D. H. (1983). *Writing: Teachers and children at work.* Portsmouth, New Hampshire: Heinemann Educational Books.

# 28

## "así no se pone sí"
## (that's not how you write "sí")

RENÉ GALINDO

Every school day presents an opportunity to learn, not only on the part of the students but also on the part of the teacher. Evaluation can be looked at as a two-way street. In one direction is the evaluation of the student's learning, in the other direction is the evaluation of the teacher's own learning. This particular account describes my own understanding of literacy development and the literacy events in which my students were participating. This two-way traffic provides a channel for communication in which information that is gathered from one side of the street can complement the decisions being made on the other side. What a teacher learns from his or her students about how children's knowledge of literacy develops helps that teacher become a better-informed evaluator of the students' learning.

Evaluation can also be looked at as an ongoing process that takes place during the children's actual involvement in literacy events. Part of the emphasis of evaluation as an ongoing process is the realization that most forms of evaluation are one-shot measures and might not be indicative of what students know. Ongoing evaluation gives the teacher the opportunity to observe the child learning on different days and in different social situations.

Evaluation of children's reading and writing should take place while they are actually reading and writing and not in situations that are supposed to simulate actual reading and writing. This makes it possible for the teacher to learn about how children use the many resources that are available to them from their classmates and from print material. Information obtained in these contexts not only helps the teacher learn about the students' use of written language but also provides information about how students apply their knowledge to expand their literacy.

The specific examples of evaluation and learning covered in this chapter are: the evaluation of a second grader's spelling strategies, the evaluation of children's choices of language use during literacy events, and the evaluation of the literacy event itself. Through a personal narrative of my own classroom experience spread out over

Reprinted with permission from *The Whole Language Evaluation Book*, edited by Kenneth Goodman, Yetta Goodman, and Wendy Hood. Copyright © 1989 by Heinemann Educational Books, Inc.

two years, I describe my experience of looking at evaluation as an ongoing process on a two-way street.

After school one day, as I was reading through my students' journals, I began to notice that several students in my first-grade bilingual classroom were learning how to read and write in both Spanish and English. I was surprised because these students were receiving their reading instruction only in Spanish. My classroom was composed of twelve bilingual students and fourteen monolingual students. During "formal" reading instruction the students were grouped by their dominant language; out of four reading groups, two were learning how to read in English and two in Spanish. At different times of the day the students were also grouped in mixed language groups composed of children of different language and academic abilities. At that time I thought that a student had to learn how to read in one language before learning to read in another. But through what I was seeing in the students' journals my preconceived notions of how children develop biliteracy were challenged. My understanding of biliteracy did not explain how the children were learning to read and write in two languages at the same time.

My students challenged me with the question: How can bilingual children develop simultaneous biliteracy while receiving reading instruction only in Spanish? I decided to start looking for an answer. My students had been writing in dialogue journals containing a narrative of some kind. These were usually personal narratives, but sometimes the children wrote fictional narratives or a song that they liked. After they had finished their journal entries, they would read their journal to one other student. When each student finished reading, the other would write a question or comment. The two students would carry on an oral and written dialogue until they decided that they had finished. They would then repeat the procedure with the other student's journal. From the beginning of the school year I had also been writing in my journal and sharing it with a different student each day. But when I started thinking about the biliteracy question, I stopped writing in my journal and began close observations of the bilingual children's writing in order to begin to understand the literacy development that was taking place in my classroom.

## PARTICIPANT OBSERVATION

Participant observation is a research method that is used in ethnographic studies. In participant observation the researcher participates directly with the people he or she is studying in the activities in which they are engaged. The purposes of this method are outlined by Peter Woods:

*The central idea of participation is to penetrate the experiences of others within a group or institution. How better to do this than by assuming a real role within the group or institution, and contributing towards its interests or functions, and personally experiencing these things in conjunction with others? Access to all group activities is assumed, and one can observe from the closest range, including*

*monitoring one's own experiences and thought process. Again,*
*teachers are ideally placed for this, for they already occupy a role*
*within their own institution. (1986, p. 33)*

Participating directly with people in the activities under investigation
is the central aspect of participant observation. In this way the
investigator hopes to achieve a view of the processes involved in the
activities that would otherwise not be possible. The perspective of the
researcher in participant observation is more similar to that of the
other participants in the activity. As Woods points out, the research
methodology of participant observation is very suitable for classroom
teachers because teachers already assume a real role.

The teacher is a participant in the classroom in the sense that he or
she is there all the time and has a well-defined role in the class. The
teacher serves as the leader or organizer of instructional activities.
The teacher also participates sometimes by actually doing the activity
along with the students. But there's a difference between being a
participant-observer and being a classroom teacher. A classroom
teacher does not become a participant-observer merely by occupying
the role of classroom teacher. In order to be a participant-observer a
teacher must first be aware of the differences that exist between being
an ordinary participant in an event and a participant-observer. James
Spradley mentions this difference in his book, *Participant Observation*:
"The participant-observer comes to the social situation with two
purposes: (1) to engage in activities appropriate to the situation and
(2) to observe the activities, people, and physical aspects of the
situation" (1980, p. 54). The second purpose is what differentiates
participant observation from ordinary participation. In my case I was
interested in noticing details that I might not have noticed had it not
been for the questions that I was trying to answer about biliteracy.
How, for example, did the choice of a writing partner influence the
choice of the language in which to write? How did oral dialogue
affect written dialogue and vice versa? Keeping these questions in
mind while I observed or participated with the children made my
participation different from the ordinary.

Another important difference is that "unlike most ordinary participants, the participant-observer will keep a detailed record of both
objective observations and subjective feelings" (Spradley, 1980,
p. 58). The records that I kept included audio tapes of the students'
interaction, the students' journal writing, and observational notes.
These notes included contextual information that would not have
been recorded by the audio tape about the interaction that influenced
what or how the children were writing.

Participant observation exists along a continuum moving from
passive participation at one end (being present at the scene but not
interacting with anyone else) to active participation at about the
midpoint (doing what the other people are doing) to complete participant observation (studying a situation in which the researcher is
already an ordinary participant). The continuum moves from only
observing interaction to full participation in the interaction.

The classroom teacher is in a unique position to be a participant-observer. The students expect the teacher to be interested and to be paying close attention to whatever might be going on in the classroom. It is not difficult for the teacher to interrupt whatever is taking place between children as they work on an activity and to ask questions about what they are doing or learning. By contrast an outsider would need considerable time to be able to develop that type of relationship with the students. The students have come to learn through their school experience that teachers ask many questions and evaluate students' participation in the activities as well as the final product. When I participated in the activity of dialogue journals, I was not the leader of the activity. I was doing the same thing as the rest of the class; I was writing in my journal and sharing it with another student, or I was sitting next to some children, observing and writing notes. I set the tape recorder next to us and taped the interaction. I was not involved in observational note taking since I was writing in my journal. When I was writing, I was highlighting the participation aspect of participant observation.

When I became interested in the development of biliteracy, I decided to stop writing in my journal in order to observe the students more closely. I was interested in the interaction between the students and hoped to find out how that interaction affected what they wrote. During this time I was more of an observer than a participant. I didn't want to participate directly in their decisions about written language use. Since I was the classroom teacher, it was easy for them to assume that I would tell them what to do or would answer their questions. But I was interested in finding out how they would go about solving their questions about written language. So I would redirect the question back to them or suggest that they ask their writing partner or the other students who were sitting at the table with them.

Every day I selected a different bilingual student to observe. I would sit next to the student as he or she began to write. I then followed the student as he or she selected someone with whom to share the journal. I observed their interactions and took notes on their writing as they shared their journals.

After I had the opportunity to observe and tape the twelve bilingual students, I begun again to write and share my journal with the students. I realized that writing in my journal alongside my students gave me an opportunity to interact with them in a manner not possible when I was only observing them. At the beginning of the year I had written in my journal as a way to introduce dialogue journal writing to the students and to show them the high priority that I placed on the journal writing. Now I was writing in my journal again in order to become a direct participant in the interaction that I was interested in observing.

At the beginning of my observations I didn't want to interrupt the interaction between the students. But after several months of observations, issues besides biliteracy attracted my interest. I began to wonder about spelling strategies, the role of social interaction in written language concept development, and code switching in writing. Whenever I saw these issues highlighted in the students' interactions, I would question them about what they were doing. I felt that I had been a passive observer long enough to gain a sense of their interaction. Now I was interested in understanding their thinking as they wrote and talked about what they had written. I tried to do this by asking them why they wrote something a certain way or why they had decided to react way they did to their partners' suggestions or comments. (Later in the chapter I list some examples of the kinds of questions I asked.) The children didn't find it unusual that I was asking them questions while they were writing. They expected the teacher to be interested in what they were doing. It would have been more unusual for me to be a passive observer, not asking any questions.

The students enjoyed and looked forward to their turn to sit with me at one of the tables to talk and share our journals. There would almost always be other students at the table who would join our conversation, and our writing time was full of talk about our topics and the events in our lives that we were writing about or other anecdotes that we shared.

Three examples from my classroom illustrate how these experiences also permitted evaluation to emerge as a part of this process. The first example shows my evaluation of the development of Don's spelling strategies. The second highlights my evaluation of code switching in children's writing. The last looks at my evaluation of the instructional activity of dialogue journals.

## EVALUATION OF DON'S SPELLING STRATEGIES

I was concerned about Don's spelling development because his spelling ability was progressing at a much slower rate than average for the class. When it was Don's turn to be observed, I made a point of observing his spelling strategies. What I saw helped me understand and feel better about Don's spelling development.

The students in my class used a spelling strategy that made use of their knowledge of the initial sounds of their names and of popular childhood figures such as E.T. Don often used this strategy. He began by looking at the student name cards that were taped above the alphabet. Above each letter of the alphabet I had placed a card on which the students had correspondingly written their names. First names and last names were written on separate cards. As time went on, Don was able to make use of this knowledge of letter-sound correspondence wihout having to look at the cards. He was able to use the students' names as a mnemonic device in order to help him remember and use initial sounds. While writing, Don would exchange information about how to spell a word by saying, "*r* like in Richard," "*a* like in Anthony," "*t* like in Tony." Don also used the dictionaries in the classroom, and more often than the other students. In addition

Don used as resources for his spelling his previous writing in his journal.

On one occasion Don wanted to spell may name in his journal. He was writing about the time I had given his rabbit some food. As he got to the place where he was going to write my name, he stopped writing and started turning pages in his journal. He found a page where he had previously written my name. He then copied my name onto the page where he was writing about his rabbit. I then asked him how he had been able to spell my name on the previous page. He told me that another student had helped him spell it. Don often made use of his classmates as resources for spelling, but this time he was able to spell my name without asking for help from his friends. After using his journal writing as a spelling resource a few more times, he won't have to turn the pages to look for the spelling of my name; he will have learned how to spell it without relying on any outside resources. Don's spelling strategy is an example of learning in the zone of proximal development. The zone of proximal development is that area of learning in which someone is able to do something with the help of more capable peers. "It defines those functions that are not yet matured but are in the process of maturation. It is the level of potential development" (Vygotsky, 1978, p. 86). Using this strategy Don moves from the point where he must ask his friends how to spell my name (help is provided by more capable peers) to where he is able to help himself by seeing how he had previously spelled it in his journal (help through the symbolic system of writing) to where he will be able to spell my name without having to look at his journal (Don as an independent speller of my name).

Another spelling strategy that Don used was to consult the writing in other people's journals. One time the girl with whom he was sharing his journal was writing about getting to use the reading loft in the reading teacher's room. Don wrote in her journal, "¿Qué es una loft?" (What is a loft?) As he was writing in his own journal he needed to use the word *loft*, so he looked for the place in his partner's journal where she had written the word. He then copied it into his own journal.

Observation of this kind yields richer information than a conventional spelling test. This information makes it possible to take more facts into consideration when I have to evaluate Don's spelling ability. A spelling test would have been able to tell me only which of certain words Don knows how to spell and which he doesn't. Instead I was able to learn about the different strategies that Don uses when he needs to spell a word that he doesn't know. Before evaluating Don's spelling ability I had been concerned about his slow spelling development compared to that of the other children. After learning about his spelling strategies I was relieved because I saw that Don was making use of different resources in the classroom—dictionaries, environmental print, his own knowledge of sound-symbol relationships through the mnemonic of students' names—and asking for help from his friends. When I learned that Don was making use of such a wide variety of strategies, I felt that his spelling ability would continue to grow because he had different options to try and because he was moving toward being able to spell the words that he was learning without the help of his friends.

## EVALUATION OF CHILDREN'S CODE SWITCHING

Another area that I began to focus on was code switching in children's writing. (For an example of such code switching, see Figure 28–1.) Since mine was a bilingual class, the students were able to switch back and forth from Spanish to English as they were talking to one another or to me. There are many studies that look at children's code switching in oral language (Duran, 1981) but very few about code switching in children's writing (Edelsky, 1986). I decided to focus on this area because I thought that it might give me valuable information about the choices that the children were making in using English or Spanish in oral and written language. As a result I would have a clearer idea about their development of biliteracy. I was also interested in discovering how individuals varied in their use of Spanish and English in their writing, for I had noticed that some students seemed to code switch more than others.

An example of code switching in writing involved two first-grade girls. They were writing back and forth to each other as I sat next to them observing and audio-taping their interaction. Mary had just finished reading her narrative to Rosalinda. The narrative was written entirely in Spanish. Rosalinda then wrote back to Mary, "A mi me gusta la canción Yes o No" (I like the song yes or no). Rosalinda wanted Mary to tell her if she liked the song that they had mentioned in their writing. Mary was to indicate her answer either by writing her response or by circling the word *yes* or the word *no*. This type of opinion survey was widely used by the children in their journals. When Rosalinda read back what she wrote to Mary, she orally substituted the word *sí* for *yes* even though she had written the

---

**Figure 28–1**
An Example of Code Switching

ANOCe mí PLPL
me í VL LDLr
UNDOLr
Y NO meDO
DiNero
AND HiS
NNS Mí DLD
THe eND Mar.7

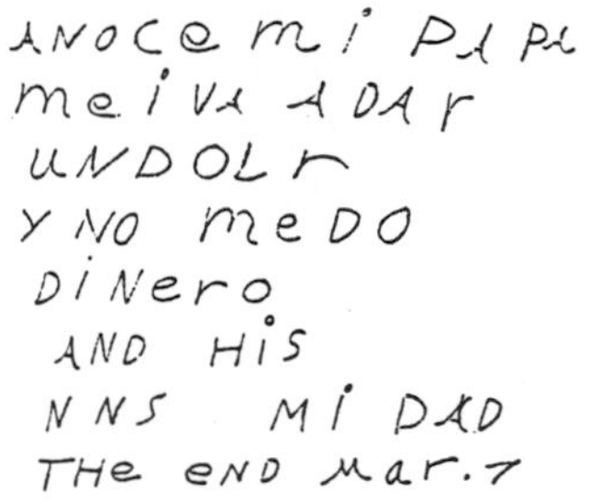

Last night my father
was going to give me
a dollar
and he didn't
give me money
and he's
nice my dad
The end.

English word *yes* in Mary's journal. Mary noticed that Rosalinda had written "yes" but read it as "*sí*." She told Rosalinda, "Así no se pone sí" (That's not how you write "*sí*"). Mary then erased Rosalinda's "yes" and wrote "sí." (Since the word *no* is spelled the same in Spanish and English and is pronounced almost identically, it was not an issue in their discussion.)

I then asked Mary why she had erased Rosalinda's "yes." Mary said, "Porque aquí era en Spanish" (Because here it was in Spanish). Notice that Mary code switched the last word, saying "Spanish" instead of "*español*." She meant that until Rosalinda had written the word *yes* in her journal, the whole narrative and written dialogue had been in Spanish. I then asked Rosalinda, "¿Cuándo escribes en español, puedes escribir en inglés?" (When you write in Spanish, can you write in English?) Rosalinda nodded her head yes. Without my having to ask her, Mary said, "Yo no" (Not me). I then asked Rosalinda, "¿Y por qué tú sí? (And why do you do it?) Rosalinda then answered, "Porque también es como una canción (Because it's also like a song). I'm not sure what she meant by that. Maybe she was saying that when you're talking in one language you can then start singing in the other, or she might have been referring to a specific song that contained code switching. I'm reasonably certain that by using songs to back up her opinion, she was saying that code switching was very common for her in oral language and was saying by implication that if you can code switch in oral language, you can also code switch in written language. She then said, "Porque si no quieres escribir en inglés puedes escribir en español" (Because if you don't want to write in English, you can write in Spanish). Here she was pointing out the role of choice in language use.

Later that day I asked Mary and Rosalinda separately about their opinions of code switching in writing. Both of them were able to summarize their views. Rosalinda said, "If I want to I can." Again she was saying that code switching in writing is a personal choice, like code switching in speaking. Mary said, "Cuando rayo en inglés o español no me gusta que me rayen en el otro" (When I write in English or in Spanish, I don't like them to write in the other one). Mary stressed the "no me gusta" (I don't like it) part of her answer. She was saying that when a text in her journal was written in one language, she didn't like the classmate with whom she was sharing to switch to the other language.

Both Mary and Rosalinda code switched very often when they were speaking. But in this case written language allowed Mary to be able to monitor the written conversation in a way that isn't possible in an oral conversation. She was able to do this because she had a graphic record of the written conversation in her journal. When Rosalinda wrote the word *yes*, Mary was able to see it and read it. She was also able to *see* that the remainder of the text was written entirely in Spanish. The word *yes* stood out. The written dialogue was also different from an oral dialogue because it was recorded in a journal. Mary owned the journal, and she could make decisions about what was going to be in her journal. Because she and her partner were writing in Mary's journal, Mary was able to erase the word *yes* and write the word *sí* without having to ask Rosalinda for permission. In other words, Mary "didn't like it," so she erased it.

This example demonstrates the difference of opinion that can exist between two students when it comes to code switching in writing. Both of the students were able to back up their position, Rosalinda by comparing code switching in writing to code switching in oral language (songs) and Mary by saying that she didn't like to see a switch in writing from one language to the other. I was surprised to learn that children as young as these first graders were able to express their opinions about language use as clearly as they did. These children had very clear and very different ideas about code switching. Being present during this interaction and being able to talk to them about it while they were writing and afterwards gave me the opportunity to learn their views on code switching, views I would not have been able to learn about through other forms of evaluation.

Code switching in oral language is very common in the Hispanic community in which these children live. The opinions that both of these first-grade girls expressed reflect common views in the community. Mary's opinion that one shouldn't switch languages is held by many people who feel that if someone is speaking in one language they should then complete what they are talking about in that language and not switch back and forth between languages. Other people hold more relaxed attitudes towards code switching similar to Rosalinda's, that code switching is a common part of the communicative behavior of bilingual speakers. Rosalinda and Mary helped me to think about the influence that language use in the community has on language use in the classroom, that the different patterns of language use found in the community are present in the classroom. They also helped me review my opinions about code switching. I code switch often in speaking and writing. My own oral and written language use in the classroom is also part of the community's language patterns. My students' opinions of language use helped me realize that I would have to look not only at what was going on inside the classroom but also at the literacy events outside the classroom. I interviewed my students' parents to find out about their experiences and their siblings' experiences with reading and writing at home. Those findings supported my growing understanding of emergent biliteracy.

## EVALUATION OF DIALOGUE JOURNALS

As a participant-observer during the writing of dialogue journals I was able to evaluate not only the children's writing but also the use of dialogue journals as an instructional activity. (For an example of such a journal, see Figure 28–2). One of the purposes of dialogue jounals is to provide a context in which social interaction among students of different academic and linguistic abilities can take place. This context provides opportunities for biliteracy and the development

Figure 28−2
A Dialogue Journal (Excerpt)

Mart

yono Meisevatara XD U Y Tou u

KSiFeu L
esce

*Lupe:* Yo no me quise levantar en esta mañana.
(I didn't want to get up this morning.)
*Luis:* Why didn't you want to get up?
*Lupe:* Because I feel lazy.

of written language concepts (Teberosky, 1982). It also provides an opportunity for the students to work in zones of proximal development with one another. In these zones the students are able to work on aspects of literacy learning in collaboration with more capable peers (Vygotsky, 1978). My observations of students writing together in their journals provided many examples of their sharing their ideas of the written system with one another. Such examples include the first exploratory use of cursive writing in their journals by some first graders as well as the exploration of the relationships between intonation and punctuation by second graders. The participant aspect of participant observation allowed me firsthand experience in the interchange of ideas about writing. This took place when I wrote in my own journal and then shared it with a student. When I was directly involved in writing in my own journal and responding to another, I had the opportunity to be directly involved in the interaction, not as a teacher observing my students but as one of the many people in the classroom writing and talking about one another's journal entries. This direct participation allowed me to evaluate the effectiveness of dialogue journals as a means for the interchange of written language concepts.

One such example involved Mónica and myself. Through this interaction I was able to get a glimpse into her view of adults as users of written language. Mónica had written in her journal about her three-year-old brother, José. In her journal entry Mónica had mentioned that she called her brother a "dum-dum." When Mónica had finished reading her journal entry to me, I wrote a question in her journal asking her whether her brother called her any names. We then initiated an oral and written conversation about her brother's language learning:

**Me**: ¿Le dijiste dum-dum a tu hermanito? (Did you call your brother a dum-dum?)

**Mónica**: Sí porque se miraba como un crazy. (Yes, because he looked like a crazy.)

**Me**: ¿Qué te dice tu hermanito a ti cuando se quiere reir de ti? (What does your brother call you when he wants to laugh at you?)

**Monica**: Titopo. (baby talk)

**Me**: ¿Qué quiere decir eso? (What does that mean?)

**Monica**: Yo creo que, ha-ha! Que fea! (I think, ha-ha how ugly!)

**Me**: ¿Y cómo aprendió decir eso? (And how did he learn to say that?)

**Monica**: No sé pero mí papi le anda diciendo muchas cosas. (I don't know, but my dad is telling him a lot of things.)

**Me**: ¿Y cómo sabe lo que quiere decir las palabras? (And how does he know what the words mean?)

**Monica**: Porque yo lo leyó. (Because I read them to him.)

**Me**: Pero yo estaba hablando de palabras cuando están platicando. (But I was talking about words when you're speaking.)

**Monica**: Oh, yo no sabía, pero sí estás libre. (Oh, I didn't know, but you're free.)

**Me**: ¿De qué estás hablando cuando dices que estoy libre? (What are you talking about when you say that I'm free?)

**Monica**: De que tienes muchas palabras tú. Pero no se que tienes mucho libre de palabras. (That you have a lot of words. But I don't know that you have a lot of free words.)

**Me**: ¿Cómo que libre? (What do you mean by free?)

**Monica**: Pues libre de que tienes muchas palabras en tu mente. Pero no se que yo tendrá. (Well, free in that you have a lot of words in your mind. But I don't know if I'll have any.)

**Me**: ¿Sabes si tienes palabras en tu mente? (Do you know if you have words in your mind?)

**Monica**: No se. (I don't know.)

**Me**: ¿Entonces cómo sabes que yo tengo palabras en mi mente? (Then how do you know that I have words in my mind?)

**Monica**: Porque hablas mucho. (Because you talk a lot.)

**Me**: ¿Y tú no hablas mucho? (And you don't talk a lot?)

**Monica**: Sí, pero no tanto. (Yes, but not that much.)

**Me**: ¿Y el José tiene palabras libre o de qué clase? (And José, does he have free words or what kind?)

**Monica**: Babies' palabras, no más. (Only babies' words.)

**Me**: ¿Y entiendes palabras de babies? (And do you understand babies' words?)

**Monica**: Pues no más de José. (Well, only José's.)

During recess, which followed our writing time, I asked Mónica more questions about what she meant by "free words." From that conversation, along with what we wrote about in her journal, I was able to piece together a rough idea of what she meant. She was using "free words" to mean the speaking, reading, and writing vocabulary available to a person from his or her knowledge without having to rely on outside resources such as dictionaries. Before this interchange with Mónica, I had never wondered how young children might think about what must seem to them the impressive number of words an adult can say, read, and write without seeming to have to consult any resources. I'm still not quite sure why Mónica chose to use the image of "free words" to describe her conception of adult knowledge of oral and written language, but it had some important metaphoric meaning to her.

Once again, as happened when I began to think about the development of biliteracy, I was presented with a question by one of my students. How do children view adults' knowledge of the written system (especially the influential adults in their lives such as parents and teachers), and how does it influence the way they view and approach literacy? I'm still thinking about that question. Mónica helped me evaluate the usefulness of dialogue journals as a context in which to challenge and expand not ony children's written language concepts but also the teacher's. I could evaluate my purpose in using dialogue journals not only by observing what the children were learning about written language but also by being able to participate directly in the activity myself. This direct participation made it possible for me to expand my own knowledge of children's views of written language, and as a result I found out through firsthand experience that the journals were providing an effective context for the development of written language concepts.

## CONCLUSION

The children's journals in my classroom introduced me to evaluation as a two-way street. They did this by forcing me to examine my assumptions about the way in which bilingual children develop biliteracy. Realizing my lack of understanding made it possible for me to assume the role of a learner and to allow my students to show me what they were doing during literacy events. Evaluation calls upon the teacher to learn not only about what his or her students know and are learning but also to learn about his or her conceptions about how children use and expand what they know. Becoming a participant-observer gave me the opportunity to learn about my students and also about my own ideas of the development of biliteracy. It put me into the interaction taking place between the children, and sometimes between the children and myself, as they were writing and talking about their writing. Throughout the school year, through this interaction I was able to learn about my student's literacy learning by observing and participating with them in situations in which they were using written language for meaningful purposes and in which they could make use of all the resources available to them. When I learned about Don's spelling strategies, I realized that he made greater use of different kinds of resources for spelling than most of the other students in the class. By using a wide variety of resources, he was expanding his knowledge of written language. When he used the dictionary, he used his knowledge of alphabetical order; his use of his classmates' names utilized his knowledge of letter-sound relationships; searching through his journal for a word that he wanted to spell made use of his knowledge of reading. Don helped me learn that spelling is not just a narrow use of written language knowledge but that it is tied to different aspects of our language knowledge.

The code-switching episode with Rosalinda and Mary helped me to learn about the variations that exist among speakers and about the ability of young children to express their views of language use. The exchange between Mónica and myself helped me to think about children's conceptions of adult literacy. My experience with my students has helped me to learn about the development of literacy in children. But equally important, it has shown me that I have much to learn about children's use of oral and written language and that evaluation is a two-way street in which teachers can evaluate not only their students' learning but also their own.

## REFERENCES

Duran, R. *Latino Language and Communicative Behavior*. Norwood, NJ: Ablex, 1981.

Edelsky, C. *Writing in a Bilingual Program: Habia Una Vez*. Norwood, NJ: Ablex, 1986.

Spradley, J. *Participant Observation*. New York: Holt, Rinehart & Winston, 1980.

Teberosky, A. "Construccion de Esctitura Atraves de la Interaccion Grupal." In *Nuevas Perspectivas sobres los Proce sas de Lectura y Escritura*. Ed. by E. Ferreiro and M. Gomez Palacio. Mexico City: Siglo Veintiuno Editores, 1982.

Vygotsky, L. *Mind in Society*. Ed. by M. Cole, S. Scribner, V. J. Steiner, and E. Souberman. Cambridge, MA: Harvard University Press, 1978.

Woods, P. *Inside Schools: Ethnography in Educational Research*. London: Routledge & Kegan Paul, 1986.

**thinking throughout
the process
self-evaluation
in writing**

SUSAN STIRES

Seven years ago, at the beginning of the first year of our school writing project, most of my intermediate-level learning disabled students considered themselves failures as writers. But as they focused on expressing meaning and communicating with others in their writing throughout the year, they began to experience success, and both their concept of themselves as writers and their confidence in their abilities changed as their understanding, knowledge, and skill increased. As Donald Graves (1985) has written, "Although writing process work helps all writers, it seems to be particularly successful with people who see themselves disenfranchised from literacy" (36).

My students learned to write and to evaluate their writing. For ongoing evaluation, or what Thomas Hilgers (1986b) calls "forming," they evaluated pieces of writing in process, particularly during revision or editing. They also evaluated their pieces as products, which Hilgers calls "summing up." For overall evaluation we looked at their collected writing every nine weeks and at the end of the year. They chose the pieces they liked best and least and talked about the reasons for their choices. At the end of that first year, I asked my students to write a self-evaluation in which they would tell how they changed or grew as writers from September to June. I also asked them to choose their best pieces for the year and tell why they selected as they did. They were to include the discoveries they had made about their own processes as writers. They had their folders to refer to and were allowed time to read and think about their writing. Except for the fact that this was an assigned topic for a specific audience—the student and me—this piece was to be written like other pieces during writing workshop; that is, it was to be developed over time, and each student was to draft, revise, confer, and edit. Shawn, a fourth grader, who had not considered himself a writer at the beginning of the year because of his spelling problems, wrote the reflective self-evaluation in Figure 29–1.

Reprinted with permission from *Stories to Grow On: Demonstrations of Language Learning in K–8 Classrooms*, edited by Julie M. Jensen. Copyright © 1989 by Heinemann Educational Books, Inc.

**Figure 29–1**
Shawn's Self-Evaluation

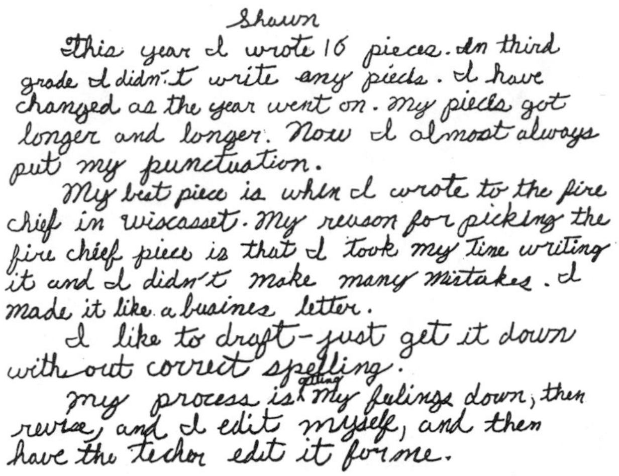

> Shawn
> This year I wrote 16 pieces. In third
> grade I didn't write any pieds. I have
> changed as the year went on. My pieces got
> longer and longer. Now I almost always
> put my punctuation.
> My best piece is when I wrote to the fire
> chief in wiscasset. My reason for picking the
> fire chief piece is that I took my time writing
> it and I didn't make many mistakes. I
> made it like a busines letter.
> I like to draft—just get it down
> with out correct spelling.
> My process is my felings down, then
> revise, and I edit myself, and then
> have the techer edit it for me.

By contrast, the following text was written by a fourth grader on a recent state assessment.

| ORIGINAL TEXT | CONVENTIONAL FORM |
|---|---|
| At Harry      Harry an I fun at<br>  he hous | At Harry's<br>Harry and I [had] fun at his house. |
| A. T. is a nise kib      an Harry<br>to. we did sone brakbansing | A. T. is a nice kid, and Harry [is]<br>too. We did some breakdancing |
| in a talint shoe we had alt<br>  of fun. I wish I was out<br>  side rite now. Sens I am not<br>  I will stoq thingcing a<br>  bowt it. I hope you relis<br>  I am not having fun good<br>    day. O I for got my<br>      frund's Ron and Jonhe<br>      Thay bo not hav mech<br>      more but I bo not<br>      care      thay ar real nise<br>      and Heath      he has<br>  a Irning bisa dlute so<br>    bo Rod. I hav bislexeal-<br>    u      you bo not no hou hrd-<br>This is fore me. | in a talent show. We had a lot<br>of fun. I wish I was outside<br>right now. Since I am not<br>I will stop thinking about<br>it. I hope you realize<br>I am not having fun [a good<br>day]. Oh, I forgot my<br>friends, Ron and John<br>They do not have much<br>more, but I do not<br>care. They are real nice<br>and Heath [is too]. He has<br>a learning disability. So<br>does Rod. I have dyslexia.<br>You do not know how hard<br>this is for me. |

This state writing test is designed so that students can have the time and materials to draft, revise, and self-edit before writing their final copies into the test booklet. The students are given a writing prompt, in this case to write about a memory of having a good time with a friend or friends. Although this student attempted to stick to the topic, he was overwhelmed by the task and used writing to "talk" to the reader. Although he has strengths as a writer, he does not appear to know what they are or how to use them in this situation. His evaluation of himself is that he is dyslexic and is therefore excluded from this process. He is disenfranchised from literacy.

The primary students I now teach have labels like L.D., E.D., and E.M.R., but they are unaware of them. They value themselves as readers and writers because they know about their own reading and writing processes and because I value them as readers and writers. Obviously, I value them because they are inherently valuable, but I also overtly value them so that their other teachers will do likewise, and so that they will continue to value themselves. My kindergarten through third-grade students are considered to be the least sophisticated language users in the school, but in many ways they are no different from primary students in the regular program.

## WRITING AND RESPONDING

I provide time and opportunities for my students to make evaluative responses to questions, both formally in publishing conferences and interviews and informally as the occasions arise during conferences and other talks. I also share things about my own processes that help them evaluate theirs, and encourage them by laughing, or rolling my eyes, or running over to get a book in which a professional writer has done something similar to the student writer. My students' comments about their writing and reading have always been important to me. They know I value that they have to say, including their evaluations, because I listen to them, record what they say, and use the information they provide to plan activities, help them work with each other, and build their concepts of themselves as writers.

Of course, I am not the only teacher in the room. When I meet with my students in small groups, everyone is a teacher. Some of my students stay in their classrooms for writing, and I go to them, assisting their teachers. In this way, they receive responses from a large group—just as Danny did last year. His most consistent answer to why he chose to publish a particular book was, "The other kids will like it." Having an effect on a group in some way, attracting interest, revealing knowledge, or gaining approval, drives self-evaluation.

When I studied my students' self-evaluations, I learned that they occurred naturally at all stages of the writing process, from prewriting, to writing, to rewriting. In the next three sections, I will relate a few of the many situations in which students evaluated their writing. Most of the students featured are my primary resource room students; the rest are primary students in classrooms where I worked when my students were mainstreamed for writing. I have limited my examples to recorded teacher/student interactions, although another fertile area is student/student or group interactions.

## EVALUATING BEGINNINGS: DRAWING, WRITING, TOPICS, AND MODES

As a kindergartner, Kevin doesn't first select a topic and then begin to draw or talk about it. For him, drawing functions as the rehearsal for his writing and usually determines topic selection; in many ways, the drawing *is* the writing. If he were asked the question "What are you going to write about?" he would give the classic answer "I don't know. I haven't drawed it yet." When I talked to Kevin, he was already working on a second drawing, having rejected his first one (Figure 29–2). After we had talked about the one he was working on I asked him to tell me about the first one. He explained, "This is messed up." I asked what happened, and he continued, "The guy's head is too small inside the car. Donnie thought so, too. I'm writing on this one 'cause it's okay."

For Sarah, too, drawing and writing are closely combined in her evaluation of her piece (Figure 29–3). She had read her random string of letters as "The fisherman has crabs, fish, lobsters, and more crabs." When I asked her to tell me more about it, she simply said that it was nice. Thinking that she might be referring to the colors or to some other aspect of the drawing because she loves to draw, I asked, "What makes it nice?" She said, "It is about a fisherman, and I was at the Fisherman's Forum." Sarah's dad is a fisherman and her family had just attended this state meeting. Her evaluation was based on nontextual considerations, which Thomas Newkirk (1988) identifies as the experience depicted and the evaluation of the experience.

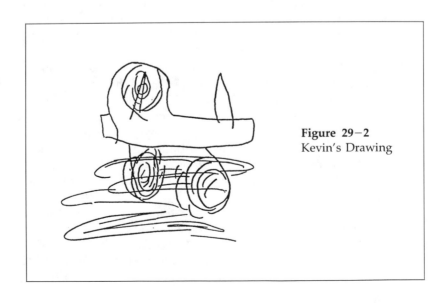

**Figure 29–2**
Kevin's Drawing

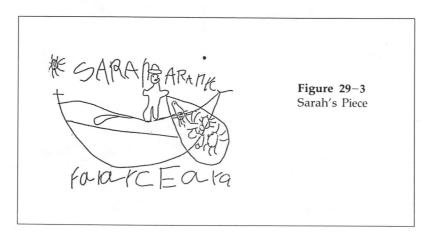

**Figure 29–3**
Sarah's Piece

Sarah was extending herself beyond the concreteness of the drawing; in fact, her evaluation existed before the drawing.

By first grade, topic selection has become a highly conscious act because students have internalized the question "What are you going to write about next?" Erik was a first grader in a classroom where several of my students were mainstreamed for writing. When I came to work with them, I often talked with Erik, who always had something he wanted to write about. One day in the spring, when he didn't know what to write next, I told him that sometimes when I am stuck, I write down three or four topics. I showed him how I think about each one and decide on the one that interests me most. Erik chose to adopt this suggestion but developed his own book format. When he finished writing it, he called me over to share it. He was excited because this kind of writing, or visual thinking, had been fun and had yielded him a topic (Figure 29–4). Throughout his book he evaluated the topics that came to mind and rejected them because he had already written about them—until he came to Boston. After he had shared his book with his classmate Elizabeth and me, he began to write about Boston.

When Nathan was in first grade, his mother had to be hospitalized for an extended period of time, and he was confused by the whole experience. The day she left he had difficulty saying good-bye to her, so a few days later I asked him if he'd like to write her a letter. He said he didn't know how, he had never written one before. I told him that I would like to write to her too, and we could do our letters together. He wrote the date and greeting according to my example, but he knew enough to write "Dear Mom" rather than "Dear Linda." Nathan was very happy and asked, "Can I put this in one of those things [an envelope]? Can I mail it? She'll like my letter!" At this point we talked about what he wanted to say, and I told him that in a letter it is nice to ask how the other person is and tell the person something about yourself. He proceeded to write the letter in Figure 29–5. It says: "I'm fine, but I hurt my knee. How are you?" As soon as he was finished, Nathan began looking for an envelope.

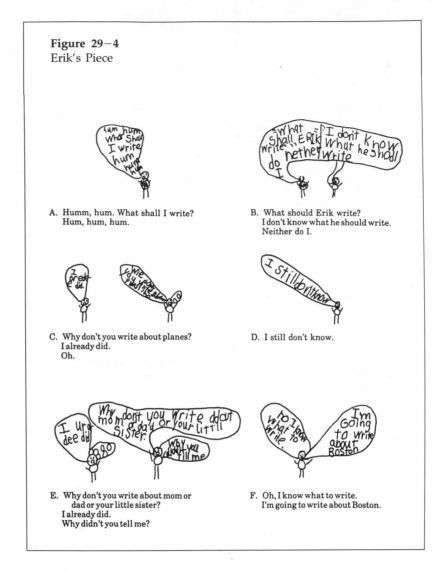

**Figure 29—4**
Erik's Piece

A. Humm, hum. What shall I write?
   Hum, hum, hum.

B. What should Erik write?
   I don't know what he should write.
   Neither do I.

C. Why don't you write about planes?
   I already did.
   Oh.

D. I still don't know.

E. Why don't you write about mom or
   dad or your little sister?
   I already did.
   Why didn't you tell me?

F. Oh, I know what to write.
   I'm going to write about Boston.

Even at the earliest stages in the development of a piece of writing, students are thinking critically about the drawings they will make, the experiences they will represent, the topics they will select, and the forms these will take. This critical thinking continues as they begin to draft their pieces of writing.

## MIDWAY EVALUATIONS: RESPONDING TO QUESTIONS OF PROCESS, CONTENT, AND AUDIENCE DURING DRAFTING AND REVISING

Jason is in the same classroom as Erik, and although he too was not one of my resource room students, I often talked with him about his writing. Once, when I asked him how his writing was going, he said, "Now this page I'm really proud of. Do you know how long it took

> June 16, 198
>
> D R  M O M J
> I M  F I N  B + I
> h r t  M I  N E
> H O  Γ  U ?
> Nathan  LOV,XO

**Figure 29—5**
Nathan's Letter

me to do this page? Three days!" (Figure 29—6). The syntax shows that Jason wrote this page over a period of time. He evaluated his writing through the investment of time he had made. Jason still struggles with letter formation—he had turned his *m's* right side up because they looked like *w*'s—and spelling, although he used *-ing*, which he had recently learned. I agreed with Jason's evaluation and told him that I certainly could see why he was proud of that page in his book on fishing.

It took Joel, a third grader, one reading period to complete his piece on Halley's Comet (Figure 29—7). He had been "reading"

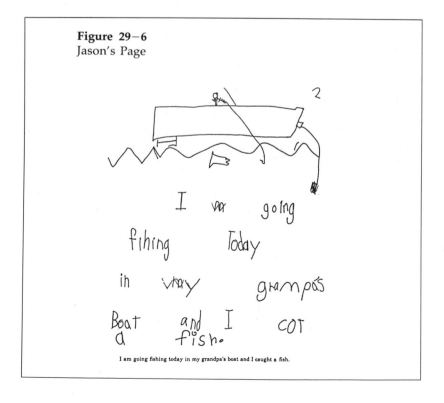

**Figure 29—6**
Jason's Page

I am going fishing today in my grandpa's boat and I caught a fish.

**Figure 29—7**
Joel's Piece

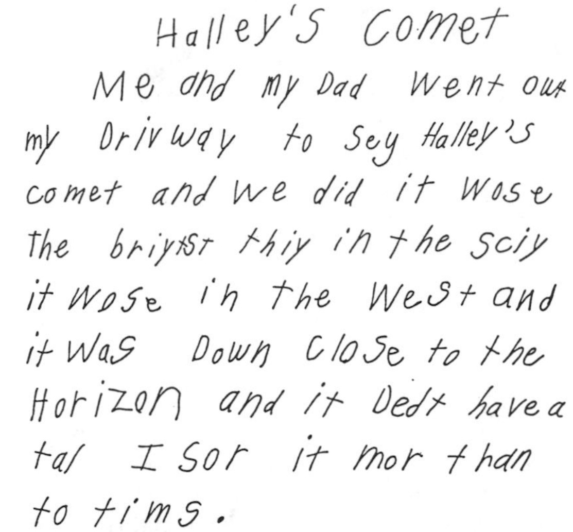

> Halley's Comet
> Me and my Dad Went out
> my Drivway to Sey Halley's
> comet and we did it Wose
> the briytsr thiy ih the sciy
> it Wose ih the West and
> it Was Down Close to the
> Horizon and it Dedt have a
> tal I sor it mor than
> to tims.

Halley's Comet
Me and my dad went out my driveway to see Halley's comet
and we did. It was the brightest thing in the sky. It was in
the west and it was down close to the horizon and it didn't
have a tail. I saw it more than two times.

about the comet in the *National Geographic World Magazine* and in every other book either he or I could find. He also talked about his own sightings. I suggested that he write about his experiences so he could share them with others. Two days later he produced his comet piece and shared it with me. I repeated back to Joel the main content of his piece to check his meaning and then asked him what he was going to do next. He said he was going to put it away because it was just to help him remember. Now he wanted to read more. Although I had hoped that Joel might want to develop this piece of writing, I realized that it was a page in a field notebook in his self-selected study of Halley's Comet. He had no reason to revise. He next wrote about Edmund Halley in his effort to use writing to learn.

The outcome of David's piece about his dad was similar (Figure 29—8). It was written like any other piece during writing time, but once David had shared it with me, and I had reflected back what I had heard, he wanted to put it away. I realized that it was a page in a personal journal, and there was no reason to revise.

Amelia, a student in a third-grade classroom in which I was working with some of my mainstreamed students, was writing an essay on nature for a local contest. When she read her piece on flowers to me, I repeated what I had heard in her piece back to her so that she could listen to its content and sequence. When I repeated her line "picking too many flowers can destroy nature," I asked if she knew of certain flowers that shouldn't be picked at all. She answered, "Lady's slippers! I

---

**Figure 29–8**
David's Piece

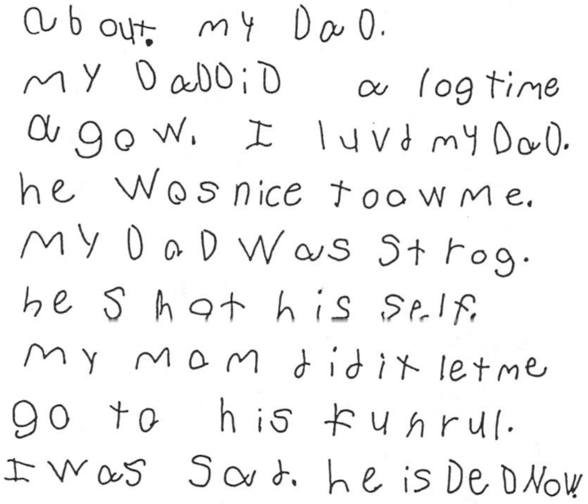

a b out my Da 0.
m Y D aDD i D   a   l og time
a  g o  W.   I   l u V d m Y Da 0.
he   W a s n i c e   t oo w M e.
M Y   D a D   W a s   S t  r o g.
h e   S  h  at   h i s   Se lf.
M y   M a M   d i d i t   l e t m e
g o   t a   h i s   f u h r u l.
I W a S   S a d.   h e   i s  D e D N o w

About My Dad
My dad died a long time ago. I loved my dad. He was nice to
me. My dad was strong. He shot himself. My mom didn't let
me go to his funeral. I was sad. He is dead now.

---

didn't tell about lady's slippers." There was a pause and she said, "I didn't tell about my favorite flower, bluets. You can pick them. At my grandmother's and great-grandmother's house, the yard is full of bluets." There was another pause and Amelia said, "I'm going to add that to make this really good!"

When Joel read his biographical sketch of his grandfather (Figure 29–9), I asked him about the statements "He had four planes" and "he stopped flying in 1985," because I doubted their validity. Joel had been my student for five years, and I knew his family very well. His piece went through his revision as well as editing by his classroom teacher, but those statements did not change until he was writing his final copy. He came over to me and, referring to the statement about the four planes, said, "Maybe I should leave that out. I want this to be right. I can't check with my grampy. He went to Florida yesterday." I also noticed that Joel had changed 1985 to 1945 in his effort to validate his writing.

B. J. came to me from a special school when he was in third grade. Although he was capable of writing, B.J. had never written much other than his name and the date or to practice handwriting because the curriculum did not provide for it. He began writing by drawing and labeling and moved rapidly to expanded text. By January, I was able to move him back to the classroom for reading and writing and was there to support him. He wrote a poem about the space shuttle disaster to express how he was feeling (Figure 29–10). After I had reflected back what I had heard in the poem, I asked him about how he had written it. I wondered if his use of the acrostic was conscious;

**Figure 29—9**
Joel's Biographical Sketch

Lewis Johnson

My grampy, Lewis Johnson was born in Portland in 1126. He worked in a shipyard before he went in the service. He went into the Army Air Corps, and that is where he learned how to fly. He started flying in 1945 and stopped flying in 1945. He was in World War II. After the war he was a boatbuilder and then built his own boat. He had two children: Larry and Linda. He got married in 1946 to Frances childs. They built their own hose.

I had taught it to him at Christmas time in an attempt to interest him in writing poetry—despite its formulaic approach. He thought hard for a few minutes and then said, "I thought about each line before I wrote it down. Then I wrote it out and thought about the next line." I asked, "Did you do anything else?" He answered, "When it was all done, I read it over to see if it showed all my feelings. That was when I added 'and a lot of puzzles,' because they can't figure out what caused it. Then it had all my feelings." What B. J. didn't consciously realize was that one of his lines was inspired by one of the lines in John Gillespie Magee's "High Flight": "Put out my hand and touched the face of God." B. J. added his poem to a bulletin board dedicated to the astronauts.

Questions about audience don't have much effect on kindergartners, but I begin to ask them anyway. When Daniel was working on his book about his baby brother, Shawn (Figure 29—11), I asked him who might be interested in reading it. Daniel blinked and didn't reply, so I moved on. When Daniel finished writing his book a day later, he brought it over to me and announced, "This book is great. It's about Shawn!" I blinked in surprise because it was unusual for Daniel to make such strong statements, even though his voice was quiet and controlled. He then added, "My parents want to see it. I

**Figure 29—10**
B. J.'s Poem

### Space Shuttle

School teacher is ready,
people look happy to see 7 People goup in space,
astronauts were going to learn about Halleys comet.
challenger went up,
exploded in the air and a lot of Puzzles.


Sad Feelings happening Now,
high school kids Feel the pain in them,
up to see God to touch hands.
time to go on with the space Progam,
tv shows keep showing all around,
let people think back about the happy things,
every one did Feel the Pain in them.

By B.J.
3rd Grade

told them all about it." Daniel proceeded to write a whole series of books about his family: Michael (his older brother), Daddy, Mommy, Nana, and Grampy. At the end of the series, Daniel interviewed me with the kind of questions I often used on him.

**Daniel**: How did I get so good at writing?
**S**: What do you think?
**D**: I don't know.
**S**: I think it is because you write all the time. You practice a lot.
**D**: I think I do pretty good. [*Daniel paused and then brought up another concern.*] I got to learn to read. I can read the easy books you taught me [predictable books], but I can't read other books I try to read [unfamiliar].

Self-evaluations during the actual writing of a piece usually occur as the student looks over, reads, or otherwise reflects on the writing. For some students the process—the investment of time, how a piece is written, or whom it is for—is significant. For others, content—its significance, its completeness, or its validity—is most important. Revisions in content do or do not occur, depending on the students' evaluation. In conferences, we can help students think through their writing, but their revisualizing of it depends on their evaluation of what they have already written.

**Figure 29–11**
Daniel's Book

MiBABEBOOK

SHAUN·CROLEiNG

SHAUNCLIMEiNG UNtHEtABAL

SHAUN·PLE·iNG THE·LEP

A. Shawn crawling

B. Shawn climbing on the table

C. Shawn pulling the lamp

SHAUNPECEiNG· iRtHE·LETL·PES·AF DRt

SHAUNSiCLi·iNG HES BADAL

SHAUNLCEiNG ATTHE·FEHE TAC

D. Shawn picking up little pieces of dirt

E. Shawn sucking his bottle

F. Shawn looking at the fish tank

## END POINT EVALUATIONS: EDITING AND PUBLISHING DECISIONS

The editing/publishing conference with primary students is a rich time for self-evaluation. When my students complete five or so drafted booklets, they select what they consider to be their best story to be typed with conventional spelling and other forms and bound in an attractive cover. They illustrate the book and share it with the class and their families; then it is put on display in the classroom. There are many other forms of publication, but this is the type referred to in this section.

When I asked Stephanie, who is Erik and Jason's first grade class-mate, why she chose to publish "My Friends," she answered, "I like this one. I like making people. Rae publishes her books on people, and she teaches me how to draw. Her people books are my favorites. Rae draws people good. Her mother is an artist."

Anticipating my question about what he would like to publish, Bryan, a first grader, had already made his decision. When I asked him why he had chosen this particular piece (Figure 29–12), he replied, "Well, I like drawing pumpkins; it's all about pumpkins. See, it says (*and he read*], 'Pumpkin, pumpkin, pumpkin, pumpkin, pumpkin.'" Then he paused as he suddenly realized that the text was the same for each picture and added, "Every one is doing something different!" He showed me the pictures and told me about them. Although I had been suggesting to Bryan that he could write a book on a single topic since last spring, this was the first time he had done so; since then I have "nudged" him—Mary Ellen Giacobbe's word for consistent suggesting—to write about the differences among the pictures.

William, a first grader, had a very difficult time last spring choosing which book to publish. He liked two of them, "Bigfoot" and "André," equally well. "Bigfoot" had his friends in it, and "André," he said, was "good and funny." I remembered when William had shared "André" with the group. Everyone who had been to see the famous seal shared their experiences, and we had all laughed a lot together. I could see what William meant, so I published both books.

**Figure 29–12**
Bryan's Book

Some students choose to publish a particular book because they have achieved control over conventions. Nathan chose to publish his book about the YMCA because he liked the Y and because the book had sentences with periods. I had been "nudging" him toward sentences for a long time and had taught him the use of the period when he wrote the Y book.

During an editing conference, after I had taught Joel to put in the addresses on a business letter (Figure 29−13), he looked at me and said, "Now I know why I didn't get anything from that cereal company. I didn't put on any addresses." (He was referring to when he had written a letter at home asking for free materials.) When he got his poster on Halley's Comet, he came and told me that it had arrived and that he was glad he did his letter "right."

Of course, control over conventions is cause for self-evaluation at any time. Donnie showed me that he knew how to write "cb" for *cub* rather than "kb" because *car* and *cabin* sound like *k* but use *c* in spelling (Figure 29−14). James brought over a page in his book, which he read as "Me bowling," and remarked, "I sounded it out all by myself!"

When young children are asked to select and finalize a piece of writing by publishing it, they are evaluating the product, what Thomas Hilger calls "summing up." For some, it is the illustrated part of the

---

**Figure 29−13**
Joel's Letter

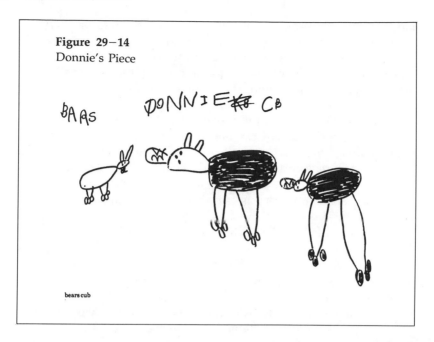

**Figure 29—14**
Donnie's Piece

BARS

DONNIE C

bears cub

piece that makes it best; for others, it is the written text. For still others, especially young children, it is the control over conventions that marks their best. Their reasons will shift as their perception about what is good shifts, and in accordance with what they are trying to do, but two that remain fairly constant are their liking for the subject and the response the writing brings from others.

## EVALUATION, RESPONSIBILITY, AND GROWTH

Student self-evaluation is a natural part of writing and responding. Evaluation occurs at all stages of the writing process, and it is crucial to the writer's engagement in the same piece or to the pursuit of the same subject in different pieces. Besides engagement, these evaluations are essential for two other reasons: they give the writer control and ownership over the writing, and they provide the basis for teaching — for planning and assessing teacher response. I cannot imagine how I could teach students without having these "windows on their minds."

For a long time, a part of me thought that the "real" evaluation must occur at the final stages of writing and that it was my responsibility. I even used to feel a little bit guilty about my students' involvement, particularly because some of the teachers walked around armed with grade books and always seemed to know what was A, B, C, or D without any input from their students. Although I knew that evaluation is more complex than that and believed that ultimately the responsibility for it is with the writer, I still thought I had to be in charge.

Linda Rief, middle school teacher from Oyster River School in Durham, New Hampshire, convinced me that it is as necessary for kids to have control over evaluation as it is for them to have control over topic choice. In 1980, when I first heard that kids were choosing their own topics, I thought it was heresy, but my students quickly showed me how valid it was. And as a result of researching students' self-evaluation and uncovering my own assumptions, I have recognized that *all evaluations, at all stages of the process, are real evaluations*. I know that I play a part in the process, but I do not control it.

Getting down what kids say and do in evaluating their writing as well as what others say and do that affects their evaluations is a challenge. Stepping outside myself and watching what we do together is a bigger challenge. In tracing her own development as a teacher-researcher, Nancie Atwell has said that she first conducted research to confirm her beliefs and theories. Second, she emphasized herself less and instead followed what her kids did in their literary endeavors. Third, she watched what she and her students did collaboratively as they found ways to query and form theories together. By looking at writing samples and at the responses and behaviors of both my students and myself, I have attempted that third stage of teacher research. In teaching, I will continue to untangle the web of inter-active response by doing research. The more closely I look at self-evaluation, the more I learn about my teaching and the more my students learn about their writing.

## REFERENCES

Atwell, Nancie. 1986. "A More Principled Practice: The Teacher Researcher." Speech, "New Directions in Composition Scholarship," University of New Hampshire, Durham, N.H. October.

Genishi, Celia, and Anne Haas Dyson. 1985 *Language Assessment in Early Years*. Norwood, N.J.: Ablex.

Graves, Donald. 1985. "All Children Can Write." *Learning Disabilities Focus* 1:36−43.

Hilgers, Thomas. 1986a. "How Children Change as Critical Evaluators of Writing: Four Three-Year Case Studies." *Research in the Teaching of English* 20:36−55.

―――. 1986b. "Writer's Evaluations of Writing: A Comparison of Criteria Used by Primary-School and College Students." Speech, "New Directions in Composition Scholarship," University of New Hampshire, Durham, N.H. October.

Newkirk, Thomas. 1988. "Young Writers as Critical Readers." In *Understanding Writing: Ways of Observing, Learning, and Teaching*, ed. Thomas Newkirk and Nancie Atwell. 2d. ed. Portsmouth, N.H.: Heinemann.

Stires, Susan. 1983a. "Disabled Writers: A Positive Approach." In *Teaching All the Children to Write*, ed. James Collins, Buffalo, N.Y.: New York State English Council.

―――. 1983b. "Real Audiences and Contexts for LD Writers." *Academic Therapy* 18:561−68.

# recipe for process

LESLIE FUNKHOUSER

Serves up to 25.

## FILLING

- Ability to Negotiate
- Choices
- Extended Time
- Listening
- Boundaries
- Shared Responsibilities

## BOUNDARIES

Mix one adult and up to 25 students.
Discuss the importance of boundaries to insure a learning environment
    for all.
Set up rules together.
Limit these to four or less.
Try them out.
Discuss their importance as the year progresses.
Refrigerate if not needed.

## SHARED RESPONSIBILITIES

Think about all the jobs that you do in one day during school time.
Can any be delegated to children?
At first, relinguish calm, efficiency, and perfection.
Teach the children about the job.
Help them if they need help while learning.
Cook on low for about five weeks and you will begin to ask yourself,
    "Why am I here?"

### ABILITY TO NEGOTIATE

We as teachers often need answers to daily dilemmas ... the pokey
worker, the talker, the child constantly seeking attention. The
children often have good solutions for our daily problems. Consult
them for advice. They can learn that a smooth day means help from
*all*.
Listen in ... they negotiate contracts with one another constantly.
Remove from heat when boiling stage is reached.

### CHOICES

Mix a combination of possibilities with a few of your high expectations.
Discuss why it is necessary to self-evaluate frequently.
Provide extremes to insure success for all and challenge for all.
Work hard each day to learn more about each child's decisions.
Save a dash of "no" for times your mixture begins to break down.

### LISTENING

We all need to know a good listener.
Listening is hearing another's tales, feelings, ideas, and questions.
It does not involve evaluation, judgement, or agreement.
Your response is merely a clarification of what you heard.
Your questions are tools for gathering more information.
Ice with a smooth stroke so that the recipient feels proud and deliciously
topped.

### EXTENDED TIME

Fight to block out the guilt and worries about the curriculum to
cover, deadlines to meet, benchmarks in the year to prove student
competencies.
Live each day as if it were the most significant in the year.
Flavor with laughter.

Mix together, risk, fail, think about what you've learned. Share your
knowledge with others!

# PART 4
## final reflections

The other day, a colleague in teacher education mused aloud about perceptions of what makes "real" research: "Dr. ——— in the biology department is doing research on the brains of slugs. She has money from the university—a huge grant—to purchase the equipment she needs to create the lab environment where she can pursue her work."

"Now, I'm not doubting the importance of her work," he went on, "but I work with teachers who want to study how the *human* brain works—how a child learns—in the laboratory of the classroom. For some reason, many people don't consider this 'real' research and few are willing to fund these teacher-researchers or to help them set up the kinds of learning environments they need."

The knowledge generated from teacher inquiry must be accorded the respect it deserves. *Nancie Atwell* argues passionately for the potential of teacher research for informing theory. Rather than considering research by practitioners an intriguing novelty, she claims that the teaching profession can build from the wonderings that teachers pursue.

*Susan Ohanian* reinforces Atwell's call for the integration of research into the real world of the classroom, stressing the importance of the warm and human learning environments and the unplanned teaching moments that are such an important part of good classrooms. We close this collection by echoing Ohanian's reminder of what it means to be a teacher, with "the tantalizing vagueness and the lumps in the throat, the poetry and true purpose of our calling."

# "wonderings to pursue"
## the writing teacher as researcher

NANCIE ATWELL

# 31

Whenever something happens that rankles me as a teacher, I try to imagine it happening to a member of some other profession. When teachers are forbidden to use the school photocopier, I try to imagine a hospital where doctors cannot make copies of patient records. Or when school board members impose a phonics program they read about in *Reader's Digest* on a group of whole language teachers, I try to imagine the board of a hospital outlawing psychoanalytic approaches in favor of primal screams and exorcism.

When I read some of the research published in our professional journals—inquiries that ignore or condescend to teachers in the classroom—I try to imagine medical research without doctors, without practitioners in the field who will read and use its findings in their practice. When I find myself arguing about whether a classroom teacher can ever really be a real researcher, I try to imagine the field of psychoanalysis without the case studies of practicing analysts— Freud or Jung or Erikson, for example. Finally, when I talk with classroom teachers who do not read or conduct research or see any benefit to studying their students' writing, I try to imagine a visit to my daughter's pediatrician when Anne's doctor didn't observe her play, test her reflexes, ask questions about her behavior and development, then compare it all with her notes of Anne's previous visits.

I want to explore two issues in this chapter: why classroom teachers' research is important to the teachers conducting it, and why teacher research is an important scholarly development for the profession as a whole, for what it adds to our knowledge of children's composing. Along the way I will briefly trace the development of the teacher-researcher movement and share some of the specific insights of practicing teacher-researchers.

I am the teacher-researcher I know best. For six years I studied the writing of eighth graders. Over these six years, the nature of the questions I asked in my classroom changed, as my understandings of research have changed. In the beginning I wanted to know, What should I do in my classroom? What will happen when I do it? I wanted to measure the effects of my teaching and prove my methods.

My research was inevitably some variation of the same question: When I perform—say, write in my journal when I tell students to write in theirs—what wonderful things will my students do? I was like the instructor in Veronica Geng's *New Yorker* essay, "Teaching Poetry Writing to Singles":

*I started the class by saying what I was going to do was get them to write words in lines of uneven length on a piece of paper (I didn't want to scare them with the formal term "poem") and then I would write a book about how much I had helped them (1984).*

The focus was on my methods. The focus was on me. It was a truncated version of classroom research.

Then, as I started looking—really looking, through the prism of the stunning naturalistic studies of children's writing of the last decade—my teaching methods took a back seat. My students climbed up front and became my focus. I conducted research to learn from them about their uses and views of written language. My questions became, What will I observe students doing? How will I make sense of my observations? For example, when I observed students—to my surprise—easily developing their own topics for writing, I interviewed them about the sources of their best ideas, then categorized their responses to describe an environment that helped writers generate their own subjects (Atwell 1985).

Over the past few years my students and I came to sit together in the front seat. Classroom research became a matter of learning *with them*, of collaborating with eighth graders as a writer and reader who wonders about writing and reading. Together we asked, What will we do, say, see, think? What sense will we make of our observations? One January, two girls instigated a network of kids writing letters to each other about their reading. This was in addition to dialogue journals between readers and me. At the end of the school year students categorized the kinds of literary talk in which they engaged with me and with each other, noted the differences, and helped me theorize about the reasons. Our work became part of *In the Middle* (1987).

The things I learned with students in the research community of the classroom continually changed my teaching. We learned about the ways we learn, about what writers and readers really do and need, and the context—what happened every day in that room—changed. The classroom became a communal "scribble" to borrow a word from Jerry Harste (1984), one that students and I revised together through each school year. My collaborators helped me break the lockstep of set-it-up-and-evaluate-it, set-it-up-and-evaluate-it, that characterizes much public school teaching. And they helped me to shut up—to stop talking at whole groups from the front of the room and to start moving among students, observing and listening. It is difficult to study kids' behaviors if the kids rarely initiate anything. Once I gave class time over to students' writing, reading, and choices and began to discover what they could do on their own and together, finding ways to collaborate with them in inquiry was the next logical step.

All the while that my activity in the classroom changed, my professional activity outside the classroom was changing, too. I read all the writing theory and relevant research I could lay my hands on. For me, as for many other classroom teachers, "relevant" meant process-observational studies of young writers, readers, and speakers such as those found in Bissex (1980), Calkins (1983), Clay (1975), Emig (1971), Graves (1975, 1981), Heath (1983), Perl (1979), Shaughnessy (1977), Sommers (1980), Sowers (1979), and Taylor (1983). These studies were in every way unlike the experimental design research I had read in English education courses. Context was so fully explained and explored in the process-observational studies that I could understand why teachers and learners were teaching and learning. These were not the teacher-proof methods that research had promised me in the past, methods that made me feel like a fool when I failed or, worse, made me look at my students as fools when they failed. (Do you remember transformational sentence combining?) Instead, they were explorations of principles underlying practices.

It was a joy to read Calkins' (1979, 1980) early articles about "Andrea" and Bissex's GNYS AT WRK (1980) from front to back, to follow the happy stories of Susie Schibles and Paul Bissex. It was almost as much fun to read from back to front, to retrace Lucy's and Glenda's methodologies and to tease out how they had gone about studying one child's language over time. From there it was a small step to conduct case studies of my own students in collaboration with other teachers at my school, and then to write about our observations, their significances, and the theoretical framework guiding our perspectives.

The big picture for teacher research parallels my story. The last decade has witnessed a dramatic increase in the number of inquiries by classroom teachers. The first collection of such studies, Jon Nixon's A Teacher's Guide to Action Research (1981), is built upon the British action research movement of the 1960s and 70s. In the United States Errors and Expectations (1977), Mina Shaughnessy's careful observations and analyses of her basic writing students' prose, gave teachers at every level a model not only for teaching writing but for scholarly activity in one's own classroom. As celebrated as the model has become, it is still often difficult for doctoral candidates at many of our schools of education to propose studying their own students. A friend doing her graduate work waged a year-long campaign to conduct dissertation research in one of her university composition classes. Her advisor admonished her, "Who do you think you are, Mina Shaughnessy?" Public school teachers operate under other kinds of constraints — recess duty in sub-Arctic temperatures, an astonishing assortment of middle-management bureaucrats whose job it is to dictate our curricula — but we generally have the power and freedom to explore the questions that intrigue us.

Many graduate schools of English and education have been our allies, encouraging and enabling teachers' research by collaborating with us, helping us to shape our questions as formal inquiries, and sharing their methods for gathering and analyzing data. Since 1979, Dixie Goswami, my teacher and the director of the Program in Writing at the Bread Loaf School of English, has worked with hundreds of teachers from across the country in investigating our classrooms and communities. Glenda Bissex works with cadres of teacher-researchers in schools throughout Vermont and at the Northeastern University Martha's Vineyard Writing Program where she guides teachers through a year-long course in case study design. Among others, Jerome Harste, Virginia Woodward, and Carolyn Burke at Indiana University; Anne Dyson, and Mary K. Healy at Berkeley; Ken and Yetta Goodman at the University of Arizona; Nancy Wilson, Carla Asher, and Sondra Perl at Herbert Lehman College; and Donald Graves, Thomas Newkirk, and Jane Hansen at the University of New Hampshire, collaborate with classroom teachers and encourage in every way teachers' systematic inquiries. The National Council of Teachers of English (NCTE) Research Foundation offers grants of up to $1,500 to teachers proposing research they would like to conduct in their classrooms and rigorously reviews and assists with teachers' studies. At Teachers College, under a grant from the Edwin Gould Foundation, Lucy Calkins and her associates assist thirty new teacher-researchers each year, from shaping their questions to writing up their findings. Two-thirds of the studies conducted by Calkins' first group of teacher-researchers have now been published, many of these in *Language Arts*.

To read *Language Arts* now, as compared with five years ago, is to read a different journal. Once almost exclusively the domain of university researchers and full-time graduate students, it is now rich with firsthand accounts written by teachers of students' development and processes as writers and readers. Heinemann Educational Books is publishing *Workshop*, a new annual about the teaching of writing and reading, with teacher-researchers as its sole contributors (Atwell 1989, 1990). And Heinemann's latest catalogue offers a number of anthologies of classroom teachers' research. Perhaps the three most widely read and cited are *Understanding Writing* (Newkirk and Atwell 1988), *Breaking Ground* (Hansen, Newkirk, and Graves 1985), and *Seeing for Ourselves* (Bissex and Bullock 1987). These volumes are a far cry from the typical NCTE idea book featuring teachers' atheoretical, two-paragraph recipes for language arts activities, with the prose "texturized" by someone at Headquarters.

When I look closely at the articles in the Heinemann texts, I am struck by the variety and complexity of the questions teachers are asking and the meticulousness with which they are pursuing answers in the midst of their teaching. And I do mean in the midst. Research and teaching go hand in hand, and data arises naturally from an interactive community where an adult and a classroom of children spend their day discussing, interpreting, analyzing, informing, criticizing, collaborating, inventing, and, most significantly, questioning.

As Glenda Bissex recently wrote, teacher's research begins less "with a hypothesis to test," and more with "a wondering to pursue" (1987).

In published examples of teacher inquiries, the wonderings commonly take two forms: I wonder what will happen, or what is happening, with this child, and I wonder what the pattern is among this group of children. The first wondering leads to case studies of individual learners, and the second to accounts of clusters of behavior among many learners in relation to a particular phenomenon. Both kinds of study reveal data from which the whole profession can learn: information about children's constructs as writers and readers, their development, and the factors that shape development.

I will highlight several examples of each kind of inquiry from teacher-researchers' studies on which I draw in my own research, teaching, and work with teachers. I hope they will demonstrate the sort of modest, naturalistic inquiries classroom teachers can take on, as well as give the flavor of the uniqueness of perspective and experience that characterizes teacher research.

Carol Avery and Ellen Blackburn Karelitz are first grade teachers who studied individual writers in their classrooms. Each of their cases focuses on a different aspect of a child's literacy, and each adds to our knowledge of primary children's writing and reading development.

Carol taught at the William Nitrauer School in Lancaster, Pennsylvania. In her article "Lori 'Figures It Out': A Young Writer Learns to Read" (1985), she traces the language development of a hesitant, reticent six-year-old, the kind of child easily lost in the shuffle of a public school classroom. Carol pursues a wondering about how such a child will progress. In excerpts from her teaching journal, interviews with Lori, and samples of Lori's writing and reading, Carol follows her student's growth to independence. She corroborates and extends Bissex's finding that early writing precedes early reading, all the while offering a highly specific portrait of the classroom in which Lori grew. Here is one excerpt, which begins with an entry from Carol's journal:

> ... I think I function best when I help maintain the atmosphere, remind them of all the strategies they could use and then step back. As I move among them, answering their questions and responding to their successes, I sometimes feel I'm an intruder. There's a danger that I might throw them off by asking them to deal with my priorities and I know that would be a mistake at this point. No schooling prepared me for the powerful unfolding that is taking place around me.

And then Carol moves into a description of Lori:

> Writing with her own invented spelling reinforced and expanded Lori's knowledge of letter-sound relationships. She now wrote several letters in succession to form words. FLAW stood for flower; san for sun; Pamn for Pac-man.... The regular practice through daily writing developed both her auditory and visual skills. As she wrote,

*she became aware not only of the use of phonics, but of a visual approximation of the word she was writing.*

*The stage was set for Lori to read. With great delight, she began applying strategies she had devised when writing to decode words in other print materials. "This book's a bit hard for me to read," she began one day, and then added brightly, "But I can read of because I already· knowed that word." A few days later Lori found the word* flower *in a book. "Does this say* flower*?" she asked me. I nodded. "I thought so. You know why? 'Cause I remembered those letters were in* flower *from when I did my writing." Another day she said, "I found the word* go *and the word* the*." It was a large step. She was overcoming her bafflement of print.*

*By the end of October, Lori was using the sight words she had acquired from her writing, consonant sounds to attack words she didn't know, picture and context clues, and her memory of the text to read a complete book,* Rosie's Walk *by Pat Hutchins. Lori was interested in the book because I had read it to the class. She spent five days mastering it and came to me, eager to share her accomplishment. As she read, she ... stopped to elaborate on the story line with observations of the pictures. Independently, Lori had decoded and then memorized the text, and although she did not know many of the words in isolation, the context provided support ... It was the context and reading for meaning that were important to her. She had successfully transferred to this task her accumulated knowledge of written language and the decoding strategies she had used when she read her own writing (Bissex, 1980).*

*When she finished the book, she looked at me and smiled. I smiled and nodded in acknowledgement. She did not need praise; the learning had brought its own reward. "What will you read next?" I asked.*

*Lori had cracked the code. She tore into reading materials and, in November, read eleven separate titles to me. She selected what she read herself and quickly learned what was too hard. Usually she chose materials in which she knew some words and used context and graphic clues to decode the rest. One day in early December she brought a small paper book to me and said with amazement and elation, "I just picked this book and I can read it all! I didn't have to figure out any of the words 'cause I knowed them all already!"*

Carol takes Lori, and us, from this point to June, when Lori independently read E. B. White's *Charlotte's Web* and made her own first attempt at writing fiction. Teachers learn from Carol Avery about the language potential of a supposedly unremarkable child. They also learn the perspective and methods of a remarkable teacher.

In "The Rhythm of Writing Development" (1988), teacher-researcher Ellen Blackburn Karelitz, formerly of the Edward Devotion School in Brookline, Massachusetts, captures the moments of breakthrough for Daniel, one of her first graders, and gives other primary teachers a prism for looking at their students' drawing and narratives. At the start of the school year, drawing was Daniel's primary means for organizing his writing. His drawings at this time were formulaic and static, and his writing consisted of labels of his four favorite motifs: house, flower, tree, sun. Ellen speculated that "since Danny couldn't draw the action of his personal experiences, he couldn't write about them."

In November, Danny drew a tree, his "standard lollypop tree with a round green ball at the top" (see Figure 31−1) and wrote the message, "Tree. The tree is dead. The tree is bare." Ellen nudged. "Danny, you said that the tree was bare in your writing, but look at the tree you drew . . . it looks green." Danny drew a spindly tree on the back of his paper (see Figure 31−2) and wrote the word "Bare."

"For the first time," Ellen wrote, "the words controlled the picture

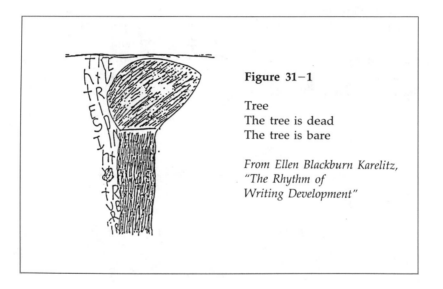

**Figure 31−1**

Tree
The tree is dead
The tree is bare

*From Ellen Blackburn Karelitz,*
*"The Rhythm of*
*Writing Development"*

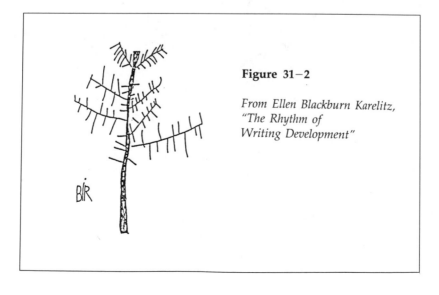

**Figure 31−2**

*From Ellen Blackburn Karelitz,*
*"The Rhythm of*
*Writing Development"*

rather than the picture controlling the words. Danny had broken his dependence on schema and revised his drawing. Two days later he wrote 'Snow Melting'" (see Figure 31–3). Here, the picture no longer dominates. "Danny had learned that the words can carry the message. He was no longer limited by his pictures." In this case, ordering an event "became a useful way for Danny to organize his writing." Ellen proceeds to characterize and theorize about the different styles Daniel used throughout the remainder of the school year. Her observations helped Ellen, and later other teachers, recognize the wide range of formulas that beginning writers use to organize their writing. Because she learned, we too learn to observe children's patterns, "anticipate signs of change, and know when intervention would be most effective." She concludes, "It is a delicate art."

Neither of these studies results in teacher-proof practices. Instead, as Ellen Karelitz concluded, we are witness to a "delicate art": teachers learning how to observe, anticipate, make sense of, and respond to the behaviors of young children. And neither claims to be the definitive study of primary-level writers and readers. Instead, they both add to our growing fund of knowledge of what is possible for six-year-olds and their teachers.

**Figure 31–3**

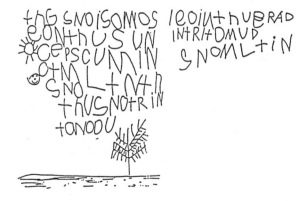

The snow is almost gone.
The sun keeps coming out, melting the snow.
The snow turns into water.
It goes into the ground and turns into mud.

*From Ellen Blackburn Karelitz,*
*"The Rhythm of*
*Writing Development"*

A second approach to classroom inquiry begins with a wider focus on a group or class of writers, then narrows to examine a particular component of behavior among group members, and moves from there to explore implications of the particular pattern. One of the first examples of this model—one of the first reports of teacher-conducted research—was Mary Ellen Giacobbe's investigation (1981) of the patterns of invented spellings among her newly arrived first graders at Atkinson Academy in Atkinson, New Hampshire, a school where there is no kindergarten. Giacobbe's work helped break new ground in many primary classrooms by showing teachers that instruction in writing could begin the first day of school and need not wait for proficiency in reading. Primary children's invented spellings and the publication of their writing as books for the classroom library are now so commonplace that it is easy to forget how recently we believed that young children must learn to read before they are allowed to write.

In September, Giacobbe asked each first grader to spell twenty words representing "as many different initial and final consonants and long and short vowels as possible." Figure 31–4 shows the class spelling pattern for four of the twenty words. Giacobbe discovered

|  | rag | five | buzz | doctor |
|---|---|---|---|---|
| Ellen | rag· | fiv | Bozo | Dokr |
| Helen | ro | FS | B | D |
| Frank | F | F | P | D |
| Greg | Reg | Fly | Bis | Dldi |
| John | RAKG | FAF | 8AS | DADDR |
| Brian | rog | 7if | das | dodr |
| Jennifer | RAG | FIve | BIS | DOCTR |
| Lisa | RAG | FOW | BAS | DOCTR |
| Kelly | RIS | FtV | BIS | DIR |
| Bob | RAG | FA | BSS | DIr |
| Carl | RaG | FiFv | Bis | DOKR |
| Linda | RAG | ViN | BST | DKT |
| Sarah | RAG | FIV | BIZ | DOR |
| Diane | Rag | fuv | buz | Dorsc |
| Donna | rag | foif | Bus | Doud |
| David | Rag | Fiv | Baz | Doctr |
| Jeremy | RAG | FiVE | Buzz | DOCTR |
| Ed | RAG- | FiVE | Buzz | DOCTOR |
| Mark | iA | FF | BS | DT |
| Susah | raG | Fiv | BU | DOD |

**Figure 31–4**
Class Spelling Patterns—First Week of School

*From Mary Ellen Giacobbe, "Who Says Children Can't Write the First Week of School?"*

that most of her children felt this was an activity they could do, all wrote from left to right, and most already knew initial and final consonant sounds and were able to use them in writing words. Her students took off from there to use invented spelling to write their own stories, which Giacobbe published as books for the classroom library. Children's writing became their reading. The data transformed the ways other kindergarten and first-grade teachers approached writing and reading in their classrooms because it revealed what children knew and could do, rather than working from the familiar deficit model perspective of what children do not know and cannot do. It also gave teachers of young writers a simple method they could use when pursuing wonderings about patterns among their students' spellings. Primary teachers at my school administered Mary Ellen's assessment to their students in September, January, and June as one way of observing children's growth as writers.

Another study that helps teachers look at patterns in their students' writing is Judith Hilliker's research on repetitions in her kindergartners' drawing and texts (1988). In an article cited often in examinations of beginning writing, Judy, a teacher at Oyster River Elementary School in Durham, New Hampshire, describes how four kindergarteners made the transition from simple labelling of their drawings to beginning narrative. She documented the repetitions of theme in the drawings that accompanied the four children's writing (see Figure 31–5) by painstakingly hand-copying five months' worth of text and drawing so patterns could be more easily discerned.

Judy Hilliker's research uncovered the value of this repetition. Three of the four children she looked at wrote their first narratives based on one of their major drawing themes. She wrote, " . . . with each redrawing, the meaning that the picture represents for the child becomes more dense and elaborate. As the associations that the children make with their drawings grow, the writing bursts the confines of the one-word label. Beginning narrative emerges." She concluded:

*Next year I won't be discouraged by the repetition I find in the children's writing books. Instead of asking them to draw something different, I'll ask them to tell me more about their picture. By exploring favorite themes in depth, rather than trying something new every day, the young writer discovers the need to move from labeling to more complex modes of expression.*

Judy's audience of primary teachers learns a new way of considering beginning writers' repetitions, and they learn to be patient with children's need to address one theme many times.

Teachers of older writers and readers are learning lessons from the ways eighth graders at Boothbay Region Elementary School taught me. In my teaching log one week I noted six casual references by students to new things they had tried in their writing because of something they had read, liked, and remembered. For example,

*Alan asked me in writing workshop to respond to his lead. He said, "I*

**Table 31–1**
Theme Repetition in the Drawings of Writing Products, November–March

| Child | Theme | No. of Repetitions | Percent of Content |
|---|---|---|---|
| Claire | Sun | | |
| | sun alone | 37 | |
| | sun and other elements | 12 | |
| | | — | |
| | | 49 | Sun 43% |
| Liza | People | | |
| | self | 9 | |
| | family members | 9 | |
| | friends | 7 | |
| | unspecified | 2 | |
| | | — | |
| | | 27 | People 42% |
| | Animals | 10 | Animals 16% |
| Ian | Vehicles | | |
| | boat | 15 | |
| | rocket | 6 | |
| | wheeled vehicle | 5 | |
| | | — | |
| | | 26 | Vehicles 25% |
| | People | | |
| | self | | |
| | family members | 7 | |
| | friends | 5 | |
| | unspecified | 7 | |
| | | 5 | |
| | | — | |
| | | 24 | People 23% |
| Paul | Holidays | | |
| | Christmas | 8 | |
| | Easter | 12 | |
| | | — | |
| | | 20 | Holidays 31% |
| | Little Faces | 17 | Little Faces 26% |

*from Judith Hilliker, Labelling to Beginning Narrative.*

*think my lead is fouled up. It doesn't really attract my attention like the books you read to us. I'm trying to tell too much about the whole camp. Maybe I should just begin with the lecture by the Detroit Pistons' coach. That way people will get some good stuff right from the start, like in* One Fat Summer.*"*

The benefits of documenting observations of what students say and do in the writing classroom quickly become apparent to teachers who keep logs. I found the pattern emerging only because I had captured in my log what kids had said, and could reflect on my notes later on.

My students used the six examples of "borrowing" (Karelitz 1984) as a jumping-off point to more closely characterize and analyze the connections they were making between their writing and reading. I interviewed every eighth grader and asked, "As a writer, do you think you learn from other authors' writing, from what you read?" Every eighth grader said yes. Then each student researched and answered my two follow-up questions: If so, who has influenced your writing? What kinds of things do you do differently because of this author?

Three students and I sorted, re-sorted, and categorized the seventy-three responses. To briefly summarize our findings, we found writers borrowing from three sources: professional authors (e.g., C. S. Lewis, Madeleine L'Engle, e. e. cummings, Lois Lowry), other eighth graders' writing, and my own. The students' borrowings took three forms.

They borrowed genre, trying a new mode after reading another author's writing. For example, Amanda wrote a ghost story after reading Mary Bolte's tales in *Haunted New England*, Timmy tried his hand at a regional tall tale because of Marshall Dodge's *Bert and I*, and Danny wrote "Kevin", which is an ode to the star of our junior high football team that parodied Bryan Adams' song "Heaven." Students showed how they had internalized the conventions and structures of particular literary forms. They were able to do this with a wide variety of literature readily available, plenty of sustained time in school to choose from and dip into that literature, and extensive, informal talk with me about what authors do.

Students also borrowed topics or themes, piggybacking on another author's writing. For example, S. E. Hinton's popular novel *The Out-siders* gave rise to at least five separate pieces of writing. Damon wrote a short story decrying urban violence, Daniel wrote a series of personal experience narratives about his adventures with his friends — boys on their own without adults; and Rhonda wrote an essay about the dangers of stereotyping kids because of where they live and what they wear. Rachel wrote a poem from the perspective of Dally Winston, the character in *The Outsiders* most on the outside of polite society, and Tara consciously incorporated a theme into her story "Beautiful Mountains" because, she said, "I wanted to make other people stop and think about things when they read my stories like I did when I read S. E. Hinton." The context was ripe — again, students chose their own texts and topics — for students to borrow from what captivated them as readers in creating ideas and information of their own.

Finally, students borrowed techniques, adopting a new style because of a way another writer had written. Sandy's short story about a girl's first date was written in first person using extremely short paragraphs, in the same style as the novels of Bruce and Carol Hart, which she had just finished reading. Robert Frost's poem "A Time to Talk" was the epigraph in Laura's essay for a Rotary Club competition because another student, Luanne, had used a poem similarly in a prize-winning essay the previous year. And Heather, fan of novelist Susan Beth Pfeffer, began to look at her own life as material to be contemplated and shaped in stories. The conclusion of Heather's non-fiction narrative "True or False" was subtle and ambiguous, as Heather explained, "like Susan Pfeffer's writing. I hope it will leave you thinking."

I learned from this research why reading and writing belong together. Time and again my students demonstrated the phenomenon Frank Smith calls "reading like a writer" (1983). I learned they did not need me to sponsor structured exercises in order for them to forge connections. Other teachers are learning what is possible when their students are given a wide range of literary resources and models from which to choose and opportunities to discover and act on their own intentions as readers and writers.

In a recent address at Bread Loaf James Britton said that teaching itself is an act of inquiry. Six years ago I wouldn't have known what he was talking about. Now, I cannot imagine teaching without conducting research. Nor can I imagine conducting research without teaching. The satisfaction of simultaneously teaching and learning from students will keep drawing me back to the classroom. It is firsthand experience that fuels my best insights—when I look and look again at data in which I am personally involved. David Hawkins has written that "... to be the best scientific observers we must be at once the best providers for and the best teachers of those whom we would study" (1974). Observing without teaching would mean depriving myself of a prime source of knowledge, that which comes from providing "the material and social environment, and the adult guidance, under which the engagement of children with their world is most intrinsically satisfying and most conducive to the development we would study" (Hawkins, ibid.); in short, the knowledge that comes from teaching.

In considering the future of teacher research, one of my fears is that classroom inquiry will go and is, in fact, already going the way of writing process: that it is being co-opted, watered down, and bastardized as textbook publishers have worked their special magic on the language of writing process by incorporating it in their latest materials without conveying the sense behind it. An article in a recent *English Journal* epitomizes this trend. In "Using an Experimental Design—Just the Thing for That Rainy Day," Donlan (1986) reminds teachers of the ostensible purpose of research—"to see if under certain conditions you can change human behavior"—then gives step-by-step instructions to incipient teacher-researchers.

*Step One: Find a problem.* ("Are boys better spellers than girls? Is outlining better than clustering?")

*Step Two: Put together two sets of materials.* (For example, develop a new unit on "The Raven" that parallels your old unit on "The Raven.")

*Step Three: Randomly assign your students to the two treatments.* ("Use your seating chart.")

*Step Four: Assign the treatments.* ("You should be careful to avoid

helping either group because it could bias the experiment.")
*Step Five: Administer a test.* (It "could consist of an essay, but a
recognition test is better since it can be scored more readily.")
*Step Six: Tabulate the results.* ("Whichever group achieves the higher
score has received the more effective treatment.")

In *Seeing for Ourselves* Glenda Bissex writes about what teacher
research is *not* (1987). To add to Glenda's list, teacher research is not
theory-stripped, context-stripped method testing. We need to reject
impoverished models that turn classroom inquiry into a pseudo-
scientific horse race.

Nor is teacher research putting on airs. Given the sheer quality of
the good stuff, the question, But is it real research? becomes irrelevant.
Lucy Calkins wrote recently about teacher research: "Fifteen years
ago, Graves and Emig created a tremendous breakthrough for the
field of composition because they pulled their chairs alongside of
students, in order to observe and understand how students learn to
write. The time has come for another breakthrough" (1985).

We are surely on the verge of that next breakthrough. The list of
teacher-researchers who inform our profession and their own teaching
grows: Avery, Karelitz, Giacobbe, and Hilliker, and also Marilyn
Boutwell (1983), Amanda Branscombe (1987), Lynda Chittenden
(1982), Elizabeth Cornell (1987), Kathy Matthews (1985; 1988), Vera
Milz (1982), Linda Rief (1985; 1988), Tom Romano (1987), Susan
Stires (1988), and Jack Wilde (1985; 1988). Their work is a joyful
addition to composition scholarship. It is characterized by careful
data gathering, descriptions of context, and connections to related
research. It is theory-driven, and it is rich in anecdote and specifics.

Teacher research is not charming. It is not English education's
version of children dressing up in their parents' clothing. But teacher
research is full of voice — ours and our students' — and it is written in
English.

Teacher research is not a self-actualization movement, a way for
teachers to feel good about themselves. But it does lead to intense
personal satisfaction, to the pleasure every mind finds in uncovering
a problem, teasing out the pattern, breaking through to new meaning,
and furthering others' understandings.

And teacher research most definitely is not a secret we keep from
students for fear that they may skew our findings. It is a model that
shows our students how adults can function as lifelong learners. It is
an attitude of "I want to know," and as Harste, Woodward, and
Burke have written, of "I can find out" (1984).

Frederick Crews (1984) wrote recently about a feature of Mina
Shaughnessy's *Errors and Expectations* (1977) that generally goes
unnoticed. He reread the remarkable "after" samples of Shaughnessy's
students' prose and, of course, credited her remarkable teaching.
But, he says, there is something else going on in that good writing,
"namely, a desire on the part of Shaughnessy's students to *become
like her*, to 'try on' her mind, echoing her way of putting the world
into syntax" (1986).

Like many teachers, I have come to mark my life by school holidays. A line that began to crop up in my conversations with eighth graders around Columbus Day was, "This is interesting, what you did here. How did you come up with it?" By Thanksgiving they asked me, "Excuse me, but is this interesting?" and by Easter, it was an imperative: "Yo. Come here. You'll be interested in this." Perhaps the most powerful outcome of teacher research is the possibility that our students, like Shaughnessy's, will try on our minds, echoing our way of putting the world into wonderings.

## REFERENCES

Atwell, Nancie, ed. *Workshop 2: Beyond the Basal*. Portsmouth, NH: Heinemann, 1990.

———, ed. *Workshop 1: Writing and Literature*. Portsmouth, NH: Heinemann, 1989.

———. *In the Middle: Writing, Reading and Learning with Adolescents*. Portsmouth, NH: Boynton/Cook, 1987.

———. "Everyone Sits at a Big Desk: Discovering Topics for Writing." *English Journal* 74 (September 1985):35–39.

Avery, Carol. "Lori 'Figures It Out': A Young Writer Learns to Read." In *Breaking Ground: Teachers Relate Reading and Writing in the Elementary School*, Jane Hansen, Thomas Newkirk, and Donald Graves, eds. Portsmouth, NH: Heinemann, 1985:15–28.

Bissex, Glenda. *GNYS AT WRK: A Child Learns to Write and Read*. Cambridge, MA: Harvard University Press, 1980.

Bissex, Glenda, and Richard Bullock, eds. *Seeing for Ourselves: Case Study Research by Teachers of Writing*. Portsmouth, NH: Heinemann, 1987.

Boutwell, Marilyn. "Reading and Writing Process: A Reciprocal Agreement." *Language Arts* 60 (November 1983):723–30.

Branscombe, Amanda. "I Gave My Classroom Away." In *Reclaiming the Classroom: Teacher Research as an Agency for Change*, Dixie Goswami and Peter Stillman, eds. Portsmouth, NH: Boynton/Cook, 1987:206–19.

Calkins, Lucy M. "Forming Research Communities Among Naturalistic Researchers." In *Perspective on Research and Scholarship in Composition*, Ben W. McClelland and Timothy R. Donovan, eds. New York: MLA, 1985:125–44.

———. *Lessons from a Child*. Portsmouth, NH: Heinemann, 1983.

———. "Children Learn the Writer's Craft." *Language Arts* 57 (February 1980):207–13.

———. "Andrea Learns to Make Writing Hard." *Language Arts* 56 (September 1979):569–76.

Chittenden, Lynda. "What If All the Whales Are Gone Before We Become Friends?" In *What's Going On?*, Mary Barr, Pat D'Arcy, and Mary K. Healy, eds. Portsmouth, NH: Boynton/Cook, 1982:36–51.

Clay, Marie. *What Did I Write?* Portsmouth, NH: Heinemann, 1975.

Cornell, Elizabeth. "The Effect of Poetry in a First-Grade Classroom."

In *Seeing for Ourselves: Case-Study Research by Teachers of Writing*. Glenda Bissex and Richard Bullock, eds. Portsmouth, NH: Heinemann, 1987:103–126.

Crews, Frederick. "Theory for Whose Sake?" In *The National Writing Project Quarterly* Volume 8, Number 4 (October 1986):4–9.

Donlan, Dan. "Using an Experimental Design—Just the Thing for That Rainy Day." *English Journal* 74 (March 1986):113–115.

Emig, Janet. *The Composing Processes of Twelfth Graders*. Urbana, IL: NCTE, 1971.

Geng, Veronica. *Partners*. New York: Harper and Row, 1984.

Giacobbe, Mary Ellen. "Who Says That Children Can't Write the First Week of School?" *Learning Magazine* (September 1981):130–32.

Graves, Donald H. "An Examination of the Writing Process of Seven Year Old Children." *Research in the Teaching of English* 9 (1975):227–241.

———. *A Case Study Observing the Development of Primary Children's Composing, Spelling, and Motor Behaviors During the Writing Process; Final Report*. NIE Grant No. G–78–0174. Durham, NH: University of New Hampshire, 1981.

Hansen, Jane, Thomas Newkirk, and Donald Graves, eds. *Breaking Ground: Teachers Relate Reading and Writing in the Elementary School*. Portsmouth NH: Heinemann, 1985.

Harste, Jerome, Virginia Woodward, and Carolyn Burke. *Language Stories & Literacy Lessons*. Portsmouth, NH: Heinemann, 1984.

Hawkins, David. *The Informed Vision: Essays on Learning and Human Nature*. New York: Agathon Press, 1974.

Heath, Shirley. *Ways with Words: Language, Life and Work in Communities and Classrooms*. Cambridge, MA: Cambridge University Press, 1983.

Hilliker, Judith. "Labeling to Beginning Narrative." In *Understanding Writing: Ways of Observing, Learning, & Teaching*, 2d edition. Thomas Newkirk and Nancie Atwell, eds. Portsmouth, NH: Heinemann, 1988:14–22.

Karelitz, Ellen Blackburn. "Common Ground: Developing Relationships Between Reading and Writing." *Language Arts* 61 (April 1984):367–75.

———. "The Rhythm of Writing Development." In *Understanding Writing: Ways of Observing, Learning, & Teaching*, 2d edition, Thomas Newkirk and Nancie Atwell, eds. Portsmouth, NH: Heinemann, 1988: 40–46.

Matthews, Kathy. "Beyond the Writing Table," In *Breaking Ground: Teachers Relate Reading and Writing in the Elementary School*. Jane Hansen, Thomas Newkirk, and Donald Graves, eds. Portsmouth, NH: Heinemann, 1985.

———. "A Child Composes," In *Understanding Writing: Ways of Observing, Learning, & Teaching*, 2d ed. Thomas Newkirk and Nancie Atwell, eds. Portsmouth, NH: Heinemann, 1988.

Milz, Vera. *Young Children Write: The Beginnings*. Tucson, AZ: Center for Research and Development, University of Arizona, 1982.

Newkirk, Thomas, and Nancie Atwell, eds. *Understanding Writing: Ways of Observing, Learning, and Teaching*, 2d ed. Portsmouth, NH: Heinemann, 1988.

Nixon, Jon. *A Teacher's Guide to Action Research*. London: Grant McIntyre, 1981.

Perl, Sondra. "The Composing Processes of Unskilled College Writers." *Research in the Teaching of English* 13 (1979):317−36.

Rief, Linda. "Why Can't We Live Like the Monarch Butterfly?" In *Breaking Ground: Teachers Relate Reading and Writing in the Elementary School*, Jane Hansen, Thomas Newkirk, and Donald Graves, eds. Portsmouth, NH: Heinemann, 1985.

———. ". . . because of Robert Frost." *Language Arts* 65 (February 1988):236−37.

Romano, Tom. *Clearing The Way: Working with Teenage Writers*. Portsmouth, NH: Heinemann, 1987.

Shaughnessy, Mina. *Errors and Expectations*. New York: Oxford University Press, 1977.

Smith, Frank. "Reading like a Writer." *Language Arts* 60 (September 1983):558−67.

Sommers, Nancy. "Revision Strategies of Student Writers and Experienced Writers." *College Composition and Communication* 31 (1980):378−88.

Sowers, Susan. "A Six-Year-Old's Writing Process: The First Half of First Grade." *Language Arts* 56 (December 1979):829−35.

Stires, Susan. "Reading and Talking: 'Special' Readers Show They Know." In *Understanding Writing: Ways of Observing, Learning and Teaching*, 2d ed. Thomas Newkirk and Nancie Atwell, eds. Portsmouth, NH: Heinemann, 1988:207−15.

Taylor, Denny. *Family Literacy: Young Children Learning to Read and Write*. Portsmouth, NH: Heinemann, 1983.

Wilde, Jack. "Play, Power, and Plausibility: The Growth of Fiction Writers." In *Breaking Ground: Teachers Relate Reading and Writing in the Elementary School*. Jane Hansen, Thomas Newkirk and Donald Graves, eds. Portsmouth, NH: Heinemann, 1985:121−31.

———. "The Written Report: Old Wine in New Bubbles." In *Understanding Writing*, 2d ed. Thomas Newkirk and Nancie Atwell, eds. Portsmouth, NH: Heinemann, 1988:179−90.

# 32

## the tantalizing vagueness of teaching

SUSAN OHANIAN

In 1916, Robert Frost wrote his friend and fellow-poet Louis Untermeyer that a poem "begins as a lump in the throat." Frost also noted that a poem is "at its best when it is a tantalizing vagueness." I feel the same way about teaching.

That's why I become uncomfortable and even irate when committeepersons insist that a good teacher's performance can be charted and graphed, and then rewarded accordingly.

If someone appears in my doorway and says, "I'm going to examine your anticipatory sets," I wonder if I have the right to make one phone call first. Teachers have been polite too long to managerial types, fellows with bulging briefcases of checklists with terms like *praise as positive reinforcer, demonstration of mastery, time on task*, and other slimy slugs of that ilk.

We are teachers. Teachers. Teachers. We traffic in words and ideas and feelings and hopes, not in goods or systems, not even in five-tiered career ladders. I hear the blizzard of words spewed forth about teacher competency and I want to ask, "Why me?"

Do we see such high-level scrutiny of other professions — of doctors, for example? After all, their collegial cover-ups are notorious — and life-threatening. Yet I can't pick up my morning newspaper and find out what my surgeon's operating mortality rate is. Nor do I know what percentage of his diagnoses are correct. Would the AMA sponsor the idea of box scores for doctors' performances — or merit pay?

But if *teachers* can prove they are competent, say our education managers, society will pay them accordingly. Hah. American values simply aren't skewed that way. Sports figures might easily get $500,000 — or $5,000,000 — to hit around a little white ball. But teachers can't command much — mainly because we don't have any special skills that are observable. What we do looks fairly easy; most people feel they could do the *teaching part*, though they acknowledge that putting up with the kids all day might be a bit difficult. Our real skills, of course, are secret. Nobody ever knows when we hit a home run or win a Grand Slam, and that's why we can never be paid what we're worth.

It doesn't take the perception of a parsnip to realize that teachers didn't enter the calling to get rich. Yet these education managers persist in ignoring—and even eliminating—the very qualities that did lead us into the fold. They talk a lot about skills, for example, but don't mention a sense of humor or a tolerance for ambiguity or an enjoyment of children.

Behaviorists have long insisted that they can deliver the carefully delineated subskills of learning. Now they are marketing a similar package for teaching. Some administrators label this move to standardize teaching as a clarion call for excellence. A lot of us veteran teachers see it as an ultimately catastrophic worship of systems at the expense of people.

I am particularly bothered by the growing popularity of teacher evaluation forms that are supposed to be objective, systematic, impersonal. Such forms tell no more about essential teacher qualities than do a box of jujubes. The time is past due for teachers to stand up and say "No! Your checklists and timetables run counter to what goes on in a vital, stimulating, nurturing classroom." The time is past due for the professors of education to step down from their ivory towers and to become involved in what's happening in the schools. If they form one more committee or draft one more recommendation, let it be on the importance of human relations in the classroom. Let them form a task force to protect teachers . . . and children.

The education managers who hand out competency tests and who write up official classroom observations make a critical mistake. They insist that prospective teachers should prove what they know. But we veteran teachers realize that the hard part of being a teacher has nothing to do with facts. Yes, teachers need to know where the apostrophes should land, but more important, they need to be nurturing human beings. They must be optimistic and enthusiastic about the possibilities of the children in their care. They must be flexible and able to bounce back after 63 defeats—ready and even anxious to try again.

I'm not much interested in seeing how a teacher carefully structures her lesson so that the kids stick to the objectives and the bell always rings in the right place—just after she makes her summary and gives the prelude for what will come tomorrow. I want to find out if that teacher is tough and loving and clever and flexible. I want to be sure she's more nurturing than a halibut. . . . What does she do when a kid vomits (all over those neat lesson plans)? Or an indignant parent rushes in denouncing the homework? Or the worst troublemaker breaks his arm and needs special help? Or the movie-projector bulb burns out, and the replacements have to come from Taiwan? Or somebody spots a cockroach under her desk?

A teacher's talents for dealing with crises aren't easily revealed on an evaluation report or rewarded on a salary schedule. And neither are those special moments that a teacher savors. So don't yield to the number crunchers—even when they dangle a golden carrot in front of you. Remember that the most wonderful joys of teaching happen in the blink of an eye and are often unplanned and unexpected. You can miss their importance and lose their sustenance if your eyes are glassily fixed on the objective you promised your principal you'd deliver that day. When you maintain a sharp eye and the ability to jump off the assigned task, the rewards are many—when a child discovers a well-turned phrase; or a mother phones and says, "Our whole family enjoyed the homework. Please send more"; or the shiest child in the room announces *she* wants to be the narrator in the class play; or the class bully smiles over a quiet poem. Our joy is in the daily practice of our craft, not in the year-end test scores or the paycheck. When outside experts ignore this, then we must stop and remind ourselves. We must talk, not of time on task but of the tantalizing vagueness and the lumps in the throat, the poetry and true purpose of our calling.

# ACKNOWLEDGMENTS AND FURTHER RESOURCES

We would like to thank the many teachers and other colleagues who helped us hone our personal theories of what it means to be literate. Patricia McLure and Leslie Funkhouser of Mast Way School in Lee, New Hampshire, allowed us to spend extended periods of time in their classrooms. The staff at Stratham Memorial School in Stratham New Hampshire, especially first-grade teacher Chris Gaudet and sixth-grade teachers Chip Nelson and Donna Lee, also graciously opened their doors to us. Nancy Winterbourne of Molalla Primary School in Molalla, Oregon, and Marie Greve of Maple Lane Elementary School in Claymont, Delaware, continue to enrich our knowledge of literacy and teaching through the time we spend in their classrooms.

Donald Graves, Jane Hansen, Donald Murray, and Tom Newkirk first introduced us to many of the authors whose works are included in these pages. Special thanks go to Tim Gillespie, Yetta Goodman, Louise Rosenblatt, and Patrick Shannon, who made the interviewing phase of the book a pleasure.

Philippa Stratton, Dawne Boyer, and Bob Thomas have been patient and generous with their time from the conception of this text. Final thanks go to our husbands, David Power and James Whitney, who tolerate enormous phone bills and our constant babblings about literacy.

---

For more information on emergent literacy, we recommend *Language Stories & Literacy Lessons* (Heinemann, 1984) by Jerome Harste, Virginia Woodward, and Carolyn Burke, a fine summary of many of their long-term research projects.

*Write From the Start* (E. P. Dutton, 1985) by Donald Graves and Virginia Stuart is a useful resource for both parents and teachers who seek to understand how current theory is being applied in classrooms throughout the world.

*The Craft of Children's Writing* (Heinemann, 1984) by Judith Newman is a short and accessible text which we often loan to parents or teachers who want a brief introduction to children's writing.

Theory comes to life in the classrooms of Tom Romano and Nancie Atwell. Romano's *Clearing the Way* (Heinemann, 1987) details his work with high school students, and Atwell's *In the Middle: Writing, Reading, and Learning with Adolescents* (Boynton/Cook, 1987) chronicles her experience with middle-school students in Boothbay Harbor, Maine. We've used these texts in courses for elementary teachers, and students love them.

Two other classic works on writing programs in action are:

*The Art of Teaching Writing* (Heinemann, 1985) by Lucy Calkins, and *Writing: Teachers and Children At Work* (Heinemann, 1983) by Donald Graves.

The teacher-as-researcher movement continues to blossom. Teachers interested in getting a research program started would find these texts helpful:

*Seeing For Ourselves: Case-Study Research by Teachers of Writing* (Heinemann, 1987) edited by Glenda Bissex and Richard Bullock, contains an introduction to teacher research and numerous studies by teachers.

*Reclaiming the Classroom: Teacher Research As An Agency For Change* (Heinemann, 1987) edited by Dixie Goswami and Peter Stillman, also contains many teacher researcher studies. These articles are supplemented by numerous theoretical essays by researchers like Shirley Brice Heath, Janet Emig, and Garth Boomer.

*Growing Up Literate: Learning from Inner-City Families* (Heinemann, 1989) by Denny Taylor and Catherine Dorsey-Gaines, is a research study of children learning to read and write in a northeastern city. Of particular interest to teacher researchers is the methodological appendix, which explains how Taylor and Dorsey-Gaines collected and analyzed their data.

Teachers interested in reading accounts of how teachers have changed their classrooms through research and close observation will be interested in these collections:

*Breaking Ground: Teachers Relate Reading and Writing in the Elementary School* (Heinemann, 1985) edited by Jane Hansen, Tom Newkirk, and Donald Graves.

*Understanding Writing: Ways of Observing, Learning, & Teaching,* 2nd edition (Heinemann, 1988) edited by Tom Newkirk and Nancie Atwell.

*The Whole Language Evaluation Book* (Heinemann, 1988) edited by Ken Goodman, Yetta Goodman, and Wendy Hood.

*Workshop* is the title of a collection of articles edited by Nancie Atwell for Heinemann and published annually. All articles in the collections are research studies by and for teachers.

As teachers develop their reading and writing abilities, they often look for resources to help them improve these abilities. William

Zinsser and Donald Murray are two expert writers who give wonderful advice to teachers. Some of their most helpful texts are:

*On Writing Well* (1985) and *Writing to Learn* (Harper and Row, 1989) by William Zinsser.

*A Writer Teaches Writing* (Houghton Mifflin, 1986) and *Read To Write* (Holt, Rinehart and Winston, 1985) by Donald Murray.

Another book of advice which is still relevant despite its original publication date is *Becoming a Writer* (1936) by Dorothea Brandt.

Two series of books provide unique views of writers developing their craft:

The *Writers At Work* series of *Paris Review* interviews are compilations of interviews with writers throughout this century. The latest collection, *Women Writers at Work* (Penguin Books, 1989), edited by George Plimpton, includes authors Nadine Gordimer, Joan Didion, Anne Sexton, Eudora Welty, and Joyce Carol Oates.

The *Poets On Poetry* series, (University of Michigan Press) includes over thirty volumes, each representing a different poet's work. Every volume contains essays by the poet and interviews with the poet. Among the poets included in the series are Robert Bly, Marge Piercy, Maxine Kumin, Tess Gallagher, and William Stafford.

An area of growing concern to teachers is that of cultural diversity. The following research studies look specifically at how cultural differences within society affect literacy:

*Ways With Words* (Cambridge, 1983) by Shirley Brice Heath is a summary of a ten-year study of rural white, black, and middle class whites in the Piedmont range of the eastern United States.

*The Meaning Makers: Children Learning Language and Using Language To Learn* (Heinemann, 1985) by Gordon Wells is an analysis of his ten-year study of different classes of children in England in and out of school.

*Narrative, Literacy and Face In Interethnic Communication* (Ablex, 1981) by Ron Scollon and Suzanne B. K. Scollon is an analysis of communication among Alaskan natives and whites.

Some of the most practical information on implementing holistic literacy programs is included in:

*Reading Process and Practice: From Socio-psycholinguistics to Whole Language* (Heinemann, 1987) by Constance Weaver, is a comprehensive overview of how reading theory translates to classroom practice. The book is filled with interesting activities and includes a listing of professional organizations and addresses for teachers interested in learning more about new literacy theories.

*Ideas and Insights* (NCTE 1987) edited by Dorothy Watson, includes contributions from whole language projects attempted by teachers and researchers throughout the country.

*For the Good of the Earth and Sun* (Heinemann, 1989) by Georgia Heard, is a beautifully written text that demonstrates how to help students enjoy reading and writing poetry.

*Children and ESL: Integrating Perspectives* (Teachers of English to Speakers of Other Languages, 1986) edited by Rigg and Enright, is a fine collection of articles that explores both the theory and practice of reading and writing process instruction with children for whom English is a second language.

*Response and Analysis: Teaching Literature in Junior and Senior High School* (Boynton/Cook, 1988) by Robert Probst draws heavily on the work of Louise Rosenblatt, and demonstrates how teachers can encourage their students to *respond* to their texts. This book's discussion of visual literacy and media competency is the best one we know of, and has implications for teachers at all grade levels.